Longfellow in Love

Longfellow in Love

*Passion and Tragedy
in the Life of the Poet*

EDWARD M. CIFELLI

McFarland & Company, Inc., Publishers
Jefferson, North Carolina

Frontispiece: Longfellow in 1854, age 47. Engraving after a portrait by Samuel Laurence (courtesy National Park Service. Longfellow House—Washington's Headquarters National Historic Site, LONG 20579).

LIBRARY OF CONGRESS CATALOGUING-IN-PUBLICATION DATA

Names: Cifelli, Edward M., author.
Title: Longfellow in love : passion and tragedy in the life of the poet / Edward M. Cifelli.
Description: Jefferson, North Carolina : McFarland & Company, Inc., Publishers, 2018. | Includes bibliographical references and index.
Identifiers: LCCN 2018029774 | ISBN 9781476675053 (softcover : acid free paper) ∞
Subjects: LCSH: Longfellow, Henry Wadsworth, 1807–1882—Relations with women. | Longfellow, Henry Wadsworth, 1807–1882—Marriage. | Longfellow, Fanny Appleton, 1817–1861. | Longfellow, Mary Storer Potter, 1812–1835. | Poets, American—19th century—Biography.
Classification: LCC PS2282 .C54 2018 | DDC 811/.3 [B]—dc23
LC record available at https://lccn.loc.gov/2018029774

BRITISH LIBRARY CATALOGUING DATA ARE AVAILABLE

ISBN (print) 978-1-4766-7505-3
ISBN (ebook) 978-1-4766-3423-4

© 2018 Edward M. Cifelli. All rights reserved

No part of this book may be reproduced or transmitted in any form or by any means, electronic or mechanical, including photocopying or recording, or by any information storage and retrieval system, without permission in writing from the publisher.

Front cover: (left) *Henry W. Longfellow* by Cephus Giovanni Thompson, 1840; (right) *Frances Appleton* by G.P.A. Healy, 1834 (both paintings courtesy of the National Park Service)

Printed in the United States of America

McFarland & Company, Inc., Publishers
 Box 611, Jefferson, North Carolina 28640
 www.mcfarlandpub.com

To the members of the NYU Biography Seminar in the 1990s—led by the brilliant and unmerciful tag team of Ken Silverman and Brenda Wineapple. Great talk, great inspiration—and great dinners at the Grand Ticino on Thompson Street in the West Village.

"My nature craves sympathy—not of friendship, but of Love. This want of my nature is unsatisfied. And the love of some good being is as necessary to my existence as the air I breathe. To tell you the whole truth—I saw in Switzerland and traveled with a fair lady—whom I now love passionately (strange, will this sound to yr. ears) and have loved ever since I knew her. A glorious and beautiful being—young—and a woman *not* of talent but of *genius*! Indeed a most rare, sweet woman whose name is Fanny Appleton."
—Letter to George W. Greene January 6, 1838

Acknowledgments

Scholarship on Henry Wadsworth Longfellow began in the middle of the nineteenth century and has continued, despite fluctuations in his reputation in the twentieth century, through to the current revived interest in the twenty-first. It is a privilege to single out a few scholars for special thanks, Andrew Hilen first and foremost for his six-volume *Letters of Henry Wadsworth Longfellow*. Others include Samuel Longfellow, Thomas Wentworth Higginson, Herbert S. Gorman, Lawrance Thompson, Newton Arvin, Edward Wagenknecht, and more recently, Dana Gioia, Charles C. Calhoun, and the scholar most responsible for the current Longfellow revival, Christoph Irmscher. It is harder to estimate the place of Louise Hall Tharp, the prolific popular biographer whose work on the Appleton family is exhaustive and readable—and from what I can determine, mostly dependable. She was an amateur, not a professional, university-trained scholar, but in 1959 she received an honorary Doctorate in Literature from Northeastern University, a well-deserved honor to a scholar who learned her craft and professionalism on the fly. I am grateful for the work she left behind on the Appleton family. I apologize to the many authors not named here, but the list of Longfellow scholars is long and impressive, and the best I can do to suggest the breadth of their interests and the depth of their studies is my bibliography. To them all I owe a debt of thanks.

For specific help on particular problems, I would like to send along my deep appreciation to the following people and institutions: From the Houghton Library at Harvard University: Leslie Morris, Curator of Modern Books and Manuscripts; also from Harvard, Reference Librarians James Capobianco and Susan Halpert; from Saint Leo University Library (Dade City, Florida): Cristina Martinez; from the Longfellow House: archivist Christine Wirth; from the Pejepscot Historical Society: Rebecca Roche (now at the Maine Maritime Museum); from the Maine Historical Society, Jamie Kingman Rice and Sofia Yalouris; from the New York Public Library: Lea Jordan; from the Archibald S. Alexander Library, Rutgers University: Stephanie Bartz; from the Special Collections Department of the University of Iowa Libraries: Denise Anderson; from the *Mississippi Quarterly*: Managing Editor Laura E. West; from the Boston Public Library: Reference Librarian Tonya Stafford; and from the Zephyrhills Public Library in Zephyrhills, Florida, a full team of professionals and volunteers: Director Andi Figart (now at the New Port Richey Public Library), Peggy Panak, Debbie Lopez, Victoria DeGeorge, and Dede Hammond. I am also obliged to Gilbert Muller for help with a Frances Bryant reference. For psychological insights into Longfellow, thanks go to Dr. Frank Ancona, professor of literature and psychology, and Dr. Larry Lentchner, clinical psychologist. A special thanks goes to Tracy Bernstein at the Signet Division of New American Library, who put this book in motion when she asked me in 2003 to write a new preface to *Evangeline and Selected Tales and Poems*. Last, thanks to Samantha Halsey for her expertise and tireless work as a copy specialist. And yet, despite all the collective good work of these fine people and many others who have helped me along the way, errors have no doubt crept in. They are mine, of course, and mine alone.

Finally and happily, thanks to my family, to my daughters Lisa and Laura, to their spouses, Heather Strout and Steven Stibich, and to six wonderful grandchildren: Elizabeth Louise, Julia Rose, Madeline Jill, Joseph Edward, David Robert, and Thomas Patrick. Most of all, I owe more than I can say to the lovely Roberta Louise, my wife and partner for fifty-one years now. I don't know how I got so lucky.

Table of Contents

Acknowledgments	vii
Preface	1
Prologue: December 2, 1834	3

Part One: Mary Storer Potter

1. From Portland and Brunswick to Paris, Madrid and Rome	5
2. "Her Ladyship"	41
3. "Utter darkness"	59
4. The "Being Beauteous"	79

Part Two: Frances Elizabeth Appleton

5. The Rogue and the Professor	93
6. Longo and Carlo	115
7. The Dark Lady and the Mad Man	130
8. The Cure	149
9. The Miracle	179

Part Three: "Ever and forever, thy Fanny"

10. From Craigie House to Longfellow House	192
11. Evangeline, Minnehaha and Priscilla	226
12. July 9, 1861	242
Chapter Notes	263
Bibliography	280
Index	283

Preface

Henry Wadsworth Longfellow wrote poetry for a huge audience that lined up to buy his books on their publication dates. He became in the process our first full-scale literary celebrity, signing autographs by the thousands and speaking patiently and politely to fans from all over the world who came to his door or stopped him when he was out walking. He even answered fan mail. He was not just admired, but beloved by readers who cared both for his tightly built poems and the morally secure universe they were set in. It was personal—people liked him and his poems.

All that popularity might suggest to some that Longfellow had to make intellectual or poetic compromises in order to secure the reader's favor and to achieve public acclaim, but that wasn't the case. He was in fact uncompromising when it came to connecting readers to the glories of European history and art—the same sort of literary cross-fertilization T.S. Eliot, part of the Modernist generation that replaced Longfellow's, insisted on in his famous "Tradition and the Individual Talent." This "historical sense," Eliot maintained, "involves a perception, not only of the pastness of the past, but of its presence"—which was Longfellow's stock in trade.[1] By connecting readers of his own time to works from the Western literary tradition in his translations and in his poems, and also by preserving complicated verse forms native to a half dozen European literatures, Longfellow lived historical tradition by embracing it, praising the past by putting it into his present.

The self, however, gets lost in this sort of poetry. Eliot thought that was only natural, commenting that poetry "is not the expression of personality, but an escape from personality."[2] Here, too, Longfellow would have agreed, for he was deeply suspicious of poetry that, as he put it, "addresses itself to our passions and internal senses—to our feelings, not to the mental faculty of poetical taste."[3] Private, reserved, and restrained, Henry Longfellow kept his personal life to himself, which, of course, separated him from most twentieth-century poets who came after him, in both senses of the term— like the self-absorbed Confessionals for example, or the formalist-bashing

Beats. Twentieth-century literary critics smugly dismissed the extraordinary success of Longfellow as the less-than-worthy achievements of a poet-entrepreneur. They agreed that what he needed was more emotion and less craft, more America and less Europe, more poverty and less profit. They thought they were attacking Longfellow's poetry from the unassailable moral high ground, which proved to be, however, an ungracious and ungenerous position to occupy.

What Longfellow's critics didn't take into account was the man himself, who was personable, generous, and warm, a man who loved close friendships, fine wines, operatic songs, and stylish clothes. Nor did they take into account the poetry that readers everywhere wanted to memorize so they would have the poems with them forever. Henry Longfellow loved to linger over the sensuous pleasure of good cigars and the ethereal beauty of belles-lettres. And he loved the company of beautiful women, which is both the biographical starting point of this book—and the cause of his greatest suffering. This is the story of Longfellow and his youthful romances in Spain and Italy; it is the story of his first marriage to Mary Storer Potter; it is the story of his grand passion for Frances Elizabeth Appleton; and it is the story of a happy marriage too, one set against the explosive tensions of pre–Civil War America, which eventually changed the couple from principled pacifists to equally principled supporters of armed resistance. And overlaid onto the romances, the travel, the friendships, the professorships at Bowdoin and Harvard, and the explosive politics was the poetry that turned Henry Wadsworth Longfellow into an unprecedented and unparalleled cultural icon.

Earlier Longfellow biographers from the nineteenth to the twenty-first centuries have painted a portrait of a man apart, cool and aloof, which hardly matches up with the passionate man who appears in this book, the man who lied to his parents and hid his romances during his early years abroad; who blamed himself for the tragedy that befell his first wife; who struggled with his emotions and a broken heart during the late 1830s and early 1840s; and who finally married again, but once again with a tragic ending. This is a book that puts the women Longfellow loved, especially the brilliant and beautiful, beguiling and bewildering Fanny Appleton, at the center of his story—and thus it is a book that presents Longfellow through a new lens, one that also gives his poetry and career a new look. Longfellow in love is neither restrained, nor private, nor reserved.

Prologue

December 2, 1834

Henry Longfellow paused when he looked down at the letter marked "Confidential" from Josiah Quincy, president of Harvard University. The letter was dated December 1, 1834, and had reached him the next day in Brunswick, Maine, where Longfellow was professor of languages at Bowdoin College. Harvard's Smith Professor of Modern Languages, the esteemed George Ticknor, was resigning, and "the duty of nominating to that office," Quincy wrote stiffly, "devolves upon me." He'd given the matter of replacing Ticknor "great deliberation," he continued without much noticeable enthusiasm, and "my determination is made to nominate you." The job paid $1,500 and residence in Cambridge was required, he wrote, and then stopped short to say he'd "be obliged by an early answer." Oh, and there was one other thing, he seemed to remember as a last-minute afterthought: if he wanted to spend a year or so in Europe "for the purpose of a more perfect attainment of the German," at his own expense, of course, "Mr. Ticknor will retain his office until your return."[1]

The advantage was Quincy's because he knew Longfellow was very interested in a one-way ticket out of parochial Bowdoin College and small-town Brunswick. A year and a half earlier, in June 1833, Henry had actually set his sights on Ticknor's job, putting a desperate, long-distance, three-party inquiry in motion (through his hometown minister in Portland, Maine to the Harvard Law School dean, who knew Longfellow's father), wondering if he might be considered for a position as Professor Ticknor's assistant.[2] He was hoping his foot in the door might lead to something more, but that inquiry fizzled out at once. The next year he took the bold step of enlisting Ticknor's help in the form of a letter of recommendation for a position he was considering at New York University, but that too sputtered out. Ticknor, whose special interest was Spanish literature (which he would write a three-volume history of in 1849 plus a second edition five years later and two expanded editions after that), had actually known Longfellow since May 1826, when as a young college graduate, Longfellow had tracked him down at dinner in Boston one night to ask for a letter of introduction to Washington Irving. Henry needed that letter for an upcoming work (and pleasure) European tour that would last three and a half years before he returned to take up his teaching duties in modern languages at Bowdoin in 1829.

Longfellow was in 1829 embarking on a career similar to Ticknor's, but with the frontier roughness of Brunswick, Maine as his destination instead of the intellectual cachet of Cambridge and the urban sophistication of Boston. In 1834, when Ticknor was preparing to leave Harvard and to pick a successor, he remembered Longfellow, perhaps especially for his work on Spanish literature, translations mostly, plus an article in *The North American Review* on the "Moral and Devotional Poetry of Spain" (1832). The younger man and the older man had enough history, in fact, for Ticknor to know in 1834 that there wasn't another candidate like Henry Longfellow to take over the Smith professorship, not another candidate he could recommend to Josiah Quincy with so much certainty and confidence.

Yes, Henry was definitely interested in replacing Ticknor, was even more interested in moving out of Brunswick, and was perhaps most interested in taking up residence in Cambridge and Boston, already in the 1830s a pulsing heartbeat of American culture. Returning to Europe was merely an attractive, irresistible bonus.

PART ONE: MARY STORER POTTER

1

From Portland and Brunswick to Paris, Madrid and Rome

Henry Longfellow hadn't always been so eager to leave Brunswick, of course. Bowdoin was a college he'd been proud of once upon a time—and was proud of still, in a manner of speaking. Grandfather Longfellow, a long-time judge in the area, had helped select the site for the new college back in 1796, and his son, Henry's father, had been elected early on to the school's Board of Trustees. Bowdoin was a family affair, then, and it was also where Henry had built his reputation as a hard-worker and a budding literary star.

He'd been admitted to the nineteen-year-old school in 1821, when he was 14, but his family elected to keep him home that year, in a sort of distance-learning arrangement with Bowdoin, either because of his youth, as is generally thought, or because his 16-year-old brother Stephen, also admitted in 1821, needed another year of home supervision. (A one-year delay wasn't enough for Stephen, who immediately gave in to hard drinking and academic sluggishness once he got on campus.) Bowdoin wasn't far from the family home in Portland, only a thirty-mile coach ride, but it may as well have been a hundred and thirty, the road being rough to travel, and a good five to six hours away. So Henry spent the 1821–22 school year as he had spent every other since 1813, at the Portland Academy, a still-young school at the time, characterized by one historian as "celebrated" and by another, with a wry smile, as "elegantly named."[1] Henry had been bright and diligent there—by 1814, when he was 7, he had already gone through half his Latin grammar and was more advanced than many boys twice his age.

Certainly Henry's childhood in Portland had been promising in every way. His father provided well; the family on both sides was well positioned socially; and even his pre-school introduction to books boded well. His mother, Zilpah, who had descended from *Mayflower* pilgrims John Alden and Priscilla Mullins, introduced him to books in the family library: tales from the *Arabian Nights, Robinson Crusoe, Don Quixote,* and the *Vicar of Wakefield,* among others. In poetry, he was brought up on Alexander Pope, John Dryden, and New England's own prodigy poet, William Cullen Bryant. He thrilled most, though, to the words and music of Sir Walter Scott.[2] He also took piano, flute, and voice lessons at home, the Longfellows owning the first piano in Portland. When that is totaled up and his studies at the Portland Academy are added in (advanced Latin, basic Greek, and fundamentals of algebra in 1815), it's easier to see how the young man, at least according to the admission standards of the day, was ready for college at age 14.[3]

Henry and Stephen moved to the village of Brunswick in September 1822, joining Bowdoin's distinguished, thirty-eight-man class of 1825. The college had the right Harvard look to it—that is, it had a quadrangle with Georgian brick buildings on it: Massachusetts Hall (1802), Maine Hall (1808), and Winthrop Hall (1822).[4] There was also a spare-looking wooden building (without either paint or heat), which served as a chapel and doubled as a library for an hour a day—and a fifth building, also of wood, which was set back and served as the residence of President William Allen, a Congregationalist minister.

Allen, a sturdy scholar who had compiled the *American Biographical and Historical Dictionary* (1809) and who also wrote uninspired religious poetry, had been chosen to lead the school because of his Christian conservatism, which is to say he was a staunch opponent of the liberal Unitarianism that was working its way from Harvard to the hinterlands in the first decades of the nineteenth century. (It was clear to the Bowdoin administration that the Harvard model was serviceable only to a degree.) Allen's job at Bowdoin was to breathe fire and brimstone on campus, which made him very unpopular among the students, including Hawthorne, who snarled that Allen was "a short, thick little lump of a man," and Longfellow, who, quoting James Thomson in "The Castle of Indolence" (1748), called him "a little, round, fat, oily man of God"—and one who was perhaps a tad too interested in young girls:

> He had a roguish twinkle in his eye,
> Which shone all glittering with ungodly dew,
> When a tight damsel chanced to trippen by;
> But when observed, he shrunk into his mew,
> And straight would recollect his piety anew.[5]

When it came to religion, young Longfellow simply could not warm to the debate boiling up around him, either in Portland or Brunswick, choosing in the end (with the help of his father's request in a letter to Allen) to attend a tiny off-campus Unitarian service instead of Allen's on-campus Congregationalist one. Zilpah had come from a traditional Congregational background, a spiritually conservative family force perhaps, but she eventually gave way in the family circle to her husband who leaned left on religious matters, no doubt because he'd been a Harvard classmate of William Ellery Channing (class of 1798), the father of American Unitarianism and its leading spokesman in the first half of the nineteenth century. It made more than one kind of sense for the Longfellows to be Unitarians, though it wasn't a subject that occupied Henry's mind very often.

Henry's intellectual pursuits, however, did occupy him—day and night at Bowdoin. The days had ritualized routines: prayers at six, first recitation, breakfast, midday recitations, noon dinner, study hour, and a final recitation.[6] In the evenings the boys were supposed to remain in their rooms for study, an unenforceable rule that Henry normally followed anyway, but which his brother did not, usually heading off to nearby Ward's Tavern instead, a beacon of hospitality run by an attractive 30-year-old woman, who was quick to extend credit to the students and, in the words of one historian, provided "other comforts that students might desire."[7] After evening study—or carousal—there were end-of-day prayers back in the chapel. It was a punishing weekly routine, if followed, but Longfellow thrived on it and made himself into one of the school's top students—the sober, restrained, and respectable son of a college trustee. He wanted his father and his school to be proud of him.

Henry had liked Bowdoin from the start, reporting back to his parents in September 1822 that he was already "comfortably settled," "well contented," and "much pleased with a College Life," especially with the many "agreeable companions" he'd already met.[8] Six months later, in March, he joined the Peucinian Society, a literary, oratorical, and fraternal organization for the class's academic overachievers, as distinguished from the hard-drinking underachievers in the Athenaean Society. Brother Stephen, Nathaniel Hawthorne, and Franklin Pierce all joined the Athenaeans. Longfellow's later life showed he was as drawn to wine, women, and song as his undergraduate friends and acquaintances had been, but during his college years, when he was in his middle teens, according to an unnamed classmate quoted by Thomas Higginson, he thought girls "something enshrined and holy, to be gazed at and talked with, and nothing further."[9] There were a number of girls in his circle whom he flirted with in letters and in person, like "my sweet friend" and "my fair cousin," Caroline Doane, who sounds more like a confidante than a girlfriend, or Mary Elizabeth Knight, whom he called "one of the sweetest and most elegant girls, that I ever beheld," but who interested him a tad less than Susan Codman, whom he called "that excellent piece of divinity."[10] They were all in fact, "enshrined and holy."

During his college years, however, Henry wanted—needed and demanded—a more controlled life of study and discipline. And so he followed the rules—which meant he joined the Peucinians, didn't smuggle alcohol into his room to thaw the iciness of Maine winters, didn't get involved with the young women of Brunswick, and didn't much care about smoking cigars or walking more than was allowed on the Sabbath. Bowdoin and the Peucinian Society were perfect for a boy whose father was a lawyer, a member of Congress (1823–25), and a college trustee; perfect too for a young neo-Federalist like Henry, a serious-minded boy who wanted to behave as he was expected to.

In late October 1823, Henry wrote his sister Anne that he'd been selected by President Allen for an important role in the December Exhibition, a debate between him and future lawyer and U.S. senator, James W. Bradbury: "English Dialogue between a North American Savage and an English Emigrant."[11] Henry took the savage's role. He was disappointed because he had thought his way through some of the same material when he was 13 for a poem he was then writing about the 1725 Battle of Pequawket, also known as Lovewell's Fight, an infamous (according to local interpretation) Indian ambush near his Grandfather Wadsworth's home in Hiram. He had written in "The Battle of Lovell's Pond" not so much about the "the savage's yell," but rather about the New England "warriors" sent to fight the Indians, the ones who "fought for their country" and "died in their glory." Having to take the savage's position in the December Exhibition three years later presented something of a moral dilemma, but it was nonetheless "a very fine subject both to write and speak upon," he explained to his sister. It wasn't the side he had wanted, but he was proud to have been given such a high honor and had "every reason to be satisfied and well pleased."[12]

At the debate, Henry was Chief Metacom, who had led a tribal alliance to drive the white invaders off Indian lands in 1675–76. Metacom was known as King Philip and the brutal and bloody conflict came to be known as King Philip's War. In August 1676, Metacom, only 38, was shot through the heart by a fellow Indian working with the white men. He was then beheaded, hacked to pieces, and hung from four trees for the birds to eat. One hand went to the Indian who killed him—which he ghoulishly preserved in a jar and dragged out to get free drinks at taverns. His head was put on a spike and displayed at Plymouth Colony Fort for twenty-five years as a gruesome warning to young warriors hoping for revenge.[13] But to 16-year-old Henry Longfellow, King Philip got what he deserved; the real heroes of the story were the New England settlers, the hard-working stewards of the land. Finding something good to say about King Philip at the December Exhibition was going to be difficult.

1. From Portland and Brunswick to Paris, Madrid and Rome   9

But he did it. According to Bradbury, who played Miles Standish, Longfellow argued "that the continent was given by the Great Spirit to the Indians, and that the English were wrongful intruders."[14] For his part, Bradbury vented an Old Testament rage and a seventeenth-century New England racism typical of the time: "Go, tell your ungrateful comrades the world declares the spread of the white people at the expense of the red is the triumph of peace over violence. Tell them to cease their outrages upon the civilized world or but a few days and they shall be swept from the earth." To which, Longfellow replied with the sorrow of a defeated leader of a defeated nation: "Lo! I hear sighing and sobbing: 'tis the death song of a mighty nation, the last requiem over the grave of the fallen."[15] The words are moving, but they are actually toned down from the ones he wanted to use to describe what he had by the time of the debate come to see as the calamity that had befallen Native American peoples and cultures.

Accounting for Longfellow's change of heart and mind between the 1820 "Battle of Lovell's Pond" and the 1823 December Exhibition was a book he read to prepare for his role as Metacom, John Heckewelder's 1818 *Account of the History, Manners, and Customs of the Indian Nations Who Once Inhabited Pennsylvania and the Neighboring States*. The book was a revelation to the young man, dramatically transforming him into something like an 1820s civil rights spokesman. He wrote his mother on November 9 that he had just read Heckewelder's book and found it "a very interesting volume" because it "exhibits in a new and more agreeable light the character of this reviled and persecuted race."[16] Heckewelder described Indians collectively as "a race possessing magnanimity, generosity, benevolence, and pure religion without hypocrisy." For Longfellow, Heckewelder's was an unexpected, topsy-turvy position, but one that was very persuasive.

Henry continued in his letter to his mother with more of the same strong language: Indians had been "most barbarously maltreated by the whites, both in word and deed." Were they really "cruel, malicious, [and] wicked"? Had white people for their own land-grabbing reasons exaggerated Indian cruelties—or made them up? Find a copy of the book and read it as soon as possible, he advised his mother. See for yourself "what a noble race have been almost entirely cut off and exterminated from the face of the earth, by the coming of the whites." It would take thirty years before Longfellow would get around to writing *The Song of Hiawatha*, but the seeds were sown in late 1823, when he perhaps surprised himself by speaking so proudly and eloquently for noble Chief Metacom, King Philip, at Bowdoin's December Exhibition.

At 27 Maine Hall, where he lived in 1824–25, Longfellow resumed his studies and his place among the Peucinians. That formal and sober role no doubt made him appear more reserved and maybe at times more like a man apart than perhaps he was—or wanted to be. One classmate spoke of him as "uniformly regular and studious in his habits, rather disinclined to general intercourse.... Such was his temperament that it appeared easy for him to avoid the unworthy."[17] Speaking to the same point in a December 1824 letter to his father, he admitted "I am not very fond of conversation, and have no great talent for it...."[18] And then six years later, he wrote to George W. Greene that he had made very few friends in Brunswick, which was just as he wished it: "My circle of acquaintances in town is very limited, and I have taken great pains that it should be so—I am on very intimate terms in three families, and that is quite enough. I don't care for general society. I like *intimate footings*."[19]

Aloof as he may have appeared as an undergraduate in the early 1820s or as a professor in the late 1820s and early 1830s, Henry Longfellow was also welcoming and forthcoming, attractive in his habits, which his daughter Alice once called, "very simple and regular": "Indeed, order and regularity were essential to him in every way, and anything like hurry and confusion most distasteful. Everything he touched fell into order at once, and he lived in an atmosphere of serenity that was felt by all who approached him."[20] And he cut a good figure too, as Alice went on to point out: "He was punctilious and careful about his dress, never appearing at home in anything that was at all untidy or unattractive, nor would he allow this in his family. He was fond of elegance, and very observant and appreciative of the dress and appearance of all women.[21]

In addition to his carefully tidy appearance, he had an attractive look. According to one description, he had during his teenage college years, a "complexion light and delicate as a maiden's, with a slight bloom upon the cheek"; he had a "nose rather prominent..., eyes clear and blue..., [and a] head covered with a profusion of brown hair waving loosely."[22] Earlier, at the Portland Academy, he'd been described as "a very handsome boy" whose "eyes were full of expression" and who had "a frankness about him that won you at once." James Bradbury at Bowdoin, noted that he "was always a gentleman in his deportment, and a model in his character and habits." Zilpah, in an 1825 letter to her husband off in Washington, took it a motherly step further: "Henry is beloved by all," she wrote, "his conduct is very correct, and he gives much pleasure to his friends...." Whether Longfellow is most accurately characterized by a winning frankness or an off-putting coolness, he was enjoying a full life at Bowdoin College and was looking forward to a bright future. He had every reason to be proud of his school (and himself) in 1824 and 1825— the more so because he was already piling up impressive publications, poetry and prose, that added even more luster and depth to his college successes.

Poetry writing, like piano playing, was a skill most young ladies and gentlemen learned as a natural part of their educations in the nineteenth century, when poetry fit easily into people's everyday lives and was a widely admired expression of cultural achievement, even if it wasn't considered a wise career choice.[23] Henry and his brother and sisters all wrote poetry, but Henry was drawn to it more completely, compellingly, than anyone else in his family or circle of friends. And he clearly had a greater technical and imaginative talent for it too. Henry's first published poem appeared when he was 13 in the *Portland Gazette*, on November 17, 1820, "The Battle of Lovell's Pond." He gave it a half-signature, HENRY, hoping no doubt to take credit if any was forthcoming, but aiming at the same time to avoid censure if it came to that. His nervous near-anonymity was preserved by carefully dropping the poem off at the newspaper office when no one was around.

Longfellow had received the story from Grandfather Wadsworth as a tale of treacherous Indians killing innocent white settlers, but that version, popular among white settlers of course, carefully avoided any mention of white atrocities committed against the Indians, which explains the one-sidedness of Henry's poem. What preteen boy, after all, challenges his grandfather when the grandfather is spinning mythic, country-forming tales of war and courage and sacrifice? There had also been a similar poem on the same subject by Thomas C. Upham a year earlier that Longfellow knew and tried to improve upon with his own proud flourish about the white warriors: "They are dead; but they live in each Patriot's breast, / And their names are engraven on honor's bright crest." The poem had a short life, except perhaps as a first footnote to Longfellow scholarship, but it was harshly dealt with by the father of a friend, Frederic Mellen. Longfellow was visiting Frederic when Judge Prentiss Mellen picked up the *Gazette* of November 17 and asked if anyone had read the new poem, which he then summarily trashed: "Very stiff, remarkably stiff; moreover, it is all borrowed, every word of it."[24] Young Longfellow caught his breath and kept his silence, not admitting to being that HENRY.

Two months later, on January 22, 1821, Henry published a sonnet "Winter" in the *Gazette*, which he signed even more anonymously as H. He was still very much a local boy from Portland, secure in the love of his hometown's glories and wonders, proud of his new state just admitted to the Union. He pitied anyone who had to travel away from there:

> And ah! how hard the helpless wanderer's lot
> Who roams alone upon some hostile strand,
> And sighs to tread once more his native land,
> To meet those friends by memory ne'er forgot,
> And hail, yet once again, that fertile spot,
> Where Friendship binds him with her strongest bands.

Then, with his Bowdoin studies pressing harder, Henry worked less often on his poems between 1821 and 1823, although they began appearing again during his junior and senior years, in 1824 and 1825.

His father disapproved, however, and tried to redirect his son to the law, his own career path—or if not that, to one of the other professions, though Henry resisted them all, especially medicine because, as he explained to his father in a letter of March 1824, he had trouble understanding lectures on "Chemical Affinity" in Professor Parker Cleaveland's class—and anyway, as he put it, "there are quite enough [doctors] in the world without me."[25] He was hoping to be allowed to pursue his literary interests, such a preposterous notion that he couldn't quite write the words, dancing around the subject in his letter to his father: "I am curious to know what you do intend to make of me! Whether I am to study a profession or not! and if so, what profession?" The closest he came to his real meaning was an indirect mention: "I hope your ideas upon this subject will agree with mine, for I have a particular and strong predilection for one course of life, to which you I fear will not agree."

From August 28 to September 25, 1824, the *Portland Advertiser* published three of Henry's poems, 152 lines in all. From March to October 1825, *The United States Literary Gazette* published his five-part series called "The Lay Monastery," where Henry complained that in America the literary man could not live by his pen alone, which meant he had to compromise his calling by becoming a lawyer or preacher as well—something, anything, to avoid poverty and maybe even to make a proper way for himself in the world.[26] It was a subject much on his mind as he looked into the future and saw a long and boring legal career stretching out before him, not the literary life he desperately wanted for himself. And as all this was looming just ahead after graduation in September 1825, young Longfellow was feeling keenly both burdens—not just the dreary prospect of a life in the law, but more deeply still, a young man's mourning over the death of his dream.

It was *The United States Literary Gazette* that gave Longfellow enough courage to think he might buck the odds and actually get launched on a literary career. The *Gazette*, the end product of several magazine mergers in Boston and New York in the early 1820s, lasted only two years, but during that time, Longfellow appeared frequently—in all there were twenty-four of his poems, essays, and book reviews with fourteen of the poems collected in the 1826 *Miscellaneous Poems Selected from the United States Literary Gazette*. In November 1824, Theophilus Parsons, editor of *USLG*, had written to the 17-year-old Longfellow, then in his senior year at Bowdoin, asking him to become a regular, paid contributor to the *Gazette*—thus unwittingly playing into Longfellow's fantasy. "Almost all the poetry we print," Parsons explained,

1. From Portland and Brunswick to Paris, Madrid and Rome 13

"is sent to us gratis…, but the beauty of your poetry makes me wish to obtain your regular aid." He asked Longfellow what sort of work he might submit and how many pages he would require so they could discuss what "amount of compensation" would be appropriate. In the end the compensation totaled $43.67—not that the final figure mattered much to the young, sought-after poet whose head was bursting with ambitious plans and whose heart was flush with a growing self-confidence and a justifiable pride. Someone was offering him money to write poetry.[27]

Also toward the end of his junior year, Longfellow was deeply involved in a translation of Horace, work he'd been enjoying more than any other "since the commencement of my college life," as he wrote to his father on March 13, 1824. He was actually running together his assignments in Latin and Rhetoric and coming up with verse translations that were so good that one of the college trustees, Benjamin Orr, took notice and eagerly discussed the talented student with his co-trustee, Stephen Longfellow. It was a conversation that would be picked up a year later when the college was searching for its first professor of modern languages—and Henry's name came up.[28] In the meantime, Henry continued with his varied publications, including a poem, a dramatic piece, and an essay for James McHenry, editor of the *American Monthly Magazine*, who praised his work lavishly and promised (falsely as it turned out) to pay handsome rates for more of Henry's work.[29] In addition there were several publications in the *USLG*, a Latin Oration delivered on October 29, 1824, and a 400-line poem on "The Poetry of the Dark Ages" to celebrate the founding of the Peucinian Society. Henry Longfellow had become an engine of undergraduate productivity. But graduation for Bowdoin's class of 1825 was just around the corner. Decisions had to be made.

Midway through his senior year, on December 5, 1824, Henry gathered up his courage and broached the subject of his future in another letter to his father in Washington. He wanted to spend the year after graduation at Harvard, where he would study history, become familiar with "the best authors in polite literature," and take up Italian, without which, he said, "I shall be shut out from one of the most beautiful departments of letters."[30] After that, he said, he'd get a job at "some literary periodical publication" and earn his living. It made sense to the 17-year-old because, as he poured it out to his father, "I most eagerly aspire after future eminence in literature[;] my whole soul burns most ardently for it, and every earthly thought centers in it." Not only had he "a very strong predilection for literary pursuits," he said, but, and this was hard to say to his father, "I am unwilling to engage in the study of the Law.…" He couldn't have put the matter more clearly, but to drive home the point, the young man told his father about the *United States Literary*

Gazette and the high praise of Theophilus Parsons, who had already invited him to become a "regular correspondent" and written that his "literary talents are of no ordinary character." He was begging his father to free him from the study of law. He wanted something better.

But by December 31, still not having heard back from his father, Henry regretted the strong language of his earlier letter: "I must confess that I feel rather ashamed of sending it...." But the longer he went on in his second letter, the more inclined he was to say again what he had said earlier, and he was particularly anxious about what his father might think about the year at Harvard that he wanted. Yes, he conceded, a profession might be all right, but not divinity or medicine—the law might work, he bargained, but he wondered if it was possible for him to study law "with all that eagerness which in these times is so very necessary to success? I fear that I could not!"[31]

Henry could have saved himself the trouble of writing his apologetic letter of the 31st because his father actually did respond to his earlier plea—not to Henry's liking—in a letter dated December 26. Stephen conceded that a literary life would be "very pleasant" for his son, but as Henry did not have the good fortune to have been born rich, he had to get a real job because their young country didn't have enough "wealth & munificence" to support "merely literary men."[32] Case closed. It would be the law for Henry—but Stephen Longfellow did bend to his son's plea for one year of studying belles-lettres at Harvard, so there was something for the young poet to look forward to, one glorious year of serious literary study before a lifetime of probate court.

Hoping to prove to his father that a literary career was far more likely to become a reality than his father had predicted, Henry tried to enlist the support of his number one fan, Theophilus Parsons at the *Literary Gazette*. He explained to Parsons that he wanted "in some way" to become associated with a literary periodical and hoped there might be a spot for him at the *Gazette*. And with Commencement creeping up, Henry was also in a hurry: "Pray write me as soon as possible, as it is of some importance for me to be acquainted with my prospects in this way before commencement."[33]

Parsons, however, took the wind out of Henry's sails with a sobering, hope-crushing assessment of the literary career he was still daydreaming about: "I should think it would be exceedingly difficult for anyone to earn a living by literature, just now."[34] It was a long letter, friendly in its way, but Henry Longfellow could not have missed the point: What he and all men of "taste & talent" had, Parsons said, was impressive, of course, but it came to nothing more than "unripened intellect ... grounded partly on vanity." It was sheer "folly" for Henry to pursue a literary career, Parsons went on, a fact that Henry would figure out for himself "sooner or later"—but "for your sake I wish it may be *sooner*." And then, as if to clarify a point that might still be open to misinterpretation, he put a dagger in young Henry's heart: "Get through your present delusion as soon as you can."

There was one very much more hopeful assessment that Longfellow would have valued very highly, had he known of it. William Cullen Bryant wrote in the July 1825 *New York Review* praising the good poetry Parsons was publishing in the *United States Literary Gazette*: "We might cite in proof of what we advance, the 'April Day,' the 'Hymn of the Moravian Nuns,' and the 'Sunrise on the Hills,' all by H.W.L., we know not who he is...."[35] But Henry's talent, so nicely underscored by Bryant, wasn't the issue, only whether or not he could earn his living by it. And on that question Bryant the poet, who would have a long career first as a lawyer and then as newspaper editor, was silent. Which spoke volumes.

At least, Henry thought after Parsons had taken him down a few pegs, he'd managed to get a year at Harvard before he had to settle into the law—that was a victory right there. He'd take his chances on the year after that. Maybe something would turn up.

Then surprisingly, it did. By Commencement on September 7, 1825, when Henry graduated third in his class and delivered the Third Oration on "Our Native Writers," he was already the topic of conversation among several school trustees. Many of them seemed to arrive at the same conclusion at the same time: something should be worked out for the bright and accomplished graduate, Stephen Longfellow's son, Henry.

As it turned out, the college was planning to begin a program in modern languages, the initial funding coming from a $1,000 donation for that purpose made some years earlier, and trustee Stephen Longfellow saw an opportunity. Maybe he could get his friends at the college to support Henry as a candidate for the professorship that went along with the new program. It wasn't a perfect solution—as a professor Henry wasn't exactly embarking on a literary life, and Stephen would be denied his son's presence in his law offices, but it was a compromise that made sense. It wasn't a perfect solution for some college administrators either, first because modern language study was far from routine in American colleges in 1825. In fact, because the study of Greek and Latin was so deeply entrenched, there were only three other schools in the country that offered it, William and Mary, the University of Virginia (which was just beginning its program), and Harvard. After all the political maneuvering and debating had been played out, however, those for and against the appointment were able to agree on two points: Henry was very young—and seriously unprepared for the job.

Negotiations continued, however, and despite lingering reservations, an offer was finally made, Stephen in the end successfully trading on his connections at the college to win the day for his son. There were, of course, strings attached. To that point the only European language Henry had was a plodding undergraduate relationship with French, so the young graduate had to go to Europe, at his own expense, for two years; learn Spanish, German, and maybe Italian; perfect his French; and then come home to assume his duties as head of the new program. But even though the rough outline for the offer had been negotiated and agreed upon, it wasn't an ironclad agreement and nothing was in writing. If it all worked out according to plan, Henry would begin his career as professor of foreign languages at Bowdoin when he was two or three years older and when he had a firm, hopefully fluent, knowledge of three or four European languages to go along with his improved French.[36]

It was a tall order, and some at the college may have doubted the young man would return fully prepared, which would allow them down the line to squirm out of the deal and appoint someone else. But Henry saw none of the potential downside and focused instead on his unbelievable good fortune. Stephen saw it the same way, and as to the expense, it was to be a loan against Henry's future inheritance and had to be measured against whatever would have been spent on Henry's year at Harvard.[37] So the strings attached to Henry's appointment were very much to the liking of father and son, who were both justifiably pleased with themselves, one for his grades and reputation, the other for brokering the deal and giving his son some at least of what he wanted most in the world. Bowdoin was their school, and they were both proud to be part of it.

Although his immediate future was settled by October 1825, Henry had to wait until spring for the best Atlantic crossing weather. During the fall and winter months, the trip was planned and re-planned; lists of what to take were written up, reconsidered, and written up again; and the adventure lying ahead was imagined and re-imagined. It was heady stuff.

Finally, Henry Longfellow left home at age 19 in April 1826, making a few stops to visit friends and pick up letters of introduction in Boston, Albany, and Philadelphia before arriving in New York where he would set sail on the packet *Cadmus* for Le Havre de Grace in France on May 15. He would return to New York forty months later at age 22, on August 11, 1829, able to speak and read French, Spanish, and Italian; read Portuguese; and get by in German. He had proven by then to be an extraordinary student of languages, eagerly taking in Old World cultures while he absorbed challenging new grammars and whole vocabularies. Even his father would be impressed with the knowledge Henry had when he returned to begin his professorship. As to the forty months themselves, they went by quickly, especially his time in Madrid, where he probably fell in love with Florencia González, and then in Rome, where he definitely fell in love with Giulia Persiani.

The sexual temptations of Europe worried Henry's parents as they prepared themselves and their inexperienced son for his upcoming journey. Tucked into his luggage when he left home were letters from both his mother and father. His mother worried openly. She told him how much she already missed his "elastic step" and "cheerful voice" and reminded him to "hold fast [his] integrity" and "purity of heart," which she was afraid he would lose.[38] He was young after all—bright, good looking, engaging, attracted to pretty girls in Portland—and there he was, grown but not tested, heading off for an open-ended stay in romantic Paris. What mother wouldn't be worried? She finished her letter with a desperate appeal: "I feel as if you were going into a thousand perils. You must be very watchful & guard against every temptation." His father was just as concerned. "Let not the solicitations of pleasure," he urged solemnly, "nor the allurements of vice lead you from the path of virtue." And with those final words of parenting, Zilpah and Stephen reluctantly let go, and Henry left on his great adventure. There would be awkward attempts at transatlantic parenting over the next couple of years, but Henry Wadsworth Longfellow had left home. He was young and very much dependent on his father's money, but he was on his own. He arrived in France on June 14.

It took five days by public transportation, a barge-sized coach known as a "diligence" that had to be towed along by five horses, for Longfellow to travel the 135 miles to Paris. To see more of the countryside en route, he sat up top where he also had a good view of "a nut-brown village beauty of sweet sixteen," seated right across from him.[39] She was a "brunette," as he later recorded it, "decked out with a staid white Norman cap, nicely starched and plaited." She also wore "a rosary and cross..., a linsey-woolsey gown, and wooden shoes." She held his attention until late in the afternoon of his first day on the road, when the diligence stopped at Rouen for the evening.

As the sun set, Henry set out to get a first impression of the city, with its "air of antiquity ... that breathed of the Middle Ages."[40] Then suddenly he found himself at the city's ancient Cathedral of Notre Dame.

> It completely overwhelmed my imagination, and I stood for a long time motionless, gazing entranced upon the stupendous edifice. I had before seen no specimen of Gothic architecture; and the massive towers before me, the lofty windows of stained glass, the low portal, with its receding arches and rude statues, all produced upon my untravelled mind an impression of awful sublimity. When I entered the church, the impression

was still more deep and solemn. It was the hour of vespers. The religious twilight of the place, the lamps that burned on the distant altar, the kneeling crowd, the tinkling bell, and the chant of the evening service that rolled along the vaulted roof in broken and repeated echoes, filled me with new and intense emotions.

It had been a glorious first day in Europe, in France, on the diligence, and at his first gothic cathedral—all made better by a "nut-brown village beauty" wearing a rosary and smiling at him.

Once arrived in Paris, Henry made his way immediately to the boardinghouse of a Madame Potet where a cousin of his, Eben Storer from Portland, was staying with five other American students and where a room had already been prepared for him. Henry wasted no time getting down to business, his parents' warnings still fresh on his mind. But almost immediately after he arrived in Paris, he began to worry about expenses that were mounting up too quickly, he thought. His room and board came to a fixed $36 a month, he reported to his father on June 20, but when he figured in the extra costs for "washing," "other charges for my clothing," and "many little incidental expenses," the total might come to as much as $600 a year, he wrote.[41] It seemed a lot.

He was asking his father for guidance, but learning instead that, with letters taking weeks to months getting to Portland and just as long getting back to Paris, he was going to have to make decisions on his own—a frightening realization at first, but clearly a liberating one as well. Despite the worrisome expense, Madame Potet's was his best option, he explained to his father, at least with respect to learning French, because at a hotel he would be shut up in his room for long stretches, and at Madame Potet's there was a French-only rule during meals, and he was able to go in the evening to the parlor to practice his conversational skills with Madame Potet herself, "one of the best women in the world," and with her two daughters, ages 8 and 13, who made faraway Paris more like Portland for him. But then he reported with an attempted savoir faire he hadn't earned yet, that the younger daughter was actually engaged to a 21-year-old "gentleman." This, he said as offhandedly as he could, "may seem strange to all of you, tho' it is the common custom in France." The older daughter, he continued along more conventional lines, "performs most elegantly on the Piano-forte, which adds much to our pleasures here."[42]

Paris in the summer, however, was hot, and while he was able to practice his French, the people Henry had hoped to meet were mostly out of town, which put him in something of a holding pattern that gave him time to become more familiar with his surroundings. He went to museums and theaters, and once he traveled the ten miles to Montmorency to visit Rousseau's "Hermitage," which seventy-five years earlier the Swiss romantic had settled

1. From Portland and Brunswick to Paris, Madrid and Rome   19

into for five years of serious writing. Henry wrote to his brother Stephen on July 23 that after five weeks in Paris, he felt himself fitting in and was at that point "half-way between a Frenchman and a New Englander."[43] At least he was beginning to look like a Frenchman, he wrote, wearing "a long-waisted thin coat—claret-coloured—and a pair of linen pantaloons" that on Sundays he accessorized with "a little hard French hat—glossy—and brushed—and rolled up at the sides.... In this garb I jostle along amongst the crowds of the Luxembourg." Henry told his brother too about all the "carryings on" on the boulevards, "the most attractive places of resort of a warm summer's evening." You could find anything there "at all hours of the day and evening"—musicians, "men with monkeys," "Turks in the oriental costume," "Frenchmen with curling whiskers," and rows "where the ladies sit to be looked at it."

But none of it was good news to Stephen senior. Was the boy having too much fun? Had he forgotten already why he was in France? Had he forgotten who was paying for all this carrying on? And what sort of costume was he wearing? He wagged his finger at his Frenchified son in a letter of September 24: "It seems that you have changed your costume to that of a Parisian.... You should remember that you are an American, and as you are a visitor for a short time only in a place, you should retain your own National Costume."[44] And all these worries came barely a month after Stephen had written to complain about Henry's slow progress in French and his heavy expenses—"more than I had been led to expect."[45] Further, he was worried about Paris's "temptations and allurements": "Go but little into company," he advised his son desperately, "& be careful to associate with none but the virtuous." This long-distance parenting was proving difficult, impossible really, and Stephen was second-guessing himself about having engineered it all and wishing as well that he had micro-managed at least the financial details.

Henry knew he'd been reprimanded in both letters from his father, but he calmly brushed aside his father's concerns in a letter to his brother (though it was at least partly for his father's benefit) two months later, in November. All the talk of his French outfit had been "nothing but a joke," he wrote, "my queer figure in French clothes"—and as to his French, he said once and for all, it "comes on famously."[46] Everything was fine. But here, Henry saw, was a case where the slowness of the mails was working to his benefit, for a scolding that travels by sea over the Atlantic and takes about two months to arrive, loses a lot of its sting.

In August Henry left Madame Potet and Paris to stay at a sanatorium (a *maison de santé*) in Auteuil, just outside of town, a place one biographer called "a shelter for invalids and hypochondriacs"—perfect, the scholar thought, for a homesick young man, though Henry himself denied that he was suffering at all and was just in search of a break: "How sweet is solitude!"⁴⁷ But there was plenty to do there, plenty of people to break the solitude, and he later wrote that he mixed "with some enthusiasm into all the rural sports and merrimakes of the village," including what he called the "rural dances" that he made it a point "never to miss." If he was homesick, he was doing what he could to combat it—and pretty young women were part of the remedy. He noticed, for example, "a noisy group of girls"; "the village maiden whirling round and round" the carrousel; the "goodly dames of Passy"; and a wedding with a "blushing bride, with downcast eyes, clad in a white robe and slippers, and wearing a wreath of white roses in her hair." If he was after sweet solitude, he apparently thought it best found with one or more of the "goodly dames of Passy."

When Henry returned to Paris in September, he gave up on Madame Potet's boardinghouse, where he determined it was impossible to avoid English, and settled in with a family that spoke only French, but this too proved to be a poor choice, and he reported to his mother in a letter of October 19, that he had been "discontented, unhappy" and then more strongly, that he'd been so "melancholy—down-hearted—dispirited—almost disconsolate" that he took himself on a ten-day vacation to "leave my cares behind me."⁴⁸ "I shouldered my knapsack," he told his mother, "and made an excursion on foot upon the beautiful banks of the Loire," which he knew he should not have done without permission, but which seemed, he wrote, deflecting criticism, like a good idea both for his French and his pocketbook. He was blameless and homesick. It was a long, chatty letter to a faraway mother who was bound to be sympathetic to her favorite son's unhappiness. He signed it, "Most affectionately your absent son, Henri."

When he told the same story to his brother a week later, Henry sounded less homesick as he added a description of his hike through what he called "the romantic borders of the Loire and Cher," and confessed to being interested in a girl he met there.⁴⁹ He was "loitering along," he said, when he came upon "a band of the villagers" returning home after a day's work. "I of course wished them a good evening—and finding that the girls of the party were going to [a] village at a short distance I joined myself to the band." But there was a "secret," he confided to his brother: "I wanted to get into one of the cottages if possible—in order, you know—to study character." The key to his plan was getting an invitation. "I addressed myself to the girl who was walking beside me—told her I had a flute in my sack, and asked her if she should like to dance. Now laugh long and loud! What do you suppose the answer was? She said she liked to dance but she did not know what a flute was! Lord!—what a havoc that made among my romantic ideas!" He told the story as a funny anecdote and laughed off the sexual possibilities of a pretty girl dancing to the music of his flute.

At about the same time, Henry wrote to his friend Patrick Greenleaf, who had spent an evening with Susan Codman of Portland, whom Henry had called an "excellent piece of divinity" back in 1826.

> I actually envied you the pleasure you had enjoyed—and perhaps that covetousness was justifiable in me, who am thus cut off from all that innocent and purifying intercourse with the young and beautiful that you are surrounded with and in whose society I have found better lessons of virtue than in all the sermons I ever heard. Indeed there is no book in which I read with so much interest as the face of a woman. This is a very gallant confession—but you know my old habits—and when I find myself so shut out of the world of my old friends—the thoughts of former intimacy now finished and in some instances finished forever come over me like a cloud.[50]

Whatever he meant by his "old habits," Henry clearly missed the "innocent and purifying intercourse" with the girls back in Portland, Susan Codman chief among them.

There are nine unrecovered letters to "that excellent piece of divinity," ones that might justify the juicy rumors in Portland that an engagement was imminent.[51] Miss Codman, however, had other ideas and broke off their relationship in a letter of March 8, 1830, after Henry had returned to Portland from Europe. In the letter she quoted a few overwrought lines from the pen of poet Caroline Sheridan Norton:

> I do not love thee!—no! I do not love thee!
> And yet when thou art absent I am sad;
> And envy even the bright blue sky above thee,
> Whose quiet stars may see thee and be glad.

Whatever Susan's real charms, she was not above striking a romantically mournful pose, writing a trite if heartfelt Dear John letter, and embellishing her feelings with Norton's sentimental and syrupy music playing quietly in the background.[52] The mention of her name, however, by Patrick Greenleaf in his 1826 letter had brought back feelings of "former intimacy" that he clearly missed six months after leaving home and living halfway across the world. It was hard to avoid moments of isolation and loneliness. Homesickness.

Henry pushed on with his travels in France in the fall of 1826, the proud recipient of a Phi Beta Kappa key (that he could not actually collect until 1829) and a Master of Arts degree that was conferred pro forma by Bowdoin at the 1826 commencement.[53] But Henry never got satisfactorily squared away either in Paris or the French countryside. No matter where he lived—the boarding house, sanatorium, or other temporary residences—there were problems that may or may not have stemmed from his learning of French. About a decade later when he thought back to his time in France, he said at first that he'd been happy there, but then he corrected himself: "No, not happy; I was not happy then, I was too young and feverish, never satisfied with the present, and reaching out my hands to grasp the future, as a child tries to grasp a star."[54]

From week to week through the fall of 1826 Henry seemed to change his mind about his progress and what he wanted to do next. On October 2, he reported to his father that French was much more difficult than he had originally anticipated and that he'd had "no idea, that it was indeed so difficult to learn a language," which in turn cast an entirely different light on his plans to study Spanish, Italian, and German in his short, two-year stay in Europe.[55] By October 19, however, that had changed and he reported to his father that he could converse in French "tolerably well." And on November 19, he wrote to his brother (without the defensive self-explanations that creep into his letters to his father) that "French comes on famously."

For the next four months, the conversation home was always about which languages to study and which countries to visit. Would Spain be next? Italy? Germany? For a while Henry favored Germany, but his father reminded him of the necessity of Spanish for his preparation to teach at Bowdoin.[56] Henry, however, had by then determined that Spain was too dangerous for travelers: "That country is filled with all the horrors of a civil war," he wrote to his father. "It is as much as one's life is worth to visit it. We get most terrible accounts from every quarter—and as I never desired to come to my end by the dagger of an assassin or the pistol of a robber, I think it at least prudent to leave Spain like the 'man who fell upon thieves' and pass[ed] by on t'other side.' Indeed I have given up all hope of visiting it."[57] But then Henry changed his mind about Germany and went back to favoring Spain and Italy. Or maybe Italy and Spain. And thus the flip-flopping continued, accompanied by letters from his father that took a couple of months to cross the Atlantic, always arriving to complicate and change matters he'd already more or less decided for himself.

And then in February 1827, Henry met Pierre Irving, the nephew of Washington Irving, who was then living in Madrid and working on his biography of Christopher Columbus, and the matter was finally settled. It would be Spain after all. Pierre, who had just arrived from Spain, soothed Longfellow's concerns about the safety of travelers and arranged for the not-yet-20-year-old Henry to meet his literary idol, the revered author of *The Sketch-Book*. It was too tempting to be resisted—regardless of the dangers, if they were in fact real. And happily, Spain was where his father wanted him to go.

1. From Portland and Brunswick to Paris, Madrid and Rome   23

Henry sent a final letter home on February 13 to say he was ready to move on: "I must say that I am well satisfied with the knowledge I have acquired of the French language. My friends all tell me that I have a good pronunciation.... I am confident that I have done well."[58] It was time to exchange Paris for Madrid.

Longfellow left Paris on February 15, 1827, and arrived in Madrid on March 9, stopping on the way in Bordeaux, "the most beautiful city I have seen in France," he wrote to his father on February 26. He wasn't sorry to be leaving France, he confessed, perhaps owing to a mysterious "secret disappointment lurking in my heart—at having found more perplexities to escape—and more difficulties to encounter than I had anticipated." The disappointment was real even if the perplexities and difficulties were left vague. Regardless, he told his father, "I look forward to a happier life in Spain."[59]

Which he had. Henry spent the next six months enjoying Madrid, learning Spanish, getting to know Washington Irving, and very possibly falling in love for the first time. It's hard to know which of these occupations pleased him most. Irving was "one of those men who put you at ease with them in a moment," he wrote to his father. "He makes no ceremony whatever with one—and of course is a very fine man in society—all mirth and good humor."[60] His writing, of course, spoke for itself, but in Madrid Longfellow was able to see first-hand something else, the older man's self-discipline, which put him at his writing desk every day before dawn. No stranger to hard work and long hours, Longfellow saw a vision of himself in future years, for Irving already was what Longfellow hoped to become, an esteemed and best-selling American writer steeped in European languages, literary traditions, and culture.

Madrid, warm and friendly, so different from Paris, worked its way permanently into Longfellow's heart despite "a glorious fit of rheumatism" that came along with some bad weather in March and April, as he wrote to his sister Elizabeth.[61] He loved the place, he said, and he loved too "perhaps the most courteous people in the world." Once again, this was in happy contrast to Paris. "I find a more frank and sincere feeling of kindness towards me as a stranger here in Spain," he went on to his sister, "than I ever found in France." But as he wrote in some travel notes that he included with his letter of March 20 to his father, there was something beyond courtesy and kindness to please him:

> The Basque girls are very beautiful—they are literally "nut brown maids".... They have most beautiful dark eyes—fine teeth—a sun-burnt complexion—and glossy black hair—parted over the forehead—gathered behind the ears—and falling down to the knees in a large beautiful braid.... One [maid] in particular—whose image haunts me

still—[was] a most cheerful looking girl—in the dress of the peasantry—her hair braided—and a large gipsy straw hat thrown over her shoulder.[62]

About a year later, he advised his close friend José Cortés in Madrid to "be careful about the young girls, for there are some very pretty ones in Spain."[63] The advice was offered with a friendly wink and a broad grin as Cortés would have known that Spanish beauties were, as Henry had found them, a joy, a temptation, an excitement.

During Longfellow's six months in Madrid, he spent most of his time with the American diplomatic community, which made him feel completely welcome. First among them was attaché Washington Irving himself, but there were others too, like the United States minister to Spain, Alexander H. Everett, and his wife, plus a small group of foreign service workers and book lovers connected to the embassy. Chief among these was a 24-year-old naval officer, Lieutenant Alexander Slidell, who was then doing research for Washington Irving's in-progress biography of Christopher Columbus. Longfellow and Slidell became close friends at once, with Slidell, three years older than Longfellow, suggesting that he take rooms in Madrid with Señor Don Valentín González and his family. Then, while his rooms were being prepared, Longfellow and Slidell took a ten-day trip together (by foot, mule, and wagon) to the Guadarrama Mountains to see the Escorial, some twenty-six miles out of town, which Longfellow described as "at once a Palace, a Convent—and a Sepulchre." The Escorial cast a spell over him, he wrote his sister Elizabeth, with its "gloomy arches" that put him into a "pleasant kind of melancholy."[64]

When at length it came time for him to move into his rooms on the Calle de la Montera with the González family, Henry found himself rather suddenly under quite a different spell, the beguiling charms of the González daughter, Florencia, whom he described in a letter home on March 20, as "a young lady about eighteen—who has already become quite a sister to me." When he wrote his sister Elizabeth on May 15, Florencia had lost a couple of years and became "a young lady of 'sweet sixteen' with the romantic name of Florence." Their relationship, he had told his father with an unnoticed double entendre, was strictly aboveboard: "Under her attentions," he said, "I hope to find the acquisition of the Spanish a delightful task."[65]

The young couple walked early most days, before the heat, sometimes to the downtown Prado area, sometimes to the busy hub called the Puerta del Sol, Florencia regaling Henry with stories and gossip. They went often to the bullfights too, which Henry embraced with the same lusty enthusiasm as the crowds—and his companion.[66] Florencia, Henry wrote to his mother on July 16, was "one of the sweetest-tempered little girls that I have ever met with," a girl who had "the grace of Spanish women and the beauty of their

1. From Portland and Brunswick to Paris, Madrid and Rome   25

language." He found her conversation "quite fascinating," he told his mother, pausing for an instant and then adding: "I confess that I feel very little desire to leave Madrid."[67]

For her part, Florencia, whether she was 16 or 18, and whether or not she made Henry's study of Spanish "a delightful task," seems also to have fallen under the spell of her steady companion, a boy who had, in addition to his "joyous temperament," according to Slidell "sunny locks, a fresh complexion, and a clear blue eye."[68] And of course she was a dark beauty in her own right. Slidell is thought to have used her as the model for his description of the Spanish woman in his memoir *A Year in Spain* (1829). "The Spanish woman is, indeed, a most fascinating creature," he wrote, one who had a "mellow olive" complexion with skin that was "smooth and rich." Her face was "round, full, and well proportioned." Her eyes were "large, black, brilliant." She wore an expression of "sadness and melancholy." She is at her best, according to Slidell, "when she meets an acquaintance and makes an effort to please, opening her full-orbed and enkindling eyes" and parting her "rich lips to make room for the contrasting pearl of her teeth, or to give passage to some honied word." In short, she was irresistible: "The heart must be more than adamant that can withstand her blandishments."[69]

It's hard to say if Henry had a heart "adamant" enough to withstand Florencia's "blandishments," to know, that is, exactly how much of a couple Henry and Florencia became in the summer of 1827. But almost as though he intended to settle the matter, Slidell completed his picture of the Spanish woman with a description of her uncontrollable, hot-blooded passion—for chastity among Spanish women, he wrote, "is yet not universal."[70] This "decline in morals," Slidell mused, is perhaps due to "the poverty of the country" or possibly to "the passions enkindled by an ardent clime." Either way, the ingredients for romance were in place: two young and attractive people under the same roof and the young woman not being bound by American conventions of chastity—all that and "an ardent clime." The situation was combustible. But whether or not their relationship became sexual is still an open question. We do know that in the summer of 1827, after all that close proximity to Florencia González, Henry Longfellow seems to have found "the acquisition of the Spanish" within his reach—and we may surmise it was indeed "a delightful task."[71]

Thinking always about where he would be going next, Longfellow kept up a regular correspondence on the subject with his parents, just as he had done months earlier from Paris, a sort of travel-patter that tried at once to justify his decisions and explain his changes of mind, while he dutifully asked his parents what he should do next and where he should go. On May

13, 1827, a couple of months after his arrival in Madrid, he explained to his mother what he was doing in Spain at all when she had thought he'd be in Italy: "To be sure, it was my own fault: as I wrote you from Paris, that I should go there first. But after forming twenty different plans—comparing them together as many different times—considering and reconsidering—reading old letters from home, and consulting your wishes—and the best method of attaining the end for which I crossed the sea—I concluded that it would be more advantageous to visit Spain first, and trust to future circumstances for a poetic pilgrimage through Italy."[72] By the summer of 1827, he was leaning toward going to Germany next, although his father thought perhaps he should go back to France. Henry worried that his father might not take the news about Germany well: "Pray do not think me too changeable in my designs—many of them are rather suggestions than mature plans—but rest assured that I shall do what will result most to my advantage, so far as I am capable of judging."[73]

Germany made the most sense, Henry thought. And Italy, as tempting as it was, couldn't measure up to the romance he had found in Spain—or so he felt at the time. It was Germany and the German language and the German universities that were most important to his career—hadn't George Ticknor back in Boston said as much? He needed to study at the University of Göttingen, to learn first-hand about the still-new German, text-first approach to scholarship, which had come so highly touted. His parents, however, thought otherwise, his mother fearing that he'd be killed in one of those famous German student duels, reports of which had traveled all the way to Portland. His father had become convinced that Spanish was more important to his son's education than German and Italian combined. No, German was too far afield to be helpful to their son's plan to become a professor of languages at Bowdoin, where few had even heard of the intellectual currents at the University of Göttingen, and where there was no one, Zilpah thought, for him to speak German with.[74]

As letters and questions were always months away from being answered, Henry's letters home sound a little disconnected—perhaps even disingenuous. The long delays gave him a clear path to do whatever he wanted, which suited him just fine. In the end, on September 2, 1827, he left Madrid with Germany as his next intended stop, although he took the long way around, a three-month journey through the south of Spain, through the region of La Mancha and then to Seville and Cadiz on his way to British Gibraltar, where he had determined to sail for Marseilles and then go by coach to Germany.

But it was a difficult trip—twelve sweltering days on a crowded public coach, a lingering fever in Seville, and a long horseback ride to Gibraltar where he missed his connecting ship for Marseilles. In desperation, he booked passage on a different ship for Malaga, which was at least one small step on the way to Marseilles—and Germany. Malaga, he suddenly realized when he got there, was only eighty-five miles from Granada and the famous Alhambra, which he took a week in November to visit. It was so moving that he felt pangs of loneliness, a desire to share the beauty and romance, perhaps with Florencia, perhaps with Susan Codman, or perhaps with someone else from Portland or Brunswick: "How much I wanted in those happy moments some early bosom friend to share those feelings with me!" And then, after a slight pause, he added sadly, "How many solitary moments a traveler has!"[75]

When Henry got to Marseilles on about December 7, two letters from his father, dated August 25 and September 10, were waiting for him—and everything changed once again. The letters said George Ticknor had convinced Stephen that German was essential to Henry's career plans after all, and that Henry should therefore spend one more year abroad. Further, Stephen told his son that with colder weather coming on, it might be best for Henry to enjoy the winter of 1828 in sunny Italy before heading up to Göttingen in time for the warmer seasons. It would be expensive, of course, and Henry must recall that he was spending his inheritance, but still, his father wrote, he should not miss the opportunity of seeing and learning all he could while he was still in Europe. Who knew when or even if Henry would find himself abroad again? It was a generous offer, perhaps even a loving one, and Stephen even managed a softer tone than usual: "I am disposed to do all in my power to make your education as perfect as possible."[76]

His father's instructions were clear—late arriving, but clear—and they made too much sense for Henry to object, even though he was already travel-weary by then and not so sure about another year away from home. He wrote back on December 14 that had he known his father's wishes earlier, he would have sailed directly to Naples from Gibraltar rather than to Marseilles, but he formed a new plan on the spot: he'd go by land to Florence, "where I hope to master the Italian in a very short time," and then, when spring arrived, he thought he might shoot down to Rome and Naples for a while and then head up to Venice, "pass through the Tyrol and down the Rhine to Göttingen"— or maybe, he thought again, he'd go "from Venice to Milan and through Switzerland." He'd get to Germany one way or another. But the extra year away from home seemed to bear down on him at that point, and he added a softer tone of his own, a tired-out sigh perhaps, at the end of the letter: "Tell mama and all the family, not forgetting my good Aunt Lucia—that before I left them I did not know how much I loved them."[77]

On December 16, Longfellow left Marseilles on a nine-day overland journey of some 250 miles to Genoa, his first destination in Italy, with big-city layovers at Toulon and Nice along the way. Traveling with him were three officers from the United States schooner *Porpoise* plus a "young gentleman, by the name of Greene—a grandson of the old General [Nathanael Greene]" as Henry described him to his father just before leaving Marseilles, adding that taken altogether, they were an "excellent company to travel with." But George Washington Greene became much more in Longfellow's life than an agreeable traveling companion, for this marked the beginning of a friendship that lasted half a century.[78]

Greene, born in Newport, Rhode Island, was at various times the United States Consul in Rome (1837–1845), a professor of languages at Brown University (1848–1852), and a member of the Rhode Island state legislature (late 1860s). He also wrote a thick, three-volume *Life of Nathanael Greene* (1867–1871). He was talented, hard working, and accomplished, but he could never measure up to his friend's achievements, never become financially secure, never earn a lasting reputation in any of the careers he worked at. Perhaps worse for his self-esteem, he became later in life dependent on Longfellow, who loved his bosom friend so much that he bought a home for him in East Greenwich, Rhode Island in about 1865 and put up half the expensive costs of publishing the *Life of Nathanael Greene*. For George Washington Greene, gratitude and humiliation in the later years of his relationship with Longfellow mingled with a deep and loving, but very complicated earlier friendship. Regardless of how their relationship may have drifted at the end, however, the beginning was a joy, and in *Outre-Mer* Longfellow wrote that his journey with Greene to Genoa was "written in my memory with a sunbeam": the "sunny landscapes," the "peasant girls, with their broad-brimmed hats of straw," the "mouldering arches of the Roman aqueducts," the "shadowy apparitions of the past," and more. "I have not colors bright enough for such landscapes," he wrote.[79]

Longfellow and Greene arrived in Genoa, The City of Palaces, on Christmas Eve and took rooms at the *Hotel des Quatres Nations* "with a terrace overlooking the [Ligurian] sea." The night was "beautiful," Longfellow wrote in his journal: "The moon is shining sweetly upon the sea—and here and there a boatman's lantern glimmers upon the silent wave."[80] He was content at that point, happy in Greene's company—and for a while at least, less anxious about heading the wrong way to Germany. Later that night, he and Greene attended midnight mass at the *Annunziata*, the city's baroque basilica, where he saw a veiled woman "earnestly conversing" with a "young man wrapped in a cloak": "Beware, poor girl, thought I, lest thy gentle nature prove thy undoing! Perhaps, alas, thou art already undone!" Even in a Catholic basilica in

Genoa, Italy, in the happy company of a good new friend, Longfellow picked out a beautiful girl and thought momentarily about her moral condition—and perhaps examined his own while he was at it.[81]

From Genoa the new traveling companions continued south another 110 miles to La Spezia, Pisa, and Livorno before reluctantly parting, Longfellow heading 45 miles inland to "Florence the Fair," as he put it, while Greene went nearly 200 miles farther south to Rome, where Longfellow promised they would see each other again in a few weeks.[82]

Florence was an overwhelmingly beautiful, culturally significant stop for American travelers in Italy, especially for the ones who'd never seen European art and architecture. But Henry had. For him Florence had to compete with the artistic and architectural beauties of Paris and Madrid, where he had also first experienced the Old World's Roman Catholic, high-church ritual and splendor. Then, too, Longfellow had met and grown fond of his literary mentor Washington Irving in Madrid—and he'd romanced Florencia González too. He'd also made friends with Alexander Slidell and the other members of the American embassy. It hardly mattered to him that other visitors to Florence were overwhelmed by the city's sublime beauties or that by 1828 Americans were eagerly visiting the city on their grand tours through Europe. He remembered ruefully his own dreams of visiting Italy and falling under its spell, because now that he had finally arrived, he was depressed at the thought of all that he'd left behind, including his new friend George Greene, and by the prospect of a lonely winter stretching ahead.[83] He was drawn for a while to the stories of the Florentine Giovanni Boccaccio in *The Decameron*, but not even all those lusty tales of romping lovers could raise his spirits.

Contributing to his gloominess, Henry felt sharply that Italy was merely extending his journey, keeping him from Germany, and ultimately delaying his return home. There was, of course, his obligation to learn a new language and absorb another culture, but turning to self-discipline and rigorous intellectual routines, characteristics that had served him well for many years, was not enough to make him happy in Florence. Instead, he felt trapped, stalled in his progress. He wanted to get on with the real business waiting for him in Germany, a business that he thought would take yet another full year once he actually began his studies there. Impatience and loneliness were setting in, and it was becoming more and more difficult for him to control his unhappiness.

Then too, there was another problem, for even though he was living with a Florentine family on the Piazza Novella, he was having more trouble with the Italian language than he had thought he would. After two weeks, he reported to his father that "the language is more grammatically spoken here than elsewhere, but the accent is very harsh." Taken all in all, Italian was "very easy to read, and not very difficult to understand," he said, but he couldn't keep Spanish words out of his speech, a pesky problem, he reported, "which perplexes me very much."[84] The harshness of the Florentine pronunciation and the problem of putting in Spanish words when the Italian didn't come immediately to mind added up to yet another frustration in Italy. "The fact was," as he summarized it for his mother later, "I got quite out of humor with the language and concluded that I would not give further attention to speaking—but would make my way through Italy with the little I had acquired—and be contented with reading, without making much pretension to speaking it."[85]

He came to think the problem was Florence itself, for although the city stood shoulder-to-shoulder with Rome in popularity among American travelers and expatriates (many saying it reminded them of Boston), and although the city was famous for galleries like the Uffizi and the Pitti Palace, and for being the birthplace of Dante and the final resting place of Michelangelo and Galileo, Henry found it disappointing on several counts.[86] He poured out his feelings to his mother: "I suppose the very names of Florence—the Arno—and Vallombrosa [a Benedictine abbey near Florence] are full of romance and poetry for you who have not seen them." He thought his family imagined him "sitting at night in the shadow of some olive grove—watching the rising moon—and listening to the song of the Italian boatman, or the chime of a convent bell!" But that wasn't even close to the real life he was living in Florence. "Can you believe that the Arno—'that glassy river / Rolling his crystal tide through classic vales'—is a stream of yellow, muddy water almost entirely dry in Summer!"[87] It was a harsh disillusionment for Longfellow, who had written a poem called "Italian Scenery" back in December 1824 for the *United States Literary Gazette*, in which he rhapsodized about "the beauty of that silent river."[88] But that was long before he'd actually seen it. It was all very disappointing.

He did admit to liking the "very excellent society in Florence," though it was mostly the French and English he liked, especially a Mrs. Derby, who managed to get him introduced to Princess Charlotte, the daughter, he bragged openly, of Joseph Bonaparte, and the wife of Prince Napoleon, "son of Louis, former king of Holland." Also part of his heady January social set was Bonaparte's wife, the Countess of Survilliers, and a group of their titled friends, all of whom Henry was duly impressed with.[89] But the charms of Florentine society weren't enough to keep him happy.

By the twenty-third, he had become so discontented and disillusioned with Italy, so "anxious to get into Germany," he wrote to his mother, that he decided to cut his time in Florence short. "I must confess it. I am travelling through Italy without any enthusiasm—and just curiosity enough to keep me awake! I feel no excitement—no—nothing of the romantic feeling which everybody else has—or pretends to have. The fact is I am homesick for Spain."[90] He added that he didn't think he'd have much time to write home during the weeks just ahead, and with mail from Italy to the United States being notoriously slow anyway, he thought he'd be at loose ends for a while, at least "until I anchor at a German University." He was feeling more and more cut off, and desperate to move on.

On February 6, about a month ahead of schedule, Henry boarded a public, sight-seeing coach with two priests and a Corsican all headed south to Rome. Florence had left Henry cold—literally as well as figuratively, with January temperatures regularly dipping into the mid-thirties overnight and sometimes not getting up to fifty by midday. The slow trip south, made in an uncomfortable mix of cold and rain, at first did nothing to improve the young man's mood; on the morning of the ninth, the fourth of his bumpy six-day journey, Longfellow grumbled in his journal, "bad coffee—bad breakfast—bad humour."[91]

On the eleventh, however, he entered Rome—and his spirits began to rise at once. "In the morning as we approached the city—saw several ruins by the roadside which announced the approach to the eternal city."[92] And by good fortune, he continued in his journal, he had arrived for the last week of Carnival: "the city echoes with gaiety." The main street, the Corso, he wrote with a pleasant excitement, was "crowded with carriages and walking gentry." But there was more than Carnival to mark the change from Florence to Rome, for very soon now he'd be back in the company of Greene, whom he had sorely missed. Rome, with its warmer temperatures and layers of allure, was suddenly and unexpectedly becoming, in the phrase of Henry Adams a few years later, "seductive beyond resistance."[93]

Henry, still thinking his stay in Rome would be short, met with Greene, who recommended he stay with him at the home of Innocenzo and Marianna Persiani, plus their son and three daughters, on the magnificent Piazza Navona. Longfellow's room looked out over the piazza, "the very heart of the city," he called it, "and one of the largest and most magnificent squares of modern Rome."[94] It was in fact a long oval, originally designed in the first century as a track for Roman games and races. Some fifteen hundred years later it had been made into a marketplace and was still, according to Longfellow when he got there, an "animated and curious scene," filled with "gaily-decked stalls," "piles of fruits and vegetables," "pyramids of flowers," and the "deafening clamor" of the shoppers. Just looking out his window at the lively scene below, as Henry would put it *Outre-Mer*, was "a source of infinite enjoyment."

But there was more to look at than a busy marketplace because in 1651 Gian Lorenzo Bernini had erected one of his masterpieces, the *Fountain of the Four Rivers*, a celebration in stone of the Nile, the Danube, the Ganges, and the widest river in the world, the *Rio de la Plata* in South America. And rising over the entire square was the church of St. Agnes in Agony, named for the 13-year-old virgin martyr who had been beheaded in the square rather than sacrifice her purity, a story that touched Longfellow's romantic heart. The nearly two thousand-year-old history of the square, the splendor of Bernini's fountain, the story of Agnes, the renewed friendship with Greene, and the large and loving Persiani family—all combined at once to brighten Longfellow's view of Italy, the place he had reported to his mother not three weeks earlier that he had no enthusiasm for and barely enough curiosity about to keep him awake.

The most important reason for Henry's sudden change of heart, however, was Giulia Persiani, the eldest of the Persiani daughters. She was then 24, three years older than Henry, and had been both married and widowed while still in her teens. It wasn't long before Henry and Giulia were an obvious couple.[95] When he wrote to his mother at the end of March, however, Henry merely mentioned that he was boarding with "the same family" Greene was. But, "such a delightful family!" he added. " I feel that I am now in it by peculiar privilege." Warming to the story of his good fortune, Henry got around to the Persiani daughters: "There are three young ladies—who have all been excellently educated—and speak besides their native tongue—both English and French. They are great musicians, also ... one plays the harp with great perfection—the other the piano with the skill of a professor—and both sing...."[96] The entire Persiani family in fact was "so very kind—so very genteel" and they introduced him into "so much good society" and helped him so much with his Italian and French, that he enthusiastically announced a very unexpected travel change: "I shall make my residence in Italy something longer than I had intended on leaving Florence." He hadn't been entirely honest with his mother in his explanation for prolonging his stay in Italy—but he was a man in love, which drove him to take a few liberties with the truth. In the presence of Giulia Persiani, Henry's conscience, which had been relentlessly nagging him to Germany, gave way to his heart. The young man would remain with Giulia, in and around Rome, for the rest of 1828.

But his conscience put up a good fight. For one thing, the 21-year-old Longfellow was ever mindful of his father's pocketbook, which was being stretched uncomfortably into a third year of study in Europe. He knew he was dawdling in Italy, that he was there merely to remain close to Giulia— and that troubled him. Beyond the continuing study of Italian (and he had already confessed he'd given up on that), there was no good reason to stay in Italy after the spring thaw made Germany warm enough to begin his studies there. But if he was troubled, he was also powerless to break free. His feelings had changed so dramatically that he felt compelled to begin, starting with his March letter to his mother, a series of evasions, half-truths, and outright lies to justify his prolonged stay in the Eternal City. His relationship with Giulia had taken precedence over everything else at that point.

Of Giulia herself, Henry said very little, guarded as he always was about his private life. Perhaps too the good New England boy was afraid to confess his feelings for an Italian woman, beautiful on many levels, but not someone to get involved with. Or perhaps it was all right to get involved as long as one kept the affair quiet, certainly out of his letters. If his relationship with Giulia had become widely known as a true affair of the heart, all his plans might be seriously compromised—even Bowdoin and the job waiting for him in small-town, small-minded Brunswick might be in jeopardy. Discretion was a good idea.

No matter how much he tried to hide it from his parents, however, his affair with Giulia was real. In October 1839, a decade later and in the midst of a different courtship that wasn't going well at all, he wrote directly and longingly of his earlier, more successful, love affair in a letter to Greene, saying that a Miss Hinkley "has lately returned from Italy and brought the story of my romantic passion for Madame Giulia in days gone by," thus confirming the relationship while being careful not to say too much.[97] Three months later, at the tail end of a long letter to Greene, he asked pointedly about the Persiani family's "*hot* daughter," [Longfellow's emphasis] remarking that "Magrini," who had been one of his 1828 acquaintances in Rome, "amuses every American he can get hold of with my *amour* with Giulia. No one returns now from Rome without *that* story. I am glad of it."[98] At the end of 1828, when he had finally and unhappily left Rome and Giulia behind, Longfellow wrote to Greene from Venice that he'd "fallen unawares into a long train of melancholy reflexion. Excuse me—but I feel so sad and down-hearted, that let my thoughts be scattered as they may, they finally concentrate in the same point. You will understand me. I have purposely avoided the subject in my letter: it is too painful for me to dwell upon: though I assure you it haunts me continually."[99] As late as August 1842, he wrote again to Greene recalling Giulia as his "*antiqua flamma*" and adding "I want to see her once more."[100] These unguarded glimpses into Longfellow's heart are scattered but unmistakable expressions of the feelings he'd once had for Giulia Persiani. Their romance in 1828 remains in semi-darkness, but not in doubt.

Meanwhile, as spring turned into summer, Henry fell into a deeply satisfying pattern. In the mornings with Giulia and sometimes other members of the family, he would visit "the wonders of Rome," like studying the "miracles of ancient and modern art" or reading literary treasures "at the public libraries." They were always back in time for what the family called "breakfast"—at noon. The late meal was at eight, followed by the always-lively *conversazioni*, which Longfellow described as evenings "enlivened with music, and the meeting of travelers, artists, and literary men from every quarter of the globe." Before bed he would head off to his chamber to read a few "gloomy pages of Dante." But every morning he was up early once again, ready to rediscover Rome and Giulia.

On July 11, Henry wrote to his mother that he hadn't heard anything from home in six months and was "in doubt which way to move—whether homeward—or to Paris, or to Germany," which meant, he said, that "I shall remain where I am until I get letters."[101] It was true that he had not received instructions, but of course that really wasn't the point. He had left Paris, Madrid, and Florence on his own, when he felt the time was right, but in Rome, even though he knew he was delaying his required trip to Germany, the time was not right. This time, in love with Giulia, he didn't want to go anywhere, wanted instead to spend his days and nights with her on the romantic Piazza Navona. Only five months earlier in the cold of Florence he had been homesick and heartsick for Spain and Florencia González. But by July, Italy and Giulia Persiani had replaced them both in his heart.

In August Henry's relationship with Giulia took another turn. He reported to his father that an upper respiratory condition in early July had turned into flu symptoms and finally revealed itself as the dreaded Roman Fever, malaria, from the Italian phrase for bad air.[102] Longfellow traced the progress of his illness on August 4, from the country town of Ariccia, about sixteen miles from Rome, where he'd gone to recover. But before he got around to the story of his illness, he repeated by rote his already worn-out disclaimer: he'd hoped that long before then he'd be up in Germany at the University of Göttingen, but circumstances beyond his control had prolonged his stay in Italy—and anyway, he hadn't received any instructions from home since the beginning of January, and he hadn't been able to get any of his usual lines of credit to pay for the trip north and his time in Germany. So what was he to do? The "unaccountable silence" from home he wrote, had been "very unpleasant" and top to bottom he'd been "greatly incommoded." He was, of course, doing exactly what he wanted by prolonging his time with Giulia in Rome, but he knew perfectly well that he couldn't explain himself honestly and that he would be better off pushing the blame onto his father and the bankers who had hamstrung him. There was nothing else he could do but wait in Rome for instructions, he falsely complained, and "thus week after week slipped away."[103]

And then he got around to his sickness. Rome, he reminded his father, was "very unhealthy for foreigners" in the summer. And so it had proved to be for him. He'd taken a "violent cold" early in July, he said, but hadn't worried about it until he began feeling "a little feverish at night" which prompted him to what he called (without further explanation) "the usual remedy ... to throw open the pores." After a day or two, he decided he was cured and left his sick room only to relapse, which prompted the visit of a doctor, who couldn't stem the "raging fever" that had returned. A second doctor was called in, but to no avail, and in the end, "we were obliged to let it have its course and come to a crisis." The official diagnosis, Henry reported to his father, was "an inflammatory rheumatic fever," which had grown "very high and dangerous."

But whether it was malaria or "inflammatory rheumatic fever," he owed his life to his nurse, Giulia Persiani, he wrote to his father. He wanted that to be perfectly clear. All the doctoring he had gone through might have come to nothing, "had I not very fortunately been situated in a very kind family, whose attentions were most zealous and unremitting. Indeed, next to [the] hand of Providence, it is to the care of this most excellent and kind hearted family, that I owe my life." Of them all, he said, he was "most indebted to the ever-watchful care of Mrs. Giulia, the oldest daughter, who having the freedom of a married woman, which the other daughters had not, was of course my nurse—and a better one I think could not be found. It is to her, I may say, I owe my life." Henry was taking great care in his letter to his father to explain that his relationship with Giulia (omitting the key point that she was a widow) was aboveboard. It was Giulia, Henry went on, who had "administered to me a gentle dose of medicine" when he was "gasping for breath," and it was she who "prevented the surgeon from bleeding me a fourth time." He was trying to shift his father's attention away from the fact that he was still lingering in Italy and put it instead on his pitiable condition that was finally improving under the watchful care of his nurse, who could now be brought out into the open, although even here Henry was careful to underscore her supposedly married condition. It was brilliantly ingenious and forgivably disingenuous.

The real purpose of the letter was not his illness, but to tell his parents and his extended Portland family about the girl in Rome he'd fallen in love with. He was positioning Giulia to best advantage just in case things progressed with her and his feelings grew even more intense and he actually returned home with her as his wife, a long shot, he would have realized, yet not altogether out of the question—and irresistible for a young man in love to think about. His parents would remember fondly how important Giulia had been to their son's recovery—so how could they not love her as he did? This motivation may even have been strong enough for him to make the whole thing up, or to exaggerate some minor illness into a near-death experience. Henry's letters home actually suggest as much.

He'd written to his mother in apparent good health on July 11 from Rome, saying that he'd already spent "a few days in the country, at the village of Ariccia" and that "every day I made some excursion to the neighbouring villages and convents."[104] There was not a word about the "violent cold" he'd told his father he had "in the beginning of July" or the "raging fever" he'd had or the life and death crisis that he escaped only by the grace of God and Giulia Persiani.[105] All those details seem to have been manufactured between July 11 and August 4. He put the finishing touches into his August 4 letter to his father: he was staying in Ariccia for a while longer, he wrote, because "the air is pure and delightfully cool—even in the heat of August." His strength, he said, was "slowly returning," but, and this was the key, he had no intention of traveling to Germany "until I find myself entirely restored."[106] It may all have been a fiction, but he'd found a way to paint a saintly portrait of Giulia for his parents—and he had also bought a little more time with her in Rome.

By early September, Henry had settled once again into his comfortable life at the Piazza Navona. So comfortable had he become in his domestic arrangements, in fact, that he wrote but a single letter (to his mother in November) over the next three and a half months.[107] This almost certainly speaks to his happiness at spending every day and night with Giulia, an idyllic romantic time for them both, but the lack of letters also means there is no way to reconstruct his daily activities, no way to know what he was doing or thinking—about himself, his intention to head up to Germany, his responses to Rome, or his feelings about Giulia. Longfellow had created a comfort zone for himself, wanting nothing more than to stay exactly where he was, doing exactly what he was doing—and to remain happily in love. But the honeymoon had an expiration date.

The one letter that has survived from the fall 1828 was to his mother on November 27. Henry was on the defensive immediately because he was answering her letter of April 12, which he had received "not long ago" because she had sent it to Germany, where she thought he would be, and it had taken extra months to drift southward to him in Rome. He was also embarrassed that everyone at home was congratulating him on having finally met up with his Portland friend Edward Preble, who was already at the University of Göttingen and waiting for Longfellow's arrival. But of course Henry was still idling in Rome with Giulia. He was forced to confess to his mother that "my happy meeting with Preble" would have to wait until the spring 1829, at which

1. From Portland and Brunswick to Paris, Madrid and Rome 37

point he would actually be heading home because unless he stretched his European tour into an impossible fourth year, he wouldn't have time to visit very long with Preble or study German very seriously. It was a shame, he told his mother, that the anticipated meeting with Preble was unlikely to come to much: "I suppose we shall meet, only to say farewell."[108]

He made small talk in the rest of his letter to his mother: winter activities in Rome are "becoming quite gay"; Christmas vendors lined the Piazza Navona; there were dances in the gardens of the Villa Borghese; and November had brought the "melancholy festival of the Dead." He was sorry to hear of his sister Elizabeth's illness, which he hoped had by then been "favourably terminated." (She would die of consumption five months later.) It was an uncomfortable letter for him to write, seeing, as he clearly did at that point, just how much trouble he was in at home. There is no mention of a letter from his father, nor is there a letter to him, but Henry had no doubt that his father was furious that he had wasted so much time and money in Italy when he could have been studying in Germany—which is where he should have been for at least six months by then. They all knew that, even Henry. Especially Henry.

And then early in December, Henry finally got a letter from his father. It was dated September 15, and contained catastrophic news. The administration at Bowdoin College had decided to reduce their offer to a six hundred-dollar instructorship instead of a one thousand dollar professorship—an intolerable loss of money and status.[109] No one was sure what had gone wrong, but some speculated that the money saved would go toward a new chapel, while others thought the reduced offer was owing to a lingering anger that Henry had rejected Bowdoin's orthodox Christianity in favor of wide open Unitarianism.[110] Not that Longfellow cared what they were going to do with the money they would be saving on his salary. Taken all in all, it was the worst possible news and it jolted Longfellow back into forceful action. Everything came suddenly into focus again. He packed his bags immediately, said his heart-broken goodbyes to Giulia (with who-knows-what promises for the future), and headed north to Venice, with Dresden as his intended next destination. Longfellow's love affair with Italy and with Giulia Persiani was very suddenly but very decidedly over.[111]

On the nineteenth, in Venice, he wrote his measured but angry reply to his father's news, which had caused him "great pain," he said:

> They say I am too young! Were they not aware of this three years ago? If I am not capable of performing the duties of the office, they may be very sure of my not accepting it. I know not in what light they may look upon it, but for my own part I do not in the least regard it as a favor conferred upon me. It is no sinecure: and if my services are an equivalent to my salary, there is no favor done me—if they be not, I do not desire

the situation. If they think I would accept the place they offer me—as I presume they do—they are much mistaken in my character. No sir—I am not yet reduced to this. I am not a dog to eat the crumbs that fall from such a table. Excuse my warmth, but I feel rather hurt and indignant. It is a pitiful policy.[112]

Certainly, he went on, he had fulfilled his end of the bargain being already "familiarly conversant" with French and Spanish. He read Portuguese "without difficulty," and his Italian was so good that the hotel staff in Venice took him for a native. Did his father really think he should accept such an insulting offer? "No, I think you cannot." And for himself, he added, "I have the greatest abhorrence to such a step." When he wrote to his mother the next day, he reported that he'd had a bad trip up to Venice, but that hardly mattered, he said, when he tallied up the "melancholy catalogue of my woes."[113] High on that catalogue, of course, was his misery at having to leave Giulia behind so suddenly, but that was hardly something he could spell out in a letter to his mother.

When it came to practical matters, Henry had already worked out a new plan. He'd be heading up to Dresden first, he told his father in the letter of the nineteenth, and then go to Göttingen in search of "a competent knowledge of German," which he felt sure he could learn quickly. "The time is short," he had written to his father, "but short as it is I hope to turn it to good advantage." He was sorry to have caused so much concern, but he was back on track for Germany: "I have only to assure you that whatever suspicions my long stay in Italy may have occasioned you, they are wholly without foundation." If his father suspected something was keeping his son in Italy longer than he should have been there, it had to be the "solicitations of pleasure" and the "allurements of vice" that he had warned his son about back in April 1826. Henry would have quarreled with his father about Giulia Persiani as an allurement of vice, but contrary to Henry's claim of innocence, his father's suspicions were clearly not "without foundation."

Henry's mind, however, was busily refocusing on his new plans, both for Germany and his return to Portland and Brunswick. For his immediate post–Rome future, he'd be in travel mode: Bologna, Ferrara, Padua, Venice, and Trieste; coming up were Vienna, Prague, Dresden, and Göttingen. He was suddenly back to pursuing his goals with clarity and purpose. By mid-January he was writing a book proposal to Carey & Lea, publishers in Philadelphia. He had in mind "a series of papers upon the scenes and customs of my Native Land," which he said would be "in the stile of Irving's Sketch Book of Old England." The book did not get written, but Longfellow's creative juices were flowing for the first time in a long while. Something was brewing, even if he didn't know quite what form it would take. Or when he'd get to it.[114]

After spending Christmas in Venice, Longfellow left for Trieste the next day and found himself in Vienna on January 3, counting down his few remaining months in Europe, although he wasn't sure quite yet when he'd be heading back home—or what he would find there. After Vienna came Prague and then one of his most anticipated destinations, Dresden, where he was headed because he had letters of introduction written by Washington Irving and an anticipation of social connections that he hoped would ease his loneliness in a new city.[115]

But his tutored progress in German, which he had tried half-heartedly to learn on his own in Italy, did not go well in Dresden. For all practical purposes German was a completely new language for him, a problem made worse by his need to learn it quickly. He had written to his father on December 19 that he didn't want to return home "without a competent knowledge of German," but he realized once in Dresden how unlikely that would be. After a month, Henry felt himself as displaced as he had been in Florence, just about a full year earlier. But it was worse now because he was tormented by the injustice of Bowdoin's betrayal. On January 28, he wrote in his journal, "Feel decidedly blue—blue—deep blue...."[116]

A month later from Göttingen his anger spilled over once again. He wrote to his father that the more he thought about Bowdoin's treatment of him, "the more I am dissatisfied"[117] He ranted on: "I dislike the manner in which things are conducted there. Their illiberality in point of religion—and their narrow-minded views upon many other points, need no comment. Had I the means of a bare subsistence, I would *now* refuse a Professorship there." About ten days later he told his father that Bowdoin College was "too limited and superficial"—that he wanted to establish a university (which he capitalized and italicized) in Portland based on the German model. And without the position at Bowdoin he'd been preparing for for the last three years, he wasn't even sure he wanted to go back home at all. Göttingen and his reunion with Edward Preble had in fact changed his mind about German and Germany—and he asked his father if perhaps it might not be best under the circumstances for him "to lengthen a little my absence." Preble had made all the difference. "[M]eeting with an old and good friend, has given new elasticity to my spirits," he wrote. He added, perhaps stretching the point, that he was happy. Happy or not, a new enthusiasm had begun seeping into his letters.

In April, during a university vacation, Henry traveled to London, and when he returned to Göttingen, he wrote to his father. He made a pair of important announcements, first that he was working on a European sketch book (a work that became *Outre-Mer* six years later in 1835), and second that he was still interested in the job at Bowdoin, despite the way he'd been treated and despite the complexity of the German language, which he said "is beyond measure difficult." Clearly with a few months to think it over, Henry realized the position at Bowdoin was one he still wanted: "If I can have the Professorship at Bow. Coll.—I should like it," he told his father, "but I must have it on fair grounds: with the same privileges as the other professors. No state of probation—and no calling me a boy—and [no] retrenching my salary."[118]

It wasn't certain how long he would be remaining in Germany, but he'd had ample time to think about Bowdoin's reduced offer—and had decided that he wanted to fight for his job. Perhaps he had simply matured. "The farther I advance the more I see to be done—and the less time to do it in. The more, too, am I persuaded of the charlatanism of literary men. For the rest—my fervent wish is—and has long been, to return home. I would not remain for a moment, were it not from the persuasion of its necessity."

To his mother in a separate letter on the same day, Henry small-talked his journey "through Flanders to London and back by the way of Holland." There was a steady stream of travel stops, Cassel, Mayence, Cologne, Coblenz, Aix-la-Chapelle, Waterloo, Brussels, Calais, and finally Dover, Canterbury, and London, where he stayed a week. The return trip took him to Rotterdam, Delft, the Hague, Leyden, Haarlem, Amsterdam, and Utrecht. He especially liked Holland, whose women caught his eye. They weren't "handsome," he wrote, but "they possess that beauty which springs from health and [a] quiet peaceful life."[119] Notably, there isn't a hint of homesickness for Rome—or of lovesickness for Giulia Persiani.

While he was traveling, thinking about his uncertain position at Bowdoin, learning German, and trying to figure out how much longer he had in Europe, his favorite sister Elizabeth, only 20, after nine months of ailing and three of suffering, died of consumption on May 5. The news, however, was slow crossing the Atlantic. In mid-June an earlier letter from his father reached Henry that Elizabeth was not improving and was not by then expected to. Stephen wanted his son home as soon as possible. That settled all the outstanding questions. Henry abruptly left Göttingen for Paris, where news of Elizabeth's death reached him, and from Paris he traveled immediately to Liverpool for passage home, arriving in New York on August 11, 1829. He'd been gone nearly three and a half years.

2

"Her Ladyship"

A week after arriving in New York, Longfellow was in Boston, and a week after that he was back in Portland among his family and friends, the long-lost son finally returned to take his proper place in the world. What place that might be, however, was still uncertain. And he had to be concerned too about how well he would readjust to Portland and Brunswick after living so long in Paris, Madrid, and Rome. He was still only 22, but he had gone from being a college boy from small towns in Maine to a cosmopolitan man of the world—one who had learned five languages, absorbed the nuances of four faraway cultures, and been swept up by gothic cathedrals, Catholic pageantry, and Old World timelessness. And of course he'd fallen in love too. Could he ever find happiness again in provincial Portland? Could he find intellectual stimulation at a backwater college like Bowdoin? Could he form friendships like the ones he'd enjoyed abroad? These were the big questions that hung in the air when Longfellow finally reached home at the end of August 1829.

The actual homecoming was, of course, a happy affair that did not immediately register the rumbling discontent Henry would feel soon afterward. The position at Bowdoin, though reduced in size and salary, was still open, and his father for one thought Henry should accept it. The "guardians of the Institution," Stephen had tried to reassure his son back in April, still thought highly of him—despite his tender years.[1] He advised his son to take the position for a year while he thought through his options for permanent employment. And in late August Longfellow did indeed still want the job—but he was adamant, or perhaps merely stubborn, about the conditions under which he would accept it.

He took a chance and on the 27th sent a brief note to President Allen to reject the school's lowered offer: "I am sorry," he wrote, "that under the existing circumstances, I cannot accept the appointment."[2] He would certainly have accepted the original offer of a professorship at the same salary the other professors were receiving, but after having spent more than three years in

Europe learning five languages for his new post "at great expense," he pointed out, "I cannot accept a subordinate station with a salary so disproportionate to the duties required." The letter worked. The trustees wrote back immediately, on September 1, counter-offering a package just good enough for Longfellow to accept without losing face—he accepted the new offer on September 2. So despite the agonizing uncertainty he'd lived with for the past year, Henry had managed to get his job back in a matter of days once he arrived in Portland.

The compromise that had been worked out specified that Longfellow would indeed have the rank of professor, but the trustees asked for an "apprenticeship" before the rank was formalized. As to salary, they offered $800, higher than an instructor's salary but lower than a professor's, and then offered an additional $100 if he would serve as college librarian as well. Longfellow was placated and didn't care at the time that the trustees also requested that he teach underclassmen should the need arise.[3] With all the details worked out, mostly to his satisfaction, Henry Wadsworth Longfellow, four years after the position had been offered and one year after it had been withdrawn, was finally introduced to the college community and the world at large as Bowdoin College's first Professor of Modern Languages.

While this professional mini-drama was playing itself out, Longfellow's private life took a new turn as well. He met Mary Storer Potter.

Henry Longfellow was an attractive catch for any girl in Portland or Brunswick. He was not tall at five-eight, but he was slender and erect, which made him look taller, and he had blue eyes, chestnut hair, and a clean-shaven face to go with a gentle manner and personal warmth. He was always carefully dressed with an eye to fashion and color—too carefully dressed some thought—and he smoked a pipe and swung a slender cane as he walked. He was the picture of

Portrait of Longfellow at Bowdoin College ca. 1829 by Thomas Badger (Collections of Maine Historical Society, #4119).

style, courtesy, and dignity. Marriage eligible women of both cities saw a man with boyish good looks and good prospects. He turned heads on his nightly walks down Brunswick's Federal Street on his way to visit Parker Cleaveland.[4]

Longfellow was attractive, too, because he came from a good family, that is, one with means and one with a good genealogical underpinning, six of his ancestors on his mother's side, including John Alden and Priscilla Mullins, going all the way back to the *Mayflower*. His more immediate family on both sides was equally prominent and proud. Grandfather Longfellow, always smartly dressed, had been a nine-time elected judge in the Massachusetts General Court in Boston and later served fourteen years on the Court of Common Pleas. Henry's father graduated from Harvard in 1798, studied law under Salmon Chase, passed the bar in 1801, and became a prominent lawyer in Portland.[5] He served as a delegate to the Hartford Convention in 1814, represented his district in the Massachusetts General Court in 1814 and 1815 (before Maine joined the Union in 1820), was a member of the United States House of Representatives from 1823–1825, and was also a member of the Maine legislature in 1826. Also doing his public duty, he served as a trustee of Bowdoin College from 1817 to 1836. The Longfellows were a distinguished family.

But for all that, they weren't as famously distinguished as his mother's family. Grandfather Peleg Wadsworth was born in 1748, graduated from Harvard in 1769, and joined the American forces during the Revolution. As Brigadier General in 1779, he made a name for himself at the otherwise disastrous Penobscot naval expedition, landing a force and laying siege to Fort George for two weeks. When British reinforcements drove Wadsworth and his men from their positions, he led them on a long retreat, eventually working his way through the dense Maine forests to safety. The next year, when he was 32, he was put in charge of the forces defending the Maine province—and that is when he earned his lasting fame as an American Revolutionary War hero.

While Wadsworth and his staff slept on the night of February 17, 1781, a force of twenty-five British soldiers attacked. Wadsworth led his men in resistance until he was shot in the left arm. Bleeding and in great pain, he was led off to captivity at Fort George. As to the rest of the story, it's hard to separate facts from legends. It was said that when his arm had healed sufficiently, though not completely, Wadsworth escaped during a raging storm, tight-roping his way across rafters above unsuspecting guards in the room below. Ever so slowly, he worked his way outside where he got past the sentries, scaled a steep grade, and once again reached a dark and dangerous forest that had to be passed through to safety. Peleg Wadsworth had become at that point a bonafide war hero. In 1784, he moved his family to Portland, where his daughter Zilpah met and married (in 1804) young Stephen Longfellow, and that union produced Henry in 1807, who had become by September 1829, one of Portland's most eligible bachelors.

The local girl who won Henry's heart, Mary Storer Potter, turned out to be from a good family too.[6] Her father was the Honorable Barrett Potter, a judge in Cumberland County known for over-protecting his three daughters after their mother died in about 1827, leaving him a lonely man who tried to compensate for the death of his wife by instituting strict household rules for his daughters, like the one forbidding them to receive letters from young suitors, who were then forced to smuggle them in.[7] A graduate of Dartmouth College in 1796, Potter had been a lawyer in nearby Gorham before partnering with Salmon Chase in Portland and then becoming a twenty-five-year judge of the probate court. He had, perhaps, more status than money, but he presided over a good Portland family. His wife, Mary's mother, was Anne Storer, described at the time as "lovely," but "frail and delicate," a woman whose early death had not come as a surprise.[8]

"Her ladyship," Mary Storer Potter (Collections of Maine Historical Society, #4115).

Like all the women in her family (or so people regularly remarked), Mary was a pretty girl, which shows through the not-very-good portrait of her in the Maine Historical Society. There we see a young woman with delicate features, a thin neck, and long fingers. She is wearing a heavy, expensive-looking brown dress with lace at the neckline and cuff; her hair is fashionably arranged; and she has a full complement of jewels—necklace, bracelet, and ring. She is looking off into the near distance with clear, bright eyes. As to Mary's education, she was steered by her father away from Greek and Latin in favor of more practical subjects for girls, like French and mathematics. In her personal library were books like *A Legacy for Young Ladies, Consisting of Miscellaneous Pieces, in Prose and Verse, by the Late Mrs. Barbauld* (1826), which included essays on beauty and fashion, plus Mrs. Barbauld's thoughts on "female studies," which she said should not include "the learned languages" because they "require a great deal more time than a young woman can conveniently spare."[9] It isn't known if Judge Potter knew about Mrs. Barbauld's thoughts on "female studies" or if the ideas had slipped into general circulation by the 1820s, but either way, Mary was spared the classical languages.

Mary was the Potters' second daughter and had grown up on Free Street, a block or two from the Longfellows' home on Congress Street. Born five years after Henry in 1812, she'd been for a time a schoolmate of his at the Portland Academy.[10] She would have been 7 and Longfellow 12 in 1819, making them at best nodding acquaintances, she perhaps more likely to have noticed the older boy in school than he the younger girl. Later she and her sister Eliza attended Miss Cushing's "female school" in Hingham, Massachusetts, where she revealed "a thoughtful and well-trained mind," one that responded to writers like pre-romantic poets William Cowper and Edward Young, as well as to the more recent, full-blown romantics like Samuel Taylor Coleridge and Percy Bysshe Shelley.[11]

By the time Henry returned to Portland, Mary had developed into a beautiful 17-year-old. She was described as having "dark hair and deep blue eyes," her personality "modest, intensely polite, [and] quiet." Longfellow's brother Samuel wrote that Mary's deep blue eyes "lighted a countenance singularly attractive." A couple of years later, a neighbor in Brunswick described her as "a lovely woman in character and appearance, gentle, refined, and graceful, with an attractive manner that won all hearts." It was universally agreed that Mary Potter was a catch in her own right, an excellent match for young Professor Longfellow, even though she was generally thought to have a weak constitution (as her mother had had) and to be subject to what was later described as "chronic ennui."[12]

On his first Sunday back from Europe, according to family tradition, Henry saw Miss Mary Potter at church, wearing by one account a "brown silk dress over crinoline and a very handsome Paisley shawl." He was instantly smitten, so smitten that he followed her silently and from a discreet distance back to her home, which turned out to be the old Potter residence he knew so well from his childhood.[13] That afternoon he asked his sister Anne, who was a close friend of Mary's and who had become his special confidante after the death of Elizabeth, to walk him over to Mary's house and introduce him. He needed to meet the great beauty staying at the Potter home.

It was the beginning of an ardent but difficult courtship—difficult at least by comparison to the ease with which he had courted Giulia Persiani, right under the approving nose of her father.[14] Thomas Wentworth Higginson, later a student of Longfellow, a famous abolitionist, and the literary mentor of Emily Dickinson, glossed over the difficulties facing the couple when he reported that once they met that Sunday afternoon, the rest of the Longfellow-Potter courtship "followed as in a novel."[15] Perhaps it did. But Judge Potter, who was said to have sown his own wild oats as a young man, was a suspicious father who stood tall as an obstacle to be overcome, and it took a full year before the couple could announce their engagement and another year after that before the wedding, which didn't take place until September 14, 1831.

With the watchful judge lurking in the not-too-distant background, Henry was forced to use his sister Anne to deliver letters, notes, invitations, and the like to Mary, who eagerly looked forward to receiving them.[16] Even this little of their courtship has to be drawn from slight evidence, however, like the note he wrote to Anne dated July 13, 1830, asking her to deliver his acceptance of Mary's invitation for "the Ball tomorrow evening." But, he reminded Anne, the message had to be kept a secret for "if the Judge finds out that I have written a letter to his daughter, he will stand on the defensive": "So please hand it to her ladyship when no one is nigh—and she may do as she pleases about making it public."[17] It isn't easy to tell if the odd courtship became more of a happy game or a frustrating problem—but Henry was confident. He was a respectable and respectful young man with good prospects and parents—and because the legal community in Portland was a closed club, the judge and his father were close friends. It made sense that if he could just be patient, something good might yet come of his feelings for Miss Mary Potter.[18]

Perhaps showing patience wasn't too difficult during the remaining months of 1829 and the first half of 1830 because Henry was in Brunswick most of the time and Mary was back in Portland. Their commitment to each other gradually grew as month gave on to month, however, which meant their frustrations at the separation also gradually grew more and more difficult to endure. To dull the pain, perhaps, Henry spent as much time as he could at the home of Professor Parker Cleaveland, where he smoked a pipe with the older man and gossiped about Bowdoin characters and school politics—and where Cleaveland's three daughters would occasionally sing songs around the piano, no doubt putting Henry in mind of cozy family evenings at his own home, and maybe even reminding him of those happy *conversazioni* with the Persianis in Rome. Being married to Mary and living in Brunswick became fixed in his mind and imagination as the perfect domestic arrangement, but owing to the distance between Brunswick and Portland

and the judge's slowness at accepting his daughter's wishes, Henry's dream of a happy home life seemed to drift further away with each passing month.

If Judge Potter became a troublesome personal problem for Henry in Portland, there were other problems he was dealing with in Brunswick. For one thing, he'd been barred from rooming at any of the private residences near campus, where the other professors lived, because of his unusual "apprenticeship" status, which in turn forced him to take a dormitory room at Maine Hall where, adding insult to injury, he had to serve as proctor.[19] Except for the addition of a brick dining hall, the school itself looked much the same as it had when Henry was a student there, although the heat of campus politics had gone up a few degrees, which put Longfellow in a delicate position. He was remembered as a Unitarian maverick among the fire and brimstone Congregationalists who ran the school. It was a serious enough breach to become a factor in the college's effort to oust him from his promised professorship in 1828—even before it had begun. Henry's Brunswick issues were as unyielding as his Portland issues.

The theological and political backstory at Bowdoin did not, however, alter Henry's day-to-day affairs as the college's first professor of modern languages, which required that he establish a new program and prepare courses in French and Spanish for juniors and seniors.[20] His typical workday, he told Greene, began early and ended late: "I rise at six in the morning and hear a French recitation (Sophs) immediately. At seven I breakfast and am then master of my time till eleven—when I hear a Spanish lesson (Senior Class). After recitation I take a lunch—and at 12 o'clock go into the Library where I remain till one. I am then at leisure for the afternoon till five when I have another French recitation (Juniors)—at six I take coffee—walk and visit friends till nine—study till twelve, and then sleep till six—when I begin the same round again." He told Greene he was leading "a very sober, jog-trot kind of life."[21]

Henry was the youngest member of the faculty, which probably accounts for some part of his popularity among students, who saw him as less of a "martinet" than his colleagues, more of the "gentle, forgetful type of professor."[22] His classroom persona, an extension of his natural courtesy and personal charm, was also appealing. One of his 1830 students said Longfellow treated them all in a manner that was "perfectly simple, frank, and manly" and that "he neither sought popularity, nor repelled it."[23] Another student wrote: "We were fond of him from the start; his speech charmed us; his earnest and dignified demeanor inspired us. A better teacher, a more sympathetic friend, never addressed a class of young men."

Once told to "admonish" a student for an unrecorded infraction, Henry took the boy aside and began a conversation about French literature that lasted long enough for him to forget the reason he had sought the student out in the first place, at which point he had to call back over his shoulder: "Ah! I was near forgetting. The faculty voted last night that I should admonish you..., and you will consider yourself admonished." On another occasion, when a boy in recitation was being helped by a nearby fellow student, Longfellow replied dryly, "Your recitation reminds me of the Spanish theater, where the prompter performs a more important part than the actor."[24] It was true that Henry Longfellow was easy-going and good-natured, more student-friendly than many of the older professors, but there was something else to like about him—he was proud of his new profession, which was both thrilling and obvious to the entire college community when he rose to deliver the August 1830 commencement speech.

This was the ceremony when Longfellow rose formally to the rank of Professor of Modern Languages—the rise in status that allowed him to take up residence at the Fales House on the corner of Potter and Maine, right across from campus. Listeners to Longfellow's speech that day no doubt arched an eyebrow and stifled a yawn when they saw the unpromising title in the program: "The Origin and Growth of the Languages of Southern Europe and of Their Literature." They were relieved, however, to hear a promising opening: "When a man's duty and his inclination go hand in hand, surely he has no small reason to rejoice." And they had to be more pleased yet to hear the college's newest professor swell with pride over his new position: "I regard the profession of teacher in a far more noble and elevated point of view than many do. I cannot help believing that he who bends in a right direction the pliant disposition of the young..., does something for the welfare of his country and something for the great interests of humanity."[25] This was school teaching on a grand, even heroic scale.

Longfellow followed up by modeling his professorship after Bowdoin's most famous professor, his friend the geologist Parker Cleaveland, whose first edition of *Mineralogy and Geology* in 1816 would dominate the field for years and earn him the title "Father of American Mineralogy." That was the sort of scholar-teacher Henry wanted to be. He had to adapt the Cleaveland model to language and literature, but that was easier than it might seem. He began by preparing French, Spanish, and Italian texts and translations for publication and classroom use, six in all between 1830 and 1832. The primary purpose of the books was to provide classroom resources for students, but the books helped keep the languages fresh for him—and producing books (even if they had little chance of earning much money) did put the idea of book publishing into the range of subjects he was interested in—and would soon enough profit from. Then, too, he thought he was bridging the gap between being a professor and having a literary career, which was a goal he had heard so often from his father and others that was not achievable in America. Being a professor and being a literary man may not have been exactly the same thing, but they were close enough to be united in Longfellow's imagination in the early 1830s as he launched his teaching career.

This determined thrust into professionalism was what one biographer called Longfellow's "intensive period of scholarly devotion."[26] At the heart of it were six long articles for the *North American Review*, including studies on the languages and literatures of France, England, Spain, and Italy.[27] This was professionalism that went beyond teaching to include a familiarity with his subject so deep and inherently valuable as to deserve publication in something very like the modern notion of what the scholar-teacher should do. Henry Longfellow was setting the bar high.

The *North American Review* articles, however, were specialized essays for a limited audience in a low-circulation periodical—and so they were therefore never popular in anything like the way his later poetry would be. One of them, however, deserved a better fate, his review-essay of Sidney's *The Defence of Poetry*. It was here Longfellow wrote about the features of American life that were keeping poetry from being more highly valued and more widely circulated.[28]

Ours is a country, Longfellow said, that sees art as a decorative overlay to the more important business of preparing men for useful occupations. "With us, the spirit of the age is clamorous for utility, for visible, tangible utility, for bare, brawny, muscular utility." We are too busy with money-making projects and "contrivances for bodily enjoyments" to see "the true glory of a nation," which is its "moral and intellectual preeminence." But such a lofty goal was impossible when literary people in America were generally thought to have an "effeminate and unmanly character." Poetry, Longfellow said, came in for special criticism in America because "it unfits for the common duties of life and the intercourse of this matter-of-fact world." What was needed was a robust American literature, one that was more muscular and manly, something more fit for American life, something that had an "intensely national tone."[29]

But he wasn't thinking of his own poetry, at least not consciously. Longfellow had in fact written very few poems after announcing to Caroline Doane in an 1826 letter that he was going to stop publishing them.[30] Being on the road for three and a half years and focusing his attention on learning languages, absorbing new cultures, and making new friends had left little time for writing anything more than letters home. When he wrote about "intensely national" poems in his 1832 comments on Sidney's *Defence of Poetry*, he was speaking more as a scholar of poetry than as a poet himself.

And yet the review-essay on Sidney may well have reminded him of what had prompted him to poetry in the early 1820s—his desire for a literary career. He never forgot how dismissive his father had been back in December 1824, when he replied to Henry's plea for a literary career that it would no doubt be "very pleasant" for rich people, which, he pointed out, they were not. No, his father had written, Henry had to get a real job because their young country didn't have enough "wealth & munificence" to support "merely literary men." Deep in the background of his essay on Sidney's *Defence* was the desire to prove his father wrong, to do what no one thought it was possible to do, earn his living as a poet. Nothing would be sweeter than to do what no one thought could be done—what his own father thought could not be done—to become a wealthy poet. It was an impossible dream, but hidden in the pages of his review-essay was the germ of a hope that maybe one day his might be the robust, manly voice America needed.

All this airy theorizing, however, was far removed from Longfellow's work as a classroom teacher at Bowdoin, where he daily bent "in a right direction the pliant disposition of the young," as he so loftily put it in his August 1830 commencement speech. His first courses in 1829 were in elementary French and Spanish for upperclassmen.[31] In October 1829, however, he described to his old friend Alexander Slidell his busy schedule, probably to excuse himself for not having written earlier, but perhaps to complain a little about the work. He'd been so busy with getting squared away and reestablishing himself with old friends, he wrote to Slidell, that his vacation time had been "completely consumed," and the teaching itself when it began, kept him "very much occupied." Why, he even had the library to take charge of, which occupied still another hour every day. And on top of everything else, he was translating new material for classes (and later publication), all of which combined to put him at the limits of his endurance—and patience. His Bowdoin work schedule didn't even leave enough time to write a proper letter, he wrote to Slidell: "I hate the sight of pen, ink, and paper."[32]

At the same time Longfellow was, as he put in his December 20, 1829, letter to his father, "thick-sown with occupations," he was also pursuing the slender 17-year-old Mary Potter, although with his schedule in Brunswick, her residence in Portland, and her ever-vigilant, over-protective father on constant duty, progress was slow. Without their letters back and forth and without her diary, and without any comment by Longfellow in his own journal, all we know for certain is that by September 26, 1830, they had become engaged, for on that day we have a self-conscious and awkward letter from Longfellow to Mary's father.

Henry had visited the judge a few days earlier to ask formally for Mary's hand and was elated and relieved to get the hardly-automatic judicial approval, but he'd hoped for another visit before heading back to Brunswick, a time perhaps when he might get a little closer to his future father-in-law. There hadn't been time, however, for that second visit, and so he wrote a stiffly formal, man-to-man letter instead. There were, he announced, a few things he had "wished to express" but hadn't. First, he began, was "the grateful acknowledgment I owe you, for the confidence you have reposed in me in placing in my hands the happiness of a daughter, and in part your own." The sentence was tortured, the sentiment solicitous, but Henry pushed on. He hoped "most ardently" that the judge would never have the "slightest occasion" to think his confidence had been "misplaced": "I certainly believe you never will have: and this belief is founded upon the attachment I feel for Mary, in whom I find the inestimable virtues of a pure heart and guileless disposition—qualities which not only excite an ardent affection, but which tend to make it as durable as it is ardent."[33] Writing to his fiancée's father, Henry might be excused for replacing his lover's passion with an "ardent affection" and ignoring Mary's physical charms in order to praise her "pure heart and guileless disposition." It was clearly hard to pick just the right words and tone for this sort of letter. He did his faltering best.

Portrait of Henry Wadsworth Longfellow, ca. 1835 (courtesy National Park Service. Longfellow House—Washington's Headquarters National Historic Site, LONG 4153).

For her part, the soon-to-be-wed Mary Potter was more excited. In June 1831, she wrote to her sister that she and Henry hadn't seen each other for three weeks, but she was holding on, she said, "with the spirit of a martyr" because she knew the wedding was coming up shortly. Soon the moment would arrive "when I shall never be separated from him," she went on. "Every time we meet I see some new point in his character, for which I love him better, if possible, than before. I certainly never imagined that I could find in this world so good and affectionate a person, and one who would love me so much. He answers much better to a being of my imagination than one of real life."[34] Her words speak more to Henry's love for Mary than his own had done. They were in love, Mary had made clear, and this was high romance.

The September 1830 engagement announcement was followed by an August 31, 1831, wedding announcement in the same church where the ceremony would take place two weeks later, Portland's First Parish Unitarian Church. The bride was 19 and the groom 24. Three days before the wedding, Longfellow wrote from Brunswick to his sister Mary in Portland that he had invited "two young ladies to pass the present week with you, and to be of the wedding party. They are Martha Anne Cleaveland and Mary Fales."[35] It sounds like a casual affair this wedding, one that could accommodate late changes with an easy shifting of place cards, but unfortunately we know almost nothing at all about the wedding itself, which may have something to do with the fact that the Longfellow family had two weddings in the space of a month, for Henry's brother Stephen married Marianne Preble on August 17. It was a double swirl of matrimonial activity.

Henry and Mary with just a few family members present were married by the Rev. Ichabod Nichols. According to one report, Mary wore "a gown of shot gray silk with a little gray bonnet with two white ostrich plumes curling down over the brim."[36] A few days later, when the husband and wife arrived in Brunswick, Mary met Alpheus Packard, Professor of Latin and Greek at Bowdoin, who described her as "an attractive person, blooming in health and beauty, the graceful bride of a very attractive and elegant young man."[37]

That the young couple was busy getting to know each other in the fall of 1831 is suggested by Longfellow's correspondence, which tailed off markedly. Then, in January he took his young bride with him on a business trip to Cambridge where he had scheduled conversations about publishing his foreign language grammars and readers. It is unknown how much honeymooning pleasure got mixed in with publishing business.[38]

There was one dark cloud, however, for by the time of his wedding on September 14, 1831, Longfellow was already deeply disillusioned by his career choice—or perhaps just by Bowdoin. He preferred to think the latter, but it came to the same thing: he was unhappy. It is likely he maintained his high-minded opinion of teaching and believed still in the principles he had sketched out in his August 1830 commencement speech—but day-to-day teaching in backwater Brunswick proved too stultifying to keep young Longfellow happy. In a January 1831 letter to James Berdan, whom he had met in Paris, he complained about living "in this land of Barbarians—this miserable Down East." He said he was "living in exile."[39] Later that year, on August 21, just before his wedding, he complained to his sister Anne that there was virtually no time at all between the upcoming wedding and the day on which he had "to commence grinding in the knowledge mill again."[40] He went on: "You call it a dog's life: it is indeed—my dear Anne: I do not believe that I was born for such a lot. I have aimed higher than this: and I cannot believe that all my aspirations are to terminate in the drudgery of a situation, which gives me no opportunity to distinguish myself, and in point of worldly gain, does not even pay me for my labor." And then, topping off his complaints, he remembered he was stuck in Brunswick, Maine: "One loses ground so fast in these out of the way places: the mind has no stimulus to exertion—grows sluggish in its movements and narrow in its sphere—and there's the end of a man."

In January 1832, on Henry's trip to Cambridge to make arrangements to publish his foreign language books, he also met Cornelius Conway Felton, then a new Harvard tutor in the classics. The two men liked each other immediately. Henry thought that if he ever did get a position at Harvard, he would already have one good friend there. In fact, Harvard was a recurring fantasy. Back in July 1826, he had written to his father from Paris that the Reverend Nichols in Portland had mentioned that he'd spoken to Henry's "*friends at Cambridge*," who had taken "an interest in my situation abroad."[41] It was a puzzling comment, Henry said, and he wasn't sure what importance to give it—though it sounded hopeful. "I thought he intended to hint, that he had a plan for obtaining a situation for me at Harvard—as being more to my taste than Brunswick." He wanted to know if his father had any information about such a position, or if he would ask Nichols for some clarification. Not surprisingly, considering the trouble Stephen had gone through to get Bowdoin to offer his son a professorship, Stephen let the question go unanswered. Clearly though, young Longfellow had been thinking about Harvard for years by the time he met Cornelius Felton in 1832. It would indeed be a wonderful thing to work with him there.

On June 2, 1832, George Greene wrote to Henry suggesting that he apply for the chairmanship of the Department of Modern Languages at New York University—so he could take Longfellow's place at Bowdoin. "Your suggestions concerning the chair of Mod. Lang. in the University of New York please me very much," Longfellow wrote back. "I would gladly make the exchange; and yet I know not why I say so, for I know nothing of the proposed endowments in the N. York University, nor of the salary, or tuition, or perquisites of the Professors.... Of course I cannot decide upon this point without first knowing all the circumstances of the case.... You see how coolly I weigh matters."[42] He may have weighed the matter coolly, but he nevertheless remained hot to leave Bowdoin: "Next September completes 3 years, that I have been laboring on in this little solitude," he continued, "and I now feel a strong desire to tread a stage on which I can take longer strides, and *spout* to a larger audience."

Nothing came of the New York University opening, which turned out to be just another of Henry's frustrating "opportunities" over the next couple of years that briefly promised his early release from Bowdoin. In July 1833, he toyed with two long shots, opening a school for young women in New York and becoming secretary to the American legation in Madrid. When he sought the aid of his old friend, the one-time Ambassador in Madrid, Alexander Everett, he learned the position had already been filled. Then deflating Henry further, Everett added that no political position was likely for any New Englander while Andrew Jackson was still president.[43] Henry was clearly grasping at straws, but his growing disappointment at having to remain at Bowdoin demanded that he pursue every avenue of escape. He had worked himself up to the point where any offer from anyone to do just about anything would have happily moved him to pack his bags.

He inquired after a position teaching modern languages at the University of Virginia in February 1834, the same month and year he thought about (and decided against) buying and running the Round Hill School in Northampton, Massachusetts, a well-known school for boys that had opened under the guidance of George Bancroft and Joseph Cogswell in 1823 and would close in 1834, when no buyer could be found. Mary thought the Round Hill School too much of a financial risk, but felt bad for Henry that she couldn't get behind the move: "The poor fellow has set his heart upon it & I believe he detests Brunswick most cordially."[44]

That spring Longfellow actually resigned—more or less. He submitted his letter of resignation saying that he'd be leaving as soon as he lined something else up, but that continued to be an elusive goal as nothing came of any of his inquiries—so he remained unhappily in place. In the summer of 1834, a professorship at New York University rose again as a possible alternative to his Bowdoin job, and this time Longfellow got a letter of recommendation from George Ticknor himself, who wrote on June 18: "He writes & speaks Spanish, with a degree of fluency & exactness, which I have known in no other American.... His knowledge of Spanish Literature is extensive & to be relied upon; and several publications he has made on the subject have been accompanied with poetical translations of much spirit and fidelity." And then, to round off the letter of praise, Ticknor added that Longfellow was "an accomplished general scholar, particularly in modern literature; and full of activity and eagerness in the pursuit of knowledge." He even looked good: "His general appearance, address & manners are very prepossessing; his temper amiable; and his character without blemish."[45] This was promising.

Henry went so far as to go to New York to discuss the job, which turned out, however, to be something less than he had hoped. In fact, as he reported to George Morris, founder of the *New York Mirror*, "This professorship, if created, will be without a salary, tuition for instruction and lectures only being given," which meant, he continued, that "I shall be obliged to look for my support, in part at least, to sources disconnected with the University...."[46] He was asking if Morris might have work for him in case the job materialized and he still needed to support himself. New York was already a literary hub, and it was not unreasonable for Longfellow to think there might be something for him there, as long as he remained flexible and persistent—but once again, nothing came of his efforts, and he found himself in September 1834 lining up for yet another year at Bowdoin College in Brunswick, Maine. His heavy sighs were desperate and audible.

If Henry's professional life had stalled at Bowdoin, his personal life in Brunswick was much happier. He had enjoyed living alone at the Fales House in 1830–31, a marked improvement over his dormitory year, 1829–30, but he wasn't happy about having to move his bride there after their wedding in September 1831—their need for privacy at least as important as his stated reason, that Mary wouldn't want to take all her meals in the boarding house's common dining room. Unfortunately, nothing more suitable turned up. It was a pity, but for the time being, as he explained in a letter to his sister Anne, "there is no remedy."[47] Mary, who may have been disappointed, tried not to show it in a letter written to her sisters in Portland shortly after she moved into the boarding house: "I like it as well as I can upon so short a residence here [Brunswick]. The ladies have been very kind and polite to me, and it would be very wrong for me not to be contented and happy with such a husband and so pleasant a home."[48]

A year later, however, in October 1832, Henry moved his wife into the Robert Dunlap House at 25 Federal Street, which Zilpah described as being "surrounded by shrubbery ... a charming quiet place."[49] Located very near campus, the Dunlap House was indeed a big step up, large enough for the young professor to have a quiet place to write and do school work, and secluded enough to give the young couple their long-desired privacy. It was even big enough for the occasional out-of-town guest. It was perfect, though the move itself had to be postponed for a few days with Mary, in Henry's words, "confined to her chamber."[50] Nothing, however, not the one-year wait or Mary's moving-week confinement, could dampen Henry's spirits. He wrote to Charles Folsom at the Harvard University Press, "I have at length got seated in my new house. It is one of the pleasantest in town, and one of the most convenient. It suits me *exactly*."[51] Husband and wife both felt more settled than they had in a year at the boarding house. "Little Mary," as Henry called her, finally had a nest of her own, and they began their second year together with the exaggerated joy of a young couple getting a slightly delayed start in one of the "pleasantest" houses in Brunswick. It had been worth the wait.

To Mary, Henry was "a good little dear," as she put it in an April 1834 letter to her sister-in-law Anne."[52] She approved of almost everything he did, she wrote, except perhaps for his smoking, and she was pleased to report that Henry was attending meetings of the Temperance Society and was looking into vegetarianism as it was then being advocated by Dr. Reuben Mussey in his popular medical campaigns against alcohol, tobacco, and meat—good health through self-denial. Always attracted to fine wines, aromatic cigars, and hearty meals, including meat of course, Longfellow was at the same time on the permanent lookout for Spartan regimens like fad diets, water treatments, calisthenics, even boxing lessons, all designed to restore his health, which he often felt to be on the edge of total collapse. The result was that Henry and Mary enjoyed a mostly sober and meatless marriage, restrictions that in reality had little impact on the limited social life they had, like their evenings with the Cleaveland family when Cleaveland played the harpsichord and Henry accompanied on flute. At home Mary took an active interest in her husband's work, sometimes copying literary passages for him to use in his lecturing and writing, although one friend noted that Mary wasn't herself in the least interested in learning another language: "She is satisfied to have her husband do all the studying and her happiness consists in being by his side."[53] Theirs was a quietly happy marriage.

Then, rather suddenly, Longfellow began writing poetry again. He hadn't precisely given up on poems, of course, but had instead been busy, as a professor of foreign languages, translating them for his students and preparing grammars in both French and Italian. And Europe, as he later put it in a letter to Nathaniel Hawthorne who was then in England, had been too all-consuming for him to write poetry: "Can you work with your pen," he asked, "in those fascinating, foreign climes? I never could."[54] In 1833 the first of his books to come out was a straight translation of the fifteenth-century Spanish poet Jorge Manrique, *Coplas por la muerte de su padre*, some 500 lines divided up into seventy-five *coplas* (couplets or stanzas) on the death of his father, who had himself been an honored Spanish poet who had died in 1476. Added to that volume were seven translated sonnets, including "To-morrow," by

Lope de Vega, about how he kept God outside in the "unhealthy dews" instead of letting Him into his heart and soul, which de Vega says he'll do "to-morrow"—but never does. It may have been the self-examining confessional nature of the poem that drew Longfellow to it—or perhaps the poem was merely an irresistible challenge to translate, with its spiritual uncertainties and emotional nuances in Spanish that needed to find English equivalents. Either way, Longfellow's rendering of it into English played a role, along with the other poems in *Coplas*, in the reawakening of his long dormant poetic impulse.[55]

There was something else moving poetry to the forefront of his mind, his Phi Beta Kappa poems. He'd delivered the first one, "The Past and the Present," at the 1829 Bowdoin PBK meeting, then revised it when asked again for the 1832 commencement, which went so well that he was invited to give it yet again to the PBK society at Harvard in the fall of 1833. The poem and performance at Harvard were reviewed in the *Boston Daily Advertiser*: "After giving a rapid and brilliant sketch of the intellectual characteristics of what are called the dark ages, he entered upon a still more interesting one of the peculiarities of our own. The prevailing modes of education afforded him opportunities for satire, which were not lost, and he concluded with a fine poetical display of the great moral objects, which all intellectual education is intended to subserve."[56] In the midst of the translations of Spanish poetry and the PBK work, Longfellow wrote to Folsom to complain once again about teaching: "I am out of humor with matters and things in general. This teaching boys their a, b, c, is growing somewhat irksome.... I mean to turn author and write a book—not a *grammar*."[57] Thomas Wentworth Higginson wrote of all this suddenly renewed literary activity of Longfellow's in the early 1830s that it wasn't unreasonable "to recognize something of his young wife's influence." Love, he thought, had gotten Longfellow's creative juices to flow once again.[58]

In prose, Longfellow was working on something else that was light years away from teaching boys their a, b, c's, a series of Irving-like travel sketches that he published anonymously in July 1835 as *Outre-Mer: A Pilgrimage beyond the Sea*. The title, he explained in the first chapter, had come from the age of the crusaders and meant "the Land beyond the Sea," which was how they referred to the Holy Land. "I, too, in a certain sense, have been a pilgrim of Outre-Mer; for to my youthful imagination the Old World was a kind of Holy Land."[59] The book came to a slightly fictionalized, twenty-seven-chapter account of his own travels to Paris, Madrid, and Rome—as well as to a few other exotic ports of call he'd visited in his three and a half years abroad.

Once again Longfellow knew he was engaged in a project that satisfied him in ways his grammars and articles for the *North American Review* had not. He had written of it to Greene on March 9, 1833: "Well, I am writing a book—a kind of Sketch Book of France, Spain, Germany, and Italy—composed of descriptions—sketches of character—tales illustrating manners and customs, and tales illustrating nothing in particular."[60] He knew he was working on a book that, like his translations of Manrique's *Coplas* and de Vega's "To-Morrow," fed the artist within him, not the professor. The textbooks and the articles he'd written for the *North American Review* were suitable exercises that kept him professionally engaged—and potentially desirable as a candidate for a new teaching position somewhere far from Brunswick. Their importance could not be downplayed, and he understood that. But the *Coplas* and the PBK poems had triggered a renewed interest in publishing poetry, while *Outre-Mer* was a foray into the prose stylings of his literary hero, Washington Irving. He was coming to realize, as he said to Greene, that "it requires but little courage to publish grammars and school-books—but in the department of *fine-writing*, or attempts at fine writing, it requires vastly more courage." He was in fact in the process of reinventing himself.

If "fine writing" cost more courage, it also paid vastly greater dividends, potentially in dollars and cents, but also in soul-satisfaction—ample rewards for the hours invested. By 1864 *Outre-Mer* had sold 6,060 copies, a very good sale for the time.[61] Part of the book's success was owing to its travel-book descriptions of far off Europe, its beauty and mystery, for readers who would never get there. But it was successful too because it reminded readers of Irving's popular *Sketch-Book*; that is, it was written in a form and style the public had already taken into their hearts and homes. Longfellow had made a couple of sound business and artistic decisions—and been talented enough to bring it off.

By the end of November 1834, Henry Longfellow, professor, translator, poet, author, and settled-down married man, was impatient for the changes he could sense on the horizon—his ticket out of Brunswick. He thought he was ready.

3

"Utter darkness"

It was just then, on December 2, 1834, that Bowdoin's first professor of modern languages received the letter marked "Confidential" from President Josiah Quincy of Harvard, inviting him to take George Ticknor's place as the Smith Professor of Modern Languages. It was too good to be true, though the offer made perfect sense. Ticknor, the acknowledged master on Spanish literature, had been impressed with Longfellow's 1833 translation of Manrique's *Coplas*, which had been prefaced by a reprint of his article from *The North American Review* on the "Moral and Devotional Poetry of Spain." It was almost as though Henry had done the work as an audition—and then got the part. And why not? He'd earned it. He wrote to his father immediately: "Good fortune comes at last; and I certainly shall not reject it."[1]

The position paid 50 percent more than Longfellow was earning at Bowdoin, but in truth, he probably would have taken 50 percent less to exchange Brunswick for Cambridge. This was his fantasy job that had somehow become a reality, the perfect cure for his deepening depression. He'd be continuing his work as a professor, which he hoped would be better with Harvard students than it had been with the boys from Bowdoin, and he and Mary would be living in the sophisticated Cambridge/Boston urban center, with all its cultural and artistic benefits. But best of all, he didn't have to start until after he returned from a year or two in Europe where Quincy thought he might go to work on his German. Whenever he began teaching, Henry would be in charge of four instructors who were teaching five languages, though his exact duties were still being worked out. He hoped to learn more at the interview he was invited to after Christmas.

The only outstanding question was whether or not he would take the opportunity to study German before beginning his duties at Harvard—and Henry was fairly certain he would. There were a few issues, however, that had to be resolved, like how he would pay for it and how he would convince Mary to come with him. And then there was his father, who rose as an obstacle. Stephen was openly against the proposed trip to Germany, mostly for financial reasons. The increase in salary would be eaten up by the higher cost of living in Boston, he said, which meant that the expense of the European trip would never be fully recovered.[2] In the end, Longfellow managed to put together just enough money to pay for the trip, tapping his savings, selling books and furniture, and borrowing most of the rest from his father.[3]

Zilpah probably had more personal reservations. She had lost her 16-year-old daughter, Ellen, in August, and now Henry, only thirty miles away in Brunswick was about to move to Cambridge, more than a hundred miles away, which was bad enough, but even that long journey was better than being completely cut off from her favorite son for a year or more. Presumably Judge Barrett shared some of these geographical reservations, but he had to be worried about Mary's delicate health most of all, to say nothing of the dangers associated with an Atlantic crossing. Would all this prove to be too much for his fragile daughter, so like her mother after all?

Mary herself was aware that she could remain in Brunswick or Portland while Henry studied in Germany—and she was at first leaning that way, but she gradually changed her mind, in part because Henry downplayed the dangers of an Atlantic crossing and emphasized instead what people liked to call "the healthful benefits of sea air." That, plus the thought of seeing romantic Europe with her husband instead of being separated from him for a year or more, persuaded her to take a chance. And there was something else that may well have been the clincher: Henry had agreed (for an unknown fee that helped make the trip possible) to be the official escort of Mary's friends, Clara Crowninshield and Mary Goddard. On February 21, 1835, Mary wrote with her changed mindset to Maria Greene, wife of George Greene, about her upcoming trip: "I anticipate much pleasure, especially as a friend of mine, Miss Crowninshield, will accompany us. She is almost like a sister to us, and I shall enjoy myself much more having a lady with us."[4]

And so, with his wife finally on board, the last piece of Henry's plans for a northern European tour had fallen into place, although with a party of four, he knew his work time would necessarily be compromised. Still, it had been a complicated business to arrange and this was the best he could do on short notice. He was pleased with himself, happy about the sudden change in his fortune, and ready to enjoy Europe with his wife of four years.

Mary Goddard, who planned to stay with the Longfellow party only until the late summer, when she was to meet up with her brother and continue touring with him, was the daughter of a wealthy Boston businessman who had married Mary Longfellow's aunt, thus making the two Marys first cousins. Twenty-four-year-old Clara Crowninshield, born on February 8, 1811, was an illegitimate but independently wealthy young woman, and a longtime and close friend of Mary's. Her father George Crowninshield was from a socially prominent and prosperous Salem family that had made a fortune in shipping and trade. He was unmarried and known locally for being colorful, if not downright eccentric, as he drove about town in his snappy curricle—a two-seater pulled along by two expensive horses. He wore his hair in a pigtail, topped it off with a rakish beaver hat, and sported a fashionable waistcoat and boots with tassels. He was also known for *Cleopatra's Barge*, a 191-ton yacht he had built in 1816, and which he famously cruised throughout the Mediterranean. Unfortunately, he was also known for his untimely death aboard the *Barge* on November 26, 1817, at age 52. Clara's mother was Elizabeth Rowell, about whom little is known besides being George Crowninshield's "kept Mistress."5

Clara Crowninshield. From the sketch by Maria Röhl, Stockholm, 1835 (courtesy National Park Service. Longfellow House—Washington's Headquarters National Historic Site, LONG 6008).

Clara was unexpectedly provided for in her father's will and ultimately received more than $15,000, with her affairs put in the hands of an attorney who was also named her guardian and who managed over the next several years to increase her fortune through good investments enabling her to live comfortably, if not lavishly, for the rest of her life. Elizabeth Rowell allowed her daughter to be cared for in this fashion and later married a Salem baker and raised a family, thus achieving a measure of respectability—and falling completely out of sight.

George Crowninshield, perhaps feeling death approaching in November 1817, spent his last ten days with the woman he called his wife and the 6-year-old daughter he'd come to love. He drew up a new will shortly before his death, and though later challenged by his siblings, who received some $60,000 each, his bequest to his illegitimate daughter was allowed to stand—and Clara Crowninshield's life took an unpredicted turn: she would never be quite respectable, but she was cared for and educated by guardians who always kept her best interests in mind. In 1819 Clara was sent off to the Miss Cushing's "female seminary," the same well-regarded boarding school in Hingham,

Massachusetts that Mary and Eliza Potter were attending. They all studied together and developed a taste for literature—and they also became fast friends, Clara developing a kind of family relationship with the Potter girls on her frequent visits to Portland.[6]

When Mary and Henry married and moved to Brunswick, Clara spent long stretches at a time with them, sometimes seeming to be a nearly permanent part of the Federal Street household. While the ladies tended to a variety of quiet evening duties, they could hear Henry and his friends talk about Swedenborgianism, modern poetry, or Andrew Jackson, whom everyone denounced. They were all amused by Señor Cortés, Longfellow's friend from Madrid, who, Mary said, "keeps us laughing from morning till night."[7] And when the subject came around to Henry's new job, Clara's enthusiasm for the proposed trip was contagious, probably even more persuasive than Henry's loving logic.

The Longfellow party boarded the packet *Philadelphia* in New York harbor to begin their journey to London on April 10, 1835, the same month *Outre-Mer*, about his first European pilgrimage, was being published anonymously by Harper & Brothers in New York. On May 8, after a month of choppy seas and miserable seasickness, Henry managed to lead the ladies ashore at Portsmouth. He'd been sick for the entire journey and had had "hardly a moment's comfort on board," Mary reported to Zilpah. In fact, she said, "none of the passengers were nearly so sick as he."[8] It wasn't much as signs go, but neither did it get the long journey off on the right foot.

From Portsmouth the travelers took the public coach to London, some seventy miles away, arriving on May 12 for a three-week stay. Henry, as always dressed to the nines, acted the tour guide for his three ladies, taking them on the sixteenth, for example, on a walk to Regent's Park and from there by coach to find a Mr. Adams, a famous watchmaker. Henry mixed in a little book buying for his department at Harvard, which had authorized him to spend 200 pounds on volumes for the college library.[9] As to the actual study of languages, his primary reason for being abroad, he'd defer that to his arrival in the various countries on their long journey. Their first three weeks would be mostly given over to London sightseeing.

After that busy day on the sixteenth, Henry wrote to his father like a man who'd been forced to surrender business to pleasure. He'd really had no choice, he explained, it was simply beyond his control. All that squiring and tourism "consumed the day," he complained half-seriously.[10] "You can do nothing before 10 o'clock in the morning, and then the distances from point to point are so great—London is on so vast and magnificent a scale, that it is impossible [to see very many sights] in the course of a day, and at night you are so thoroughly tired, that you sleep late into the next morning." Between sightseeing and occasional hours browsing bookshops, the days in London flew by.

On the twenty-seventh, Henry took the ladies to the National Gallery, where, as Clara wrote in her diary, "it was whispered about that the Queen [Adelaide] was soon to pass!"[11] They ran to a window in time to see the queen's carriage go by, complete "with 4 footmen behind in pointed caps and coats covered with strips of gilt." According to the whispers, Clara continued, the Queen was on her way "to attend the examination of children," and the ladies concluded that it would be taking place at St. Paul's, which caused them to change their earlier plans to see the ongoing construction of the Thames Tunnel. They raced to St. Paul's only to discover the Queen was elsewhere. "Then we won't go in," Longfellow said, "in a tone of chagrin," as Clara recorded it in her diary. He "hurried away," Clara said, "vexed that we should have thrown away so much time in a fruitless chase."

Mary was enjoying herself and wrote a chatty letter to Zilpah on the 31st to say that they'd been spending their time "very delightfully in London," but like her husband, she complained that there was so much to do and so little time to do it. She wrote about their visit to see Mrs. Mary Skinner, the patron of Portland writer Nathaniel Parker Willis:

> Last Monday we passed very delightfully at Shirley Park, near the little village of Croydon. The ride is through a very beautiful country. We passed several gipsy encampments, in the most picturesque situations. Shirley Park is a truly delightful place. The house, which is a very fine one, is placed on a beautiful spot, & there are fine views from all sides of it. Mrs. Skinner, the lady of the place, is a very agreeable amiable lady—she took us all over the grounds in her carriage, & was very kind & attentive to us. Her house is thronged with visitors, the great, the fashionable, & the *literati* all pay their court to her.[12]

Longfellow was pleased and relieved that Mary was so happy and healthy. It was better, he knew, that he had been the one to suffer seasickness on the crossing, not his "Little Mary"—and here she was enjoying London too. He'd been right to insist that she be by his side on this important journey that was rapidly turning into a delayed honeymoon. Not surprisingly Mary became pregnant, possibly at sea in April or more likely on dry land in London in May. Henry was smart enough to know that he should be enjoying London with his beautiful young wife and putting off his duties until later. They were a happy couple.

Henry had a few letters of introduction, but they proved mostly disappointing, as for example the meeting with John Bowring, the multi-talented linguist who had invited Longfellow over to breakfast—and then ignored him in favor of reading his mail. He had a similar experience with the dandified and lisping Edward Bulwer, still basking in the 1834 success of *The Last Days of Pompeii*, who was leaving his house when Longfellow arrived with his letter of introduction from the Philadelphia publisher, Willis Gaylord Clark. Bulwer barely broke stride, casually fingering the offered letter and stammering a hurried new invitation, all the while squeezing past Longfellow on his way out the door. "Shall I record it?" Longfellow wrote in his journal, "I felt a little piqued at such a cold reception."[13]

Henry also met with Willis, who had become nearly as phony as Bulwer—and even more popular. Henry wrote to Greene that Willis's "orbit is *high* among the stars and *garters* of the fashionable zodiac," but though he'd been "very polite," Henry went on, "it was evident that I hung heavy upon his skirts, like a country cousin."[14] Then too there was Willis's poetry that Henry found "too artificial" because it "has now lost one of its greatest charms for me—its sincerity." Mary wrote home on May 24 that Willis's appearance had improved since the last time she had seen him, but that he was nonetheless too much the foppish man about town. Making him even shallower, she thought, was his way of jumping from party to party where his female admirers always gathered eagerly around him.[15] Even his sister Sara, who became the international literary sensation Fanny Fern, grew to hate him—he had refused to help her when she was getting started as a writer so she slammed him as the self-absorbed brother in her best-selling autobiographical novel *Ruth Hall* in 1854.

Meeting up with Willis had not been especially memorable, but it may have remained the literary high point of the early going if it hadn't been for Henry's meeting in the last week or so of May with Jane and Thomas Carlyle. Emerson had written Longfellow's letter of introduction, which Henry brought around to the Carlyle house outside London in Chelsea on May 21, but Carlyle was out so the new Harvard professor was entertained instead by Jane, who took a great interest in this American so far from home. Longfellow wrote in his journal of Jane that she was a "sweet simple, lovely woman, with long black tresses, and a downcast, timid look"—he called her a "wild-flower from the Highlands of Scotland." Mary was equally taken with Jane, whom she called "a lovely woman with very simple & pleasing manners. She is also very talented & accomplished, & how delightful it is to see such modesty combined with such power to please."[16]

A few days later, Carlyle came calling on Longfellow and whisked him back to Chelsea for a long visit that same night. He gave Longfellow a copy of his *Life of Schiller*, which brought Henry around to studying German and German literature, at once beginning to fulfill his obligation to Harvard, and more importantly discovering a literary vein he would mine for the rest of his life. He read the book in a single sitting on May 31, and wrote in his journal that he hoped when he finally got to sleep that he would get up with as much enthusiasm for the book as he had when he had finished reading it.

Carlyle the man made an even deeper impression than Carlyle the writer, not only on Longfellow, but on Mary and Clara as well. He was unprepossessing physically, "a tall man—with coal-black hair—brown complexion," wearing "an old blue coat—brown trousers—and carpet socks upon his feet," Longfellow wrote. His manner was "awkward—almost clownish." But his conversation, Longfellow gushed, "is glorious—so natural—and bearing the stamp of so free and original a mind."[17] Clara had a similar response: "He was tall and awkward in his appearance and his countenance did not betray inward cultivation, but as soon as he began to converse his original mind beamed forth.... I *hung* upon every word he let fall."[18] But it was Mary

This portrait of a young woman is described in the catalogue at Craigie House as "possibly a portrait of Mary Storer Potter Longfellow" (courtesy National Park Service. Longfellow House—Washington's Headquarters National Historic Site, LONG 4423).

who captured the Carlyles best in a letter to Zilpah: "Oh dear! I do not know as I shall be able to speak to you when I return, I see so many lords and ladies! But in reality these lords and ladies are not half as agreeable people as some of Henry's literary friends. Mr. and Mrs. Carlyle have more genuine worth and talent than half of the nobility in London. Mr. Carlyle's literary fame is very high, and she is a very talented woman—but they are people after my own heart—not the least pretension about them."[19]

On June 9, from the Thames, Longfellow and the ladies boarded the packet *William Joliffe* for Hamburg, the start of a difficult eighteen-day journey to Stockholm. Mary, who had begun having what she thought might be flu symptoms, was not eager to exchange the comforts of London for the discomforts of sailing ships and bouncing carriages with a final destination a country where she would not even be understood.[20] She was concerned about what might lie ahead, fearful perhaps that what she was calling the "ague" might actually be another pregnancy—and yet there was no alternative to pushing on to Stockholm. She decided to delay telling Henry her concerns, at least for the time being, and tried to continue enjoying herself. She'd make the best of it.

But it was hard going. Hamburg was a three-day, 500-mile journey away, followed by a too-brief, two-day rest at the comfortable *Hotel de Russe*. And then, in the blink of an eye, they were boarding a coach for Lübeck, some fifty miles and twelve hours northeast of Hamburg, a "horrible road," Clara wrote in her diary, "the terror of all travelers."[21] They stopped once for food and a brief rest, but then it was back on the road to Lübeck, where they were finally able to stretch their legs and have a decent meal. But then they were on the coach again, another eleven miles to the coastal town of Travemunde where they crossed by steamboat overnight to Copenhagen. By then, however, the company was worn out—and they all found Copenhagen dull. "As you walk up the wide, & solitary streets—and see the grass growing here and there from between the stones of the pavement—a feeling of gloom and loneliness comes over you. The city has a melancholy look," Longfellow wrote in his journal.[22] Clara called it "deserted" and said "it looks like a city of the dead."[23] So they packed once again, "for about the hundredth time since our departure from home," Clara complained in her diary, and left by steamer for Gothenburg on the southern coast of Sweden, Henry growing so concerned about Mary's "ague" that he found a place "downstairs" for her to rest as comfortably as possible. When they arrived, however, the weary travelers felt their spirits dip lower: they had missed their connecting ship to Stockholm by an hour and faced a two-week wait for the next one.

Rather than endure the long layover, and worried about Mary's condition, Longfellow took the bold step of buying a heavy, twenty-foot carriage and hiring a guide/interpreter to lead them northward to Stockholm. But not even the big Russian carriage was comfortable enough to cancel out the jolts and bumps on the steamy, 300-mile, six-day journey for the travel-weary company who'd been on the road two solid weeks already by then. Nor was there any overnight relief at the inns that provided little comfort and served meals Mary couldn't tolerate. It was toughest on Mary of course, who was becoming more visibly pregnant by the day—and showing more symptoms. They all did what they could to make her comfortable—but they could only do so much. They all felt helpless and hoped Stockholm would be a tonic. If they could only get there in time.

Finally they limped into Stockholm on June 28. Mary's travel weariness would subside as pregnancy fatigue and morning sickness took its place. She was gratefully looking forward to two months of comfortable rooms, good meals, and plenty of rest to build up reserves of strength and stamina for the rest of the journey to Germany. For the moment, however, she was looking forward to a resumption of pleasant travel routines—meeting the locals and beginning a new, perhaps slightly scaled-down round of sightseeing. It was becoming clearer by the day, however, that Mary needed attention, some quiet, old-fashioned pampering.

But apart from allowing Mary to rest up and stay warm, Stockholm proved as unpleasant as Copenhagen, too cold, rainy, and abandoned to please any of the travelers. "We are all disappointed," Clara confided to her diary on July 1: "We have seen nothing in the way of scenery to admire as yet and I have seen nothing to induce a traveller to take the trouble to come here." In fact, she concluded, "there is such a universal disappointment that nobody complains."[24]

Further coloring Longfellow's feelings about Sweden was a major disappointment. Karl Nicander, the Swedish poet who had been Henry's good friend back in 1828, in Rome, was out of town for the summer. Henry liked Nicander and had planned on seeing him regularly while he was in Stockholm, and on being introduced by him to Stockholm's literary community, but that was now off the table, which made the summer seem even longer and less attractive. And there was still another disappointment. Jakob Berzelius, the famous chemist whom Henry had met with a letter of introduction from Parker Cleaveland, was leaving Stockholm for the summer too. "So, here are two persons gone from town, upon whom I most relied for information and entertainment here," Henry wrote in his journal, "the town seems empty."[25] Things had taken a sudden turn for the worse, and then there was still a Swedish language teacher to find and the three ladies to show around and take shopping. Sweden wasn't turning out at all as he had hoped. As any of them had hoped.

Longfellow finally did arrange for Swedish lessons with Prof. Karl Lignell from the University of Uppsala, and squeezed a little Finnish in with the help of Gustaf Henrik Mellin, a novelist and clergyman friend of Nicander's, who also introduced Longfellow to the local literati, thus salvaging for him a literary tie that was practically useful, personally entertaining, and intellectually stimulating. By July 8, there was language progress to report. Learning Swedish, he wrote in his journal, was "slow work—slow work. It comes word by word—and phrase by phrase."[26] But as usual with Henry and languages, this new one came more quickly than he let on, and within a month, according to Mellin, he "was well enough at home in reading the Swedish language."[27] Henry reported to his father on the eighteenth that Swedish was "soft and musical, with an accent like the lowland Scotch." He added that it was an "easy language to read, but a difficult one to speak with correctness," but he thought, in a letter to Greene dated August 10, that Swedish "wants the energy of the German and the English."[28]

There were just enough dinners to keep the company diverted from the quiet tedium of Stockholm that summer. Henry wrote in his journal of a "right good dinner" at the home of David Erskine, the longtime American consul in Stockholm, who provided "a most hospitable welcome."[29] On August 5, Mary described some of their July days in a diary-like letter to Zilpah, whom she addressed as "My Dear Mother." She showed here and there gossipy high spirits and animated language, happy moments between unspoken pregnancy concerns. One evening, they had dinner with the Arfwedsons, father and son: "[He] is a fine old man," Mary reported. "His wife has been dead several years. The only ladies present were our countrywoman Mrs. A____ & the eldest daughter of Mr. Arfwedson—the wife of Baron S____ She is a very delicate and graceful lady, was dressed very tastefully & altogether unlike the Swedish ladies we had before seen."[30] Mary described another dinner at the home of a Mr. and Mrs. Stockoe, "excellent, kind-hearted people..., who have paid us every attention. Mrs. S. ____ sends us presents of fruits & flowers & all those little attentions which it is so agreeable to receive." But that Sunday she told Zilpah, she'd been "quite unwell" owing to "a very long walk the evening previous."[31]

Henry added a Sweden-weary P.S. to his wife's letter: "We have just returned—that is to say, day before yesterday, from a visit to the University of Uppsala, and the Iron mines of Dannemora.... We already begin to think of leaving Stockholm—and shall probably take the steamboat to Gothenburg in about three weeks. For my own part, I should like to go sooner if we could. I am disappointed in Sweden. The climate is too cold and unpleasant. I want a little warm sunshine. Something that I can feel, as well as see."[32] To Greene on August 10, he was even more frank. He'd be leaving Sweden in a couple of weeks, he wrote, "to return no more forever—I trust. From which pious ejaculation you will infer, that I have not been much pleased with my 'Summer in the North.' It is indeed so.... There is no spirit—no life—no enterprise—in a word—'no nothing.' Literature is in an abject condition.... And then it is so cold here! It is August—but it is not summer. The rain it raineth every day; and the air is like November.... 'O for a beaker full of the warm south!'"[33]

In fact, it had rained and been cold all summer. Longfellow commented on it regularly in his journal: "A drizzling rain—cold and blue devilish" (July 1); "Rain—rain—rain! drumming on the tiled roofs—splashing in the gutter" (July 28); "more rain—more rain" (July 31); "another rainy day" (August 1).

Clara commented too: "It was raining in torrents! The fates are certainly hostile to our excursion." (July 31).[34] Nothing in Sweden had gone as planned—certainly not as hoped—which would have been enough for Henry to change his itinerary on the fly, but adding to his anxiety was Mary's condition, growing more noticeable by the day. She needed warmer, more hospitable weather where she could settle in for a period of uninterrupted nesting. Stockholm would not be that place. But there were several scary legs to the upcoming journey to Germany and safety, and "knowing the delicate state of Mary's health," Henry wrote to his father-in-law Barrett Potter in December, "I came all the way from Stockholm with fear and trembling."[35]

Longfellow's journal that summer contains no references to Mary's pregnancy, and Clara's diary was equally silent about it, but G.H. Mellin, writing Nicander of his summer with the Longfellows, said very off-handedly, as though it had been the most obvious thing in the world: "Mrs. Longfellow, who was pregnant, was the most beautiful and the most agreeable of all three of Longfellow's ladies."[36] So Mary's condition was clearly seen and commonly known, even though there was unwillingness among the travelers themselves to speak or write of it—delicate New England sensibilities apparently not allowing for openness about such things. All Clara would say in her diary was that now and then Mary would not travel, or that she had not attended a dinner party, or that she did not sleep well, or that she should not go out in the rain, or that Henry didn't think her strong enough to attend the theater, or that she ate too many strawberries the day before and was "indisposed."[37]

Mary herself was only slightly more forthcoming. "I have suffered from the ague for the last two months more than ever," she wrote to sister-in-law Anne on July 15. "For six weeks I had it every night, and some nights hardly closed my eyes.... I have not suffered much since we reached here [Stockholm], till within a few days, when it returned with *renewed vigor*."[38] "Ague" was associated with the malarial symptoms of fever, chills, and sweats, perhaps not so different from what Mary was experiencing, which would have made it a convenient code word for "pregnant," a term that was still taboo in 1835.[39] Mary may well have thought she was speaking clearly when she wrote to her sister-in-law that she "suffered from the ague," but it would have been clearer yet to her husband and traveling companions, not to mention strangers like Mellin who could see plainly (and in Mellin's case speak plainly) of Mary's pregnancy.

As the truth of Mary's condition gradually became clearer, Henry drew closer to her, more protective. Previously she had been just fragile, but now she was delicate in a different way. Everything had changed. Henry had to be worried watching her day-to-day exertions; he juggled travel arrangements to make them as easy as possible for her. And where he had been up to that point pleased with himself for having persuaded Mary to travel to Europe with him—she'd been having such a good time—now he questioned himself. Why had he been so persistent? She'd had a miscarriage when she was safely home in Brunswick, but for her to be pregnant while traveling in Europe, so far from the comforts of home, from familiar surroundings, from family attention, and from access to health care she trusted, was downright dangerous. No, pregnancy on a foreign soil and on the high seas and in bumpy coaches in the hot summer sun—none of it boded well.

Late on August 26, Longfellow and the ladies began their slow retreat from Stockholm. This time, they went by sea rather than rattling coach, the steamer covering the 300 miles to Gothenburg via Sweden's extensive lake system and the still-new Göta Canal, with its miraculous but time-consuming series of seventy-two locks spanning 118 miles. On September 2 they arrived in Gothenburg only to be delayed a full week waiting for a ship with suitable sleeping accommodations for the overnight jaunt to Copenhagen. Longfellow accepted the frustrating delay with as much good grace as he could muster— that is, he knew he should get Mary as soon as possible to Germany where she could wait out her pregnancy in relative comfort and safety, but he also knew it was dangerous to rush her through the miles. "Heighho! the time drags lazily on," he wrote in Gothenburg on the seventh. "If I were not in such a hurry to get to the Rhine, I should not care a fig. But as it is, every hour is precious."[40]

In Gothenburg, Mary had good days and bad. Early in the week she wasn't well enough to take a coach ride in what Clara called "the coziest carriage I have stepped my foot into since I left London."[41] She rallied later in the week, however, and was able to accompany Henry to dinner at the home of a local politician, although she characterized the carriage trip as "a long & tedious ride"[42] Once there, she joined the others in a walk before and after dinner. She seems to have decided to do what she could, to enjoy as much as possible of her time abroad, and to carry on as normally as possible—as difficult as that might now and then be. And Henry in turn decided to be guided by how she felt and what she wanted to do. For the expectant father, the dilemma was the contradictory impulse to slow down and hurry up at the same time, but he had to be guided by Mary, how strong she felt from one day to the next. It was a fine line to travel—for both of them.

Their week in Gothenburg proved surprisingly pleasant, but at two o'clock on September 9, a cloudy and unpleasant afternoon with the threat of heavy rain blowing in the wind, the travelers sailed down a three-mile run to the pier where they were to pick up the overnight steamer to Copenhagen.

The three-mile sail was so choppy the small boat began taking on water, which frightened Mary, Clara wrote in her diary, but they arrived safely. They had an uncomfortable three-hour layover at the pier waiting for their connecting ship, which hadn't yet arrived.[43] At six they boarded the crowded steamer to Copenhagen, where they were heading simply because it was on their evacuation route out of Sweden, not because any of them was eager to see it again.

They arrived in Copenhagen mid-afternoon the next day and moved into what Mary called, "good accommodations" at the Hotel Royal.[44] Henry was immediately struck by how much better the city looked than it had in mid–June, when he thought it was all "gloom and loneliness." Now he admired the "wide and well paved" streets, and the "large and well built" houses: "It has quite a royal look," he wrote in his journal.[45] And after going to the theater that night and being impressed by the play, the house, and the audience, he wrote in his journal that "the Danes have risen fifty per cent in my esteem." He thought suddenly, and it caught him by surprise, that this was a city that might claim more of his attention than he thought it would, but before he could explore that thought or the city much further, they received bad news.

A letter arrived for Clara, who proceeded to read it aloud to the others, which they normally did with letters from home. She stopped short, however, when she came to the news that Mary Goddard's father had "taken sick suddenly and died yesterday of apoplexy."[46] Mary returned home at once, and the traveling party was reduced to three.

Almost by way of compensation, Copenhagen continued to show its best side to Henry, Mary, and Clara. Mary told Aunt Lucia on the seventeenth that "Henry would like to pass the winter here, he is now so charmed with it," adding with a smile, "coming from Sweden any place would be quite delightful."[47] Often together but sometimes separately, they saw things like the gallery of paintings and the library at the Christiansborg Palace, the Fredericksborg gardens, the Museum of Northern Antiquities, and a pair of operas.[48] On the morning of the fifteenth, Henry took his first lesson in Icelandic, "a tongue which has a harsh, sharp and disagreeable sound," he wrote in his journal, and that afternoon, he took his first lesson in Danish, which, he thought, sounded "unpleasant" because it lacked the "softness and beauty" of Swedish. Whenever he could fit them in, Henry also went on Harvard book-buying excursions. And then, on the twenty-third, the night before leaving, Henry received an invitation to join the Royal Society of Northern Antiquaries, dedicated to "the cultivation of the ancient Literature of the North," a final triumph that prompted him to write in his journal that night: "I really feel regret in leaving Copenhagen. I have passed a delightful fortnight here."[49]

Conspicuously absent from Longfellow's Copenhagen journal are any mentions of Mary or how she was getting on, private matters certainly that he never liked to reveal, even in his journal; nor are there any direct references to Mary in any of his letters, although he may have alluded to her when he announced in a letter to George Washington Pierce on September 20 that he had decided to go to Heidelberg next instead of Berlin, "for many reasons, which I will explain when I get home—perhaps."[50] The principal reason, in fact, was to replace bumpy overland carriage rides with a gentler sea passage for Mary's sake, but Longfellow wasn't inclined to go into details. Clara's Copenhagen diary doesn't mention Mary's condition either, though on the sixteenth, she wrote: "It was a beautiful afternoon but we (Mary and I) did not go out." She didn't say why.[51]

If her husband and best friend stopped mentioning her in their letters and journal entries, it is probably because they had stopped for the moment worrying about her. Mary herself implies that she was getting on very well at that point in their travels—and in her pregnancy. She wrote a long letter to Aunt Lucia on September 22, tracing out some of her activities and interests, for she was active, after all—not restricted to bed rest. She'd gone to the new palace, for example, on the fifteenth, "a fine building, the rooms very neat, most of them carpeted." On the 17th, she was along for the trip to the Museum of Northern Antiquities, "the largest in Europe," she wrote, with its "gold rings & bracelets." She was still as deeply into her travel experience as her condition would allow. And she was as smitten with the Danish capital as Henry was: "Indeed it seems now quite like London—the cries remind us of that city & it appears almost as noisy. How different from our first impression of Copenhagen!"[52]

Copenhagen had been a tonic for the weary travelers who had spent such a bad summer in Sweden, but on September 24 they had to push on again, this time boarding the *Frederik den Siette* for a one-day journey to Kiel in northern Germany and then going south some fifty miles by coach to Hamburg. The rest of the latest revised travel plan was to take the sea route from Hamburg to Holland where they would go first to Amsterdam then by coach to Rotterdam to pick up the Rhine and follow it down to Heidelberg where Henry, hoping to arrive by early October, planned on spending the winter. It seemed the least strenuous route for Mary—and it would take only a single week in all. They did not know exactly when the baby was due, but may have been guessing February or March. There was plenty of time to settle Mary into a comfortable place to finish out the pregnancy—no more difficult travel days and weeks.

They arrived on schedule in Kiel on the twenty-fifth, spent one day there, and then left for Hamburg on a coach that glided over a macadam road that was "as level as a floor," as Henry described it for his father on the twenty-ninth. You could hear the relief in his voice when he added, "So—we are safe in Hamburg once more." The next day they boarded the steamer for Amsterdam, a direction and strategy, he told his father, chosen because it would be "less fatiguing and less expensive."[53]

The strategy backfired, however, when the passage to Amsterdam was "rather rough," as Longfellow reported it on December first to Barrett Potter: "Mary was quite unwell."[54] Clara's version, however, made "rather rough" sound tame. First she complained on boarding the ship of the "odious smell of bilgewater" that was "eno' to make one sick." Then she reported on the storm they passed through: "There is a strong wind that is eno' to blow you to pieces on deck, so we stay in the cabin till we are almost suffocated and then go up and walk, fighting with the wind to keep our clothes round us. Wednesday night we had a gale which drove us along at a furious rate. The sea was boisterous and many of the ladies could not sleep from fright..."[55] Mary, Clara wrote, was "unwell in the steamer"—she'd been "quite indisposed."

Then, making matters worse, they had trouble finding a place to sleep that first night in Amsterdam, October 1. After the ship docked at about 8:30 that night, the travelers had to wait what seemed a long time to them on the wharf while their luggage eventually found its way to them, which was followed by another wait for a carriage, which took them to a hotel that didn't have rooms for them. They were tired and frustrated and out of patience as they cooled their heels in the hotel that had no vacancies, waiting for the carriage with their luggage to catch up to them. Then, with the hour getting later and later, Longfellow made a few desperate inquiries and found a place to sleep at what Clara called "this mansion," but their rooms were "up ever so many flights of steps." The storm at sea, the lateness of the hour, the frustrating delays, and the search for a place to sleep, all combined to make Mary miserable, her strength completely gone.

The next morning, Friday the second, though she remained in bed, Mary announced that "she thought she was better." Nevertheless, she kept to her bed all day Friday and Saturday, trying to rally. A doctor was called in. Clara went shopping and brought some linens to Mary's bed for her to inspect on Saturday afternoon, and Mary made an order that included a dozen napkins. For a while, "Mary felt quite pleased with her bargain and was exulting over her purchases," but then she learned the price was based on "Dutch yards and not English," which raised the price and lowered Mary's spirits. And anyway, though it was nice to have been brought into the shopping trip in this manner, Mary was keenly aware that she wanted to be out shopping, not lying in bed judging napkin quality and trying to regain her strength.

When Clara rose on Sunday morning and went to the Longfellows' room to see how Mary was feeling, she learned that Mary had spent a bad night, but for the moment was feeling better. They were hoping to leave that day, but then Mary began to fail again, and the doctor had to be called in again, this time leaving her with "some medicine in a little chunky vial."[56]

On Monday night the fifth, Clara woke in the middle of the night. "Presently I heard a tap at my door." Longfellow was there to ask if he could borrow a candle, for his had burned out. She asked what the matter was, and Longfellow answered, "Mary is sick—worse than ever." Clara asked if he'd like her to come in and help: "'No,' said he, 'you can't do any good.'" She wrote later that all through the night she "heard Mr. Longfellow's bell ring and much passing up and down the entry." When Longfellow returned to Clara's room, "he stood for a moment at the window," and when she asked if Mary had had another "ague fit," he responded: "Something worse than that." When Longfellow got to his own journal, he left this brief accounting of the miscarriage: "Was up before daylight—Mary being very ill. The very deuce to pay, and all in the dark; for it was a long time before I could muster flint, steel, and matches, and strike a light. Sent for the Dr. in a hurry; but before he arrived it was all over..."[57] Clara finally went in to see Mary and found her "looking very pale." She said she was feeling a little better by then, but that she hadn't slept all night. When Longfellow left the room to smoke a pipe, "Mary called me to her bed and related the occurrences of the night and there they were in utter darkness!"[58]

Later that morning, the 6th, after getting some desperately needed rest, Mary was smiling and looking "much better," according to Clara.[59] The doctor visited regularly for the next ten days and a nurse was hired to come in as well, but Mary improved so quickly that by the fifteenth the doctor stopped seeing her, and the travelers were just about ready to resume their journey, first to Rotterdam and then to Heidelberg. On the nineteenth, barely two weeks after Mary's miscarriage, they were all packing their belongings and preparing to leave.

The trip from Amsterdam to Rotterdam was only sixty-six miles by coach but it took three days to complete, in part to make it less strenuous for Mary, though there were other factors slowing them down as well.[60] They were supposed, for example, to leave early on Tuesday the twentieth, but carpenters had to be called in at the last minute to box up books Henry had bought but inadequately prepared for travel. They weren't able to leave until four in the cold afternoon. That first night they could manage only twelve miles before arriving at Haarlem; the second night they got to The Hague, about thirty-seven miles south. The last leg to Rotterdam, where they would pick up the Rhine into Germany, covered only seventeen miles. But as easy as it may have seemed on paper, there were early risings, inconvenient waits, long and short walks, and the uncertainties of public transportation, all followed by a search for accommodations in the new cities. Mary was once again pushed to the limit. When, on the third day, they got to Rotterdam, they "were set down in a busy street," as Clara put it. Henry asked for directions to the Hôtel Des Pays Bas and was told it was within walking distance, so they set off on foot. They went over a bridge with heavy carriage traffic, down what Clara called "a long street" which led to another just as long, and then "passed a bridge and market, kept on to the water, then turned a corner." And then "in a little while" they finally got to the hotel, which happily had rooms for them—upstairs. It was four o'clock on Thursday the twenty-second, before they collapsed into their rooms.

The next morning when Clara went into Mary's bedroom, she found Mary still in bed: "I went to her and she told me her troubles had returned. Poor child. She lay in bed all day."[61] A doctor was sent for, but he prescribed rest rather than medicine, so it didn't seem a serious relapse. They spent the day and night looking at American newspapers and magazines that had just arrived, and when the reading was done, they planned their departure for Germany on Monday, only a two-day delay from Henry's original intention to leave on Saturday.[62] Patience was needed, but at least they waited in what Clara called "fine apartments," which included a parlor that was "quite magnificent" and "the first carpeted rooms we have seen in a public house since we left England." There were also "Chinese style" paintings, "two French beds with white curtains," and "a stove with a grate in it for coal." There was even a "pleasant view of green trees." The rooms, however, faced north and were depressingly sunless for a patient too sick to get out of bed.[63]

Mary was sick overnight on Sunday, felt a little better in the morning, but was told by the doctor to settle in for three or four more days of rest. When Monday came, she was worse, and worse yet on Tuesday. She took the news badly as she was impatient to get on the road, troubled that she was holding up the plans Henry had made to get them all into Germany as soon as possible. Impatient or not, she'd never felt worse than she did that Tuesday. Her doctor called in another doctor for a consult. Clara called Mary "deadly pale" and wrote in her diary that she was "somewhat alarmed."[64] A nurse was hired. And for the next month, Mary lost ground, rallied, and then lost more ground. All talk of leaving Rotterdam ceased. Keeping Mary as comfortable as possible and as free from pain as possible became the theme of their days and nights. There were flashes of alarm, occasional glimpses into doom, but now and then there were hopeful signs too, and they all thought the rest and regimen prescribed by the doctors would get Mary back on her feet, eventually. It was emotionally and physically exhausting for all three of them.

Clara kept track of it all.[65] Regularly Mary suffered from headaches and a fever, sleepless nights, and lack of appetite. But in early November she got stronger and began "recovering famously," according to Clara, who knew at the same time it would be "several weeks yet" before they'd get back on the road. On the twentieth, however, Mary took another turn for the worse, this time with pain Clara called "rheumatism," plus fever and nausea. Two days later, she was "very feeble and suffered much pain," so much that "both the doctors came," agreeing on a treatment of "poultices for her side," which seemed to work for a while. By the twenty-fourth, her doctor grew anxious that she hadn't picked up more strength, muttering with a too-obvious foreboding that Mary was "weak, always weak." Henry was so alarmed by the doctor's words and dark expression that he followed him out of the sick room to talk. When he returned, he "spoke cheerfully to Mary," Clara wrote, "but I saw that there was a cloud upon his brow."

The next day, Wednesday the 25th, Mary was worse again. Henry went early into the sickroom and found her "feverish and agitated," according to Clara's account. While they waited for a new batch of medicine to arrive, a sedative called "eau de corme," Mary said quietly, "Henry, you will go to Heaven," showing the direction her overheated mind had taken, for by then she had intimations of what was coming. She turned to Clara, who was concerned about how long it was taking for the medicine to arrive, and said "It won't do me any good, Clara." She followed that grave assessment with a "wild, feverish look," which was too much for Clara to bear: "I turned away instantly and left her husband to settle her."

Heartbroken over Mary's rapid and visible decline, Clara rushed into her own room "to give vent to my feelings," she wrote, and then, after composing herself as well as she could, she returned to Mary, whom she found a little "more calm." Later that day, Mary seemed better yet, but Clara noted that the "bad symptom," which was Clara's phrase to avoid speaking directly about Mary's bleeding, continued.[66] After a while, Mary asked Clara to read aloud from the Old Testament, "slowly that I may think about it."

Early in the morning of the Thursday the 26th, Mary "was agitated and her heart was throbbing," according to Clara, but after another dose of medicine and after Henry sat with her a little while, "she was placid again." When her three physicians consulted with one another that morning, "they told the nurse there was but little hope," but when the nurse brought in "a number of things of her own accord which Mary relished," her fever went down and she felt well enough to tell the nurse: "How quick you have cured me."[67] Clara read to Mary from John 14: "Let not your heart be troubled," and helped her recall a stanza from a poem called "Trust and Submission" by the so-called Unitarian Pope, Andrews Norton:

> My God! I thank thee! May no thought
> E'er deem thy chastisements severe.
> But may this heart, by sorrow taught,
> Calm each wild wish, each idle fear.

The lines calmed Mary's "idle fear" so much that she asked to have them written down, which Henry did, and which she then put under her pillow. When Henry wrote to Judge Potter a few days later, he reported that Mary "loved to repeat these lines, which seemed to soothe her feelings."[68]

On Friday morning Mary woke with an appetite. She ate some "nice beef tea" with an egg, "which she relished" and which they all took as an encouraging sign.[69] She was equally pleased when Henry read aloud a letter that had arrived the day before from her sister Margaret. On Saturday morning, she had an even greater appetite and told Clara and Henry that she'd been "so hungry all night that she could not sleep."[70] But though this seemed another encouraging sign, Clara noticed how "hollow and dark" her eyes were. Henry could see it too. Up to that point, he wrote later, "I had indulged the most sanguine hopes—but now my fears overmastered them."[71] As the day wore on, Mary grew worse. They moved her when she revived a little at dinner time, but after an hour she was carried back to her bed, Clara wrote, "exhausted as before, though we kept her perfectly horizontal and she made no exertion herself." Clara watched as "Henry kissed her lips and paused when he felt no return. He pressed them again and then turned hastily from the bed. At dinner we could scarcely eat anything."[72] That night Mary rallied and felt good enough for Henry and Clara to agree that it was time to read Mary the letter from her father and sister Eliza that had arrived with Margaret's letter on Thursday. But this was to be the last of her pleasures.

Overnight Clara and Henry remained at Mary's bedside, knowing by then that despite Mary's short-lived rallies and her renewed appetite, they were on a death vigil. Henry sat with his arm around her head, now and then adding and rearranging pillows to help her breathe; Mary found just enough strength to reply "Yes, dear" whenever Henry asked if the new rearrangement was helping.[73] She was thirsty all night and "asked continually for drink," Clara recorded "and I gave it to her as fast as I could prepare it." The nurse "moistened her mouth" regularly with a syrup that Mary "reached for with the greatest eagerness." As the night wore on, however, Mary's breathing "grew more difficult," although, as Clara put it, "she seemed to be free from pain, quite free."[74] At one point, as she fought for breath, she whispered to Henry, "Why should I be troubled; if I die God will take me to himself."[75] Mary asked Henry to read from a prayer book, which he did "with the utmost composure," Clara noted. A little while later, she asked for a clergyman, Henry's friend, the Anglican priest Joseph Bosworth, to come in and pray with them.

When the end came, Mary whispered a few last words to Henry: "Tell all my friends I thought of them in my last moments. How my poor father will mourn for me. He has always been so kind to me and so have all my friends." Henry replied, "Because you have always been such a good, gentle girl." She asked if God would take her in and if she would shortly see her mother again, and Henry said yes. "Then she clasped Henry's neck with her almost lifeless arm," Clara wrote, "and said, 'Henry, it is hard to die and leave you. I remember all your kindness to me.'"[76] When Henry wrote to Barrett Potter two days later, he reported that just before she died, Mary thanked Clara "and clasping her arms affectionately round my neck, kissed me, and said 'Dear Henry, do not forget me!'" As she was dying, the Reverend Bosworth arrived, somewhere between one and two a.m. on Sunday, November 29. He and Henry and Clara, plus the nurse all knelt by Mary's bedside for a final prayer. Henry then closed one of Mary's eyes and Clara closed the other. She was already cold.

4

The "Being Beauteous"

Henry and Clara stepped out of Mary's room to exchange a few parting words with the Reverend Bosworth while the nurse tidied up the bed, the room, and the body for visitors and viewing. After seeing Bosworth out, Henry returned, kissed Mary's lips, and took the rings from her fingers. Clara then gave him some wine and had him lie down. "Now that there was no longer cause for restraint," she wrote in her diary, "he gave vent to his grief and wept bitterly till sleep came to his relief."[1] In his journal, recorded later that same day, he wrote, "my Mary—my beloved Mary—ceased to breathe." He was sure she had already become a "Saint in Heaven"—and then after the slightest pause he added: "Would that I were with her."[2]

Henry awoke after a fitful sleep when the doctor, unaware that Mary had died overnight, arrived for his morning visit. At that point, Henry made several arrangements—with the doctor for embalming the body; with the proper people for putting the body in a double coffin (lead on the inside, oak on the outside); and with the ship's captain for delivering the caskets into the care of Mary Goddard's brother William, who was to place Mary's body in what Longfellow called the "Tomb of the Mount Auburn Cemetery," which was a temporary resting place for bodies, he said, that were awaiting final burial. He explained to Goddard that when he returned, he would "purchase a spot" for her final resting place, adding that Mary's death had been "very sudden and unexpected to me. Till the last day—and almost till the last hour I cheered myself with vain hopes."[3]

"Vain hopes" hardly captures it. Mary's descent to death had been noticed by everyone, but Henry had fooled himself into thinking she would rally once again and that she would return in due time to full health and a long life. He'd been in full denial until the final weekend. In his heart he knew that if Mary was as desperately ill as she seemed to be, and if she did indeed die, he would spend the rest of his life in agonizing guilt that he was responsible, not just for Mary being in Europe in the first place, but also because he'd gotten her pregnant, which had led, in his tortured logic, to her miscarriage and death—and perhaps even worse, to the death of their unborn child. Henry's "vain hopes" for Mary's survival were all he had to hold on to.

When he told the story to Mary's father in a long letter written on December 1, he explained that the sea route from Stockholm to Amsterdam had been selected because it would be easier on Mary than the bumpy overland roads, evidence that he had taken every care to protect her. He had done the best he could, he was saying, but she had suffered the miscarriage anyway, which had led to what seemed to be her inevitable, predetermined march to death. There was nothing he could have done. Their hope for "happiness and renovated health" had been dashed into "sorrow unspeakable."[4] Four months later on March 25, Henry wrote in the sort of open language he reserved only for his old friend George Greene:

> You knew her well—you know how great my loss is. But alas! you do not know how it has prostrated me. I cannot recover my energies, either mental or bodily. I take no interest in anything—or at most only a momentary interest. All my favorite and cherished literary plans are either abandoned, or looked upon as a task which duty requires me [to] work out, as a day-laborer. Other [tasks?] and projects have begun to spring up in my mind, though as yet all is in confusion. In a word, sometimes I think I am crazed—and then I rally—and think it is only nervous debility; sometimes I sit at home and read diligently—and then for days together I hardly open a book, but stroll about over hill and dale, and am idle and indolent: and at all times and in all places I move about among men and things as if invisible, and of course as taking no part in what is going on around me.[5]

These 1835–36 months of grief and guilt are Longfellow's emotional low point, so severe and so traumatic as to reset his lifework away from the dry pleasures of literary scholarship toward the creative—and perhaps more healing—world of poetry.[6] Or that, at least, is one view of what he meant when he said he was giving up his "cherished literary plans" and thinking of new, unspecified work. He was confused, but he wasn't interested in being a "day-laborer" any longer. This life-changing transformation may have been ignited by Mary's death and the loss of his child—but it may also have been fueled by his pending professorship at Harvard. Having achieved his goal of escaping Brunswick and relocating to Cambridge and Boston, he had in a sense been promoted to a position where he could look beyond the dry-as-dust scholarly field and shift his attention to the more creatively satisfying field of poetry writing. He would remain a professor for another eighteen years, but it would be poetry that would get his best attention from that point forward, not scholarship. Success as an academic, in a manner of speaking, had freed him from having to be one.

Marking this shift is a poem from February 1838 originally titled "Evening Shadows," but which was later lengthened and finished into "Footsteps of Angels" for his first book of poems in December 1839, *Voices of the Night*. There was more than one wellspring for the pain in the poem, but the ghostly image of Mary shimmers at the center. Late in the afternoon, Longfellow wrote, before the lamps are lit, "phantoms grim and tall, / Shadows from the fitful firelight / Dance upon the parlor wall."

>   Then the forms of the departed
>   Enter at the open door;
>   The beloved, the true-hearted,
>   Come to visit me once more.

These forms he calls "the holy ones," chief among them "the Being Beauteous, / Who unto my youth was given, / More than all things else to love me, / And is now a saint in heaven."

>   With a slow and noiseless footstep
>   Comes that messenger divine,
>   Takes the vacant chair beside me,
>   Lays her gentle hand in mine.
>   And she sits and gazes at me
>   With those deep and tender eyes,
>   Like the stars, so still and saint-like,
>   Looking downward from the skies.
>   Oh, though oft depressed and lonely,
>   All my fears are laid aside,
>   If I but remember only
>   Such as these have lived and died!⁷

This beautiful-woman-back-from-the-dead poem is more directly autobiographical than is usual in Longfellow, an accounting of his lost love returning as an angel to put her hand in his and calm him. Calm is the key, of course, nothing frenzied or unbalanced here, as there is so often when Edgar Allan Poe writes of similar subjects. Longfellow, though troubled and in pain, thought it unsuitable to reproduce that exact, emotionally-stressed state of mind. Calm control was what he was after. Poe could be overwrought in his language, frenzied in his music, deranged at times, as he was in "Ulalume," for example, when the speaker is hysterically drawn to Ulalume's crypt on the anniversary of her death. Longfellow would be more temperate in his language, quieter in his music.

In the larger context, Longfellow was not only coming to terms with his loss but also announcing a new literary direction for himself—which seems the inevitably right conclusion in hindsight. But the time immediately after Mary's death was heartbreaking and uncertain, a time when Longfellow didn't any longer see how his life was going to unfold. He had gone from being a settled, married man about to have a child to a man about to begin a career in a new college, city, and state without the wife and child he was planning to build that career around. As he had written to Greene, there were some vague new projects that had sprung up, but everything was "in confusion" and there were moments, he said, when "I think I am crazed."

On December 1, 1835, two days after Mary's death, her body was embalmed in the same room she had died in by the physicians who had attended her in life. Placed deep within her dual coffins, Mary then took her last journey back to Boston where Longfellow imagined she would be waiting for him to join her in death so they could lie together forever in their final resting place at Mount Auburn. A couple of days later he wrote in his journal, "It is incredible how much consolation I draw from this thought."[8] The next day, December 2, Henry and Clara boarded the ship that would take them down the Rhine to Heidelberg. They had been through a lot together, and Henry wrote in his journal that he found in Clara "many a soothing influence" because though young, "she has known much of sorrow and sadness … and can sympathize with those who mourn."[9] And so the two of them, now perhaps an unseemly, unmarried "couple," fled Rotterdam with all its painful memories of a dying wife and friend. On board the steamer for Cologne, Clara recorded in her diary that "we had the cabin to ourselves. There are no beds or berths but a cushioned seat goes round the cabin, with here and there pillows for the heads. We wrapped our cloaks round us and lay down, Mr. Longfellow one side and I the other." Longfellow found a measure of consolation in the fact that even though Mary was gone, "Clara is still with me."[10]

Perhaps in a brave effort to strike painful memories from their minds, and no doubt to resume something like normal activities after the ordeal they had both gone through, Henry and Clara bonded further on their way to Heidelberg. There were several stops, the first at Nijmegen in the Netherlands, where Clara recorded that they stopped for the night at a hotel. "We got small rooms in an upper story, not adjoining," she confided to her diary. "Henry's room was the best and I passed the evening with him." On the fourth, they stopped in Düsseldorf, where they went ashore and took a walk, and later that night they reached Cologne, where they "had two fine rooms opening into each other."[11] The next afternoon they left by public carriage for Bonn, and that night Clara wrote in her diary that she "had a bed with a spring sacking, very comfortable" and that she and Henry had "read in our Rhine book," *Tombleson's Views of the Rhine*. They managed at least eight other stops before arriving at Heidelberg late on Friday, December 11, where they asked for adjoining rooms, although they refused ones on the first floor because they were "cheerless" and because, as Clara put it, "we preferred going upstairs."[12]

Heidelberg charmed Henry at once. With its university that dated back to 1386, it had long been established as one of Germany's premier travel destinations. Henry described it in a letter as "one of the most beautiful [cities] you will see in Europe." He said the town had "every variety of pleasant walks—from the gardens of the old castle—with its ruins and terraces to the level plain of the Rhine and the deep valley of the Neckar."[13] He took rooms for himself near the castle, which had been laid low by lightning strikes, wars, and fires, and had thus been reduced to ruins. But even in its current condition, it dominated the landscape and the lives of the locals. For one thing, the town had appropriated the castle grounds for its "public promenade." "In the evening," Longfellow explained to his father, "there is music in the gardens; you meet your friends and acquaintances there; there are shady walks and fountains; and the nightingales sing all night long." With the sole exception of the Alhambra, he went on, "I have seen nothing to compare to this ruin."[14] But despite the Harvard-driven work that faced him in Heidelberg, and despite the charming beauties of the city, Longfellow's grief dogged him day and night. "Amid all this enchantment," he wrote to his father, "a sense of loneliness hangs over me constantly. The scene of Mary's death—and the consciousness of what I lost in losing her—are ever present to my mind." But catching himself in this dark line of thought, he stopped—he wouldn't "dwell longer," he said, "on those mournful events, which so suddenly changed our tour of pleasure into a funeral procession." And yet he couldn't help himself.

Henry found rooms for Clara not far from his own, in the *pension* of a widow, Frau Hepp, who lived there with her son, daughter, and granddaughter, all of whom became Clara's German teachers and eventually her friends. The Hepps became friends of Henry too as he called on Clara nearly every day. Suitably separated, Henry and Clara were still an oddly-bonded couple, who suddenly found it a tricky business to keep up appearances.[15] Henry resumed his studies, his book-buying, and his calls on the local gentry, sometimes with Clara by his side, and thus he not only fulfilled his obligations to Harvard and Clara, but he was also able to keep his grief at bay, at least some of the time. Instinctively he understood the importance of work and self-discipline to get him through the months of mourning. And when he needed it, Clara provided a more-than-friendly shoulder to cry on.

None of it, however, was easy, as the ache over Mary's death rose up in his heart every day. About a week after arriving in Heidelberg, he wrote in his journal late in the evening: "I am sitting alone in my new home; and yet not all alone—for the spirit of her, who loved me, and who I trust still loves me—is with me. Not many days before her death she said to me: 'We shall be so happy in Heidelberg!' I feel assured of her presence—and am happy in knowing that she is so. O my beloved Mary—teach me to be good, and kind, and gentle as thou wert when here on earth."[16] Then, a little before Christmas, Longfellow received another blow: his very dear friend and classmate from Bowdoin College, George Washington Pierce, who had married his sister Anne in 1832, died of typhus fever two weeks before Mary's death. The loss of his good friend combined with the loss of his wife and doubled his depression. On January 10, he wrote in a letter: "I have a void in my heart—a constant feeling of sorrow and bereavement, and utter loneliness...."[17] Shortly after that, a letter for Mary arrived pushing him deeper into his downward spiral. He wrote in his journal: "I cannot study. One thought occupies me night and day. She is dead—she is dead! All day I am weary and sad—and at night I cry myself to sleep like a child. Not a page can I read without my thoughts wandering from it."[18]

Compounding Henry's grief was a steady dose of German writers, especially those in the so-called *Sturm und Drang* movement (usually translated as "Storm and Stress"), which had emerged as an emotional antidote to the persistent rationalism of the 1700s. It was a heart-driven, romantic reaction to a century of head-driven, neoclassical restraint. Henry was thus fulfilling his obligation to Harvard by absorbing the German language and great chunks of German literature, while at the same time, he was indulging his grief, for many of the storm-tossed, romantic stories he was reading matched his own fitful emotional state. Among these writers, Longfellow found himself drawn most to the early Goethe and Novalis, the pseudonym of Georg Philipp Friedrich Freiherr von Hardenberg.[19] In Novalis Longfellow discovered a man whose suffering had been much like his own. In love with a girl named Sophie von Kühn, he became engaged to her in 1795, but she died of consumption two years later. In 1800 Novalis wrote *Hymns to the Night*, a series of prose poems that mystically connected him once again to his beloved Sophie, much as Longfellow would reconnect with Mary in "Footsteps of Angels" in 1838–39. As Lawrance Thompson put it, Novalis "spoke an emotional language which Longfellow, schooled in New England reticence, had never learned."[20]

With Goethe's *The Sorrows of Young Werther*, Longfellow had a more complicated relationship. This was Goethe's partly autobiographical novel, written when he was only 24 in 1774. It begins with a young man desperately in love with a woman who marries another and ends with the love-stricken Werther committing suicide. *Sorrows* had been a wrenchingly popular book when it was first published and was still a powerful story more than fifty years later when Longfellow read it apparently for the first time in late 1835.

But it was also routinely criticized for its treatment of a prohibited love triangle and for Werther's "sinful" way of dealing with it. Longfellow connected with the emotionally draining story. Werther had "demons grim and terrible," Longfellow had written in his journal on December 29, 1835, words he might have used to describe his own interior condition at the same time.[21] He could not, however, bring himself to approve Werther's suicide. The book did have beauty in its "language and imagery," Henry conceded, but it was not the sort of book he could feel entirely comfortable with—there was too much "unrest and pain" to suit him: "This is not the company I love to keep."[22]

Contributing further to Longfellow's outer balance and inner turmoil was William Cullen Bryant and his family, who had been traveling in Italy and had settled in Heidelberg a couple of months before Longfellow and Clara got there. Clara had never heard of Bryant, writing in her diary on December 13 that "a Mr. Bryant [is] here also, an American with his family."[23] Bryant, however, was very well known to Longfellow.

In 1808, the year after Longfellow was born, 13-year-old Bryant had caused a stir when he wrote a scathing verse satire addressed to President Jefferson, "the scorn of every patriot name, / The country's ruin, and her council's shame!" He called the poem *The Embargo* and published it as a twelve-page pamphlet of some 244 lines, and then reissued it two years later, "*Corrected and Enlarged*" into 420 lines.[24] At issue was Jefferson's 1807 Embargo Act that had been hurriedly written, rushed through Congress, and signed into law as an economic sanction against England, which since 1803 had been attacking American ships and taking American sailors. Though designed to protect the American shipping industry and to avoid American entry into the war between England and France, the Embargo had not been thought through well enough. Not only were thousands of American sailors suddenly put out of work, but thousands of others were affected as well, from farmers who could not ship their surplus produce overseas, to ship owners who were denied markets, to dockworkers who were idled, and to all those who provided food, drink, and miscellaneous services to the stevedores and other dockyard personnel. By denying New England's shipping industry its European markets, the Embargo had crippled at least that part of the American economy and had become so unpopular and ineffectual that it was revoked by Jefferson himself shortly before he left office in March 1809. While angry New England protests were the order of the day, one coming from a 13-year-old caught everyone's attention. Bryant had become a poet, a prodigy, and a political activist before his voice changed.

It is unlikely, however, that Bryant's teenage political protest poem would have secured his reputation from his thirteenth year forward. For that he had to wait until 1817, when he was 23. During the intervening years, the young man had been working on a poem about mortality, about how one should think about death—not so much in terms of standard Christian consolation, but rather in more humanistic terms. The poem was "Thanatopsis" (a coupling of Greek words meaning "view of death"), and it was published in the *North American Review* in 1817. The opening seventeen lines and concluding sixteen were added for *Thanatopsis and Other Poems*, published in 1821, just when the 14-year-old Longfellow was beginning his college studies at Bowdoin. (He still had his early copy of the book when he heard of Bryant's death in 1878.) Bryant's reputation as a poet was peaking in the 1830s, just in time for Longfellow to draw strength from both the man and his poem when they met in December 1835.

Longfellow had been so taken with this most American poet throughout the 1820s and early1830s that, as he later wrote, "from the beginning" he'd been a "stanch friend and admirer" and that his own early poetry owed much to Bryant, "an involuntary imitation, which I most readily confess."[25] Henry may have reread "Thanatopsis" again in December 1835 or January 1836 (Bryant's poems had been reissued in 1832 and 1834)—or he may have retained the lines from his first reading of them in the early 1820s. It is possible too that he and Bryant discussed "Thanatopsis" on one of their many walks through Heidelberg. More certain, however, is that Bryant and "Thanatopsis" happened into Longfellow's life just at the moment Longfellow needed them both. Whether it had been the hand of providence that brought them together just then, or mere coincidence, Bryant's lines resonated with the grieving Longfellow: "When thoughts / Of the last bitter hour come like a blight / Over thy spirit," Bryant had written, "Go forth, under the open sky, and list / To Nature's teachings." These were words, after all, that described Henry's own healing ritual as he walked every day through the beautiful and ancient Heidelberg area.

Longfellow found more in the poem to help him through his grief, like Bryant's epiphany that though death is unavoidable and everlasting, it also opens the door to the "patriarchs of the infant world—with kings, / The powerful of the earth—the wise, the good, / Fair forms, and hoary seers of ages past, / All in one mighty sepulchre." But then came Bryant's final movement, a ringing reaffirmation of life that Longfellow needed desperately to be reminded of:

> So live, that when thy summons comes to join
> The innumerable caravan, which moves
> To that mysterious realm, where each shall take
> His chamber in the silent halls of death,

> Thou go not, like the quarry-slave at night,
> Scourged to his dungeon, but, sustained and soothed
> By an unfaltering trust, approach thy grave,
> Like one who wraps the drapery of his couch
> About him, and lies down to pleasant dreams.

Henry Longfellow, who had tended his wife during her miscarriage, final sickness, and death, and then arranged for her remains to be returned to America, could not have met anyone better equipped to help him through his initial period of mourning than the author of "Thanatopsis." Recovery may have suddenly seemed possible.

The Longfellow-Bryant friendship stretched from mid–December 1835 to mid–January 1836, barely a month in all, but plenty of time for Bryant's strong moral code and personal magnetism to become as real to Longfellow as the great man's poetry. They hiked and talked (often in German) for long hours together, exploring the beautiful city with its ruins and hills and river walks. For his part, Bryant was only slightly aware of Longfellow—if he remembered him at all. Back in July 1825, he had admired three poems signed only H.W.L. that had appeared in the *United States Literary Gazette*, but unfortunately, he said in a review, "we know not who he is...."[26] And then too, Longfellow hadn't published poetry in a decade, so Bryant can be excused if he didn't at once connect his new friend with the H.W.L. whose work he had earlier admired. But walking and talking his way through Heidelberg with Longfellow in late 1835 and early 1836, Bryant may well have had his memory jogged, which may in turn have prompted him to ask his young friend why he wasn't writing poetry anymore? It was a good question—whether it was asked or not.

Toward the end of January Bryant, who was on leave from his job as editor of New York's *Evening Post*, got news that his next-in-charge at the newspaper had became seriously ill and that he would have to cut his European travels short. It was a sad parting for Longfellow. Mrs. Bryant and her daughters, however, would be remaining in Heidelberg through all of the winter and spring, and most of the summer too, which suited Clara perfectly, for she had become fast friends with Frances Bryant and the girls, 14-year-old Fanny and 4-year-old Julia. She had liked Frances from the first day they met, on December 14, when the Bryants had come to call. Clara wrote in her diary that night that Frances had "a very pure feminine countenance" and was so "sociable" that "I felt acquainted with her in a moment." Two weeks later, she wrote, "I like them all very much and feel as much acquainted with them as if I had always known them."[27] Clara was as taken with Mrs. Bryant as Henry was with her husband.

Frances Bryant, however, was not entirely honest about her fondness for Clara. To Clara's face, Frances was so attractive that Clara fell immediately under her spell, but in her journal over the next several months, Frances secretly hissed her disapproval of Clara's relationship with Henry. To Frances, the two were an obvious couple, unmarried and traveling together. She could not have imagined what they'd gone through over the previous six months. She didn't have the benefit of knowing Clara's old friendship with Mary Potter before her marriage to Henry, didn't know how the three of them had bonded in Brunswick for months at a time when Clara took up a long-term residence with the newlyweds. She hadn't been with the happy travelers as they visited England and Scandinavia in the spring and summer of 1835, and she hadn't feared for the pregnant Mary's well being or shared the horror of her middle-of-the-night miscarriage. And Frances hadn't been there for the death vigil a month later. What she did see was Henry and Clara traveling alone together and arriving in Heidelberg on December 11. Under the circumstances, she might be excused for getting it all wrong. If she did.

The evidence for a relationship between Henry and Clara is circumstantial—suggestive here and there, but hardly conclusive. There is nothing in Clara's diary or Henry's journal to prove the point, which argues strongly against it, as does the absence of any corroborating gossip in anyone else's letters and diaries, but a romance born out of close proximity and a shared pain and suffering cannot be entirely ruled out. Frances Bryant had been thrown together with Henry and Clara for several months, an eyewitness to their behavior, and to her, they were a couple—she was sure of it. She may, of course, have been all wrong, or she may have been nothing more than a cranky busybody, but to her, the romance between Clara and Henry was so visible as to be conclusive, not even a debatable question. Moreover, even a scholar as careful and dependable as Andrew Hilen called the possibility "one of the most interesting questions dealing with [Clara's] history." Hilen acknowledged that neither Henry nor Clara convicted themselves with their own words, "and yet the experience that they shared for eighteen months," he wrote, "encompassing as it did all that lay between comedy and tragedy, must have brought them to a close understanding of one another."[28] Their few existing letters from after this period, according to Hilen, "reveal that their friendship had progressed toward intimacy as well as informality." The picture never does come into full focus, but for seven months, between December 1835 and June 1836, Henry and Clara displayed to the people of Heidelberg, and to Frances Bryant in particular, the complicated and ambiguous relationship they had with each other. For all practical purposes, they were a couple.

By the late spring and early summer of 1836, Frances was feeling so left out that she started dropping comments to that effect in her diary and in her letters to her husband in New York. On June 12, Bryant himself wrote to one Eliza Robbins that his wife had begun "to feel a little solitary." He said that Clara had been traveling to nearby cities (with Longfellow, although his name doesn't appear in the letter): "They have only eyes for each other. My poor wife," he repeated, "feels solitary." Bryant biographer Gilbert Muller in 2008 wrote that Frances had become by the spring 1836, "an increasingly irritated witness to the affair between Longfellow and Clara Crowninshield."[29] But Frances could do little but watch disapprovingly as Henry went about his business in Heidelberg, as Clara went about hers with the Hepps, and as the two of them got together for some part of nearly every day—Henry still being paid ironically to be the escort Clara Crowninshield needed to maintain respectability on her travels. They had developed by that time a very complicated relationship.

In the meantime, while Henry, Clara, and the Bryants were busy with one another in Heidelberg, Henry was also hoping to meet up with his old friend George Greene in Florence. On January 22, Longfellow wrote him a long letter explaining that he had thought Greene was in Berlin and that they'd be able to see each other there, but when he learned Greene was in Italy and beyond an immediate visit, he was forced to tell him about Mary's death in the letter. A letter, though, was unsatisfactory. What he really needed was his good friend's love and companionship: "O, my dear George; what have I not suffered during these last three months! I am completely crushed to the earth; and I have no friend with me, to cheer and console me." He was hoping to make his way to Italy for that longed-for visit, but he didn't see how it could happen: "the Alps are between us," he wrote, "and I am neither Hannibal nor Napoleon."[30] There was nothing in the letter about Clara, which probably means there was nothing to report—either that or the secret was too shameful to share, even with Greene.

February, March, and April 1836 in Heidelberg passed with routine work that interrupted Longfellow's period of mourning for a good part of every day. He did keep busy. For one thing, he was studying German all the while, grammar and conversation every day, but every day and night he was also reading volumes of German literature. That wasn't nearly enough to occupy all his hours every day, however, so he also spent February preparing a handbook or syllabus on the literature of the Middle Ages, covering the thousand years between the fifth and fifteenth centuries. The work, prepared in the ice-cold university library, was an impressive chronology (complete with commentary and notes), a testimony to Longfellow's bottomless capacity for work—and perfect for a man who was consciously building a wall against grief.[31]

Early in March, George Greene's cousin, Sam Ward, made his way to Heidelberg for two weeks, meeting Longfellow and sparking a friendship that would last nearly fifty years and be captured in some 350 spirited letters between them.[32] Ward's father was a wealthy New York banker, who was indulging his son with a multi-year tour of European wine, women, and song, which is what brought him that March to Heidelberg. It was no doubt because of his partying ways that he developed into the witty and sociable character that Longfellow grew to like so much—or perhaps he was so charismatic that parties naturally formed around him. Either way, few could resist his charms, his down-to-earth way of making a person feel special. Charles Sumner famously remarked: "I disagree with Sam Ward on almost every known topic: but, when I have talked with him five minutes, I forget everything save that he is the most delightful companion in the world." Longfellow said he had a "sixty-horse-power" temperament.[33]

Ward had swept into town during the first week or two in March and been invited at once to a reception in honor of Frances Bryant, "little dreaming," he wrote in a memoir, "I should there meet and make a friend … whose genius and culture had been so frequently praised by my cousin George W. Greene, that he was of all men the one I most desired to meet." He described Longfellow as having a "ruddy face, eloquent blue eyes, and abundant locks." He "glowed with a sweet and brilliant ensemble" and "emanated a cheerful magnetism." Ward confessed that for him, "it was a case of love at first sight…."[34] At the end of Frances Bryant's party, Henry walked Sam back to his small hotel and the two talked till dawn. Once he understood why Longfellow was in mourning, Ward took it on himself to raise his downcast spirits: "My budget of rattling talk was … a cheering and interesting peep into the social world from which his mourning had so long excluded him."[35]

> My infectious spirit of gladness came like a sound of marriage bells upon his solitude and, as one who has been wandering all day over a desert refreshes his parched lips at some bubbling spring, he drank in the story of my adventures in France and Germany, from Parisian Burgundy and French wit, to Rhine wines, carousals with poets and philosophers, and the daintier attractions of the Dresden Court. If we retired like owls at daylight it was with the promise on my part to see him at his lodgings early next afternoon.[36]

Sam Ward was a living, breathing antidote for depression.

When April came with better weather, Longfellow was eager to travel once again. He and Clara and a small party went sixty miles north to Frankfort, and from the tenth to the fourteenth they enjoyed seeing the cherry blossoms, visiting Goethe's house, and attending Henry's favorite opera, Mozart's *Don Giovanni*.[37] On the twenty-second, with Frances Bryant along, it was off to Mannheim for the paintings at the Grand Ducal Palace and a performance of Mozart's *Marriage of Figaro*.[38] In full travel mode once again, Clara revived her lapsed diary with details of their days and nights, as for example, her comment that the streets of Frankfort were "broader and better paved" than any they'd seen in Germany and that they reminded her and Henry of Boston.[39] She too was clearly glad to be on the road again.

Restless, Longfellow wrote on May 14, that he was "tired of being cooped up here in Heidelberg."[40] By June he and Clara were talking more often about moving on, Clara commenting on the sixth that "we talk of making a journey to München [Munich]...."[41] Then on the ninth, she wrote in her diary that "Mr. Longfellow was cogitating a second journey down to Geneva," whenever they finally got around to leaving Germany. "I laughed at our many projects," she wrote in almost giddy anticipation. From June 11–19, Henry and Clara, accompanied once again by their vigilant chaperone, Frances Bryant (and her daughter Fanny) made a steamboat excursion that Henry described to Sam Ward as "a Tour down the Rhine." Clara was so happy to be on the move that she wrote what came to twenty-two printed pages on the trip.[42] By then, though, Henry was intellectually and emotionally finished with Germany, at least for a while, and he was determined to leave with Clara and go to Switzerland, a trip that would include the Tyrol. All the plans were fluid and in constant rearrangement, but Longfellow wrote to Greene on June 5, that he intended to go from Munich to Milan where he was hoping to meet Greene and his wife Maria and have them join him and Clara, "because Miss Crowninshield goes with me," he reported, on a journey to Switzerland.[43]

Just then a letter from William Cullen Bryant to Frances arrived, urging her to continue her stay in Heidelberg and to make side trips as she pleased. "I do not wish you to be parsimonious. Get whatever you have occasion for, and go where you please.... If you could contrive to see Switzerland, or a part of it before you return I should be glad."[44] That same night, Clara recorded in her diary that young Fanny Bryant had come "flying in" to tell everyone that her father had written "that he wanted them to go to Switzerland" adding that they "should make the journey with us." It was the best news possible.

Frances Bryant would be once again the perfect solution for Henry and Clara. She would be the chaperone they needed to travel openly together. With Frances along, they could maintain respectability. What they didn't realize was that it was already too late to save their reputations—at least under Frances Bryant's critical eye and sharp tongue. She'd been clucking her irritation and disapproval right along in her diary at what she determined to be their public carrying-on. Her husband may have been encouraging her to travel to Switzerland, but she didn't want to go with Henry and Clara. She begged off saying she could not leave her daughters for what sounded like such a long time, but she was really saying she didn't want to be a party to what she'd already determined was Henry and Clara's open affair. Moral outrage was trumping her chance to see Switzerland. It was devastating news to Henry and Clara, who were out of chaperone options. The proprieties won out, however, and Clara was forced to remain, unhappy and abandoned, in Heidelberg, while Henry, beginning on June 25, began a two-month tour of the Tyrol and Switzerland—where he fell in love.

PART TWO: FRANCES ELIZABETH APPLETON

5

The Rogue and the Professor

Traveling alone was not a hardship for Longfellow. Back in the twenties, just out of college, when he'd traveled so extensively in France, Spain, Italy, and Germany, he'd missed his family and friends, of course, and gone through patches of loneliness and homesickness, but he always worked his way through them by keeping busy and making new friends—including Florencia González in Madrid and Giulia Persiani in Rome. He was, after all, personable, good looking, and smart, and while not exactly rich, he had means sufficient for his travel needs. People liked him.

But going on without Clara seems to have burdened him with a fresh sense of how alone he was in the world just then. Mary had been his wife, friend, and traveling companion; Clara had suffered with him and held his hand through the worst of times, bonding with him in a unique and ambiguous way. But now he was completely alone—once again. On June 20, still in Heidelberg, he wrote in his journal, "My mind has lost its sensibility and does not feel the spur. I cannot study; and therefore think I had better go home."[1] But he'd already written to Greene of his plan to meet up in Milan and had received a letter in return confirming the plan, which meant that he had an obligation, that his best friend would be waiting for him, and that he wouldn't be alone for the entire trip—so Henry decided in the end to push on without Clara. Maybe his successful travel formula from days gone by would kick in again and he'd be able to enjoy a little more of Europe before heading home, which figured to be in November, when his new job at Harvard was set to begin. It was seven months since Mary's death, still too recent for him to have recovered from the downward emotional spiral he'd been suffering through, but maybe this trip would be a step in that direction.

Henry began his journey on June 25, stopping at Stuttgart, Munich, and Salzburg on his way to Innsbruck, the capital of the state of Tyrol in western Austria, where he arrived on July 6. He immediately made arrangements with a driver and coach to take him down through the Brenner Pass into Bolzano, the capital city of South Tyrol in northern Italy, where he would then begin his drive to Milan and Greene, a total journey of some 250 miles. But on July 8, in Innsbruck, he got disappointing news. The passport officials discovered a problem with his paperwork, which had been made out for Tyrol only; they determined he could go west into Switzerland, but not south into Italy.[2] The entire affair seems to have been a small oversight or a minor red tape snag, but it was frustrating, time-consuming, and in the end, insurmountable. Meeting Greene in Milan was suddenly out of the question, so Switzerland was where he was more or less forced to go from Innsbruck. But for Henry this news came as the last in a series of disappointments: he was without Mary, without Clara, and now, once more without Greene. Three weeks later, he wrote despondently to his father: "Thus far my journey has not had much effect in cheering, or even soothing me. On the contrary," he wrote, "I have frequently thought, as I pursued my way alone, that it was the worst thing I could have done, thus to have undertaken a solitary expedition among these mountains."[3] And when his summer travels were finished, he wrote to Greene about the loneliness he had suffered through: "Those grand and solitary regions made a most melancholy impression upon my sick soul. Such a journey," he went on, "under such circumstances, proves to me, that traveling is not always a cure for sadness."[4]

But Henry wasn't being entirely honest with Greene about his "melancholy" and his "sick soul" because during his summer in Switzerland, he had met and fallen in love with 18-year-old Frances Elizabeth Appleton, although to be fair, he probably saw little in the way of any possible romance with her. True, he was exhilarated by her for two and a half weeks in August and happier with her than he had been in months, but Fanny was so young and beautiful and intelligent—not to mention wealthy—so perfect, in fact, that Henry, ten years older, already a widower, and a mere professor, may not have allowed himself to think about such a long shot love affair. Fanny had appeared suddenly in his life, welcome as sunshine after a downpour, but that was probably all there was to it. Still, he thought to himself, they had hit it off very well and she did live in Boston, so he would be able to see her when he got back and began his career at Harvard—so it was at least a theoretically possible match. Maybe he allowed himself to fantasize about her in that way, but if so, it's hard to know if he felt more elated by the prospect, depressed by its improbability, or guilt-ridden by his sudden interest in another woman so soon after his wife's death.

However it was, Fanny Appleton had clearly added a new dimension to his complicated emotional state in the summer of 1836. He may at the end of the

5. The Rogue and the Professor

summer have persuaded himself that "traveling is not always a cure for sadness," but for two and a half weeks in August, he'd been feeling anything but sad.

Frances Elizabeth Appleton was the fourth child of Nathan and Maria Appleton, who had married in 1806 and set up their first home on Park Place in Boston's then fashionable North End. He had opted in 1794, when he was 15, to join his older brother Samuel as a shopkeeper in Boston rather than become a student at Dartmouth, and six years later he was a full partner in the business. By the time he and Maria married, Nathan and Samuel were investing heavily in British textiles and other products ranging from silver watches to pocketbooks—one shipment of French goods having been worth a reported $10,000.[5]

After six years of marriage, Nathan and Maria began their family. Their first-born, Thomas Gold Appleton, was born in 1812; then came Mary in 1813; Charles Sedgwick in 1815; and Frances Elizabeth on October 6, 1817. By the time Fanny came along, the family had already moved uptown to 54 Beacon Street, overlooking the Boston Common, for Nathan's fortune had grown exponentially when he began manufacturing textiles. He had begun talks with Francis Cabot Lowell about cotton goods in 1810, talks that resulted in late 1813 in the formation of the Boston Manufacturing Company (BMC), which would shortly open its first mill at Waltham on the Charles River, some ten miles west of Boston. Appleton was among the dozen original investors, increasing his share-commitment several times over the next seven years, and for the next quarter-century he was the single most invested man in the manufacturing of New England cotton goods.[6] And his commitment to the industry's eventual profitability paid off. He and Lowell stocked the stone and brick factory at Waltham with improved modern machinery like the power loom, the dressing frame, and the double speeder, all water-powered by the Charles River and able to turn raw material into finished cotton products in the same place, a startling innovation that guaranteed speed and maximized earnings.

Frances Appleton by G.P.A. Healy, 1834 (courtesy National Park Service. Longfellow House—Washington's Headquarters National Historic Site, LONG 4437).

Nathan Appleton was especially proud of the factory system he developed to support his cotton mills and the humane way he treated the mostly young, unmarried farm girls from all over New England who worked in them. It was so successful that Charles Dickens praised it in his often-critical 1842 book, *American Notes*.[7] The girls worked long, seventy-hour weeks, but they were paid in cash, lodged in company-owned boardinghouses, and supported by a network of churches, schools, and hospitals. There were company-owned banks for them to save their money, and company-supplied libraries where they could borrow books.[8] Nathan Appleton had good reason to be proud—there were long waiting lists of young women who wanted jobs.

If Nathan Appleton's factory system was humane, it was also very profitable, and soon he and the other investors opened three new mills in Massachusetts and two more in New Hampshire. By 1821 he was in the top 7 percent of Boston's wealthiest men; by 1845 he was a millionaire and the seventh wealthiest man in town; eleven years after that he was the sixth—and cotton manufacturing grew by 1860 into a billion dollar industry.[9] Cotton was paying big dividends, which meant Nathan Appleton's fortune (increased even further by banking and railroad investments) grew faster than he could count it.

But most of that was in the future when Fanny was born in 1817, when her father was merely rich. She would grow up in the 1820s and 1830s as the pampered and entitled daughter of a New England merchant prince.

During the summers, when the Appletons were not at their Beacon Hill residence, they could usually be found enjoying the sea breezes at Nahant, a one-square-mile, near-island community connected to Lynn by a spit of land and situated between Nahant Bay to the north and Broad Sound to the south, some twenty miles from downtown Boston. Beginning the same year Fanny was born, a round-trip steamboat service ran daily across Broad Sound, giving Boston's upscale community easy access to the resort's increasingly posh hotels. When they weren't at the shore, the Appletons were at Pittsfield, the heart of the Berkshires, where they took the crisp mountain air at Elmwood, the stately homestead of Fanny's grandmother on her mother's side.

When she was 9, in 1827, Fanny wrote a letter to her 15-year-old brother Tom, the young artist in the family, that he had better not become a poet. "Miss Mallet who is the [dancing] school mistress, told me that she heard, that you were going to be a poet, and she told me to tell you, 'that you must not be a poet because if you were, you would be poor.' She said, 'that poets always turn out poor'[;] therefore I think that you had better not, if that is the case."[10] It isn't likely that at 9 and living on Beacon Street Miss Fanny had any real sense of what "poor" meant, but she knew she wasn't and that by becoming a poet, her brother might be, at least if he continued down that road. That, she knew, was a bad thing. Nor was she old enough to have an idea like this fixed firmly in her mind, though it isn't clear how much that sense of a poet's fortune, or misfortune, stayed with her as she grew rapidly into a beautiful young woman who drew all sorts of gentleman callers into her circle of admirers. She had no conception of a rich poet, after all. No one did.

In the same letter to Tom, Fanny wrote that she was going to Miss Peabody's school: "I like her very much, though I have to walk in the cold a great way, as it is in Franklin Place." She didn't say how long a walk it was, but studying with Elizabeth Peabody was probably worth it. She would eventually become an important if peculiar figure in the intellectual life of Boston, but in the 1820s, Miss Peabody's career was just getting launched. Through the years, she would become closely associated with William Ellery Channing, Bronson Alcott, Ralph Waldo Emerson, and Margaret Fuller; she was also a charter member of the Transcendental Club, an assistant of Alcott at his Temple School in Boston, the owner of the West Street Bookstore for more than a decade (where Margaret Fuller's "Conversations" took place after 1839), and the business manager of the Transcendentalist magazine, *The Dial*. In 1860 she opened her famous kindergarten for children under six, a new concept in America at the time. But in her twenties Miss Peabody lived in Boston and founded the school Fanny Appleton attended.

Peabody was a strong proponent of the classics as a proper course of study for girls as well as boys—she herself had studied Greek with Ralph Waldo Emerson. She liked to remark that "there is no sex in intellect." But Fanny didn't like her Latin lessons very much and wouldn't bother with Greek at all. She was headstrong—and there were discipline problems too. Miss Peabody tried to cut them off early by writing a letter to Nathan Appleton about his daughter: "I feel a great deal of interest in Fanny, indeed—and not the less for her faults...." The problem was that Fanny learned her lessons "with so much facility that they do not serve the purpose of disciplining her mind or occupying her time—thus leaving her mind to the invasion of every evil."[11] Miss Peabody thought it might be better for Fanny (and everyone else) if she could attend the afternoon session when she had only two other students instead of the more crowded morning session. That way, Miss Peabody wrote to Nathan, Fanny "will have more of my personal attention"—which she seemed to think would keep all those evils from invading poor Fanny's young mind.

Miss Peabody thought Mr. and Mrs. Appleton would "perceive immediate improvement" with the suggested changes, but it's doubtful anyone had high hopes, for Fanny was already known as a spirited child, strong-willed and unbroken. Nathan commented about this time that while Mary was keeping "tight to her studies," Fanny was "pretty much the same sort of rogue" she'd always been; it was a term, however, that he seemed to use with more affection than disapproval.[12] After Elizabeth Peabody closed her school rather suddenly, the result of embezzlement by a trusted employee, Fanny was sent to one run by George Barrell Emerson, a man who lectured widely on "The Education of Females." Unfortunately, Fanny's behavior there went unrecorded, so it is unknown if her young mind was still subject to "the invasion of every evil."

Nathan wasn't sure what to make of his 14-year-old daughter's New Year's Eve letter in 1831, where she sighed that life in Boston was "excessively dull at present—no parties."[13] He may even have allowed himself a smile at the thought of his favorite rogue having a little fun at his expense. It's possible he was a little more concerned two months later when Fanny was smitten with a young Cherokee Indian who came to dinner at 39 Beacon Street, a major upgrade the family had moved into in 1821.[14] Nathan, however, was in Washington, serving in Congress on the night of the dinner, which elevated Tom to the position of family host. The young man who caught Fanny's eye was a Mr. Ridge, "a young Cherokee Chief," Fanny wrote to her father, "an extremely interesting youth," a man who was "vastly agreeable" and sang them "real Indian songs."[15] But again, she was having too much obvious fun for her father to worry.

That same spring Fanny, Mary, and Tom, with an aunt as chaperone, rather than their mother Maria, who was too weak from consumption to travel, visited Nathan in Washington, passing through New York City on their way and taking "a private sitting room," according to Fanny in a letter home to her brother Charles. She added that though it had been raining, New York "looks very fine and is truly an immense city," which she liked even more at night because it was, "excessively brilliant with its gas lights." When the rain finally cleared, Fanny wrote with a rich girl's careless extravagance: "we plodded the streets and shops to see how fast money could be spent...."[16]

Then it was down to Washington, where they all got to meet President Andrew Jackson, even though the entire Appleton family disapproved of his politics. Nathan had been elected to the Twenty-second Congress (1831–1833), a Whig in spirit a year or so before the party came into existence under Henry Clay in opposition to Jackson and his Democrats. (The Whigs would be named after the English anti-monarchist party to highlight the flaws of "King Andrew.") In turn, the Whigs were attacked as the political tool of the privileged and rich, like Nathan Appleton, the perfect example of America's commercial aristocracy. Despite their differences, Jackson received Nathan Appleton and his family in the President's Mansion—but the girls were not impressed, focusing their attention mostly on Jackson's personal crudeness. Mary wrote, "I do not feel very bitter against the poor president, for we paid him a visit the other day and I found him polite enough."[17] He even had, she remarked sarcastically, the courtesy to get up and spit tobacco juice into the large fireplace instead of aiming for the small spittoon on the floor. Fanny wrote in her diary: "What an odd mixture of splendor and meanness in the President's house. A stupid, countrified servant ushered us to the luxurious drawing rooms, where the spermaceti of the last levee was still adorning the elegantly cut chandeliers and a broom stood at the side of the marble fireplace." Then she echoed her sister: "The President is courteous and polite enough but not very polished in his manners."[18]

Nathan had arranged for his children to visit Congress during one of its day-to-day deliberations, but Fanny called the House of Representatives "a somniferous place" full of "stupid debates which we took no manner of interest in." Her real complaint was that "we have not been to a single party yet," but she was premature because soon enough there were parties the girls could attend in the new finery they had recently bought in New York. Mary especially liked the cut oranges at the parties, which she called "the most elegant refreshments," and the "torpedo crackers," which were small fireworks that exploded with a lot of smoke when thrown to the ground. Mary wrote that the oranges stained her white gloves, and that the torpedo crackers "heighten much the gaiety."[19] When the smoke had cleared in early June, Fanny wrote to Susan Benjamin, "Yes, this journey is indeed over, and here am I returned at last to Boston and Beacon Street. Never did I enjoy travelling more, or appreciate the beauties of the Common and its muddy frogpond so well as now!" On another homecoming three years later, she wrote how "heartily glad" she was to get back to her house on "aristocratic Beacon Street," which she said, "loomed on us as a palazzo."[20]

Young Fanny Appleton was the daughter of a captain of industry, a member of America's privileged class, and she took everyday illustrations of her rank and status as part of the natural order. An expensive shopping spree in New York, a trip to Washington to meet the president of the United States, and living in a "palazzo" on "aristocratic Beacon Street"—all were part of the elite status her father had secured for her. She was young and rich, beautiful and brilliant—and she was determined to gather up all the available beaux and divide them up with her sister.

In the summer of 1832, Maria Appleton took the cool air at her family home in Pittsfield where she got some relief from the hacking cough and the ever-worsening shortness of breath that was slowly killing her. She died a few months later, on February 10, 1833. Mary (19) and Fanny (15) began filling in at home, taking on new social and householding responsibilities for their father. Brother Charles teased Fanny saying that despite her new role, she was still just "the infant of the family"—or maybe he was playing on the term "enfant terrible." In reality, of course, Fanny was nearly grown up by then, and as the co-hostess (or perhaps the assistant hostess) of the Appleton home in 1833, she was nearly ready to take her position in the family hierarchy. Charles continued his gentle teasing by saying that it really was silly to call her "infant" when she stood five-ten, which may have been an exaggeration for the sake of his joke, but if true would have put her a couple of inches taller than Henry ("Longo") Longfellow—whom she hadn't met yet.[21]

Nathan Appleton, busy as he was with his sprawling financial empire, had little time (and probably just as little inclination) to consider the future marriages of his two daughters, but his wife's death had forced his hand. At least a little. One thing seemed clear to him, the girls should steer clear of writers. He didn't exactly say so to them, but he did say it in a letter of parental wisdom sent to his son Tom, who had decided six weeks after his mother's death to head off to Europe. In the letter, Nathan offered guidance. With respect to money, he couldn't pretend they weren't rich, and so he told his son not to deny himself "whatever is comfortable and respectable," but at the same time, he recommended "a guarded, well-regulated ... economy."[22] With respect to "female society," Nathan said carefully, it would be "very desirable" for his son to "cultivate" only women "of a proper character." He was equally clear with his next warning: "I would recommend caution in making acquaintance with theatrical people—I mean writers." As Tom himself had a literary bent, the remark was double-edged, but even if it was only semi-serious, it is likely his daughters heard much the same message when it came to beaux: writers were bad bets—set your sights higher.

For about six weeks in the summer of 1833, perhaps to take the minds of the girls off the death of their mother three months earlier, Nathan took Fanny, Mary, Charles, and Fanny's friend Emmeline Austin on a journey around New York state, then farther north into Canada, stopping at every waterfall they came to. Their first stop was up the Hudson to West Point, where an impressive uniformed cadet was their personal guide. After that they traveled to Albany, accompanied on the boat by "a most exquisite youth, with fierce moustaches and a guitar," the girls wrote in their diary of the trip.[23] Then came a quick round-trip to Saratoga, where the young mustachioed musician serenaded the girls one evening, and they learned his name was Lispenard Stuart. According to onboard stories, he was "renowned in New

York for his splendid equipages and unmanageable horses." Young Mr. Stuart was more interesting to the Appleton girls than any of the sights. Even the splendid waterfalls came in a distant second. Until, that is, they arrived at Niagara Falls, which Fanny called "the most lovely spot in creation."[24] Then, with either an appropriate sense of how lucky she was to have seen the Falls at such a tender age, or perhaps with something more akin to a teenager's world-weary sigh of ennui, Fanny wrote in the diary, "And I, at fifteen, had seen Niagara."

From the Falls, the travelers headed northeast to Lake Ontario to pick up a steamer that took them all the way to Montreal where they met a new traveling companion, Johnny Crosby, whose family had recently joined the tour and would stay with them for another hundred and fifty miles, all the way to Montmorency Falls near Québec City, and back. The Appleton girls claimed him, but Fanny took his fancy. At the Falls, higher even than Niagara's, Fanny took Johnny's arm on the slippery fortifications that had been erected in 1759, during the French and Indian War. They stopped at a narrow opening used for guns, and Fanny leaned her sketchbook on the wall. She called it later, "a very romantic and perilous position, for we were at an immense height over the town." Young Johnny Crosby was so perfect that Fanny gushed in her diary: "We talked, laughed and sang and I was never happier in my life."

On their return journey, Fanny and Johnny spent an afternoon sightseeing from the top of a huge coach and six. Fanny wrote that it all looked "immense" from their vantage point. "We were in ecstasies—never did I enjoy a delightful afternoon more or a ride so much.... We sang all manner of songs, got into a gale of spirits...." On the last day she was to have with Johnny, she had "faintness and headache" and thought she would not be able to see him, but he wouldn't allow it. "Seignor Johnny tried every art to amuse me and at last succeeded.... I enjoyed this bright and sunny afternoon amazingly." When the Appletons separated from the Crosbys, Fanny was lovesick for a while, but with the resilience of a 15-year-old, she put aside her crush on Johnny Crosby, and by mid–July when their trip ended with a coach ride through Vermont and back to Boston, Miss Fanny was feeling herself once again.

In the winter of 1834, while Nathan was in Washington and Tom was in Europe, Fanny and Mary remained in Boston under the watchful eye of Aunt Martha Gold. Mary wrote to Tom that she'd been playing the role of "Miss Discretion and Sobriety" for so long that she intended to change direction and "set up for a coquette." Then she paused and thought about her 16-year-old sister, who, Mary told Tom, "is coming on stage." Poor Nathan, she said playfully, had a double dose of still young but soon to be marriage-age daughters to deal with. Beaux were a regular part of their lives by then, including an "indefatigable Captain" who visited the girls in the afternoons after having had too much wine at lunch, and a "half-lunatic Mr. Gerry," otherwise unidentified, who also came calling—too often. The next summer, in the midst of a record heat wave, the girls went with their father to Newport, the only beaux being the Middleton boys from South Carolina, one of whom had a talent for sketching, which he did often in the hotel dining room. He was currently working on a portrait of Fanny.[25]

But by April 1835, Fanny wrote her friend Susan Benjamin, "I have seen no beaux of late. My friend [name illegible] has quite cut me I fear, since I have not been his comely [companion?] for many a day."[26] In September she flirted happily about her marriage prospects to Robert Apthorp, whom she had long known as one of Tom's school friends from the late 1820s, and who was now showing an interest in her: "As to my 'intended,' I shall not be satisfied with even your high praises, for *par parenthese*, I am by no means flattered that you find so many [beaux] worthy of my smiles."

> I am the most fastidious person in the world and shall not be satisfied with mere everyday excellences. You have a thankless office [trying to guess the man I might marry] after all, for there is no uncertain probability that I should fancy *ever* one *selected* for me by my best friend even, either from obstinacy or unwillingness to have my free impulses swayed by a hint. Indeed, I have often felt a sort of presentiment that I should marry somebody disapproved of by all my friends, for I have universally found that those I was inclined to like best showed always the least and perhaps most unattractive portion of their character to common observers. I feel always pleased in making discoveries of characters veiled from the many, in sounding unknown seas whose pearls have not sought the hand of every careless diver.[27]

These happy marriage daydreams turned into nightmares a month later when her brother Charles, two years older than she, died of consumption two weeks after his twentieth birthday.

Charles Sedgwick Appleton had been a good-natured, sweet, and teasing brother to Fanny and had shown signs of wanting to follow in his father's footsteps before the sickness overcame him. Of course, Charles remembered all too clearly the gradual demise of his mother, who had died in 1833. At first the family paid little attention to his annual winter "flu," but in March 1835, when his cough hung on a little longer than usual, he was sent south to Charleston to regain his health. At first he reported improvement, saying that his cough was no longer "troublesome" and that he could now "walk all about town." He thought he'd like farming, he reported to his family, because it would keep him outdoors in healthy air—once he had fully recovered, that is.[28] And he reported in the same letter that he'd been visited by the 30-year-old, Harriot Coffin Sumner, who, he said, "offers to do a thousand things for me." It isn't known exactly what those things were or how devoted Miss Sumner was to the young man—but she did marry Charles's father, the 59-year-old Nathan Appleton four years later in January 1839.

In July, Tom visited Charles and reported home that he was "*decidedly better*": "His only need is moderation. He has a rather awkward unwillingness to admit weakness, illness, fatigue or anything that seems unmanly."[29] But only five days later, a doctor prescribed laudanum to calm the coughing and for the first time the previously unspoken word "consumption" entered into their conversations. Charles returned home, but his condition worsened, and he died on Sunday, October 25. Fanny, who had just turned 18, wrote to Robert Apthorp once again, but this time with the pain of a sister who had watched her brother die:

> Sunday, being a cool, invigorating [day], he seemed quite as well if not better than for some days previous and intended going to take a drive as usual, but the doctor's late visit prevented him and he determined to defer it till the afternoon. He talked occasionally and his face beamed with the peace which earth knows not of. Feeling death's shadows weighing upon him, he walked with father's assistance into the bathing room for a change of air (about one o'clock), and suffered much from want of breath.... I shall never forget the strange look of wonder, almost pity, which he gave me as ... he saw the tears which I could not restrain streaming from my eyes. It was a silent rebuke that I could mourn for what opened to him happiness ineffable.[30]

But something remarkable was a consequence of Charles's death, Fanny went on in her letter to Robert Apthorp. "We are now so desolate, with nothing to anticipate ... that father has actually sent to New York to engage our passage to sail for Europe in a fortnight! The slightest thought of it staggers and bewilders me so that I dare not yield to the excitement." Nathan Appleton had lost his wife in 1833 and his second-born son in 1835. Never one to interrupt business for pleasure, he had been until then single-minded about his work, his investments, and his profits. But this latest loss pressed heavily on him. It was time for some conspicuous consumption from one of America's captains of industry, a man who could afford a Grand Tour that was open-ended, both in time and budget. Life and death were simply too uncertain to put off pleasures like this any longer. It was time to take his girls to Europe.

On November 16, 1835, barely three weeks after Charles's death, and a week and a half before Mary Longfellow's death in faraway Rotterdam, the Appletons left Boston for New York, beginning a European journey that lasted until August 1837. They would have stayed longer had it not been for the worsening financial panic that year which forced Nathan Appleton to move his family back home where he could personally watch over his various business interests, including his so-far profitable but now suddenly vulnerable textile industry.[31] But for twenty-two months, the Appleton party of six (Nathan, his two daughters and son Tom, plus two nephews, Isaac Appleton Jewett and Willie Appleton, the latter a 20-year-old who had developed a troubling cough) all enjoyed the Grand Tour in the Grand Style. They left New York harbor on board the *Francis de Pau*, waving madly to the many friends and relatives who had gathered to see them off. Despite her sadness over her brother's recent death, Fanny's 18-year-old high spirits could not be held in check, and she kept careful track of the three-week crossing—plus everything else that followed in Europe one week at a time, one city at a time, one country at a time.[32]

Fanny took to the open seas joyfully—the noise, the sailors, the other passengers, but especially the captain, she wrote in her diary, we "fancy him vastly." He was tough with the seamen, she wrote to Robert Apthorp, "but with us he is gentlemanly, full of fun, and well informed on every subject you can propose. He has been most zealous for our accommodation, and is more active and beauish than any of the juveniles aboard, sings us sailor songs and seems to take real pleasure in giving us information about the ship and explaining all the sea-phrases, in which he thinks us wonderfully apt pupils." After dinner on their first night out, Fanny took the captain's arm for "a most delicious promenade for two hours" and by night's end she was using terms like "studding sails," "the throat and the peak," "spanker boom," and "the lazy guy." As usual, the rogue had fit right in.

They landed at Le Havre on December 9 and reached Rouen three days later. When the gentlemen went off on their own "to explore some manufactures," as Fanny put it in her diary, Fanny and Mary, guide book in hand, wandered in a different direction to see the famous gothic Cathedral of Notre Dame, enormous and awesome even without its spire that had been destroyed by lightning fourteen years earlier. Fanny was overcome by it and gushed in her diary that it could "only be equaled by Niagara!"[33] A week later, they were in Paris, where they stayed a month and met one of Tom's friends, the Baron de Poilly, whom the girls had heard so much about in letters. Fanny was happy to meet him at last: "He has the most remarkable appearance of youth, seeing that he confesses to fifty and odd; wears a flaming waistcoat and pants plaited round the waist, petticoat fashion; is tall, very handsome and dandified and has a formidable array of moustaches and whiskers."[34] A young attaché named Duff was another regular caller on the girls in Paris. Especially taken with Fanny, he teased her about her high praise of the Louvre, which he predicted she would temper once she saw the artistic treasures of Italy.[35] There were also visits from young and old men alike who called on Nathan Appleton to discuss business matters—and perhaps catch the eye of Fanny, the 18-year-old heiress.

Their time in Paris passed in a whirl of activity, even though they had to slog through some rainy weather at first. They visited the Louvre, of course, but they also experienced Italian opera for the first time, and went to the *Théâtre Français* where they saw Isaac Nathan's opera *Don Juan d'Autriche*, which so impressed Fanny that she wrote in her diary that it was "thrillingly heroic," especially the actors' "perfect ease of excellence."[36] There were several other visits to theaters, like one to the *Théâtre des Enfans* and another to a Bedouin performance that had her exclaiming that the troupe was "wonderful, wonderful, and still wonderful beyond all whooping." But it was the opera she saw on December 17, that captured her most completely, especially the celebrated soprano Giulia Grisi at the peak of her powers in *Norma*, Vincenzo Bellini's masterpiece that had premiered only four years earlier at Milan's *La Scala*. "I cannot describe the effect of that voice!" Fanny wrote in her diary. "It is forever ringing in my ears, and the whole floats through my memory as a vision filled with melody not of this earth. And her beauty and grace and tragic power!" Two weeks later she heard Grisi a second time, and though she was not as taken with Rossini's opera *Semiramide*, she thought Grisi "very majestic," especially when she was "flashing her beautiful eyes with a lightning expression of scorn, and pouring out a perfect rush and Niagara of sound." Rossini didn't do as well in Fanny's review, not his "pet machinery," not the "unnatural quirks and trills," and certainly not the "bang-bang of cymbals and drums," which she called "deafening." In the end, she wrote, "it is all glitter and noise without one clear exquisite air to haunt the memory." Frances Elizabeth Appleton knew what she liked—and what she didn't like. And why.

Nathan Appleton commissioned Jean-Baptiste Isabey, famous for his miniatures of Napoleon, to paint a somewhat larger double portrait of his daughters, which they sat for on January 12 and 17, 1836. Fanny called the 78-eight-year-old artist a "most fascinating old man" and laughed at the studio bantering between him and his wife during the sittings; she also marveled at the workmanship and beauty of the miniatures she saw there of Talleyrand, Napoleon, and others.[37] (A year later, when the Appletons returned to Paris, they went to the Art Exposition at the Louvre and were proud and pleased to see their portraits prominently displayed near the entrance.) But there was more in Paris—beaux, dinner invitations, dressmakers, and shopping. The girls bought so many dresses and cloaks that they were barely able to squeeze them all into suitcases when they boarded the two carriages Nathan had bought for their 700-hundred-mile trip from Paris to Rome, which began on January 22, the very same time Longfellow and Clara were settling into their lives without Mary in Heidelberg.

In early February, the Appletons reached Lyons, the City of Silk, so that Nathan could examine firsthand its famous mills. For a little more than thirty years, the Lyons silk industry had been boosted by the revolutionary punch-card system introduced by Joseph-Marie Jacquard, who had invented a loom that allowed layers of patterns and colors to be mass produced onto fabrics. For the practical-minded Nathan, this was the sort of travel that made sense—and showed profits. For Fanny, who was nearly as interested in the factory as her father was, there was much to be admired: "They were making rich shawls and beautiful figured satins. The pure, glossy silk looks like spun silver as they wind it off on spools—which reminded me of Lowell. We were amused to see a man ... turning the big wheel for the machinery—instead of a stream of water."[38] They left Lyons by steamer, loading the pair of carriages onto the ship's deck, and sitting in them all day during the long river journey. At night they'd go ashore for lodging, but were up again at five thirty to resume the journey. It was a "barbarous hour," Fanny thought.[39]

Fanny (right) and Mary Appleton by Jean Baptiste Isabey, 1837 (courtesy National Park Service. Longfellow House—Washington's Headquarters National Historic Site, LONG 4152).

Their next stop was Avignon, where the papacy had been relocated in the fourteenth century, and where the Appletons were one and all struck by the splendor and beauty of the Palace of the Popes. The carriages were stored for a few days while the party saw the sights in smaller rigs that got around town more easily. And then it was down-river another 200 miles to Marseilles, a steamship to Genoa, the carriages again to Pisa, and eventually, by typical travelers' fits and starts, to Rome on March 1. That day Fanny wrote in her diary, "Can I believe tonight, I shall be in the Eternal City?" She gushed that she felt "unworthy of Rome" and said she was "ashamed to come so unprepared on all its wonders," but like so many first-time American visitors to nineteenth-century Rome, she was at first revolted by it: "I am immensely disappointed in the modern people of Rome.... The women are hideous and there is a little too much dirt even for picturesqueness."[40] The gap between the real city with real people and the storied capital of the Roman Republic and Empire was greater than Fanny could at first bridge.

She knew in her heart, however, that the Colosseum at night would bring her back to romance and the picturesque. And she was right. "Somehow I cannot feel on what ground I am treading," she wrote in her diary. "My mind wants tutoring by breathing longer the atmosphere of ruins to make the Past the yesterday of the Present." Her rhapsody was interrupted by the party of young Americans she was with, including a young man, William Payne, whom she had known and liked in Philadelphia. But her American companions didn't respect the physical remains of the great symbol of Roman grandeur, which drove a wedge between her and them. What she heard from them was what she called "pygmy voices" in a cathedral:

> To me it was *desecration*.... I can never forget glimpses of wild beauty as the torches flashed along the huge arches like the glare of fiends beside the pale, celestial flooding of the clear moonlight, which spiritualized the big skeleton into an awful majesty, but I did not undertake to feel where I was, or to enjoy anything I saw. I was all wearied and disgusted[,] and what might have been an inexhaustible delight became a heavy nightmare. What is there creditable in insulting and mocking the most solemn sermon ever preached to man? Why are people ashamed of feeling strongly and deeply?[41]

The Colosseum had suddenly transformed Rome into what she had imagined it would be—and St. Peter's confirmed her conversion. Similarly the Vatican galleries replaced in her estimation what she now dismissed as the "vault-like" Louvre: "How often have I seen casts and copies, how *new* was the effect of the originals."[42] And thus by stages Fanny and Mary came to terms with modern Rome and came to love it. "It does not live like others," Fanny wrote in her diary, "on the breath of whizzing manufactories and laboring steam engines," but instead "painting in all branches; sculpture in every variety, are staple productions. The noise of the chisel certainly accords better with its shattered columns and innumerable gushing fountains than would that of saw-mills and spinning-Jennies."[43] Rome was so altogether captivating that it temporarily pushed Fanny's interest in beaux into the background, although she did have for a while the Philadelphian William Payne, who was still, she said, despite his lack of proper reverence for the Colosseum, "full of fun." There was also an Italian donkey rider who serenaded her and picked violets for her on an excursion into the countryside.

Travel was broadening, but the thrill of romance was never far from Fanny's imagination.

By May the Appleton company had reached Florence where Fanny, beginning on May 24, sat four times for a sculpture by the famous Lorenzo Bartolini, whose works on Napoleon were widely known and praised, and who by then had moved permanently to Florence. To Fanny he was "a nice old man, short and broad, with an intelligent, good-natured face and a smile that is full of drollery. He converses delightfully."[44] Fanny was especially taken with Bartolini's stories of the famous people who had sat for him, including Madame de Stael, "whose vanity (he says) was beyond all rhyme or reason." The next day she said goodbye to the old sculptor and recorded in her diary: "if he does have ugly days and makes me look solemn in clay, why he means well and talks well into the bargain."[45]

The Appletons had all been heartened by the good health of cousin William to this point, but he took a turn for the worse and his doctor recommended they hasten their departure from Florence for the cooler climate in Switzerland. By then Fanny had become fond of Florence and recorded of their departure, on June 3, when they were seen off by Bartolini himself: "Away we dash over the quaint old shop-excrescenced [sic] bridge [the *Ponte Vecchio*] through the grey swarms of fete-loving people, all staring with open mouth that on such a day there could be mortals leaving Florence. A wave of a white hat in the air and a profound bow fixed my eye gliding over the mass, and Bartolini's kind face beamed in view, looking all regret and good wishes." She swallowed her tears, she wrote in her diary, "until I reached the hill."[46]

The Appleton departure from Florence may have been hurried because of William's health, but the trip north to Switzerland was leisurely, the party not arriving in picturesque Berne until July 19. The next day, on their way to Interlaken, they were in the charming town of Thun. The girls gathered up their sketch books and equipment, settled into what Fanny called a "dashing new hotel" just outside of town, and "rushed to the windows of their room to see the view."[47]

Longfellow by July 20 had already been in Switzerland for nearly two weeks. He had picked up an occasional traveler or two on some of the legs of his journey, but for the most part he trudged on alone, first west to Zurich then south to Lake Lucerne and finally down to the Furka Pass at the foot of the Alps. After hiking a couple of days there, he headed north stopping to see waterfalls at Handeck and Giessbach, eventually working his way east to Interlaken, where he spent the night of the nineteenth. The next morning he boarded a steamboat heading west some twenty miles across Lake Thun to the town on the far shore of the same name.

There, at the Hotel Bellevue, Longfellow met a man of his father's generation who was traveling with his family to Interlaken—Nathan Appleton. The meeting triggered a surge of loneliness that was hard for Henry to put aside, for he liked the older man at once, and was disheartened that Appleton and his family were traveling east while he himself was heading west. Henry worked his way back to the Bellevue later that day, hoping for just a little more of this Boston connection. Miss Frances Elizabeth Appleton wrote in her diary, "Prof. Longfellow sends up his card to Father. Hope the venerable gentleman won't pop in on us, though I did like his *Outre-Mer*."[48] The book, plus Henry being a "professor," a snobby title that put him in the category of a "venerable gentleman" rather than a potential beau, combined to put Fanny off.[49] She needn't have worried, however, for the meeting did not take place, which produced in Henry's heart a heavy sadness: "How unlucky I am in not having met them there [Interlaken]! I had but a few moments' conversation with him and we were off for Berne." He thought for a moment about Berne in his journal and then the loneliness burst on him once again: "Good God! What a solitary, lonely being I am! Why do I travel? Every hour my heart aches with sadness. To-night I am almost crazy. I wish I were at home once more!"[50]

Over the next eleven days, Longfellow traveled to Bern, Lausanne, Vevey, Geneva, Ferney, and Chamonix (for a good view of Mont Blanc). Lausanne turned out to be very much to his liking, especially the Notre Dame Cathedral, which he called "a small but very beautiful gothic building" from the twelfth century. He paused inside at the memorial to a young woman who had died "after having been but eleven months a wife": "Tears started into my eyes when I read the inscription—and I turned away with an aching, heavy heart."[51] At Vevey he went to the château of Chillon, which he called "the most delightful prison I was ever in," praising especially its columns and arching roof. The stop at Voltaire's residence in Ferney, was prompted by a traveler's sense of duty—and a group of Frenchmen he happened to be with that day—because, as he put it, "I have neither love nor veneration for this arch-scoffer." Afterward, he and his "French companions," went in different directions, which left Henry "once more alone," as he phrased it in his journal. "I then went to several of the principal hotels, to see if by any lucky accident I might meet with some friend or even acquaintance.... Vain hope!" He returned to his hotel and wrote in his journal that he was "disappointed and low-spirited," that he was subject to "melancholy reflexions," and that he had so many "gloomy thoughts" that he thought he was going "crazy."[52] Five days later on the twenty-ninth, he wrote to his father, "thus far my journey has not had much effect in cheering, or even soothing me. On the contrary I have frequently thought, as I pursued my way alone, that it was the worst thing I could have done, thus to have undertaken a solitary expedition among these mountains."[53]

Finally, discouraged and lonely and with all the required waterfalls and cathedrals behind him, Henry began working his way back to Heidelberg and Clara—at least that was the plan. In Geneva, however, he met a Boston merchant Thomas Motley and his wife Anna, both of whom he liked very much. The threesome traveled together by public coach to Berne, Thun, and finally Interlaken once more—where, surprised, Henry ran into Nathan Appleton once again on July 31. Appleton and his family had gone from Thun to Interlaken and had remained there while Longfellow was trekking from town to town, lake to lake, waterfall to waterfall. Henry couldn't believe his good fortune to find the Appletons once again, couldn't believe how happily it had worked out. It was, he thought, as though there was "a charm about the place" that had kept the Appletons rooted there, waiting, it almost seemed, for his return.[54]

He sent his card once again to the man he'd met eleven days earlier, and this time he met the entire Appleton party. Fanny, however, wasn't impressed. She wrote in her diary that night that she had been "called down to meet Mr. Motley & Prof. L—a young man after all, or else the son of the poet."[55] There were no 18-year-old effusions over having met yet another beau to become interested in, no swooning comments on his look or his manner. She was mildly curious that he had turned out to be so young, but that was the extent of her interest.

If Henry thought a charm had been at work keeping the Appletons rooted in Interlaken until his return, Fanny was being charmed in a different sense and at the same time by a "genteel and amiable" count who had booked a band to perform for the young travelers at their hotel. Within a day or two after Longfellow arrived, there was another dance, and Fanny found herself being charmed again, this time by a different German Count, "rather well-looking but not over genteel," who dipped and whirled her so fast across the dance floor that she had to cry out in delighted mock fear for him to slow down.[56] On a different night, Fanny and Mary gave lessons in the Virginia reel and "frolicked till eleven." The girls were being thus charmed at every turn. Henry had hoped only that he might fit in with these traveling Bostonians for a day or two as he continued his journey back to Heidelberg and Clara. Nothing more. But suddenly, with the Motleys and Appletons in the picture, his "melancholy reflections" were put on hold, and the world didn't seem quite so lonely. His plans were flexible after all, so he thought he'd wait another day or two to see what might develop.

Still mourning Mary's death and still in some kind of relationship with Clara, Henry wasn't looking for another complication to his already messy emotional life. And yet he couldn't help noticing young Fanny, and the day after his arrival at Interlaken, August 1, he moved into the same *pension* she and her family were staying at.[57] After breakfast that day, a group of the Appletons invited Henry to join them for a walk to a nearby wood where they stopped at an abandoned medieval castle perfect for sketching. "And thus the time slipped pleasantly away," Longfellow recorded in his journal, sounding contented—for the first time in many months. Fanny, equally contented in her own diary, wrote that she had taken later that evening "a drive and a walk along Lake Brienz with Mr. Longfellow—quiet and lovely."[58]

That night at the hotel, however, Fanny took the dance floor with a young man she described in her diary as "a red-haired cockney who danced like a kangaroo." Later she did a highland reel "with two Scotchmen" she called "very merry," and then she took turns waltzing with them. Apparently Longfellow hadn't picked up much in the way of formal dancing instruction in Portland, for he remained on the sidelines all evening, avoiding quadrilles and waltzes alike. Or perhaps he felt he couldn't compete. He chatted only now and again with Fanny in between dances, but she was too happily out of breath to spend much time with the wallflower professor. His conversation was "quiet and lovely," but he was at a distinct disadvantage with the young heiress, who was having the time of her life dancing with young counts and merry Scotchmen.

The next morning the weather was threatening, so the girls finished their sketches from the day before, while the men fended for themselves, Longfellow reading Ludwig Uhland, a German romantic poet whose imagination, like his own, was stirred by the Middle Ages. When the weather cleared that afternoon, some of the group drove to nearby Unterseen where Longfellow and Fanny walked together and talked about the poetry of Shelley and the American Nathaniel Parker Willis, whose personal life Fanny thought "so false, so flimsy." Later she wrote in her journal that she'd had "a nice walk in the P.M. with Mr. L. to the old bridge." She'd done some sketching of "cloister-spires" and "a dark, picturesque cottage"—and then she and the professor had had "a nice talk" in the "delicious twilight."[59] For his part, Longfellow was taken with this young woman who sketched castles and cloister spires and who also discussed poetry—even the "flimsy" stuff of Willis. They'd only been together a couple of days and already Miss Fanny had his attention, as much for her conversation as her beauty. Later that night, he noted how pleasantly the time was passing—and realized that suddenly he was having a good time: "I now for the first time enjoy Switzerland."[60]

Henry jumped at the unexpected invitation to accompany the Appletons, including brother Tom (who had joined the group but had gone ahead to Zurich), for a week's travel to Lake Lucerne, Zurich, and Schaffhausen, a trip Nathan hurriedly put together for the benefit of William, whose condition had responded so well to the mountain air that it seemed a good idea to give him a little more of it. Longfellow had originally intended to be back in Heidelberg by the end of that week, but this was too tempting to resist, especially now that he was enjoying himself. On the third, "a sultry dog day," according to Fanny, they began their journey by steamer across the lake to Thun, where the Appleton carriages were being stored. When they set off in the carriages the next day for Lucerne, Longfellow thought it was his "lucky star" that had put him in the large carriage with "the two young ladies who are all intellect and feeling."[61] Along the way, Henry read the girls some Coleridge and a few ballads of Uhland, which he called "simple and strange."[62] That afternoon, they stopped by an old mill, and Henry recalled later in his journal that a young girl had brought them cherries. At the end of the day, he could say with what must have been a surprising contentment, "my soul was filled with peace and gladness," that it had been for him "a day of true and quiet enjoyment," and that the time had "glided too swiftly away." Fanny enjoyed it all too, saying with a little less enthusiasm that it had been a "very pleasant morning" and that she had "liked listening" to Henry's readings. She'd had "a very merry time."[63]

Over the next three days Henry and Fanny weren't thrown together by circumstances, but they were part of the large group that spent the night of the fifth at Lake Lucerne and that rowed the next day to the far shore where they stopped at the resort town of Brunnen. Perhaps swayed by his traveling companions, Henry enthused in his journal that Lucerne was "so beautiful! I think it is the most picturesque of all the Swiss lakes." The Appletons then took an overnight excursion up the Rigi Mountain, Henry electing to stay back in Brunnen where he and William, who had taken a turn for the worse and was suddenly bed-ridden, spent several hours together. Henry was impressed with the sickly young man, whom he called "a most gentle spirit, resigned and uncomplaining, as one who has already commenced 'his conversation in heaven.'"[64]

On the eighth Henry and Fanny paired off again on the trip to Zurich, which they reached by early evening. Brother Tom was waiting for them "with a slouched hat and a merry heart," as Henry described it.[65] He was charming and artistic too, irresistible to Henry (and most everyone else), and the two became friends at once, rowing and swimming together in the cold lake water.[66] The next night Henry and Fanny took a walk, then a boat ride, and finally back at the hotel, he translated Uhland's ballad "The Castle by the Sea" "with the assistance of Lady Fanny, who was scribe on the occasion, and made some of the best lines."[67] The tenth was steaming hot again, which led to another row into the middle of the lake with Tom: "When we jumped out of the boat we went down, down, down, 'into those depths so calm and cool.' Brother Tom is a mighty swimmer; and my element is cold water."[68]

The next day Longfellow traveled with the Appletons some thirty miles from Zurich to Schaffhausen, but William was "very feeble," Henry wrote in his journal. When they stopped for lunch, William rested and picked up enough strength to get back on the road in the afternoon. By the time they arrived in Schaffhausen, however, William had to be "carried upstairs to bed," Fanny wrote in her diary.[69] It was clear to everyone, including William himself, that he couldn't live very much longer, but still he looked at his death directly and with uncommon courage, "making his little gifts to friends with a calmness which is beautiful," Henry remarked. "How heavenly it is to die thus!"[70] That day too, Fanny and Henry walked, and talked, and shopped in Schaffhausen bookstores.

They all took turns sitting with William, Henry and Fanny sitting together more than once, bonding over William's deathbed, and one time stealing away afterward to sit beneath some trees where they talked for a while about Boston society "and such dull topics," according to Fanny.[71] On Sunday the fourteenth, Henry and Fanny sat with William all morning, Henry reading aloud from Orville Dewey's Unitarian sermons over the ringing of nearby church bells. The couple walked together along the Rhine the next day. As Fanny recorded it, they "talked about autumn, which my companion prefers to the rest of the year. So do I for the matter of thinking and the thrilling exhilaration of an Autumnal wind," though she also saw autumn as a metaphor for the beginning of the end, and determined that such thoughts were not good for her: "My mind is too morbid, and I dread delivering myself up to such influences." Their conversation went well beyond the tedious dullness of Boston society as they talked about "poetry and people living in different places." They talked on a bench until darkness settled over them, "people occasionally passing like specters, lanterns hanging in the Casino gardens." Fanny broke down—"the rushing of the river and sighing of the trees," she wrote in her diary, "undid me."[72] Henry did what he could to comfort her.

Henry and Fanny spent the sixteenth together once again: "I sallied forth with Mr. L," Fanny wrote later, wandering through town, stopping to watch the ducks, crossing the river, and finally sketching yet another castle. "Mr. L read aloud walking behind me [Wordsworth's] *The Excursion*. Decided it was too ponderous and prosaic a style for all moods, a dose to read much of at a time, like *Paradise Lost*." Later she remarked "on the unpoeticalness of the present" and was surprised when Henry disagreed. "He seemed never to have thought of it before," Fanny wrote in her diary. "We determined to discuss it fully when our wits were brighter."[73] But there would be no further discussion.

On the next day, the seventeenth, Longfellow received a desperate letter from Clara, who was beside herself with boredom and abandonment. Henry had been dallying with the Appletons—spending lazy days with his new friends, rowing and splashing in the deep lake with Tom, and falling under the spell of Miss Frances Elizabeth. It was as though Clara could tell he was late returning because he was with another woman. The urgency in her letter was clear. As Fanny put it in her diary, the letter "decides him to leave us immediately as [Clara] is out of patience awaiting an escort to America."[74] In his own journal, Henry wrote that Clara's letter "rendered it absolutely necessary for me to start for Heidelberg without further delay." Henry knew Clara was right, that he had been derelict in his duty to her and guilty too for the emotional stress he'd caused. He needed to get back, and so he gathered his things and left on a coach for Heidelberg at six that same afternoon. That night Fanny wrote that she was "quite sorry to have him go," and two days later, on the nineteenth, she wrote plaintively in her diary, "Miss Mr. L. considerably."[75]

Their brief, complicated summer romance was over. Henry had been irresistibly attracted to Fanny, but William's worsening condition had shaded the affair in somber colors rather than gay ones. He had been circumspect and courteous throughout, as was proper for a recent widower who had finally found a measure of personal comfort to take his mind off his inner misery. He did pursue the charming 18-year-old, but always with respect—for her, her father, and the memory of Mary. For Fanny, Longfellow had been a surprisingly moving interlude, a poet-professor with good looks and a sensitive manner, one to commiserate with while they waited together for William's rapidly approaching death. And though on the eighteenth Fanny did write in her diary that life was best compared to a "dungeon narrowing daily," she was surely thinking more of William's imminent death (he died on the twenty-fourth) than Henry's sudden departure.[76] But the two events had intermingled in her mind—and it no doubt came as a surprise when it burst on her that she did indeed "Miss Mr. L. considerably."

6

Longo and Carlo

The letter from Clara to Henry which had "rendered it absolutely necessary" that he return at once from Switzerland, was just the tip of the iceberg. Goaded on by Frances Bryant, who was also waiting in Heidelberg for Henry to escort her home, Clara had had enough. She'd been left behind when Henry went to Switzerland in mid–June, which had hurt and disappointed her, but by mid–August, she'd been away from home sixteen months, the last two on her own. The trip had gone on long enough, she'd been through enough, and now Henry was lollygagging around in Switzerland. It was inconsiderate, insensitive, and intolerable.

Had Clara known Henry was at that very moment falling for an 18-year-old-heiress, she would certainly have added unfaithful too—certainly to Mary's memory, but maybe to her as well. Broken-hearted when Henry left, Clara couldn't even continue with her diary that was by then three volumes long. She just wasn't up to it. But then after three weeks of loneliness, she began it again in abbreviated fashion—but broke down under the strain. On July 10, not having heard from Henry since he left, she wrote in her diary that she'd been "walking up and down the room at Mrs. Bryant's, feeling as sad as I ever did in my life, with the tears just ready to start into my eyes.... Never felt more desolate and heartsick in my life. Wept outright after dinner and felt as if I did not care what became of me." Even her landlady Frau Hepp, according to Frances Bryant, was "up in arms about Mr. L_____ not writing Clara."[1]

Frances Bryant barely managed to control her frustration and fury when she wrote in her diary for August 14 that they were all "vexed" that Henry was making them wait to begin their homeward journey—it was unthinkable, she thought, that they had to extend their already overlong stay in Heidelberg while Henry dallied in Switzerland with a family of strangers from Boston.[2] How much longer would they have to wait for him? It was unforgivable that he should keep them stuck in Heidelberg while he continued his leisurely tour through cathedrals and waterfalls. Frances was more than ready to go home, and it was Henry's fault that she couldn't.

Then there was Henry's cold disregard for Clara, his girlfriend, Frances thought. The two women had already had a heart-to-heart talk while Henry was in Switzerland about what one scholar has termed Clara's "troubled relationship" with Longfellow.[3] But Frances's concern for Clara's situation faded when Henry finally returned and preparations were made for their departure from Heidelberg. At that point, Frances stopped writing about Henry abandoning poor Clara, and all the way to Paris she wrote an inventory of their public displays of affection which angered her just as much as when there had been no displays at all. The couple's indecent behavior was way over the line, Frances thought, but worse, by having eyes only for each other, they were making her feel more isolated by the day. In Strasbourg on their way home, Frances wrote in her diary with a rising anger: "I am going to bed disgusted to see Longfellow & C again playing the fools." Two nights later she wrote: "How I wish that we had some one with us who could talk, but these lovesick children I am heartily tired of." The next night, she wrote: "It is now past nine and L & C are yet in the garden—I wish they would come in for I want to go to bed."

For his part, Longfellow seems to have been oblivious to the criticism, either because it didn't deserve comment or because it never reached his ears. He knew he had been derelict in his duty to Clara and had returned immediately to her when she summoned him—and then he put in motion all the machinery necessary for a quick departure. On the twenty-seventh, barely a week after his return, he, Clara, Frances Bryant and her two children had all put their Heidelberg affairs in order, packed their things, climbed into "a carriage and pair," and left for Baden-Baden first and eventually to Paris and Havre where they would finally leave for home on October 12.[4]

On their way to Paris, the Longfellow travelers stopped at Strasbourg on August 30, which gave Henry an opportunity to wander through another gothic cathedral, the Minster, "the great wonder of Strasbourg," as he called it. On that same day, the Appletons were also in Strasbourg, also working their way to Paris (after William's death on the twenty-fourth). Clara recorded in her diary for the thirtieth, that they "saw the Appletons of Boston," and Fanny wrote in her diary that they all had breakfast together the next day at the Appleton's hotel dining room, "then they leave."[5] Fanny described the Bryant daughter as "fair, blue-eyed" and "rather pretty," while she said Clara was merely "modest."[6] It would be another full year before Fanny and Henry would see each other again.

Three days later at nine in the evening, the Longfellow group finally arrived in Paris, worn out but looking forward to a month of fine foods, French wines, ballet, opera, and theater. After the tensions of the summer in

Heidelberg and Switzerland, Paris was a good place to decompress and prepare for their return journey. On September 4, they drove to St. Germain-en-Laye, a Paris suburb some nineteen miles from the city to see the annual country fair called *Fête des Loges*. It was a pleasant day, Henry noted in his journal, "with shifting clouds and sunshine." The ladies commented on his "good spirits," but that took him by surprise—and moved him to deny it that night in his journal. "It was the surface only," they had seen, he wrote, "stirred by the passing breeze and catching the sunshine of the moment":

> I have often observed that amid a chorus of a hundred voices at their loudest pitch—and the sound of a hundred instruments—horns and flutes and drums and trumpets and viols—that amid all this whirlwind of the vexed air, I could distinguish the melancholy vibration of a single string, touched by a finger.... Thus amid the splendor of a festival—amid the rushing noisy crowd—and choral song and sounds of gladness, and a thousand mingling emotions distinctly audible to the mind's ear, are the pulsations of some single melancholy chord of the heart touched by the finger of memory. And it has a mournful, sobbing sound.[7]

His "mournful sobbing," he was saying, had been temporarily trumped by the "sunshine of the moment"—which the ladies had carelessly mistaken as a sign of "good spirits." The ladies may be excused if they missed the subtle difference. Switzerland had actually been a crosscurrent of good and bad spirits mingling, with the good spirits dominating so often that they now and then showed clearly on his face. He couldn't hide it, despite his words to the contrary—it hadn't all been a "melancholy chord of the heart."

Henry visited Madame Potet's boarding house where he'd lived for a while in 1826; toured the *maison de santé* in Auteuil where he'd spent the month of August that same year; and attended Giacomo Meyerbeer's *Les Huguenots*, the wildly popular Grand Opera that had opened seven months earlier in Paris and which Henry wrote a one-sentence review of: "Tedious enough, though the music was at times grand." The month went speedily by, and on October 8, the Longfellow party was in Havre ready to sail, but there was a delay as they waited for a supporting wind. Henry wrote wearily in his journal that he and his group "must idle our time away in this muddy place."[8] Finally, on the twelfth, they sailed for home.

In December, after he had worked his way through landing in New York, saying final and probably awkward goodbyes to Clara, and traveling up to Cambridge, where he had begun working in mid-November, Henry shipped two trunks of Mary's clothes up to her sister Eliza in Portland. It was a painful business. "What I have suffered in getting them ready to send to you, I cannot describe," he wrote. He knew that at times he seemed "cheerful," but he assured Eliza, "there are other times when it seems to me that my heart would break." He had been so happily in love, he wrote, "that it is very hard to be alone." Friendships helped fill the void, but "how little, how unsatisfying they are to one who has been so loved as I have been!" Every day, he said, he was reminded of Mary: "the merest trifle is enough to awaken within me deep and unutterable emotions." Sometimes, he said, it is just a face or "familiar object" or "some passage in the book I am reading" that calls up "the image of my beloved wife so vividly, that I pause and burst into tears—and sometimes cannot rally again for hours."[9] It had been over a year and still his grief felt fresh and disabling, which heightened the new anxiety he felt as he faced a new job in a new college, and in a new city and state as well.

But he was ready. The new Smith Professor of Modern Languages began his tenure at Harvard on November 17, midway through the fall term, with a firm knowledge of French, Spanish, Italian, and German, plus a fair degree of fluency in Swedish, and a smattering of Danish, Dutch and Portuguese. All that plus Latin and Greek. Harvard's new department head in modern languages was well prepared for the job ahead. His professional life was in place.

His personal life was taking shape as well. He had moved to Cambridge, then still a lazy college town of some 6,000 people, a week or two earlier, settling into third-floor rooms in a boarding house on Kirkland Street ("Professors' Row"), where his friend Cornelius Felton was living. His rooms looked out onto the tree-lined street—long, leafy branches from the one in front of the house stretching in so far that he could nearly touch them from his window. Some six weeks later, Henry reported to Greene that his life there was "quiet and agreeable" and that he walked regularly the three miles into Boston, which seemed closer because he always went there with "an object in view." In fact, he continued, "all would be well with me, were it not for the excited state of my nervous system, which grows no quieter, although I have entirely discontinued smoking."[10]

He wasn't in his new rooms very long before he headed up to Portland to see his family, and from there on January 1, 1837, he wrote to his old friend and colleague Parker Cleaveland at Bowdoin that Harvard had so far been "disposed to make everything pleasant to me." All I have to do, he said, "is to oversee the various branches of my department and to lecture," and the lectures on German literature didn't actually begin until the following summer, still some six months away.[11] Overseeing his department wasn't difficult either as the instructors were all foreign-born and therefore spoke their languages natively and perfectly—and they were used to working without supervision, which they'd had to do since George Ticknor had left. Making matters still easier for the new department chairman, the instructors were already teaching all the courses, so there wasn't much classroom work for the new Smith Professor to do. On March 22, Henry wrote to his father that he'd been paid for his first quarter's work, though as yet he hadn't done anything beside preparing for a summer course and writing "The Great Metropolis" for the April *North American Review*. Gradually his duties would increase—dramatically—and gradually he would become as disenchanted with Harvard as he had been with Bowdoin, but in mid-November 1836, the future loomed pleasant and untaxing.

Snuggled away as he was in the small language department of Harvard, Longfellow also seemed largely immune to the seven-year economic depression the nation was about to suffer through beginning on the watch of President Martin Van Buren, who had been elected in 1836, been blamed for the ensuing hard times, and then been gleefully renamed Martin Van Ruin. The ailing economy turned into an epidemic of collapsed banks, closed factories, failed businesses, and laid off workers, all of which accounted for the soup kitchens that sprang up—and the rioting and looting of food stores. It was a devastating spiral that touched everyone, even Longfellow in an indirect way, for when President Quincy got around to defining his new professor's duties in July 1837, he made sure he was getting maximum production while holding down expenses. He'd be a responsible steward.

Longfellow's suddenly rigid set of duties and responsibilities fell under three headings: "to superintend, to instruct, and to lecture."[12] He had to visit classes every month, hear the recitations of every student, and suggest ways his four instructors might improve; then he was to comment on student work and hear seniors present "critical and analytical studies of their own"; and finally he was to deliver two public lectures every year. Quincy was announcing that Harvard was expecting a great deal. Henry's cushy early months had come to an abrupt end.

As Longfellow's duties became clarified at Harvard, so did his social situation in Cambridge and Boston. He certainly had time on his hands during the fall, spring, and summer that first year, so much that he wrote to his father in March that he spent most of his nights out: "There is such a social spirit here and in Boston, that I seldom see a book by candlelight. Indeed, I pass half of my evenings at least in Society: it being almost impossible to avoid it."[13]

When he ventured out into Society, of course, he made every effort to look just right. Julia Ward described him in 1837 as "remarkably youthful in his appearance"; she liked his "clear, fresh complexion, and the bright chestnut of his hair." Thomas Wentworth Higginson, a student at Harvard between 1837 and 1841, pointed out that Professor Longfellow was especially suited to what he called the Cambridge "social circle" by his "naturally cheerful temperament." And he dressed well, Higginson added—maybe too well, as "contemporary critics" routinely observed that he was "not only neat in person," but maintained "a standard of costume which made him rather exceptional." He wore "wine-colored waistcoats and light gloves" and had a fondness for colorful jackets and neckties.[14] One of his students, James Kendall Hosmer, described him after a chance meeting at the post office as "handsome, genial of countenance, and well-groomed"; he wore a silk hat, a long, double-breasted top coat, and "carefully polished" shoes. The outfit was set off with a little cane that he twirled as he walked. The boys at Harvard, according to Hosmer, though amused by his "unusual look," were at the same time charmed by Longfellow's friendly manner "and loved him much."[15] With much less love, Margaret Fuller, partly reacting to a portrait of him in his 1845 *Poems*, said he looked like "a dandy Pindar," implying that he was over-dressed in person and over-elegant in his verse. Longfellow sulked in his journal, "She is a dreary woman."[16]

Set against what Fuller had perceived as an off-putting and distancing elegance was Longfellow's compensating talent for drawing people into close friendships, which showed itself in the late 1830s and early 1840s when the Five of Clubs formed around him, attracted by his gentle manner, warm openness, and his "slightly mischievous look," according to one historian.[17] The other four were Charles Sumner (Carlo, Don Carlos or Sumnerius), Cornelius Felton (Corny or Feltonius), George Hillard (St. George or Geordie), and Henry Cleveland (Hal or Heinrich). Longfellow of course was Longo, whose five-eight stature was an irony not lost on him—or his pals.

The club met informally at Longfellow's rooms for a Saturday afternoon dinner followed by hours more of good fun, high-spirited talk, and cases of wine, with Sumner generally sleeping over to keep Longfellow company on Sundays while Henry wrote letters or prepared lectures for the next week. They were a well-matched bunch, all except Hillard single and all about the same age, with Sumner the youngest at 26 and Longfellow the oldest at 30. They were also energetic, talented, and ambitious, not just for professional advancement but for social position as well. They didn't have the right connections to support such hopes, but dreams of upward mobility nevertheless drew them to Beacon Street, a symbol of achievement they all saw as a glittering possibility. Professional and personal optimism prevailed.

Occasional crossovers into dreamy social and financial advancement were the exception for the members of the Five of Clubs, however, who at their weekly meetings mostly workshopped their books-, essays-, and poems-in-progress. They gave each other ample supplies of helpful criticism and needed encouragement. They took it a step further by publishing good reviews of one another's new work, which led some outside observers to call them, with wry smiles, the "Mutual Admiration Society."[18]

As a group they were literary but with diverse professional interests. Corny Felton was the Eliot Professor of Greek at Harvard since 1834, a man with a large frame and a rollicking good humor. Hillard was Sumner's law partner, and would be the author in 1853 of *Six Months in Italy*, which would go through twenty-one editions and become one of the best-known travel books of its time.[19] The bright and clever Cleveland was a teacher who had worked for a time at Harvard, but he was so unwell that he soon had to retire to a sick room where he slowly declined and died of consumption at age 34 in 1843. He was replaced in the club by the physician-reformer, Samuel Gridley Howe, Chev—short for "chevalier," a title given him by the King of Greece for his service during the revolution in the 1820s. Howe became director of the Perkins Institute for the Blind in 1833 and an abolitionist who supported John Brown in 1859. He was a worthy addition to the ranks.

It was the tall, handsome, and serious Charles Sumner, then lecturing at the law school, who became Longfellow's lifelong best friend, confidante, and more—especially as George Greene was stationed overseas for so many years. Sumner, like Longfellow, was even given to elegant fashions, so that the two of them made splashy entrances at parties—and provoked more than a few arched eyebrows and broad grins. Longo and Carlo became the kind of close friends who were in each other's company day and night—and for long stretches at a time, including as many weekend sleepovers in Cambridge as Sumner could arrange. But though they were intimates, it is uncertain if they were sexually intimate—or if anyone would have noticed if they had been. Mid-nineteenth-century American culture allowed for same-sex closeness, even including sexual contact, and accepted it as within the boundaries of normal behavior. As David Reynolds put it in his study of the Jacksonian era: "Same-sex affection was not considered

Longfellow by Eastman Johnson, 1846. Crayon and chalk on tan wove paper (courtesy National Park Service. Longfellow House—Washington's Headquarters National Historic Site, LONG 544).

unconventional. Men regularly slept with men, and women with women, with no eyebrows raised. People of the same sex hugged, kissed, and even, on occasion, had sex with each other without being considered a different sexual type."²⁰

The relationship between Abraham Lincoln and Joshua Speed was a case in point. They met in 1837 and lived and slept together in the same bed for the next four years without causing a public scandal that would have torpedoed Lincoln's political aspirations a century later. It was what David Reynolds in his life of Whitman called one of the common "intense mail pairings" of the time—but it never became an issue, public or private.²¹ So even if there was a romantic relationship between Longfellow and Sumner, it would not have been looked at with disapproval—and may not have been noticed or spoken of at all. One might point out as well that Sumner had the same close relationship with Howe, whose heroism in the Greek war for independence wrapped him in a romantic cloak Sumner found irresistible. They grew so close that Hillard remarked on their relationship in a letter to Longfellow, "[Sumner] is quite in love with Howe and spends so much time with him that I begin to feel the shooting pains of jealousy."²²

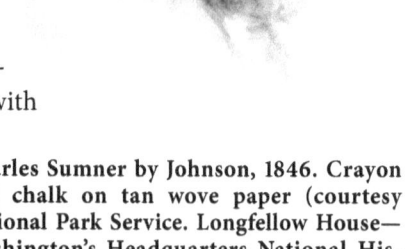

Charles Sumner by Johnson, 1846. Crayon and chalk on tan wove paper (courtesy National Park Service. Longfellow House—Washington's Headquarters National Historic Site, LONG 545).

Sumner's sexuality was, in fact, more of a question than Longfellow's or Howe's. David Donald in his Pulitzer-prize-winning biography of Sumner, wrote that "despite some mild flirtations in his youth," Sumner was "by choice and temperament a bachelor" and had never, "so far as can be determined, been in love with a woman."²³ One woman, quoted but unidentified in Edward Pierce's edition of Sumner's *Memoirs*, wrote that he "was less at ease with women than with men, and I think understood them less."²⁴ Donald, however, dismissed the gay question to a footnote: "As a young man," Donald wrote, "Sumner frequently spoke of his 'love' for male friends like Longfellow and Howe. Perhaps it ought to be explained the word in nineteenth-century usage did not imply an overt homosexual relationship, of which I have found not the slightest evidence in Sumner's entire career."[25] Forty-five pages later though, Donald admitted that "there had always been a passive, essentially feminine element in [Sumner's] composition," and that at Sumner's one, disastrous try at marriage (it lasted from October 1866 until the couple separated in June 1867) "he was probably a virgin" and "doubtless he proved an awkward and often ineffectual lover."[26]

Between 1837 and 1843, Longfellow and Sumner were especially close. The handsome Sumner was a heartthrob among the young women of his acquaintance, but he resisted their charms and preferred the company of the Five of Clubs, and particularly of Longfellow, who, despite his lifelong passion for women, was for those six years unhappily single and possibly celibate too. Under those circumstances, it may be that the two men fell in love without quite expressing it to themselves, Longfellow routinely and affectionately addressing Sumner as "Dearly beloved Charles," or "Carissimo Carlo."[27] Recent biographers of Longfellow like Charles Calhoun, for example, have concluded, much as Donald had earlier, that the love of Longfellow and Sumner was one of those nineteenth-century American attachments which "were rarely sexual but which in the years before one of the two friends married, satisfied emotional needs with an intensity that went far beyond mere comradeship."[28] Similarly, Christoph Irmscher concluded that "there is no doubt both men were strongly drawn to each other, both intellectually and emotionally."[29] Whether romantically attached or not, Longfellow and Sumner did form a club of two among the Five of Clubs and remained uncommonly close until 1874 when Sumner died.

When Longfellow decided to take new rooms in Cambridge, the one requirement was that they had to be big enough not just for his own comfort, but also for him to continue hosting the Five of Clubs. He found two large rooms on Brattle Street at what was known as Craigie House on Tory Row, where he moved in August 1837—and stayed for the rest of his life. The house was already seventy-eight years old when Longfellow moved in, a beautiful and dignified Georgian estate house set up high on spacious grounds and looking down onto the Charles River. Adding to its visible dignity, was its distinguished history, for George Washington had taken it for his headquarters in July 1775, a month after the battle of Bunker Hill, and not only directed the Continental forces for the next ten months from there, but entertained with Martha all the high-ranking military personnel who passed through—including, according to reports, a memorable anniversary party on January 6, 1776.

By 1837, however, the house had fallen on harder times. It had been bought and enlarged in 1791 by Andrew Craigie, who married Elizabeth Shaw two years later and remained there until he died in 1819, leaving his widow a mountain of debt she had to pay off by taking in boarders. Between then and her death in 1841, the Widow Craigie drifted off into a striking eccentricity. She regularly wore gray silk gowns and white muslin turbans, implored visitors to "be good," and was rumored in Cambridge to read Voltaire "in the original" deep into the night—and then to sleep late into the morning. Longfellow called her a "free thinker" and said that she loved cats—and canker worms, which now and then fell from infested elm trees onto her turban—which didn't alarm her at all: "Why, sir, they are our fellow-worms; they have as good a right to live as we have."[30] When it came time for her to die, Henry wrote his father that she wouldn't take medicine because, she said, her system was "not adapted" to it and it made her feel worse. "She is determined to die as she has lived, pretty much in her own way, without regard to the opinion of others," which summed up Elizabeth Shaw Craigie for Longfellow, who was surprised when she took ill at how fond he had become of her.[31]

But she said no when Henry inquired about taking over the rooms vacated by a law student who had just moved out. She made it a practice, she said, learned from hard experience, not to rent rooms to Harvard students, but when the youthful-looking Smith Professor of Modern Languages properly introduced himself, Madame Craigie recognized her mistake and was suitably impressed by the man who stood before her—the more so because she had a copy of his *Outre-Mer* on a nearby sideboard. And had read it. She showed him through the rooms in the house, and one by one she announced that he could not have any of them—until she got to the upstairs front rooms where Washington had lived. Longfellow could have them.

When Longfellow moved in, the only other resident was "young Habersham, of Savannah," a flute player who occupied the other upstairs suite. In the winter when Habersham returned to Georgia, Longfellow later recalled, "I remained alone with the widow in her castle."[32] The back rooms of the huge house were taken by the farmer on the estate and his wife Miriam, a woman so large that Longfellow took to calling her the "giantess," who acted as Mrs. Craigie's servant. Within a year, James Russell Lowell's elderly Aunt Sally had moved in too, her sprightly eccentricity matching nicely Mrs. Craigie's. She and Henry became fast friends who frequently had their dinners together, happily for both of them. Another tenant was the renowned Joseph E. Worcester, the lexicographer who since 1830 had become Noah Webster's chief competitor in what were quaintly called the "dictionary wars." Craigie House was developing into a bright and busy place with colorful, accomplished, and eccentric characters.

While Longfellow was enjoying his first year at Harvard with limited duties and loads of free time, the Appletons were continuing their European grand tour. They had fled the Swiss scene of William's death on August 24, 1836, and headed north to Paris, stopping first in Strasbourg, where they had run into the Longfellow party, and then, after a stop at a German spa (where the girls came down with what was diagnosed as "gastric fever") the Appletons finally got to Paris, where by December they were settled into an apartment, complete with a billiard table much to Fanny and her father's delight, near the Tuileries Palace—just in time for the winter social season.[33] They arrived in time to see the dancer Marie Taglioni on November 27, in *La Fille du Danube*, her signature role. "Saw Taglioni the other night for the first time," Fanny began her diary review. "It is well that I have seen so much dancing before hers or it would be impossible to appreciate how truly she alone is the goddess of the art. With all others it is effort, well subdued but still effort; with her it seems the breath of life…. She floats over the earth like a creature of a rarer element, and you fear, as you gaze at the weaving elasticity of her motion, that she will vanish away like a vapor and ascend to make the clouds her ballroom."[34]

Early in January, Fanny, through the good offices of a dashing, uniformed American attaché to the court, Henry Ledyard, stood in line to meet King Louis Philippe. But when the king finally came into view, he was "old and fat and ruddy," Fanny wrote in her diary, with "bleached white whiskers" and a "coal black wig."[35] He bowed and smiled to the girls before moving on. The queen Fanny dismissed as "hideous" with her "ringlets and withered Austrian visage." Their daughters were "better looking," but the Duke of Orleans, who paused before them for a word, she called "graceful, elegant."

Attaché Ledyard became a regular member of the social season that January—and Fanny danced the first quadrille with him at a ball held by the American banker Welles and his family. Dressed in white crepe with roses, Fanny also danced with the Count Rochefoucauld, but she was overheard to lament that some of the beaux who had been calling on her weren't at the Welles affair—because, as it turned out, they did their banking elsewhere. In February, John Crosby, whom Fanny had liked very much during her 1833 Lake Ontario cruise, showed up as a widower, spurring conversation that Fanny might be inclined to marry him, but she was too involved with the Paris social season at that point to want a permanent relationship. She had lost her mother, her brother, and her cousin, been through a nasty bout of gastric fever, and was just then beginning to enjoy herself again. Settling into marriage was out of the question, especially when Crosby announced that he hated the theater. It was easy for Fanny to bow out and make a half-turn toward Henry Ledyard, whom she invited to be her date for the *Barber of Seville.*

After that, Ledyard's position as Fanny's First Beau was cemented, at least for the 1837 social season in Paris. This was borne out at the court ball, which Fanny called "the most magnificent spectacle that ever dazzled my eyes."[36] She was fully into her role as the semi-aristocratic American heiress. She danced with Ledyard to the "delicious band" and sat with him during quiet moments on the balcony, always within sight of the royal family, including the princesses who were dancing with young uniformed soldiers. Ledyard led Fanny through the rooms—the throne room, the card room, and finally the room where supper was being served, where they parted company because the ladies were served first. Fanny followed all the other women into the supper room after the Queen and her Maids of Honor had passed through. Take it all in all, and Paris was a heady experience even for a rich daughter of an American merchant prince. The Appletons didn't get back to their apartment until five in the morning. And there was another ball the next night, followed by another and another and a costume party thrown in for good measure. The season wound down at the March party of Ambassador Lewis Cass, American minister to France. Fanny had danced her way through the winter, dazzled and dizzy with romance.

Back in Boston, at Tom Appleton's urging, Henry had visited Mrs. William Appleton, whose son had just died, and she introduced him to another of Fanny's aunts, Mrs. Samuel Appleton, who invited Henry to call on her whenever he was in town, which he began to do. She wrote to Fanny that she'd "seen Mr. Longfellow several times socially" but "didn't know what to think of him exactly," though she thought perhaps she'd like to become "more acquainted" with the young man. "I may like him very much." But she hadn't written her young niece to tell her that. "Your picture, which has attracted his attention always, during his visits, he likes very much—the attitude especially...."[37] She meant the pose, but it's easy to imagine that Henry, like Nathan Appleton, loved Fanny's irrepressible, billiard-playing personality, that roguish manner of hers, that daunting gleam in her eye—the double-barrel of passion and intelligence, wit and fire. Aunt Sam, as she was called, was letting Fanny know that Henry was smitten.

At one of his visits, Aunt Sam was preparing a packet of letters to send to Fanny and the others, and she asked if Henry would like to add one. He did and dated it Boston, January 8, 1837:

> My dear Miss Fanny,
> As I sat down a few evenings since to translate the piece I here send you, I remembered the time when "by the margin of fair Zurich's waters" we translated together the

little ballad of Uhland ["The Castle by the Sea"]. I remembered also, the delight you always felt in reading whatever was beautiful in his poems, and I thought it would give you pleasure to see this Elegy of Matthisson, a writer celebrated for the elegance of his style, and the pleasing melancholy of his thoughts. I therefore send it to you as a kind of Valentine; with my warmest wishes of a Happy New Year to all of you. It will serve you likewise as a German lesson, during the master's absence. He hopes to resume hereafter his instructions in the *musical tongue*.[38]

Henry was trying to rekindle the moment of their closeness the previous summer, but it had been a melancholy time that Fanny had put behind her in the glow of Attaché Ledyard and the Paris social season. She had liked the professor during their time together the previous summer, and had missed him when he left so abruptly—as if summoned home by an angry wife. And at Strasbourg, when she had last seen him, she couldn't tell if he was merely the man Clara and Mrs. Bryant needed to travel with or if he was acting as a husband watching out for his extended family. Either way, it distanced him from Fanny, who hadn't thought much about the professor since arriving in Paris. Henry Ledyard had seen to that.

Now, with the professor's letter of January 8 in her hands, she was suddenly reminded of all that "pleasing melancholy"—but probably discovered that it didn't please her any more. She was happier than she'd ever been, blossoming with Henry Ledyard at ball after Paris ball. Everything had changed. And even if it hadn't, this was a most peculiar Valentine. And what could he possibly mean calling himself her "master"? And wasn't he being presumptuous getting to her through Aunt Sam? Yes, the entire letter was slightly unsettling. A trifle off putting.

Not that Fanny cared much, either about the professor or any of the current beaux filling up her days and nights in Paris. She wasn't at all ready for a serious relationship, which disappointed her school friends back in Boston who were all atwitter about Beacon Hill romances, including the rumor being circulated that she herself was intending to marry cousin Isaac Appleton Jewett. None of it was true, Fanny reported back with unruffled self-assurance: "I will enjoy my wings a little longer."[39]

From Paris, the Appletons traveled to Belgium and the Netherlands before getting to London, where they arrived early in May. Fanny enjoyed in particular the "curious cabs," the "splendid equipages," and the English "neatness." On balance, however, the city was a dreary downgrade compared to Paris, where she'd spent such a glorious and glamorous winter.[40] But she did meet the beautiful actress Fanny Kemble at "a very delightful party" on May 11. Kemble had made her reputation as a Shakespearian actress in the early thirties, gone to America for a triumphant tour, and married a Southern gentleman, Pierce Butler in 1834. That May of 1837, Fanny Kemble was in London for a visit while her husband was tending to plantation business in Georgia. Kemble would become one of Fanny's dearest friends—and Henry's too.

The Grand Tour continued in June through England and Scotland. There were stops at Little Waldingfield, the home of Appleton ancestors, then Stratford on Avon and Oxford. At Stratford on June 14, Fanny was disappointed to see Shakespeare's house "wedged in" on a "mean, dirty street." At Oxford's Bodleian Library, the girls were "much pleased" with the lines of "quaint old portraits," Fanny singling out one she called the "gem" of the collection, "a most exquisite portrait of Mary Queen of Scots, softly painted and satisfying all one's wishes of the winning loveliness of her who wore the crown of beauty and sorrow." She thrilled at tiny details like the "infinite sweetness in the small mouth and dove-like eyes, and nothing can be more perfect than the chiseled oval of the face...."[41]

The family continued on their journey through England in late June 1837, meeting Robert Southey, the English poet laureate for nearly a quarter century, on the twentieth-ninth He was "a tall spare man in grey checked pants," according to Fanny, with a "fine halo of grey hair," all supporting a "strong and striking" but nonetheless "stiff manner."[42] The next day they were at Abbotsford, Sir Walter Scott's homestead in Scotland, and Fanny, though the famous author of the Waverley novels had died in 1832, felt near to him because there were so many "interesting relics full of his presence." Fanny hadn't said anything about Southey's poetry, but Scott's books were closer to her heart. The great writer should be revered, she wrote in her diary, "for the happiness he has conferred, the brightening of many a weary hour." She was certain Scott, whom she compared to Shakespeare in this regard, had left behind literary "high watermarks" in his depictions "of female and heroic excellence." And she knew that notwithstanding "efforts of his undervaluers to disenchant his magic influence," Scott's fame was destined to "outlive his century."[43]

Fanny Appleton shifted easily between playful caricatures and serious commentaries on the arts and the artists who created them—a combination of irreverent humor and thoughtful analysis that Henry Longfellow had seen for himself in Switzerland—and fallen in love with. He knew from the beginning that there was a lot more to this beautiful young woman than fancy gowns and grand balls, more than the glitter of the high life, more than her father's great fortune.

As much as 19-year-old Fanny had enjoyed her nearly two years visiting Old World splendors—from cataracts to cathedrals—there had also been a regular flow of letters from friends reminding her of what she was missing in Boston. Resuming her rightful place in Boston's social structure wasn't exactly a priority for Fanny, but settling back into her life amid the comforts of her Beacon Street palazzo was a pleasure to look forward to. And then, with the Panic of 1837 causing an unexpectedly long and severe recession, Nathan Appleton suddenly realized that he needed to oversee the day-to-day operations of his financial empire—in Boston, not London. Abruptly, in August, he made arrangements for the family to sail from Portsmouth, and after a month at sea, the Appletons found themselves once again in New York harbor. Fanny said her time in Europe had been a "glorious dream," but "better than a dream" because it had left them all with "a possession time can never destroy."[44] By September 1837, however, it was over and the Appletons soon found themselves once again in their posh surroundings on Beacon Street overlooking the Boston Common, a home described by Five of Clubs member George Hillard as a place of "beauty and grace and tasteful luxury."[45]

On September 28, Longfellow wrote a long, rambling letter to George Ticknor in Paris, ending with a tidbit of local interest: "In town," he said, "there is nothing new, save the late arrival of the much beloved Appletons, who have returned more beautiful than ever. Nothing has produced such a sensation here since the Boston Massacre...."[46]

7

The Dark Lady and the Mad Man

A week hadn't passed before Henry sent Fanny a bouquet of flowers he'd picked from the gardens at Craigie House—and a poem for her that he'd just written to go with them.[1] But the poem lingered on a metaphor that compared "bright flowerets" to "burning stars," both containing "wondrous truths" about the universe and the "universal being." It didn't get around to Fanny until stanza seven—and even then the connection was oblique: the poet, like the "Gorgeous flowerets," had "brilliant hopes" and "large desires, with most uncertain issues." He had "tender wishes, blossoming at night!" If the poem was really intended to restart a fire that had been out for a year already, it certainly took the long way around—and it isn't known if Fanny ever did figure out that it was about her somehow. Henry may have wondered afterward if the reference to his "large desires" and "tender wishes" stood out sufficiently in the middle of a sixty-line poem, or if his faith in Fanny's ability to fathom his real meaning was reasonable. And he had to wonder too what she would say if she did figure it out, how she would feel. He didn't give her much help either with the simple message accompanying the poem: "With many thanks and a few flowers."[2]

Through October and November, Henry pressed his case, gently but persistently, ardently but cautiously. He'd had a full year to work up an intense feeling for Miss Fanny Appleton and to fantasize a life with her, and now that she was finally back in Boston, he began immediately to woo her away from her many other suitors and to convince her to marry him—that was the plan. Even with his recently increased work schedule at Harvard, he managed to become a regular at 39 Beacon Street. He and Fanny sat for many probably awkward hours in the expensively furnished front parlor, looking through imported purple glass that opened onto a New Orleans style wrought-iron balcony high above the Frog Pond on Boston Common.[3] This was the sort of upward mobility Five of Clubs members could only dream about, a point that could not have been lost on the courting professor.

7. The Dark Lady and the Mad Man

The conversation was polite and included a German lesson here and there, idle talk about Emerson and related literati, and at least at first, recollections of their days in Switzerland. With Mary present as often as not, they all spoke French to one another.[4] When he didn't have an invitation, Henry would show up for a walk around the Common just at the time Fanny and Mary took their morning stroll, and "accidentally" bump into them. At that point they would continue walking together and find their way back to the parlor at 39 Beacon Street. It was transparent, but he wanted it to be—he was in love.

By early December, however, Fanny had already rejected him. It probably didn't take many visits from the professor for her to decide that she wanted to continue being his friend—but that she was not in love with him. There is no letter that has survived letting him down easily, so Fanny probably broke the bad news in person on one of Henry's frequent visits. A pair of Henry's still-hopeful letters from October do survive, but neither can be called a love letter, the first recommending a book of Jean Paul's and the second, addressed to "Madonna Francesca," thanking her for the "delightful day" they'd spent together "on Monday"—and recommending that she read Tennyson. He liked especially some lines from "The Lotus Eaters" that spoke of "slow-dropping veils."[5] As a soul-baring confession of long-simmering love was out of character for him and therefore out of the question, Henry was left with literary references and an ethereal mistiness, what he took to be an aesthetically pleasing romantic quality, perhaps one that embraced a tragic but winning melancholy. In Henry's mind, that's what they had shared in Switzerland, and he wanted to build on it. But Fanny thought differently.

However long it took her to do it, Fanny had cleared the air by early December. On the tenth, Henry wrote to Mary Appleton in response to a consoling letter she had written to him. The two were close, Mary being present at virtually all of Longfellow's calls on Fanny, and the German lessons being for both Appleton daughters. It had been at least a week since his last visit, and Henry asked Mary what she'd been doing in the "bright parlor": "Shall I sit there no more with you, and read in pleasant books! Are those bright autumnal mornings gone forever?"[6] Warming to the real subject of his letter, Longfellow continued in German because, as he explained himself to Mary, "a foreign voice is a kind of twilight and moonlight, wherein one may say all sorts of things to women, and so heartfully sincere!" What was this "heartfully sincere" subject he wanted to say to Mary? Mostly he wanted to tell her how much pain he was in: "It makes me quite sad in spirit when I think about it and see how the lovely dream there is ended, how the clouds dissolve and melt into tears, and everything becomes empty around me, and in my soul a gloomy night—a gloomy, starless night!" He thought, he told Mary, that perhaps when he got the bad news from Fanny, he hadn't made himself clear: "We left one another without understanding one another." He was grasping at straws, hoping that perhaps if he had made himself clearer, argued better, he might still have a chance. But as they had left it, all was lost. He asked Mary to "greet affectionately my dear, dear Fanny, whom I shall always love as my own soul. Ah! That little bit of judgment that one may have comes hardly into consideration when passion rages. How full becomes my heart!"[7]

Four days later, out of ideas, Henry sent Fanny castanets and a two-sentence note, saying he was sending them because it was impossible to give them to her directly—and that he was sorry he wouldn't be seeing her that night "at the ball."[8] He couldn't resist being in touch, but he had nothing left to say. Stunned and confused, he had declined into a sudden mourning that he seems not to have anticipated. He was in love, rejected, and trying to cope.

Sumner, who had left for Europe that same December, wasn't sure what to think as he balanced a genuine interest in Longfellow's happiness with relief that he'd have his best friend all to himself, at least for the immediate future. He wrote from Italy saying he couldn't bear seeing Henry's heart "so long in *suspense*" and encouraging his friend to either "win her or abandon her." Fanny Appleton, he said, was beautiful but daunting, her "sweetness & sensibility" mixing with what he called a "stateliness which bars approach." As one Sumner biographer put it, he "was a little afraid of the elegant and dignified Fanny Appleton," whose eyes "make you shiver, while you admire their brightness."[9]

For Christmas 1837, Henry was up in Portland, where he wrote lightly to George Hillard that rumors of his interest in Fanny Appleton had just arrived via a Portland dress maker who had been visiting someone in Boston on Beacon Street and seen him "walking by at sundry times with Madonna Francesca." He was amused because the rumors included exactly what they were both wearing on their stroll about the Common. "Thus Boston gossip comes with Boston fashions."[10]

Two weeks later he was back in Cambridge and took up the matter of his broken heart with George Greene, probably the only friend he had with whom he could, and would, let loose his feelings:

> A leaden melancholy hangs over me—and from this I pass at times into feverish excitement, bordering on madness; which confines me to my chamber for weeks. Witness last Summer—witness the present moment. My friends here think nothing of it. They say—oh, you look very well! Alas! They know not what soul-sickness is. And I have come to the conclusion, that there is very little sympathy in the world for mental suf-

fering. A wounded hand excites more commiseration than a wounded soul. The truth is this. My nature craves sympathy—not of friendship, but of Love. This want of my nature is unsatisfied. And the love of some good being is as necessary to my existence as the air I breathe. To tell you the whole truth—I saw in Switzerland and traveled with a fair lady—whom I now love passionately (strange, will this sound to yr. ears) and have loved ever since I knew her. A glorious and beautiful being—young—and a woman *not* of talent but of *genius*! Indeed a most rare, sweet woman whose name is Fanny Appleton. You saw her at Greenough's studio.[11] You cannot have forgotten her. Tall, with a pale face. Well, that pale face is my Fate. Horrible fate it is, too; for she lends no favorable ear to my passion and for my love gives me only friendship. Good friends we are—but she says she loves me not; and I have vowed to win her affection. Ah! my friend! you know not how this is interwoven into my soul. I think that among all my friends you are the *only* one, who can *understand* me, or *appreciate* me in this point. I shall win this lady, or I shall die. I feel this to be true. I am no longer a boy. All feelings—and this most of all—have become earnest with me. This is not willfulness. I cannot overcome the passion. I cannot change my nature. Ah! few know the force of *good* passions in *good* souls! The event is uncertain. You will see a good friend of mine soon—Chs. Sumner of Boston. He will tell you much more about this, than I can write.[12]

Henry had never before bared his heart and soul to anyone as he did here. It was Greene he was writing to, which partly explains it, but Greene was also in Rome, four thousand miles away, which he no doubt thought was a safe enough distance to reveal his most personal feelings. He'd been in love before, of course, but this was different, he told Greene, "I cannot overcome the passion."

During the winter of 1838, Henry now and then went to social gatherings where Fanny would be, but he was always disappointed—both because she was beyond his reach and because she was, as ever, popular with the Boston beaux. Making his pain worse, Fanny was always at her ease with him whenever they happened to meet, coolly indifferent, an attitude he tried to match but couldn't.[13] He decided to withdraw as completely from Boston as possible and to make his life more Cambridge-centered. But he couldn't stay away. Now and then he'd go to the Appleton's to lend a book or take care of some other piece of real or trumped-up social business. Seeing her was emotionally draining, what he called a series of "delicious deaths"—but so was not seeing her. Occasionally they met truly by accident, as they did on February 28, at a Boston painting exhibition. Fanny was her usual cool and composed self, while he blushed and trembled.[14]

He was relieved of the daily pressure to see her (or not to) when she left on a trip with her father to Washington, D.C., in late March, but they returned, too soon perhaps to give him any prolonged peace, in early May, and the pressure to see her returned as well. He was out on the Boston Common walking after dark on May 5, perhaps there just to see if she had come back yet, and saw lights on in the house. She was indeed home again—and he couldn't stay away. Only a few days before, on April 28, he and Felton had sat up late into the evening "talking of matters, which lie near one's soul: how to bear one's self doughtily in life's battle and make the best of things." That was good in theory, but impossible in reality. Shortly afterward he was back on the Boston Common hoping to spot Fanny and Mary walking along: "Jumped from the carriage and ran in pursuit. I was indeed rejoiced to see them." And they were pleased to see him as well. He was so set up by this upbeat, "accidental" May 12 meeting that he wrote in his journal, "A day of Paradise." A week later, though, he met "Lady Fanny" on the Common once again. They "took a turn" around the familiar streets, but "she was as cool as an East wind," he wrote in his journal that night. He could sense that she "reluctantly" asked him in for tea when they got back to 39 Beacon Street, and he therefore declined—dejectedly.[15] Pursuing Fanny had become emotional suicide for Henry—he couldn't win her love or harden himself to a life without her.

Six weeks later, on June 26, Henry spent the day in town. He went to see Fanny at home, but she was out on the Common, so he caught up to her there, and they walked a while together, he handling the encounter better than he had in recent meetings. One reason was Goethe, the subject of the June lectures he was then delivering. He was coming to terms with Goethe's lessons about pushing through youthful passion and achieving ultimate control and peace. As one biographer put it, "Goethe was teaching him to face life boldly and courageously."[16] The very next day he wrote the first six stanzas of "A Psalm of Life," completing it a month later. It spilled out of him as a series of memos to himself on what life is really about: It is not "an empty dream" but is instead "real" and "earnest." One has "to act—act in the living present" so that "each to-morrow / Find us farther than to-day." He reminded himself not to be "like dumb, driven cattle," but instead to "be a hero in the strife." And then in the poem's final quatrain, he gave himself one last life lesson:

> Let us then be up and doing,
> With a heart for any fate;
> Still achieving, still pursuing,
> Learn to labor and to wait.

He confessed in a headnote written for later collections that the poem had come "from my inmost heart," and that it expressed "my feelings at a time when I was rallying from the depression of disappointment."[17] Fanny Appleton may never have learned that she had indirectly inspired one of the best-known poems in American literary history.

With the help of Goethe and the good therapy of "A Psalm of Life," Longfellow had begun the summer of 1838 more hopefully. Fanny Appleton wasn't interested, but he had for the moment a way of dealing with it. "Look not mournfully into the Past," he would write in *Hyperion*, a book begun that September. "It comes not back again. Wisely improve the Present. It is thine. Go forth to meet the shadowy Future, without fear, and with a manly heart."[18] He spent his summer vacation back in Portland, recovering sufficiently from his broken heart to joke about it in a mock news item enclosed in a letter to George Hillard on August 16: "We understand that Professor Longw. is expected in Boston on Friday next; and that he will dine at Tremont house with a number of citizens. We are glad to learn he has recovered from his late serious accident in Beacon Street." The citizens were the Five of Clubs; the accident was Fanny Appleton.

But Henry's announced recovery was premature. He wrote from renewed despair on September 4 in his journal: "I think I was never more dejected, than now in this bright beginning of the glorious Autumn. The main-spring of Life seems to be broken, or so weak within me that it does not recover itself.... It is just a year since the Appletons returned. What a difference between my feelings *now* and *then*."[19] His health, never robust and with a tendency to eye strain, acid stomach, tooth decay, and upper respiratory infections, was a constant problem. And when that combined with his lovesickness, he found himself muddling through day-to-day activities. He wrote in his journal at the beginning of September: "A new month, a new College year, and a new book in my Journal begin today. I am neither in good health nor good spirits; being foolishly inclined to indigestion and the most unpleasing melancholy. It is a kind of sleepiness of the soul, in which I feel a general indifference to all things."[20] The malaise spilled over into his teaching, which he doesn't appear to have enjoyed very much. "Perhaps the worst thing in a College Life," he wrote in his journal on September 10, "is this having your mind constantly a play-mate for boys, constantly adapting itself to them; instead of stretching out, and grappling with men's minds."[21] But dealing with other men's minds right then would have been hard for a man who thought he might be losing his own.

Fanny, meanwhile, was having a fine time that summer at Grandmother Gold's homestead in Pittsfield in the heart of the Berkshires in western Massachusetts. She and Mary spent a few days on assignment for their father, inspecting real estate for a "summer villa" he was planning to build some fourteen miles south in Stockbridge.[22] The girls were doubly elated at the prospect because Stockbridge was also the home of Catharine Maria Sedgwick, a distant cousin, who had by 1838, gained international fame with a string of what came to be known as domestic or sentimental novels, especially *Hope Leslie* (1827), set in seventeenth-century Massachusetts. To Edgar Allan Poe she was "one of our most celebrated and most meritorious writers"; to Nathaniel Hawthorne she was just another of the "damned mob of scribbling women."[23] To Fanny Appleton, she was a constant source of pride—as a writer and a woman and a relative of distinction.

Fanny and Mary selected acreage with a view of the lazy Housatonic River dotted with local sugar maples, black birches, and stately oaks, plus mountains ranging in the distance—a breathtaking panorama. Even better, in Fanny's view, the railroad was expected soon, which would put them in convenient touch with nearby towns while remaining "at a safe distance from the afternoon bores," which is what she called the string of suitors who were a constant presence both on Beacon Street and in the Berkshires.[24]

Toward the end of August, when new guests arrived at Grandmother Gold's, the girls wandered down to Lenox, midway between Pittsfield and Stockbridge. There they stayed at the same hotel as the charismatic Fanny Kemble Butler, who, with her three-year old daughter Sarah, was up in the Berkshires to escape Philadelphia's sticky summer heat. The Appleton girls may even by then have read Kemble's best-selling *Journal of Frances Anne Butler*, which had appeared in 1835 and would have added further luster to Kemble's cachet that summer. They became friends at once, with Fanny and Mary soon feeling so perfectly at ease that they could rush into Fanny Kemble's rooms every morning to find her still in her dressing gown—everyone ready to resume the talking and laughing of the night before. When they went out riding, Fanny Kemble was striking, as Fanny Appleton reported in a letter to her best friend Emmeline Austin on September 5: "white pants (*tout à fait à la mode des messieurs*) and habit, with a black velvet jacket and cap."[25] She loved turning heads. At evening parties, sometimes at the hotel and other times at the Sedgwick home, Fanny Kemble, "always in white muslin," entertained them all by "singing old ballads with a thrilling pathos," Fanny wrote. As the celebrity actress herself put it: "We laugh and we talk, sing, play, dance and discuss," everything happily, she added, in "the absence of all form, ceremony and inconvenient conventionality whatever."[26] Fanny Appleton took it all in, fascinated by a role model who thrillingly challenged social, literary, and artistic rules.

Then too there was cousin Catharine to admire and be proud of. "I am enjoying myself excessively," Fanny wrote to Emmeline, "for it is a rare good fortune to be in the constant influence of such rich minds and noble hearts as our friends here are gifted with. Miss Sedgwick—or my own Aunty Kitty, as she is always called—you know I am enthusiastically fond of. She always seems to me a female St. John, breathing forth, on all who come near her, an atmosphere of goodness and love that is irresistibly winning and heartwarming. All the children great and small run to her ever open arms as to a sanctuary, and there is no human creature she will not bless with some corner of her great heart."[27] The Sedgwick home became headquarters for the Appleton girls, who would most evenings, after dinner, end up there. Miss Sedgwick, who had decided long ago not to marry, and who wrote strong female characters who didn't conform to type, gave Miss Frances Elizabeth Appleton another reason to think and thrill over unconventional possibilities open to women. It was, after all, at Aunt Kitty's suggestion that Fanny read Mary Wollstonecraft's *Vindication of the Rights of Women*, a book the local librarians were shocked that Fanny even showed an interest in.[28]

Fanny found in Wollstonecraft a women's rights activist who argued that women should be companions to their husbands, not mere ornaments and certainly not property, and by her example she showed that a woman could decide on a sexual relationship outside marriage, and even have a child on her own. All this was heady business for a budding Boston bluestocking like Miss Fanny Appleton, whose own life choices were just beginning to present themselves. More and more she wanted to try her wings; less and less was she tempted to settle down, especially perhaps with a German-spouting Harvard professor. Surely something more exciting was waiting in the wings.

When the summer ended, Fanny and Mary planned a big end-of-season party for all their friends, including Fanny Kemble and even Aunt Kitty, who came along as the official chaperone. Seventeen young people piled into a large carriage with buffalo-hide seats while Fanny and Mary rented a barouche, a fashionable two-seater complete with a convertible top in case of rain. Brother Tom was there too, plus two Italian refugee boys, Albinola, whom Fanny called a "useful beau" because she could practice her Italian with him, and Foresti, who was "a particular admirer" of Miss Mary.[29] They drove up to Great Barrington and Sheffield, where they stopped for lunch, then it was down to the tiny village of Salisbury, Connecticut, where they stopped for the night. It rained the next day, forcing everyone indoors where Fanny Kemble acted out scenes from Shakespeare and recited poetry. In the evening a fiddler was brought in from a neighboring town and there was dancing through the night. The next day was sunny, so the group went off to see the falls at Canaan, the equal Fanny thought of the ones she'd seen at Schaffhausen in July 1836. After three days in Salisbury, the Appleton girls, tired out from a summer of good fun and good company, all accompanied by the normal quota of eager young beaux, began their return trip to Boston and Beacon Hill.

Longfellow's spirits lifted with the September publication of "A Psalm of Life" in the *Knickerbocker*.[30] It was reprinted in New York newspapers almost at once, then picked up by the Boston papers, and soon there were editors everywhere inviting Henry to send in poems for their publications. "Psalm" was catching on with the public on a scale no American poem ever had.[31] "Young men read it with delight," Samuel Longfellow wrote in his biography of his brother, "their hearts were stirred by it as by a bugle summons." He added defensively that readers "did not stop to ask critically whether or not it passed the line which separates poetry from preaching, or whether its didactic merit was a poetic defect. It was enough that it inspired them and enlarged their lives." Sumner claimed the poem saved one of his classmates from suicide. And after the Civil War, it became even more popular as a memorized recitation piece for students—often at schools named after Longfellow. There was no end to its popularity. It was even translated into Sanskrit.[32]

Readers everywhere loved that it had a lesson, even though it was hard to pin down exactly what that was. It was uplifting and embraced a life of action—and it had an undeniable, inescapable rhyme and rhythm. It was reassuring and inspirational. It was a hit—easy to memorize and rich with quotable if slippery lines, like these which may be the most famous (and perhaps the most indecipherable) in all of nineteenth-century American poetry:

> Lives of great men all remind us
> We can make our lives sublime,
> And, departing, leave behind us
> Footprints on the sands of time.

This was poetry as it was supposed to be written, most people thought, and because the individual quatrains felt deep, they produced conversation and analysis—which proved to be the poem's undoing in the following century because the poem couldn't stand up to the closest critical scrutiny. But for the remainder of the nineteenth century and well into the twentieth, "Psalm" was read as a first-class literary achievement as well as a popular phenomenon. It appealed to a wide, public audience at every level of economic and educational and social class. And as it swept the nation, it marked the beginning of Longfellow's gradual makeover from a drab college professor into a beloved literary personality. He became a celebrity.

Miss Fanny Appleton could not have missed the transformation. She had turned down his marriage proposal, but Henry Wadsworth Longfellow was still a good friend of hers, and she no doubt spoke of how close they were whenever the "Psalm of Life" came up in conversation.

There was, however, no noticeable thaw in Fanny's cold dismissal of him. It is possible there was a trace of softening, that she may have begun thinking of Henry as the "poet" instead of the "professor," but if there was a transition here, it was so slow that Henry couldn't see much to be encouraged by. By August, however, he was displaying a healthy sense of balance and recovery in a letter to Greene: "The *Madonna Francesca* affair is all dead and buried.... I modestly think she made a mistake. But it was not her fault. She is a most noble and beautiful woman.... After this I shall not be likely to see her equal in any woman. I knew her too well, not to suffer much.... It makes men of us to suffer."[33] But two months later, in his October 22 letter to Greene, he was less inclined to put his love for Fanny in the "dead and buried" file:

> And now open your great heart, and hold it open by the four corners, while I pour into it all thoughts, all passions, all desires, which fill mine own. And first of the *"Dark Ladie,"* who holds my reason captive. As yet no sign of yielding. As stately and sublime, and beautiful as ever! While I likewise sail with the flag nailed to the mast, to sink or conquer. She has been in the country all Summer, and has at length returned to town. But we seldom meet; never except by accident. I have given up society *entirely*: and live alone here, grim as Death, with only that one great thought in my mind. Meanwhile crowds are about her; and flatterers enough; and all the splendor of fashion, and suitors manifold. My hope and faith are firm planted in my righteous cause. If there can be any difference between me and those about her—if our souls can understand each other—she will sooner or later find it so. If not—then I take this disappointment likewise by the hand; I bide my time. But my passion is mighty; *gigantic*—or it would not have survived this. Meanwhile I labor and work right on with what heart and courage I may, and despise all sympathy; and am quite reasonably cool for a mad-man.[34]

There was still some slim hope, he seemed to think, some reason to bide his time—but to be encouraged after a year of outright rejection was madness—and he knew it.

It was at this point, however, when he was "quite reasonably cool for a mad-man," that Henry made what turned out to be a near-fatal decision: he'd make public the tatters of his campaign to win Fanny Appleton's love. He'd write a German style autobiographical novel, after the fashion of Goethe perhaps, on the nobility gained through suffering, and combine that with Jean Paul Richter's romantic-sentimental-digressive style, which was running softly through his mind like a musical score as he wrote.[35] The character he based on himself, however, Paul Flemming, reveals an unhealthy desperation as he courts and is rejected by Mary Ashburton in the novel Longfellow began writing in September 1838, and called *Hyperion: A Romance* when it was published in the summer of 1839.

The desperation would have come to nothing if the story had been less popular or less transparent, but the book sold well and everyone on Beacon Hill, and everyone Henry and Fanny knew personally, understood at once who Paul and Mary were. Until that point, Henry's romantic humiliation had been limited to gossips on Beacon Hill and at Harvard, but with the appearance of the book, whatever shred of privacy Henry may have had as an unrequited lover was gone forever. Even that paled as a problem, however, compared to his worry about Fanny's reaction to being dragged onto a public stage. That was the burning question. What had he risked? He'd been a rejected suitor but still a valued friend before the book came out—what could he expect after its publication? It may have occurred to him in the summer of 1839 that he'd had a lapse in good sense when he decided to write the book a year earlier, that he'd been through too much emotional distress to trust his own decisions during the composition of this very personal book—but it was too late by then. There was nothing left to do but stand by the book.

In July 1839, about a week before the book came out, Henry sent a letter to Greene, then United States Consul in Rome, asking first if Charles Sumner, visiting Rome, had filled in the details of Henry's "*affaire du coeur* and of the Lady."[36] From his end, Henry could say only that even though Greene had probably thought his love for Fanny would fade, it had not: "I am as much in love as ever." He said there were "two mighty wills" clashing: "The lady says she *will not*! I say she *shall*!" He called it "the madness of passion": "I visit her; sometimes pass an evening alone with her. But not one word is ever spoken on a certain topic. No whining, no beseeching, but a steel-like silence. This *is* pride. So we both stand eyeing each other like lions." At that very moment, he said, she was spending her second straight summer in Stockbridge, where he thought she might be expecting him to visit her. But he wouldn't. "Such are not my tactics." He wouldn't take a step in that direction, he said stubbornly, "but next week I shall fire off a rocket, which I trust will make a commotion in that citadel."

The rocket of course was *Hyperion*, into which, he told Greene, "I have put my feelings, my hopes and sufferings for the last *three* years." He tried to be cagey telling the story about Fanny and himself through the characters of Mary and Paul, but it was a trickier business than he had banked on. "Things are shadowed forth with distinctness enough to be understood; and yet so mingled with fiction in the events set down as to raise doubt, and perplexity."[37] That was his hope. But even though he'd presented his love in a work of fiction, he went on, "the *Feelings* of the book are true." Mary Ashburton "bears a resemblance to *the lady*, without being an exact portrait; so that the reader will say 'It is! No, it is not! And yet it must be!'" He hadn't betrayed any confidences, he reassured Greene, hadn't depicted any real scenes, and he thought that just maybe the Lady might "fall in love with her own sweet image in the book." He was a man in love with a woman who didn't love him back—and he was betting against long odds that *Hyperion* would turn her around, win her love. He was desperate, delusional. The book had just the opposite effect.

Hyperion follows Longfellow's own journey through Germany and Switzerland in 1835–36, beginning with his mourning over the recent death of his wife as he worked his way through his grief traveling down the Rhine to Heidelberg and then later to Switzerland. (Notably absent is a character modeled on Clara Crowninshield.) He put himself into the romance as the lead character and speaker, Paul Flemming. With that as a starting point, *Hyperion* turns into a leisurely travel book full of literary excursions into countryside and cathedral, although its central interest is Paul Flemming's sudden and deep passion for the 21-year-old Miss Mary Ashburton, whom he meets in Interlaken, Switzerland, where she was traveling with her mother. This section, some sixty pages over nine chapters, less than a quarter of the book, is more precisely about her rejection of him—and his response.

Henry, of course, had met Fanny in Interlaken only two years earlier when she was 18 and traveling through Europe with her father. Longfellow seems to have thought when he was planning the book that he'd spin the details out as a storyline in his romance, exorcise the demons of disappointment that he'd been dealing with, and grasp at one last romantic straw. Maybe, he thought, if Fanny could see the depth and purity of his love in print, she might change her mind. This little book, then—which sold well as a handbook for travelers and remained in print for fifty years—was overloaded with emotional complications for the author.[38] The cool and reserved Henry Longfellow had never written anything before that had come close to this level of personal confession. And he worried about it even as he was doing it.

Eager but edgy as the day of publication neared, Henry told Greene that he'd probably opened the door for "tremendous censure," but he hoped as well for "equal applause."[39] He was encouraged because he thought at that moment *Hyperion* was better than anything else he'd ever written. He was excited because he knew the book was "*reality*": "My heart has been put into the printing-press and stamped on the pages." Readers would not fail to see his "agony of soul," he told Greene. "*I am in earnest*! I lay aside all sham modesty and speak to *my friend* as I really feel, having neither *time* nor *need* for apologizing because I speak what I think." And he thought that he'd been through hell:

> My wife's death—my meeting with this lady—my return and a whole year's delirium of hope, before she came [back], during which my imagination had time to forge fetters

> as strong as the threads of life—then her return and the catastrophe—and an eighteen months' struggle—humiliation—wounded pride, wounded affection—derision—conflicting feelings enough to drive one mad. Well, during the last year, and under this pressure the book has been produced. And if now and then there be a passage, which to a *well man*, in the light of sober reason may seem a little morbid, is it any wonder! I fear, my dear Greene that I have been *very* near madness and even death, within the last few months.[40]

He had told Greene a year earlier that he was "quite reasonably cool for a mad-man," but now he felt his condition had worsened.

How mad had he become? How embarrassing were his disclosures? Those were the questions he was wrestling with when the book finally appeared in black and white in early August. He had introduced Mary Ashburton into the story more than 150 pages into the book as a voice only. She enters a hotel lobby and speaks a few hushed words to her companion, but they were spoken "in a voice so musical and full of soul, that it moved the soul of Flemming, like a whisper from heaven."[41] When he sees her in the morning, Flemming is transformed immediately: "I will not disguise the truth. She is my heroine." She had a "calm, quiet face," "deep unutterable eyes," and a "striking" figure. "Every step, every attitude, was graceful, and yet lofty, as if inspired by the soul within.... And what a soul was hers! A temple dedicated to Heaven and like the Pantheon at Rome, lighted only from above." For page after page Longfellow as Flemming holds back his emotions only to have them spill out, as of their own will, a few pages further on: "Oh, there is nothing holier, in this life of ours, than the first consciousness of love, the first fluttering of its silken wings; the first rising sound and breath of wind which is so soon to sweep through the soul, to purify or to destroy!"[42]

Flemming's sanctified passion notwithstanding, Mary Ashburton "remained unmoved." At one point after his rejection, Flemming passed the place he had first met Mary. "Involuntarily he closed his eyes. They were full of tears." When he pulled himself together and got back to his hotel, he told the whole story to a traveling companion—about his broken heart and how he had made an ass of himself—but Mary, he insisted, was "very dear to me still; a beautiful, high-minded, noble woman." He couldn't help it. "I shall never cease to love her. This may be madness in me; but so it is. Alas and alas!" Flemming/Longfellow had written himself into a corner that seemed to have but a single explanation: Mary Ashburton/Fanny Appleton had been sent by God "to punish me for my sins." In the end, "he journeyed on, wrapped in desponding gloom, and mainly heedless of life going on around him. His mind was distempered."[43]

Distempered or not, Flemming returns to his travelogue for the last six chapters of the book, suffering in silence. But on the last three pages, Mary Ashburton reenters. In a replay of the first time he had heard her voice, that "whisper from heaven," Flemming hears her once again through the "thin partition" separating his room from hers in the hotel. "His heart could not be deceived; and all its wounds began to bleed afresh, like those of a murdered man when the murderer approaches." But rather than "go to her, and behold her face once more," which he wanted to do, he remained in his room. "Pride had so far gained the mastery over affection," but the nearness of her beating heart made him realize "now for the first time how weak he was, and how strong was his passion for that woman."[44]

And thus the books ends. He'd fired off his rocket, as he said he would do in his letter to Greene, and worried anew what sort of "commotion" would follow.

Henry's commotion, however, had to stand in line to get Fanny's attention when the book appeared in early August, without his name but with the coy and cautious "By the Author of *Outre-Mer*" on the title page instead. It had already been a life-changing year for Fanny. For one thing, on January 8, her 59-nine-year-old father, a widower for six years, had suddenly remarried. His new wife and Fanny's new mother was 34-four-year-old Harriot Coffin Sumner (thirteen years older than Fanny), a cousin of Charles Sumner through her father Jesse, a Boston merchant.[45] The wedding had caught Boston by surprise. Harrison Gray Otis, a one-time mayor of Boston, a United States senator, and a member of the House of Representatives, was so astounded by the news that he mailed the gossip at once to a friend in Philadelphia. Harriot, who had never been married before, was "nice" enough, Otis reported—but then couldn't resist adding, probably with a broad grin and an arched eyebrow, "There's no fool like an old fool."

Shortly after the wedding, the new Mrs. Appleton was visibly pregnant, delivering her first of three children, William Sumner, on January 11, 1840. Life at 39 Beacon Street was being totally reshuffled and rearranged, which put both Fanny and Mary in a significantly changed domestic situation. For six years they had been in charge of the household—servants, meals, parties, social events—but now there was a new wife to step in and take charge. They didn't know quite what to think, how to behave, although they certainly felt replaced and suddenly less relevant. Mary wrote to Franz Lieber guardedly, "Our new Mamma is so amiable that it would be in vain to find fault, as yet, with her entrance among us."[46] It is unclear if she meant the emphasis to be on "amiable" or "fault," but she seemed to be saying that it wouldn't do to nitpick about her new mother's faults—at least not yet anyway. At 26 and after a decade of being a sought-after Boston heiress, Mary could see that it was time for her to marry, to leave Harriot in sole charge of her own house and growing family. Fanny would have to deal with their "new Mamma" on her own. But finding a husband in the first half of 1839 wasn't as easy as perhaps Mary had thought it might be.

That summer she and Fanny once again went to the Berkshires, this time going first to the inn at Lenox, before heading to Stockbridge where they rented rooms in the home of a Mr. and Mrs. Yale. Mrs. Yale took care of their meals and laundry, while Mr. Yale watched over the their rented barouche and two horses.[47] In high spirits, they called their summer place Yale Manor, and immediately began receiving gentleman callers from Pittsfield, Lenox, and Stockbridge, all of whom had to ride or walk up a steep hill to reach them. But the Appleton girls were clearly worth the effort. Fanny loved the whole thing, especially the fact that she was away from her father and new stepmother, who were on the beach at Nahant. In every way, it was more agreeable being in Stockbridge than Boston, she bragged to Emmeline Austin in July, but mostly because she and Mary were enjoying "twenty times the independence" they would have had back home.[48]

One of the gentleman callers was Robert Mackintosh, a Scotsman born in Bombay, India, the last child of Sir James Mackintosh, who had taken the position of chief judge in Bombay in 1804. Sir James had had careers in medicine and law, written a famous defense of the French Revolution, served seven years in Bombay, and then become a Member of Parliament, professor of law, and the author of late works like his *Dissertation on the Progress of Ethical Philosophy*. He had died in 1832, leaving a legacy to be reckoned with, and Robert had dutifully set about the project of collecting his father's papers and editing his *Memoirs*, which were published in two volumes in 1835. In the summer of 1839, he was working as a British attaché in Washington, a job that left him lots of time to see the country and think about a book on the United States, which he was gathering information for when he arrived in Stockbridge. He undertook the long trek from the inn at Stockbridge all the way up the steep hill to call on the Appleton girls. Mary and he were apparently drawn to each other at once, but Fanny didn't know quite why. She couldn't warm to him—at least not at first. Maybe it had something to do with his age, 33, which put him seven years older than Mary and a whopping eleven years older than Fanny. He was older even than Longfellow.

Mackintosh, Fanny wrote in a letter to her friend Emmeline in late July, was good looking but a "puzzle." He has an "awkward figure," laughs "spasmodically," and "jerks out his words like a badly-working pump." Maybe worst of all, she thought, was his maddening habit of being "constantly *absent* when *present*." In September, Fanny was still complaining about him in her journal, about a run-in they had had when he declared Unitarianism to be "worse than Heathenism." "This eternal quizzing wears me out," she wrote. "An honest opinion deserves a like return, and you never feel sure of getting that from him. Then he contradicts all your assertions with a saucy 'oh very like,' implying 'I don't believe a word you say,' which provokes me like the buzzing of mosquitoes."[49] She interrupted her diatribe long enough to admit, reluctantly, that Mackintosh was "a good enough creature *au fond* [basically]," but then with renewed exasperation she lashed out again: "But such a combination of *gaucherie*, coolness and laziness I never encountered."[50]

It's doubtful Fanny would have cared, but her friend the professor was none too taken with Robert Mackintosh either. Longfellow wrote to Sam Ward on December 10, that though he was "but slightly acquainted with the youth," he'd found Mackintosh off-putting: "He is taciturn, modest, and bald-headed—three points worth considering in marriage."[51]

The Appleton girls ended their long summer in the Berkshires on October 5, and returned by stagecoach and railroad to Beacon Hill, where Mr. Robert Mackintosh showed up soon afterward to ask for Mary's hand in marriage. The proposal turned into an engagement and their wedding was set for December 26, barely five months after they had met and not even three short months into the future—which meant that Fanny's carefree summers with beaux and parties were over. Without her older sister at her side, it would be impossible to maintain even the minimum standard for the combination of fun and respectability Fanny had almost giddily become used to. Moreover, her issues with Mackintosh multiplied tenfold when he announced that in April he and Mary would be leaving for Scotland where they would live permanently. Fanny's disappointment with Mackintosh then exploded into angry, broken-hearted sobs as she realized she would be losing forever her older sister, her pal, her co-conspirator. At least it seemed like forever. Fanny was devastated.

On January 3, a week after the wedding, Fanny poured out her misery to Franz Lieber, the Waterloo veteran and fighter for Greek independence who had been Mary's tutor in German in 1832 and was then a professor at South Carolina College

> Yes, Mary is actually married, and certainly no union of life and soul, except the wedded one, has such oneness as that of two sisters of nearly the same age, bound to each other from birth.... You can believe, then, what I suffer in my bereaved state, how undermined has been my peace of mind and hopes of the future, for if it excites no little jealousy and loneliness to see a stranger claiming what was once all our own, this sorrow is doubly aggravated when he makes her also a stranger and steals her from her home and kindred. No one but Death and a lover can thus quietly bereave hearthsides.

She took a deep breath, suddenly realized how negative her letter had been, and shifted her ground. She thanked God that since the wedding her "feelings have attained a less selfish character. Now that it is over, I actually feel relieved, and live only in the consciousness of their supreme happiness." But the words had hardly reached the page when she wailed out a final lament: "Yesterday-week she was made a bride, and the joy- and sorrow-fraught name of Mary Appleton ceased to be known on earth!"[52]

As to the wedding itself, Fanny told Lieber, it had been a quiet affair at home without "smirking brides-maids and men," presided over by William Ellery Channing himself. Breaking down again, Fanny said that Channing's "solemn prayers were echoed by more aching hearts and streaming eyes than often hallow this most awful ceremony." Then she dropped into a description of Mary as bride. She wore a simple white muslin dress, without flowers in her hair, but holding a bouquet "next her heart." Fanny added that her sister's face was "radiant with a deep joy and trust which God grant may be eternal." Afterward, "there was the usual cutting up of cake and spasmodic attempts at hilarity" before the now-married couple went to Lexington for their wedding night.

The whole affair had left poor Fanny reeling. "Even yet, at times," she continued in her letter to Lieber, "I think it all a dream on which some gracious dawn will arise." And then, with renewed determination, she returned once again to Robert Mackintosh in order to put him in a better light. She said she'd become "warmly attached" to him, that he had a "genuine, upright, manly character" and "a true, noble heart." At that point she seems to have been reduced to the platitudes expected of her. Or maybe she was pretending admiration that she hoped would develop into truth in the future. As far as her own future was concerned, she told Lieber, she'd reached a "dead blank" and she thought as little as possible about it. "Life's kaleidoscope," she said, was full of "strange shiftings," so it was impossible to know "what a year may bring forth."[53]

The kaleidoscope had already turned up one other strange shifting that fateful summer when Robert Mackintosh had shown up and caused such a stir in her life—and that would be her own unexpected appearance in Professor Henry Longfellow's new book, *Hyperion*. A copy reached Fanny in Stockbridge in early August, sent by Longfellow himself and delivered by cousin Isaac Appleton Jewett, who had been spending time with the girls in the Berkshires before taking a trip to New York where he had happened to meet Longfellow, who was seeing *Hyperion* through the final days of prepublication in late July and early August. He had picked up a few copies prior to its official release and given one to Jewett for Fanny, who wasn't sure what to make of it at first.

A few days later, Fanny wrote to her friend Emmeline with news that Longfellow had put her into his new book—but she had trouble in the letter settling on a tone or even a message. She wrote that Longfellow had sent the book "and a rank Swiss cheese! which Mr. Charles S. [Sedgwick] says testifies his admiration, as strong and as disagreeable!"[54] But then she praised vaguely "some exquisite things" in the book before delivering another punishing blow: "it is desultory, objectless, a thing of shreds and patches like the author's mind." But then she circled around and praised once again: "The type and cool covering are fascinating; then the style is infinitely polished and sparkling with many beautiful poetical *concetti* [concepts], for his scholastic lore and vivid imagination create infinite comparisons, very just and well carried out." But she wasn't happy with the hero, "evidently himself," who "sticks ludicrously to certain particulars." One particular was wooing the heroine "by the reading of German ballads in her unwilling ears." In the end, she wrote, "the adventures have not the same zest of novelty to us as to other people, as we have had the misfortune to be behind the scenes...." She praised the "graceful chapters," but said it was "a pity they should achieve their destiny solely by enlightening the dull brains of college boys or scornful maidens." She thought there were "more shadows than sunshine" in the book.

Fanny's early misgivings soon gave way to a certainty that she had been used badly. By the time she got back to Boston, the gossip hit her full force, and she realized the damage that had been done. She wrote on November 4 to Jewett that she had been "hoisted" into a "public notoriety by a certain impertinent friend of mine." She was, she said, "entirely disgusted with the honor."[55]

Henry had wondered in his letter to Greene in July what sort of "commotion" his "rocket" would ignite. By November he had his answer. The Dark Lady was disgusted with the whole business—embarrassed, indignant, mortified, angry. With hindsight, Henry wavered between faith in the book and a horrible recognition that he had just broadcast his tale of personal romantic pain to the world. He had written to Greene that there was no "sham modesty" in the book, that his transparent "agony of soul" would be apparent, and that he believed he had written Fanny Appleton's portrait in such a way that "unless I much deceive myself" would make her "fall in love with her own sweet image in the book." He felt on solid ground: "*I am in earnest!*" he had told Greene. There was "neither *time* nor *need* for apologizing because I speak what I think."[56] But he had miscalculated, very much deceived himself. Not only did Fanny Appleton not "fall in love with her own sweet image," she resented being used as a storyline in the professor's new book. She felt violated, powerless, livid. In the end Longfellow had to retreat: he'd been a "mad-man" when he'd written it, as he told Greene in October 1838, which is to say he'd been too addled to think clearly. He'd made a terrible mistake and would have to move forward as best he could in the fall 1839, but his already dire situation with the Dark Lady had taken a fatal turn for the worse. It was finally over, "dead and buried."

8

The Cure

To work through the severe economic and emotional depressions of the late 1830s and early 1840s, Longfellow threw himself headlong into his professional lives, the one at Harvard that included all his language instruction and department responsibilities, and the one at his desk that included the writing of poems that were about to catapult him into literary sainthood. Less and less he liked the former, and more and more he felt he was on the right track with the latter. Striking a balance between them became his day-to-day challenge.

At Harvard the minutiae was maddeningly persistent. For one thing there was the teaching staff he had to supervise. The department consisted of four foreign-born instructors, who'd had no supervision at all between George Ticknor's exit and Longfellow's entrance. Two of them were fired in the spring 1838, after Longfellow's first full year, with the German instructor being replaced at once. The French instructor, however, was not, which meant Longfellow had to teach the elementary French classes himself, substantially increasing his week-to-week workload without adding much to his annual salary. Hoping the situation was temporary, Longfellow was disappointed when he was told in August 1839 that it was "inexpedient" for the college to hire anyone new to the language faculty at that time, and that "the Smith Professor ought to continue to give all the instruction required in the French language."[1] It isn't clear how much of this decision was owing to a lack of respect for the modern languages as a department (the ancient languages continued to be the backbone of a man's education) and how much was due to the economic recession that was by then stretching into its third year. Quincy as management's chief executive officer was charged with getting more production from fewer resources, which meant he wouldn't be replacing the French instructor any time soon. No, Quincy thought, it was better that Longfellow should continue teaching French. Permanently.

It was especially bad news because Longfellow's easy first year had given way to a difficult second year with very specific duties outlined by Quincy on September 21, 1837. His work would fall under the headings of superintending, instructing, and lecturing. The instructing and lecturing were clear enough, but lest there be any misunderstanding about superintendence, Quincy dipped into his inkpot for his worst educational jargon: Longfellow was to "at least once in every week, attend the recitations of one of the Instructors in his Department, and be present at the recitation of every individual studying the language taught by such Instructor; and in like manner in succession, attend the recitation of every other instructor in his department, and thus be present at, and hear the recitations of every section and individual therein, at least once in every month."[2] In short, the administrative work by itself was going to be a full-time job. But of course there was more.

Every week he also had to "give oral instruction ... in some one of the modern languages," then

Henry W. Longfellow by Cephus Giovanni Thompson. Oil on canvas, 1840 (courtesy National Park Service. Longfellow House—Washington's Headquarters National Historic Site, LONG 4127).

move on to each of the other languages one at a time, his job being to provide "commentary upon and illustration of" some work the students might reasonably be expected to understand. And then, finally, in the summer term every year he was to give two public lectures a week—or one a week during each of the first two terms. That was his workload in 1837–38. And then beginning with the fall term 1838, he'd had to take over the French classes, which brought him right back to full-time elementary classroom instruction once again.

It had made one kind of sense back when he was graduating from college and looking forward to an extended European sojourn, that college teaching might be a decent compromise between a career in law, the thought of which he could never bear, and a lifetime of literary study and writing, which he longed for but which was impossible in the 1820s. The Bowdoin teaching years had been a disaster, at least from his point of view, and now Harvard was turning out to be the same. All the compromise had done, in the end, was give him a job that eroded his spirit more and more every day with its mind-numbing monotony. It was on September 10, 1838, that he had written in his journal that the worst thing about college teaching was "having your mind constantly a play-mate for boys."[3] The depression over his professional life was rapidly catching up to the depression of his personal life. Suddenly in 1838, Longfellow became as eager to leave Harvard as he had been to leave Bowdoin in 1833—and he began looking around for a new job. Any new job would do. And then, nearly a year later in August 1839, an opportunity presented itself and Longfellow grasped at the straw.

His friend Sam Ward had married the daughter of millionaire fur-trader John Jacob Astor and recommended Henry for the job of tutoring Astor's young son for a period of six years in Germany. "Your office," he wrote to Henry on August 21, "would be to superintend his studies and see that his time is employed in the most profitable manner." Longfellow was immediately over-excited at the prospect of escaping from Harvard, putting distance between himself and Fanny Appleton, living in Germany, and resuming a life worth living—but in the end the Astors, in the words of Sam Ward, "became seized with misgivings" and decided against hiring a tutor after all.[4] It was another blow. He had worked his hopes up more than he should have, and the disappointment was hard to take. He wrote in his journal, flashing uncharacteristic anger: "Well, that is cruel, after asking me! No matter."[5] But it did matter. He wrote to his father on September 21, 1839: "My work here grows quite intolerable; and unless they make some change, I will leave them, with or without anything to do. I will not consent to have my life crushed out of me so. I had rather live a while on bread and water. I feel all the time, that I am doing wrong to stay here under such circumstances...."[6]

Intolerable as his Harvard work may have seemed to Longfellow—crushing the life out of him, as he put it—it did force him to focus on something other than his full-time obsession with Fanny Appleton, a blessing not to be dismissed lightly given his fragile emotional condition after Fanny had turned him down in the fall of 1837. He said as much in his journal for September 4, 1838: "I feel better these College work-days, when I can let my electricity off among my pupils." What he needed, he said, was "ceaseless activity" because "my heart breaks when I sit alone here so much!"[7] He knew better than to give in to melancholy and self-pity—no matter how tempting they were. He even had his own words to give him strength, for "A Psalm of Life" was published that same month of September 1838 in the *Knickerbocker Magazine*. He knew that sorrow wasn't "our destined end or way" and that each of us needed "to act, that each to-morrow / Find us farther than to-day."

That was what he'd do: act. He would put aside his impatience with Harvard and try to dig himself out of his depression. And he'd also act on his long-suppressed impulse to write poetry, to become a real part of the literary world that seemed always just out of reach. In December 1839, just when *Hyperion* was making such a brouhaha in Boston social circles and his emotional life was in a critical nosedive, he published a book of poems, his first, *Voices of the Night*, which included poems he had written in Cambridge plus a few earlier ones and some translations. The 75-cent book became an overnight success—the 900-copy first printing selling out in a month, followed by three more printings in the first year alone—all tallied up in the tight-money aftermath of the Panic of 1837. By March 31, 1857, according to a note in Longfellow's journal, American sales alone had run to 43,550 copies.[8]

Higginson remembered with pride, "the sense of triumph with which we [students] saw the proof-sheets of *Voices of the Night* brought in by the printer's devil and laid at his elbow." Hawthorne wrote to say he had read and reread the poems, and "nothing equal to some of them was ever written in this world." Sam Ward on reading "Footsteps of Angels" said it would "find an echo in every true heart." Bryant's *Evening Post* in New York, ran a review signed by J.Q.D.: "These voices of the night breathe a sweet and gentle music, such as befits the time when the moon is up, and all the air is clear, and soft, and still." There were good reviews too in the *Boston Quarterly Review* and the *New-Yorker*; the *Corsair* reported that *Voices* had earned "an elevated place in the library of American classics" and the *Southern Literary Messenger* put Longfellow "among the first of our American poets." "Everyone praises the book," Henry wrote to George Greene. "Even the Boston papers which so abused *Hyperion*, praise this highly. *Hyperion* they could not understand. This they *feel* more."[9]

What readers felt was an emotional and intellectual connection to Longfellow, a closeness to poems that radiated an inner strength of purpose delivered in elevated language and wrapped in reassuringly tight rhymes and metered verse. It was unapologetically didactic, at times openly inspirational. And it wasn't enough for readers to own a yellowing newspaper copy of "A Psalm of Life"—they wanted the book it appeared in too. Henry Longfellow couldn't have known it in December 1839, when *Voices* was published, but he had found the formula that would make him a beloved literary celebrity for generations to come. There seemed, as the next three decades unfolded, no limit to his talent, his productiveness, his success, and his reputation—whether measured by readers who lined up to read his books, critics who reviewed them, or dollars spent on them. America finally had its poet. There were a few naysayers, but they were drowned out by readers from every walk of life who believed in "A Psalm of Life"—and its author.

Coming on the heels of his monumental blunder in *Hyperion*, *Voices* had a couple of poems that ran similar risks—revealing too much of his own personal losses. There were poems like the "Prelude" that traced the loss of innocent childhood; "The Reaper and the Flowers" that had carried a subtitle in its *Knickerbocker* publication, "A Psalm of Death"; "Footsteps of Angels" that recalled Mary so clearly; "Flowers" that he'd written for Fanny; even "A Psalm of Life" that could be read as a series of prescriptions for him to move on with his life after the death of Mary and the rejection of Fanny. Had he stumbled once again? Had he been embarrassingly and openly self-absorbed—again? Was this another clumsy blunder?

One built-in protection was the way the book took shape. First of all, there were only nine new poems, four of which had to be rushed out in the fall of 1839 to make the December publication schedule—which speaks more to Longfellow's eagerness to get back to the business of poetry than his actual readiness to publish. It was as much designed to look away from his dreary students, colleagues, and "career" as it was a tentative first step in a new direction. He did have the success of "A Psalm of Life" to build on, which he no doubt thought was enough to gamble on—and his publisher, his old Portland friend John Owen, who had been at Bowdoin with him and subsequently relocated to Cambridge, agreed with him. But nine poems, including a prelude, weren't enough to make a book, so author and publisher decided to add eight more poems from his teenage years, like "The Burial of the Minisink" and "The Spirit of Poetry," both of which were written after graduation from Bowdoin in 1825 and published in 1826 and 1827 respectively in *The Atlantic Souvenir*, a Philadelphia annual. That grouping of poems ended with what he called "*L'Envoi*," another fall 1839 poem that he called a "poetical summary" of the seventeen poems just presented. But even that was too slender a book, so Longfellow added translations, his other great passion, twenty-three in all, including the long *Coplas de Manrique*. They finally had enough to publish a book that ran to 144 pages, of which only the first few were given over to new poems—and there was no character in any of them so obviously traceable as Mary Ashburton had been. The only poem that came even close to being self-revealing was "Flowers," which had been written as a love poem to Fanny but was sufficiently oblique that even she may not have recognized it as such. He was on safe ground.

Two years later, in December 1841, he took another big step forward with *Ballads and Other Poems*. That book was actually begun on December 30, 1839, when he wrote "The Wreck of the Hesperus," a ballad that had come to him in the middle of the night: "It hardly cost me an effort," Henry famously confessed in his journal. "It did not come into my mind by lines but by stanzas."[10] It was a poem, like "A Psalm of Life," destined to become a chestnut that poetry students would memorize for the next century or more—and then remember fondly for the rest of their lives as what real poetry ought to read and sound like.

By definition ballads were written imitations of folk narratives, the kind of campfire songs that were easy to remember because of their short, swinging, four-line stanzas that traditionally rhymed at the end of the second and fourth lines. Where *Voices* had announced his facility with lyrical poems, *Ballads* would do the same with narrative poems, for Longfellow was uncovering a talent for story telling in verse, and discovering too that he could manage his craft so well that few caught him at it—which was the ultimate compliment. Longfellow wrote to Greene on January 5, 1840, that he thought he'd write more ballads, as he was so pleased with "The Wreck of the Hesperus." "The *National Ballad* is a virgin soil here in New England; and there are good materials. Beside[s] I have a great notion of working upon *people's feelings*."[11]

There was something practical going through the back of Longfellow's mind too, for it made good sense to get a new book in the public's hands while they were still enamored of the first one. "Blow upon blow, is the word; and not let the iron cool," is how he would put it in a letter to his father shortly before *Ballads* was published.[12] Together, *Voices* and *Ballads* marked the beginning of a life-changing transition that would move Longfellow from college classrooms to people's living rooms. However, for the two years between those two books, Longfellow struggled with his demons—his health, his emotions, and his career.

Longfellow's closest friends all knew that he needed to fall in love again and did what they could to encourage him. In January 1840, Sam Ward in New York, fixed him up with his sister Anna. Or, rather, Henry selected Anna from among the three Ward sisters, known in New York's elite social circles as the "Graces of Bond Street."

Their relationship began when Henry went to New York late in January to deliver two lectures on Dante and one on Jean Paul Richter at the Mercantile Library Association. Public lectures like these had grown to immense popularity by then, answering a need among intellectually starved citizens for entertainment and instruction on every subject imaginable. Henry had for many years, even before the Lyceum movement began in 1826, set his sights on delivering public lectures (and would later steadfastly refuse to give them), but this one at the MLA was to be his first. Among the other speakers in the series were Ralph Waldo Emerson, Horace Mann, Richard Henry Dana, and Sam Ward himself, who was giving the last two lectures that season, on

The Doctrine of Chances.[13] Ward offered his family home to Henry while he was in town, an invitation Henry gratefully, eagerly accepted. This was the kind of society he liked, cosmopolitan, gracious, well to do, and good fun. And he'd also be meeting Sam's sisters, all of whom, like the Appleton girls, were highly prized—and single. Corny Felton knew all three and knew of course that his pal Longo was suffering from multiple layers of depression. He told Henry flatly that he was "the most insensible block in existence not to fall in love with one of those incomparable sisters...."[14]

Julia Ward, the eldest, was beautiful, with an "oval face, creamy complexion, blue eyes, and startlingly red hair." And she was also supremely talented—an opera-quality singer, a poet, a linguist—and a social activist who would write what became the anthem of the Union forces during the Civil War, "The Battle Hymn of the Republic" (1862). In the fall of 1841, Greene wrote Longfellow that word had reached him in Italy from Sam that Henry and Julia were in love, which Henry corrected on June 28, 1842: "The report in regard to Miss Julia and myself has not, and never has had the slightest foundation in fact; nor did I ever hear of it, till I received your letter." Louisa was the middle sister, the most beautiful one, according to some accounts, and the one being urged on Henry by Sam. But Longfellow, just about to turn 33, found himself drawn to Anna, the youngest Grace at 17. When he left New York to return to Cambridge, according to one biographer, he had "thoroughly convinced himself that he was in love with her," and in Ward family lore, he was so smitten that he actually proposed and Anna turned him down, saying with a slight blush, "O Mr. Longfellow, think of the difference in our ages." On May 5, 1840, expecting to see her in Cambridge with Sam, Longfellow wrote in his journal that he couldn't wait to see "my dear Anna, light as a daughter of the air." And a couple of weeks later, on May 18, he wrote in his journal, that he'd had a "long chat" with Sam and had given him a "Swiss basket" for "my dear little Annie"—then he returned home and "sat by the open window till midnight, weaving fond, foolish dreams of one who is far away and not dreaming of me." Presumably he was referring to Anna in New York, not Fanny in Boston—but he didn't exactly say so.[15]

While Longfellow was working on a play he called *The Spanish Student* in 1840, he received a letter from Sam Ward in July about the dancer Fanny Elssler, who interested Longfellow almost immediately. Elssler had taken New York by storm that summer with her sensuous "cachucha," a virtuoso solo dance in triple time complete with castanets clicking and heels blazing. Ward sent Henry a description: "She is a charming dancer. The ideal of a fascinating mistress. Her eyes charm the Pit and Boxes by a mightier spell than the boa constrictor's.... Her influence is sensual, her ensemble the incarnation of seductive attraction. She has been as often bought and sold as absolution from and by priests." Almost breathlessly, he added that "such a woman is dangerous to her sex and to humanity."[16]

Ward, however, was certainly not alone, for Elssler had that effect on everyone, even Ralph Waldo Emerson, who saw her on October 13 in *Nathalie* and joined the chorus of believers. He wrote in his journal to praise the "extreme grace of her movement ... the winning fun and spirit of all her little coquetries, [and] the beautiful erectness of her body...."[17] He recognized what he called some "incidental vices" such dancing might give rise to, especially among the college boys of Harvard who, having seen Fanny Elssler's "tripping satin slippers" might find it difficult to forget "this graceful silvery swimmer" when they got back to their "baccalaureate cells."[18] And then there was Charles Newcomb, one of the Brook Farm philosopher-farmers and a writer Emerson courted for his magazine the *Dial*, who thought the famous dancer was a "vile creature" until he saw one of her performances, whereupon he placed her picture on a wall in his bedroom—between St. Francis Xavier and St. Ignatius Loyola.[19]

When Longfellow saw Elssler perform at a benefit for the erection of the Bunker Hill Monument on October 1, he fell as quickly under her spell as everyone else had—and he decided at once to put her into *The Spanish Student*. But in his hands the sexy and seductive Elssler (made over to be the gypsy dancer Preciosa in the play) was changed from a dancer of questionable reputation to an innocent young girl misunderstood by a public that had seen her sensuous dancing and drawn its own improper conclusions. The sexy virtuoso dancer was romantically transformed into an innocently virtuous woman.[20]

That Longfellow could turn his attention in *The Spanish Student* to a comedy with a strong romantic undercurrent in 1840 is more significant for what it suggests about his mindset than about the play itself, which remains among his minor works. As a project that didn't reach into his tangled emotional life, it was a step in the direction of a renewed psychological balance—recovery. It had been three years since his broken heart, and this was a sign that perhaps he was moving on. There were other hopeful signs—the 1838 success of "A Psalm of Life," the ballads, the Five of Clubs, and young Anna Ward. Longfellow was beginning to see that this combination of interests, activities, friends, and especially a new love interest might be his salvation. But the key to these hopeful developments, the straw that stirred the drink, was the wild success of *Voices*, which had revived, after years of drab dabbling in academic essays, his old dream of a literary career. With the Dark Lady receding into the deep background (most of the time), and his physical ailments not overwhelming for the moment, Longfellow felt physically and emotionally better—all based on the potent combination of new work and new friendships.

One new friend from the late 1830s wasn't new at all, Nathaniel Hawthorne. They had graduated together in 1825 from Bowdoin, but they had barely known each other back then, Hawthorne belonging on campus to the club of drinkers and under-achievers, the Athenaean Society, while Longfellow chose the more sober club of over-achievers, the Peucinian Society. Some years later, Hawthorne told Annie Fields, wife of his and Longfellow's publisher James Fields, that, as Annie paraphrased Hawthorne: "no two young men could have been more unlike." Longfellow "was a tremendous student, and always carefully dressed," Annie remembered Hawthorne saying, "while he himself was extremely careless of his appearance, no student at all, and entirely incapable at that period of appreciating Longfellow." There hadn't been much common ground to build on back then.[21]

On March 6, 1837, however, when Hawthorne was emerging from his decade-long retreat into the twin mysteries of Puritan radicalism and successful writing, he published *Twice-told Tales*, a collection of stories that had already appeared once before in magazines and annuals.[22] Jealously observing his former classmate's secure footing and steady income as a professor at Harvard and his early literary successes as well, Hawthorne thought perhaps he could impose himself on Longfellow and hope for help getting his own much-delayed literary career launched. But it was awkward. How could he broach the subject to his fellow classmate, his peer that he hardly knew, without bending and scraping, looking like a beggar asking for crumbs? He decided to do it with grace and good humor: "We were not, it is true, so well acquainted at college that I can plead an absolute right to inflict my 'twice-told' tediousness upon you, but I have often regretted that we were not better known to each other."[23] He said his stories were meant to "repay you some part of the pleasure which I have derived from *Outre-Mer*." It was a good enough cover, but Longfellow of course recognized it as the cry for help that it was—and he graciously offered it by praising Hawthorne's work in a return letter, and then by writing a review that bent too far in its fulsome accolades. Hawthorne had asked for help, and Longfellow would provide it—if he was going to err, it would be on the side of friendship—a new friendship really.

The review was published in the *North American Review* in July. According to Longfellow, Hawthorne was a "spiritual star" who was "newly risen." And it wouldn't be long before the new star would be recognized for its "magnitude" and before it takes "its place in the heaven of poetry."[24] That set the tone, unfortunately, which only got worse when he added, "Live ever, sweet,

sweet book" (which was actually an echo of words once used to describe Sir Philip Sidney's 1590 *Arcadia*). Hawthorne's new book, Longfellow wrote, "comes from the hand of a man of genius. Everything about it has the freshness of morning and of May. These flowers and green leaves of poetry have not the dust of the highway upon them. They have been gathered fresh from the secret places of a peaceful and gentle heart." The idea of Hawthorne having "secret places" might have yielded useful observations, but Longfellow didn't pursue it except to say that in Hawthorne's stories there "flow deep waters, silent, calm, and cool." Then he sank back into empty phrases once again: "spirit of love," "lively sympathies," "delightful volume," "rejoices in his heart," "beautiful and holy." He interrupted the string of friendly inanities long enough toward the end to make it seem that something important was going on in these stories: "Sometimes, though not often, [Hawthorne] glares wildly at you with a strange and painful expression." And again: "Another characteristic of this writer is the exceeding beauty of his style. It is as clear as running waters are." But instead of developing these promising lines of thought, he ended the review with several pages of excerpts, which, following Samuel Longfellow's editorial decision in *Works* (1886), are left out of reprints, a decision that at least spares most readers the loose misreading in the final paragraph: Hawthorne had written a book of "pleasant philosophy" and "quiet humor," Longfellow wrote. And then, saving the worst for last, he concluded: "Like children we say, 'Tell us more.'"[25]

In his defense, Longfellow had come to the aid of a man he felt sorry for, a man he once knew slightly, who had endured difficult years and finally emerged from his study needing help. The review was hardly Longfellow's finest critical moment, but it was a grand gesture, one that Hawthorne was grateful for for the rest of his life. When the review came out, he wrote Longfellow with a deep sense of gratitude and relief: "Whether or no the public will agree to the praise which you bestow on me, there are at least five persons who think you the most sagacious critic on earth; viz., my mother and two sisters, my old maiden aunt, and finally, the sturdiest believer of the whole five, my own self." From that point forward, Hawthorne changed his letters from "Dear Sir" to "Dear Longfellow" and ended them with "ever your friend."[26]

The two writers would meet now and then for dinner and drinks in Boston or at Craigie House, where they gathered with Hillard and Felton on April 5, 1840. Hawthorne had brought along the Reverend Horace Conolly, an Episcopal priest, who told a story after dinner of a French Canadian couple about to be married in 1755, when British troops broke in and sent them and thousands of their countrymen on a far-reaching diaspora. Separated from her betrothed during the dispersal, the young woman spent the rest of her life looking for the man she'd been about to marry, finally reuniting with him on his deathbed many years later. Conolly long afterward remembered how interested Longfellow had been in the story and that he had said it was "the best illustration of faithfulness and the constancy of woman that I have ever heard of or read."[27] Henry asked Hawthorne's permission to use the story in a poem—if Hawthorne himself wasn't planning to use it for a novel. With permission thus granted, Longfellow put *Evangeline* on his list of poems to get around to writing. This was the way a woman should love a man, he thought. This was the ideal woman, pure of heart and unswerving in her love. Faithful and constant.

Nineteen days after being introduced by Conolly to this ideal woman, Longfellow passed Fanny Appleton on a street near her home—and as if to punctuate the end of their relationship she passed by and barely acknowledged him. Later that night, at home writing in his journal, Henry wrote solemnly, "It is ended."[28]

And for a while, it seemed to him that it was. Five months later, on September 4, he was trying to show off his newfound emotional resilience in a letter, now brave, now pathetic, to his confidante George Greene. He was facing up to despondency—and succeeding, at least partly. He announced that he had "an *agreeable surprise*—the most *dis*agreeable thing on earth to me." He was, he said, over Fanny at last, but his voice broke several times in the telling:

> We now move in separate orbs, and hardly see each other's faces once a year. The passion is dead; and can revive no more. Though on this account I lead a maimed life; yet it is better thus, than merely to have gained her consent—her cold consent—even if it could have been done. So of this no more—no more—for evermore! For though I feel deeply what it is *not* to have gained the love of such a woman—I have long ceased to think of it; and remember it only, when I see that my elasticity is nigh gone, and my temples are as white as snow. Three of the best years of my life were melted down in that fiery crucible. Yet I like to feel deep emotions. The next best thing to *complete success* is *complete failure*. Misery lies halfway between. But you have thrown me into a reverie, with your *query*, and I can write no more to-night. I shall smoke, and then to bed. I must contrive to send you *Hyperion* which is the *Apology* for my madness.[29]

Meanwhile, Fanny, "looking like a princess, reserved and self-possessed" in the words of Richard Henry Dana, was 22 in 1840, comfortably settled in as one of Boston's most sought-after prizes.[30] Her life had been changed somewhat by the marriage of her sister, by her new stepmother, and eventually by two new half-brothers and a half-sister (all born between 1840 and 1843), but she still combined youth, beauty, and station with grace, intelligence, and taste. More changes were coming, but in the early 1840s, Fanny Appleton was "like a princess" in Boston society.

In January 1840, barely two weeks after her sister married Robert Mackintosh, Fanny joined the couple on a trip to Washington D.C. where attaché Mackintosh rejoined the British embassy. They took a leisurely route, stopping first in New York, then in Philadelphia, where they visited Fanny Kemble Butler, and then journeyed the rest of the way by train to Washington.[31] Once there, Fanny began juggling beaux, like a Mr. Hudson, whom she described as "a very good-looking, merry sort of person," a Lieutenant Campbell, whom she called "extremely waggish," and the dashing Austrian attaché, Mr. Friedrichstall.[32] The young lieutenant seemed to have the upper hand but was transferred out of Washington, and Fanny decided against the attaché. Other young men, however, took their place at Fanny's side during dances and parties all through January and February. On February 25, she and her sister and brother-in-law attended a dinner party at President Van Buren's Executive Mansion, Fanny liking it better than Andrew Jackson's, which she had visited eight years earlier. She wrote to her cousin Isaac Appleton Jewett that they "dined agreeably with the President, on spicier dishes than talk." But she was "fatigued with his non-committal manner," she said, and "pitied him for the bore of being equally gracious to all visitors, even lunatics, who, he says, often come."[33]

With one party, dance, and dinner after another, including the one at the president's house, Fanny Appleton's social calendar was full. But Robert and Mary, married only two months and already expecting their first child, decided suddenly to sail for England as soon as possible, so they all left Washington at the end of February. They stopped again to see Fanny Kemble Butler in Philadelphia and by early March they were back in Boston, Mary getting ready for her transatlantic voyage. Henry Longfellow came calling on March third, but Fanny recorded in her diary that day only that she had received "a nice long visit from Mr. Prescott, fresh as a rose." As an afterthought, she added, "Prof. L in P.M."[34] It was April 24, when they passed each other silently on Beacon Hill, and he recorded in his diary, "It is ended."

That summer of 1840 Fanny went to Newport with her father, her new mother (whom she called "Mrs. Appleton"), her brother Tom, and her new half-brother Willie, who was born on January 11. Nathan had arranged for a three-month stay at a place called Marine Villa, an upscale hotel with, as Fanny described it in her diary, a "straw-carpeted, flower-perfumed, drawing room" and a "pillared piazza."[35] Fanny and her Pittsfield cousin, Fanny Wright, a summer companion taking Mary's place, wore new swim suits in the still-cold Atlantic water—and then sat on the cliffs with brother Tom while he wrote poetry and later fished for dinner.

By early July, however, Fanny was up to more serious business, as she

8. The Cure

reported to Isaac Appleton Jewett: "We have been reading the first number of *The Dial*, a magazine got up by our Transcendentalists, and as you think such things fit testers of the spirit of the times, try to get it. You will like the astonishing concentration of thought therein for so few pages. Some of the poetry resembles the 'Psalms of life' and I think it is much more creditable than these patched-up Brobdingnag newspapers."[36] When she later met Margaret Fuller, perhaps at one of the "Conversations" held at Elizabeth Peabody's West Street book shop, Fanny found Miss Fuller's explanations of Transcendentalism so intellectually stimulating that, as she put it, "the air burned blue." The summer was working out quite well—comfortable, fun, and intellectually stimulating—and the poetry had actually put her in mind of an unnamed professor she knew.[37]

Then in November Fanny ran across a poem by Longfellow in the *Knickerbocker Magazine*. She wrote on the eighth to cousin Jewett: "Have you seen the Prof's last attempt, 'The Country Blacksmith'? *very* good, especially the children looking in and the daughter singing."[38] She got the title of "The Village Blacksmith" wrong, but she knew the prof had captured an iconic figure in a sentimental tribute to values so American that printmakers Currier and Ives distributed three different versions of the scene:

> Under a spreading chestnut-tree
>   The village smithy stands;
> The smith, a mighty man is he,
>   With large and sinewy hands;
> And the muscles of his brawny arms
>   Are strong as iron bands.

Readers connected with the scene and the smithy, and connected too with what they received as the poem's attractive, common sense moral, its universal application:

> Toiling,—rejoicing,—sorrowing,
>   Onward through life he goes;
> Each morning sees some task begin,
>   Each evening sees it close;
> Something attempted, something done,
>   Has earned a night's repose.

Ironically, this was the very same formula Longfellow himself was employing to get over Fanny Appleton, and by happy accident, it turned out to be the poem that earned her praise—and perhaps softened her heart.

Two months later, however, in early February 1841, a new champion stepped up to claim the hand and heart of Fanny Appleton. The new beau was a lawyer, James Winthrop Andrews, described by brother Tom as "Fanny's adorer."[39] He wrote her a letter in which he described Fanny's "diamond eyes" and "lips of ruby hue." Would she marry him, he asked? He'd be below her window that night, he said, and at her signal, he would know that she had accepted him. Fanny, however, never showed up at the window, never gave the signal, and (probably for reasons having nothing to do with Mr. Andrews) decided soon afterward to leave the country, which she did on May 1, with her brother Tom. They would go to England to see Mary, Robert, and their new son Ronald, but Fanny's specific mission was to help poor Mary, who was having a rough postpartum period, both physically and emotionally.

Fanny and Tom took one of Samuel Cunard's new super-fast screw steamers, the *S.S. Columbia*, arriving two weeks later on May 15 in Liverpool. The next day, as Fanny put it, they "railroaded it to London" and soon after Fanny could see Mary's condition for herself.[40] "I am saddened by my poor sister's peculiarly distressing state of mind ... so pulled down from her former self—these vile nerves triumphing with the malice of Furies," Fanny wrote in her diary.[41] They tried a wide range of remedies, including the so-called curative waters at Tunbridge Wells and sea bathing. Nothing worked. But Fanny thought she saw some improvement when Mary began with homeopathy. "Of course the effect is very gradual," she admitted, but Mary seemed stronger to Fanny, able to walk longer distances—and she began to look healthier too. They walked to Hastings, a mile from the spa, to see yet another ruined castle that called out for sketching, and Mary was able to keep up well enough to be encouraged, no doubt owing as much to the presence of her sister and brother as to the exercise and the homeopathic drugs. She was so encouraged that she talked about a visit to Boston—but then changed her mind.

On October 5, Fanny and Tom headed home alone, arriving on the fifteenth—but then, three weeks later Mary showed up with her husband and son, unannounced, at 39 Beacon Street for what turned out to be a six-month visit. She happily surprised her younger sister, but her stepmother Harriot, due to deliver her second child a month later, could not have been pleased by the unexpected arrival of guests who would demand so much attention, time, and care. The household was put in an instant uproar. Fanny's job was to resume her September work at guiding Mary back to strength and health, a hard and depressing task at times, though a little easier in the friendly environs of Beacon Hill. She wrote to her friend Emmeline on December 21: "Mary is looking much better, which is some comfort to me, but her weakness seems almost to have become a lasting portion—she is often depressed at the prospect of falling into what she calls the slough of invalidism for life...."[42] With her sister's decline in constant view, Fanny may have wondered if marriage and motherhood were worth the potential cost.

Not that there was anyone at the moment she was interested in. Certainly not Henry Longfellow, whose new book, *Ballads and Other Poems* had just come out. She had liked "The Village Blacksmith," but she was still angry that he had used her so badly in *Hyperion*. She wrote to Emmeline on December 24, 1841: "The Professor has a creamy new volume of verses out—rather meager *selon moi* [in my opinion], the cream of thought being somewhat thinner than that of the binding."[43] She was being deliberately caustic, of course, probably exaggerating her feelings for the amusement of her confidante, but it was nonetheless a brilliantly bitter and biting remark, though not one Longfellow ever heard or saw. It would certainly have set his recovery back a few months.

Longfellow's recovery was actually going very well through most of 1841. During the January break at Harvard, Sumner took him on a brief holiday to Philadelphia to enjoy post-Christmas parties and dances.[44] Sumner wrote George Hillard how much fun he and Longfellow were having: "Three or four engagements for every evening," he reported exuberantly, with plenty of "beautiful virgins and wives." They had determined to leave that very day, he told Hillard, "but could we resist the polite requests & invitations of the most beautiful, gracious and distinguished here?" He winked at Hillard and gave him an elbow in the ribs as he said with a broad grin that "Longfellow actually lost his appetite by sitting by the side of a most beautiful girl at dinner—the belle of Philadelphia."[45] Maybe their old friend was snapping out of his funk at long last.

When Henry reported the Philadelphia trip to his father on February 3, he toned it down and left out the girls:

> We were received with the utmost cordiality and kindness; dined, and breakfasted, and supped—and seldom went to less than three parties in an evening. All this is very agreeable for a while; but a week satiated me; and I have come back to this place [New York] in hope of being a little more quiet. But alas! Fallacious hope! I have already received six invitations to dinner; and I know not how many to parties and Concerts &c. In fine, for the sake of change, I have turned my habits of life upside down; and do nothing but run to and fro from morning till night and from night till morning.

He then dutifully and soberly added that all the partying had become "very tiresome" and that he couldn't wait to get back to Cambridge.[46] He was, after all, the hard-working diligent son, not the hard-drinking dissolute one—but neither did he want to completely hide his good spirits or disguise the fun he'd had.

For the first nine months of 1841, in fact, Henry continued to be mostly in good spirits and good health. There was the Saturday fellowship of the Five of Clubs to enjoy; dinners with the effervescent and ever-present Felton and other occasional guests at Castle Craigie and elsewhere; and *Voices* went into its fifth printing in April. There was also Sam Ward, who came up from New York for so many short visits that he seemed to become the sixth of clubs. And of course Sumner showed up just about every weekend and lounged around, perfectly at home, while Henry worked. In March Henry wrote to his father that Sumner was at that very moment reading Italian poetry while "stretched in all his majestic length upon the sopha."[47] Three weeks earlier, Henry had written a long, chatty letter to Greene that didn't even mention Fanny Appleton. In fact, her name doesn't come up at all in his letters in the first half of 1841, and when he sent Greene a copy of *Hyperion* on June 10, he was able to say flatly that "it is a *sincere* book; showing the passage of a morbid mind into a purer and healthier state."[48]

Harvard too had become more bearable, as he explained in a letter to his father on March 21, because he was working only three days a week, had little or no preparation, and thus had "a great deal of time to myself." He added in controlled understatement, "[I] do not find it disagreeable."[49]

Except for a short visit to Portland and a few days at Nahant, Henry spent the summer in Cambridge. In early August, Ward breezed into Craigie House with his usual high spirits, and when he left, Henry wrote how much he had enjoyed seeing him: "To me it was delightful. ... We were free from care; almost joyous; the sunshine only subdued and broken by some long, sharp shadows from the Past. Come again, soon, dear Sam...."[50] Ward wrote back that he'd met a lady who wanted to know about Longfellow and asked if he was "often very unhappy," to which Ward replied: "Yes, no, not exactly, you know one has blue moments sometimes—heigho! but that isn't what I mean. 'Does he not sit abstractedly with his eyes fixed—musing mournfully to the Tune of the Psalm of Life?' Not that I ever saw Ma'am. He is generally merry & cheerful—a good deal more so than myself—likes a smiling chat & good glass of wine with a friend or ½ a dozen."[51] So there were "blue moments," what Longfellow had called "sharp shadows from the Past," but they weren't casting much darkness on his mostly sunny days. Perhaps he hadn't recovered fully, but he was showing good emotional resilience at that point, coping, and feeling better on balance. Finally.

When the new term began in September, Henry felt so good that he wrote to his father, "I never commenced a Term in better health and spirits; and I think everything will go on vigorously and harmoniously."[52] And in similar good spirits, he wrote to Ward on September 17: "This term begins beautifully with me. My lectures come in the afternoon, so that I have all these golden Autumnal mornings to myself. Believe me, I both enjoy, and improve them.... Life is sanctified by its uses."[53] As late as September 26, he was still reporting to his father that "college affairs go on smoothly." But a few days later, things took a turn for the worse.

On the thirtieth Henry wrote excitedly to Ward that he was enclosing a poem he'd just written, "Excelsior," "one of the best things, if not the best, that I have written." So far only Felton had seen it, he said, and even he "found less than usual to criticise."[54] He told Ward how the poem had come to him:

> The other night, about one o'clock, as I was smoking a cigar preparatory to going to bed, it came into my mind; but, as it was late, I thought I would not write it out until morning. Accordingly, I went to bed, but I could not sleep. That *voice* kept ringing in my ears; and finally I jumped out of my bed, lighted my lamp and set to work. The result was this poem and a dreadful cold and rheumatism, which have confined me to my chamber for two days. The idea of the poem is the Life of Genius. This you will comprehend at a glance. Many people will not comprehend it at all.

As elated as he was, the undercurrent of a "dreadful cold and rheumatism" tempered his excitement—and then signing off, he added, "I am in such great bodily pain that I cannot write a word more." Only a month earlier he'd told his father he was in "better health and spirits" than he could remember—and now he was in such "bodily pain" that he couldn't finish a letter.

Two weeks later, in the middle of October, Longfellow told Ward that his health had become so much worse that he was thinking about going to Germany for a rest and the so-called "water cure," which had been popularized in 1829 as "hydropathy," the brainchild of a German farmer named Vincenz Priessnitz, who had opened a resort and begun attracting desperate patients who could afford his therapy.[55] By the 1840s, hydropathy had become so popular that it had its own magazine, *Water-Cure Journal*, which claimed the water cure would "hasten the advent of UNIVERSAL HEALTH, VIRTUE, AND HAPPINESS."[56] It was alternative medicine, attractive to those who wanted to believe—quackery to everyone else. But Henry was a believer, mostly, and he'd begun to see the water cure as a last resort to recover his suddenly lost health. On November 14, he told Ward once again about the seriousness of his condition: "I am all unstrung, eating only bread and meat.... Not a glass of wine—not a drop of coffee—not a whiff of tobacco."[57]

No single reason explains why Henry became so suddenly unstrung. Perhaps it was due to his usual recurring ailments, like indigestion, troubled eyesight, headaches, flu symptoms, and sharp pains that were diagnosed as neuralgia. It may be too that when his nerves weren't causing actual pain, they were frayed from routine stress over college affairs, which could not continue as "smoothly" as he had told his father they were going late in September. Nor can one discount a relapse of the guilt he still felt over having been responsible for the death of Mary and their unborn child and then falling in love with another woman—who had then broken his heart. All the old wounds may have opened again at the same time—but for whatever combination of reasons, Henry Longfellow had by the end of 1841 become as damaged as he'd been in 1838.

Ward understood that Longfellow's physical problems were complicated by depression. "Yours is a strange malady," he wrote, "and you must not wonder if I look for its seat and origin in the heart and not in the stomach.... I know by experience that friendship, fame, the wine cup and literary pursuits are insufficient to fill up the place of a passion that cannot be *exaucée* [fulfilled]."[58] But sympathetic as Ward was, he thought running off to Germany in the dubious pursuit of a water cure for symptoms that seemed suspiciously psychosomatic, seemed excessive.

The high-spirited Five of Clubs all registered their amused skepticism, as well.[59] It was hard to understand how their friend Henry could so suddenly have been defeated by the miscellaneous demons he had been controlling for the best part of a year. The relapse had caught them all by surprise. But Longfellow saw the German water cure as the only path back to health, a chance for him to regroup. Yes, it was a full retreat, an admission that he was no longer able to cope either with his feelings or their physical symptoms, but how could half a year in Germany be a bad thing, he reasoned. The water cure might be a waste of time and money, a sign of weakness and gullibility, but it took him half a world away from Fanny Appleton, which his friends all thought was at the heart of his decision. So they smiled indulgently and encouraged their good friend as his plans took shape.

In early January 1842, Longfellow asked President Quincy and the Harvard Corporation for a six-month sick-leave: "I am reluctantly compelled by the state of my health to ask leave of absence from the College for six months from the first of May next. In this time I propose to visit Germany, to try the effect of certain baths, by means of which, as well as by the relaxation and the sea-voyage, I hope to reestablish my health."[60] Quincy may have heard the request as the voice of a love-sick hypochondriac who was looking to indulge himself on a paid vacation to Germany, but in April he nonetheless granted Longfellow his request with the strict understanding that he would be back to work in time for the fall term.[61]

In the last week of April, Henry sailed for France on the *Ville de Lyon*. The last letter he received before leaving was from a distraught, teary-eyed Sumner on the twenty-third: "We are all sad at your going; but I am more sad than the rest; for I lose more than they do. I am desolate. It was to me a source of pleasure and strength untold, to see you, & when I did not see you, to feel that you were near.... God bless you! My dearest friend, from my heart of hearts.... My eyes overflow as I now trace these lines. May you clutch the treasure of health; but, above all, may you be happy!"[62] Longfellow replied from New York, just before boarding for what he called his "pilgrimage": "My dear Charles, Your letter reached me this afternoon, and made my heart swell into my throat." He had put Sumner's words, he said, into his "inmost soul": "So you see, I devote my last moments and last thoughts to you. Think of me often and long.... When this reaches you I shall be rocking on the broad sea; and thinking of you all through the many long hours."[63]

With Sumner's loving words warming his heart, Henry arrived at Le Havre, revisited Paris for a few days, then took a train through many familiar locations like Antwerp, Bruges and Cologne, before arriving on June 3 at Boppard in the Rhine valley. It was there that the former Marienberg abbey and convent had been taken over by a student of Vincenz Priessnitz, a Dr. Schmitz, who had set up a cold-water health resort in 1839. Three years later, on June 6, 1842, Henry Longfellow took his place with sixty other patients at what he described as "the most elegant cold-water establishment in Germany" by which he meant "the most expensive" one.[64]

Dr. Schmitz was in fact running an expensive and punishing detox program that used water to purge evil spirits and bodily poisons out of patients— a regimen of strictly regulated submersion and abstinence.[65] Henry described the day-to-day routine to his father when he was in his third week of treatment:

> About four o'clock in the morning a servant comes in and wraps you in a blanket, then covers you up in a mass of bed-quilts. There you lie for an hour or more, until you perspire freely. You are then wheeled in an arm-chair to the bathing room, where you plunge into a large bath of running water, and remain a couple of minutes, splashing and rubbing. You then dress and walk an hour in the garden, drinking at intervals at the fountains; to the amount of four or five glasses. Next follows breakfast, which consists of bread, butter and milk, and sometimes strawberries. After breakfast another walk (or a letter, as to-day). At eleven o'clock a *douche*; which is nothing more nor less than standing under a spout. The *douches* vary from 18 to thirty-five feet in height; and are perhaps the pleasantest baths, the force of the water making you warm in an instant. The water from the hills is brought into the bathing rooms by pipes, under which you place yourself for three or four minutes. You then take another walk for an hour; then a *fliessandes Sitsbad*, or flowing bath; in which you sit for half an hour, the water flowing through continually. Then walk till one o'clock. At one dinner; very frugal, without wine or spice of any kind. After dinner, sit or walk or play billiards till five. At five another *sitsbad* as at 12; and then a long walk up the hills to the neighboring villages, till supper; which is on the table from 7 ½ to 9; and is the same as the breakfast; at 10 to bed.[66]

Every day but Sunday was the same, and Henry realized as he was describing the routine to his father, how extreme (even preposterous) the treatment sounded. He imagined his father thinking it was all "quite barbarous," but it wasn't half as bad as it sounded, he went on defensively. "To me, indeed, it is extremely pleasant. I delight in the cold baths; and have great faith in their efficacy," which he said there are "some striking proofs of," though he didn't bother mentioning what they were.

It all seemed much less pleasant three days later, however, when he wrote "MY DEAR CHARLEY" that "the water begins to work upon my nerves."[67] Henry missed Sumner more perhaps than he realized, and more intensely. The night before, he said he'd dreamed that Sumner mentioned "a certain person's name" at which point, "I fell on your neck and wept, exclaiming 'I am very unhappy.'" He added, as though it were an unimportant afterthought, that the "most amusing part of the dream was that we were in bed together."[68] Then, returning to the water working on his nerves, Longfellow wrote that his fellow patients were a "drowsy, unintellectual set," yet another reason for his unhappiness. He was in fact itching to get out, whether he was cured or not: "The Doctor says I am better; I say, I am not. I do not perceive the slightest change. *He* says I shall not get away before the end of September. *I* say, perhaps I shall."

Whether or not he was getting better, there wasn't any time in his long days of water therapy "for reading and writing," he went on in his letter to Sumner. All there was time for was "bathing, and walking in the open air, climbing mountains, and the like." Then he added, "As to the poems you speak of, it is alas! quite impossible to write them, much as I desire to do so." Here he was answering Sumner, who had written on May 15: "Oh! I long for those verses on Slavery. Write some stirring words that shall move the whole land. Send them home, and we will publish them."[69] It was a thought Longfellow had to put aside—reluctantly, he said—at least for the moment. Six weeks later nothing had changed. He wrote to Sumner once again that he didn't have time "to write a verse or a line" and that even if there were time, "there is no inspiration in dressing and undressing. Hunger and thirst figure too largely here, to leave room for poetical figures."[70]

If the water cure had begun working on his nerves and if he thought his fellow patients a drowsy bunch, as he had reported to Sumner on the twenty-fourth of June, there was also something unintentionally hopeful that leaked through in the same letter. He said he was annoyed by "the trivial tone of thought prevailing among the patients; the mean wants, the never-ending complaints, the querulous frame of mind—of which this letter, now that I think of it, is no bad specimen." That he could turn his complaint into a joke was a good sign. A few weeks later, he quipped to another correspondent that he was "following the Water-cure, and the grape-cure and every other cure under the sun, except the *sinecure*."⁷¹ There were problems with the water cure certainly, problems that Longfellow acknowledged, but he had found a way to smile about them. Maybe the baths were helping after all.

Two days later, on the twenty-sixth, however, Longfellow was back to his standard optimism about the water cure. Instead of getting on his nerves, the water-cure, he told Hillard, was "delightful." He didn't know what he'd do when he had to give up "these pleasant baths." In fact, he said, "I am never happy now, except under water." If he meant this as over-the-top sarcasm, he didn't let on, though his last sentences on the subject sound more typically earnest: "I am disappointed only in the slowness of the process. Put that down to natural impatience."⁷² He repeated the official version of how much good the treatment was doing him in a letter to his sister Anne on July 20, when he reported with "satisfaction" that he was "better": "The course of treatment agrees with me."⁷³

Perhaps it did. It was not true, however, that the routines left no time for writing. From the time he arrived in early June until he left in mid–September, he wrote thirty-six mostly long and discursive letters—among them five to Sumner, three to the others in the Five of Clubs, and two each to his father, Greene, and Ward.⁷⁴ There were also four to Catherine Eliot Norton, the Beacon Hill socialite who had married Andrews Norton and whose nephew Sam arrived at the Marienberg waterworks while Longfellow was still there. Mrs. Norton, fourteen years older than Henry, had taken an almost motherly interest in his unrewarded pursuit of Fanny Appleton, and he had turned to her often for comforting girl-trouble talk beginning in late 1837. Writing to her from Marienberg no doubt kept Fanny a little closer to the surface of his mind, which was of dubious value, but that was as close as he would come to a painful rehashing of the long, sorrowful Appleton affair. That was all in the past. There were new girls to think about. He reported to Mrs. Norton on June 12: "I saw the first beautiful woman I have seen in Germany," adding with a grin that "had there not been a table between us to check the impulse, I should have been guilty of some indiscretion."⁷⁵

This uncharacteristic quipping, punning, grinning, and laughing was a spillover from the fun-loving friendship that was developing in and around the Marienberg waterworks between Henry and a young poet who lived in nearby St. Goar, Ferdinand Freiligrath, who received ten of Henry's letters that summer, twice as many as he wrote to anyone back home. Henry met Freiligrath and his group of artist friends on a Sunday jaunt in mid–June with a fellow sufferer at the treatment center, and as he had done so often in the past when traveling, once he found a group he liked, he mixed with them freely and happily, and attached himself to them as a family member. It helped that Freiligrath reminded him of Felton, overweight and always "merry and laughter-loving."[76] Although Henry admired the 1838 collection of poems Freiligrath had published (his subjects, meters, and rhymes were all "invariably striking," he wrote), it was the family atmosphere and the intellectual companionship and the relief from the waterworks that all combined to make Longfellow embrace the strangers with all the considerable warmth and charm he was capable of.[77]

The company included Freiligrath's wife Ida and a beautiful young poet, Louise von Gall, who was spending the summer with the Freiligraths, plus a changing gallery of additional literary and artistic sorts. The inner circle took playfully silly nicknames based on Freiligrath's landlord, whose last name was Ihl, which put them in mind of the *Iliad*—and so Freiligrath became Hector and Ida became Hector's wife Andromache. The alluring and unmarried von Gall was Helen of Troy while Henry (only three years older than Freiligrath) was Nestor, the advice-giving senior citizen.[78] Everyone that summer expected a romance to blossom between Henry and Louise, so Freiligrath now and then would tease Longfellow by changing his nickname to Paris, who had once according to the myth, chosen Helen as the most beautiful woman in the world. Henry and Louise were thus Paris and Helen, one of the most famous couples in Western culture—but nothing developed between them that summer, prompting Freiligrath to write a mocking sonnet, "Brother Jonathan," in which Longfellow was said to be made of stone and was called the "cold-hearted barbarian" for not pursuing von Gall.[79] Despite all the energy spent to spark a romance, and despite Louise's obvious enticements, Henry chose to be too busy that summer with the water cure to risk yet another entanglement. But he was tempted.

Longfellow fell in so completely with his new extended family that he accompanied them on a four-day steamer trip up to Bonn and Cologne in late July, sightseeing and joking all the way, and probably flirting with Helen of Troy too. He rationalized his short holiday by saying he had reached the halfway point in his treatment and was pausing to see how much improvement there had been in his condition—and he was quick to point out to Sumner on July 22, that while he was promising himself "great pleasure" on his trip, there would be "not a drop of wine—not one cigar!" But he did drink and smoke—or at least he bought a "beautiful Meerschaum" pipe in Cologne and said in a letter to Freiligrath when he returned to the waterworks that he regretted his "flirtation" with a bottle of Maitrank wine.[80]

The four-day excursion shows that Henry was willing to abandon hydropathy and his commitment to his treatment plan, especially perhaps for a trip to Bonn and Cologne on the Rhine or "a major excursion to the lovely Wispertal [river]," which he took on August 5.[81] He reported to his sister Anne that he and his new friends also made "excursions together to old castles and ruins."[82] And to Sumner he wrote on August 8 that he'd been to half a dozen cities on the Rhine and "climbed every ruin within ten miles."[83] In fact, he took regular leaves from treatment, escaping the watery routines and indulging his passion for travel and his talent for friendships—but that wasn't enough for Freiligrath and company, who tried to pry Henry loose even more often for family dinners and tramps around the countryside. In a pair of witty sonnets, Freiligrath teased him about his "slavery to the cure" and urged him to spend less time in Marienberg and more time in St. Goar.[84] The Freiligrath lightness of touch was a welcome break from the spartan nunnery, and thus it moved the days and weeks along at a more tolerable pace for Longfellow, whose recovery, if it came at all, was no doubt as much the result of his new friends as Dr. Schmitz's cold water submersion campaign.

As skeptical as Longfellow was at times, as impatient with the treatment, his letters from Marienberg continued to show more faith in the slow benefits of the water cure than doubts about its effectiveness. He was at times defensive and sensitive to what he imagined people might be thinking about his own credulity. "What annoys me is the slowness of the *Wasserkur*," he explained to Sumner on August 8. "It does not operate with one-half the speed and vigor I imagined it would. After two months I do not find the decided advantage I anticipated. But two months are a very short time."[85] With the passage of eighteen years, the Water Cure improved markedly in his memory, for when Sumner himself was in need of therapy, Henry wrote: "*Go to Marienberg at Boppard on the Rhine*, where I should like to be now, if anything were the matter with me. *Think seriously of this*.... I cannot too strenuously urge the trial of this natural pleasant remedy. Do not disdain it!"[86] Even in the late summer of 1842, he pushed through his occasional lapses of faith and continued with the cure. He was there in Marienberg and he meant to see his therapy through to conclusion—and hopefully to restored health.

But then his health took a sudden turn for the worse. He told Freiligrath on August 15 that he'd been down with the "*grippe*" for the past week, "and have suffered night and day, violent head-ache and tooth-ache." He added that he was "heartily, *heartily*, tired of staying here."[87]

The closer he got to September, when he would have to put his return to Harvard in motion, the more he realized that he needed more time away—not in Marienberg perhaps, but in Italy, England, and maybe even Spain. After the hot German summer and the cold-water baths that he couldn't be sure were working, he was mostly hoping for a long visit to sunny Italy in the fall, full as it would be with old friends, familiar haunts, and even Giulia Persiani, who had married since he'd seen her last in 1828. He wrote to Hillard on July 22 about his hope of remaining in Europe another year, perhaps on an official book-buying mission for Harvard, and asked him to put in a good word with President Quincy.[88] He repeated the message to Sumner on the same day, adding that "the fine frenzy of traveling in Italy begins to stir within my heart. I am so near! The sunny land beckons me with all its soft allurements." This put him in mind of his current situation and prompted another short outburst: his nerves were bad, he said, and occasionally put him "out of humor" and prompted him to make "ill-natured remarks." Put it down to "the gigantic *douche*, that scourges me daily into a rather sensitive state."[89]

On September 3, Henry wrote a letter of outright lies and half-truths to Quincy requesting an extension to his leave.[90] "I thought by this time I should have recovered my health," he said, but "in this I have been disappointed." He'd arrived in Boppard at the beginning of June, he went on, and then omitting his many excursions on land and up and down the Rhine with the Freiligraths and the beautiful Louise von Gall—and leaving out as well his forbidden dalliance with wine and tobacco—he said he had "remained stationary" all summer trying to get his health back. And the treatment *was* working, but so slowly that he was "yet far from being well." That very morning his doctor had given him "a written opinion" in which he emphasized that it was "of the utmost importance" he remain for continued treatments and that "it is *absolutely necessary* I should give up all thoughts of returning home before next Summer." Under no circumstances should he engage in "severe study." There really was only one conclusion: "if I hope to be well, I *must* go on with the baths." Of course, this was bad news, he said, and he was asking for more time "with the greatest reluctance" because as he put it, he had "no desire to remain here." (He didn't mention his half-formed plan to head down to sunny Italy.) In the end, he told Quincy, it was far more important to keep his long-term health objectives in mind than to return prematurely to a "maimed life." So—could he please have an extension to his leave of absence?

Quincy probably wondered how a language teacher and an acclaimed poet could be so tone deaf as to send a letter like this—self-serving, overdramatic, and insincere. And why did his Smith Professor quote his doctor instead of sending the actual written opinion—or a copy of it? An unfriendly skeptic might have wondered if Longfellow hadn't made it all up to get his extended leave. Longfellow immediately after he mailed the letter regretted sending it, but in his journal the next day he didn't admit to botching the letter, saying only that he was "sorry" he had sent it because he was "homesick" and didn't want to stay in Europe any longer.[91] One part of him wanted the extension with time in sunny Italy; but something else was on his mind that made him want to get back as soon as possible.

What had changed sufficient to explain this sudden change of heart? One possibility is the only poem Longfellow wrote that summer (on August 25), one that would rank among his best and best known, the sonnet "Mezzo Cammin." The poem was about how little he had achieved at the biblical midpoint of his life, age 35. And though it was written a week before his letter to Quincy begging for an extension to his leave, the poem seems to have worked its way from August 25 to September 3 into his thinking, into his planning, into his heart. It seems to have retracked him. He felt on that late August day when he wrote the poem a renewed sense of mission springing up, no doubt in some measure because of his long summer of watery self-indulgence. He had wasted enough time and now recognized that he had reached a turning point in his life. It wasn't "indolence, nor pleasure," he wrote, that accounted for his previous unproductiveness, nor was it "the fret / Of restless passions." It was Mary's death, a "sorrow, and a care that almost killed," that "kept me from what I may accomplish yet." This was the critical juncture of his life, with the past below him and the future, including "the cataract of Death," above. It was such a personal poem, such an unusual self-analysis, that he kept it close to his heart—and out of print—for the rest of his life, first publication not coming until 1886. This one was for him alone:

> Half of my life is gone, and I have let
> > The years slip from me and have not fulfilled
> > The aspiration of my youth to build
> > Some tower of song with lofty parapet.
> Not indolence, nor pleasure, nor the fret
> > Of restless passions that would not be stilled,
> > But sorrow, and a care that almost killed,
> > Kept me from what I may accomplish yet;
> Though, half-way up the hill, I see the Past
> > Lying beneath me with its sounds and sights,—
> > A city in the twilight dim and vast,
> With smoking roofs, soft bells, and gleaming lights,—
> > And hear above me on the autumnal blast
> > The cataract of Death far thundering from the heights.

Just as significant as what the poem said about the "care that almost killed," the insistent "cataract of Death," and the hope that he might have more to "accomplish yet," was the absence in the poem of Fanny Appleton. At this critical moment when he was thinking about what he might yet accomplish, the Dark Lady was not part of the equation. This may well have been proof that Professor Longfellow had indeed been cured.

Mostly.

Even if Longfellow's heart still ached occasionally, he looked good and felt fine, cured for all practical purposes, despite the obviously untrue comment he'd made to Quincy that he was "far from being well." His physical health was in fact better than it had been in recent memory. For one thing, the strict water and hiking regimen had put him in the best shape of his life with a broader chest and a healthier complexion, Hillard observed a couple of months later. "Were it not for the thick sprinkling of gray among his sunny locks, he might pass for an Apollo, in the glow and prime of his manhood."[92] And as usual, he was elegant in dress, though his gloves were no doubt still, as he had put it in *Hyperion*, "a shade too light." With his good manners and open smile figured in, Longfellow at 35 presented an attractive and winning countenance for the world to know him by. In September 1842, as he was preparing to leave Marienberg, he had something else that may have been visible, a firm resolution to get back to his career—not the teaching one at Harvard, but the writing one at Craigie House. As he put it to Sumner shortly before sailing, "I come back with tremendous momentum!"[93]

Aiming for an early November return to Harvard, Longfellow left Boppard on September 18, gleefully recording in his journal the night before that his bills were paid and farewells said: "Tomorrow I'm going up the Rhine, to drink Johannesberger wine. Poor Doctor Schmitz would lose his wits, and go into fits, if he only knew what I'm going to do!"[94] He worked his way through Germany and England, arriving at last in London where he moved in with Charles Dickens for a two-week stay on October 5. The invitation went back to January when Dickens had been in Boston. "We live quietly—not uncomfortably—and among people whom I am sure you would like to know," Dickens had written to Longfellow, "as much as they would like to know you.... Let me be your London host and cicerone."[95]

When Longfellow wrote Dickens from Germany that he was hoping to be soon in London, Dickens wrote back that Henry had been eagerly expected for a month already. "Your bed is waiting to be slept in; the door is gaping hospitably to receive you. I am ready to spring towards it with open arms at the first indication of a Longfellow knock or ring."[96] He added that he had just finishing writing a book about his American travels, *American Notes*, which would be published on October 19, during Longfellow's visit, in which he said he'd "spoken very honestly and fairly," although he fully expected "many people will like me infinitely the worse" for publishing it. He was referring to his abolitionist views. "Slavery," he had written in Chapter 17, "is not a whit the more endurable because some hearts are to be found which can partially resist its hardening influences."[97] With his antislavery views fresh in his mind and the book brand new when Longfellow arrived for his two-week stay, Dickens probably indulged in the occasional rant, for this was a subject he could warm to—and then get hot over.

But controversy aside, from the fifth to the twentieth, Longfellow became part of the Dickens household, fitting himself into yet another family. Of course, Henry made time to shop for the latest in fashionable menswear—which he bought so much of that Dickens reported the London shops to be "at the point of death," after he left.[98] Longfellow's taste for dandy outfits was always fair game for pointed wit—friendly for the most part, but always double-edged.

As he prepared for his final leg home, Longfellow was turning several thoughts over in his mind. One was Dickens' ardent antislavery views in *American Notes*. It was mostly a "jovial and good-natured" book, Henry reported to Sumner on October 16, but it was also "at times very severe," especially the "grand chapter" on slavery.[99] Another thought was Sumner's pleading with him to join the antislavery battle in poetry: "Oh! I long for those verses on slavery," he had pleaded in May. Still another was Freiligrath's exotic African poems. The timing was right, too, for all these threads were intermingling just when "Mezzo Cammin" had put him firmly back on the trail of new poetry. With all these stars in alignment, it was perhaps inevitable that something worthwhile would follow.

Once back in Cambridge, Henry wrote to Freiligrath about the "boisterous passage" aboard the *Great Western* (October 23 to November 6), which had kept him imprisoned in his berth with sea-sickness for all but a few hours at sea.[100] "During this time I wrote seven poems on Slavery. I meditated upon them in the stormy, sleepless nights, and wrote them down with a pencil in the morning.... In the '*Slave's Dream*' I have borrowed one or two wild animals from your menagerie!" *Poems on Slavery* was published in thirty-one pages by John Owen about a month after Longfellow's return to Cambridge and was reprinted the next year by the New England Anti-Slavery Tract Association as an even slenderer eight-page pamphlet. The book, however, proved to be more important than its size might suggest.

Longfellow's feelings about slavery and racial intolerance in general had developed over the years in fits and starts. He was nine when the American Colonization Society was formed in 1816, an organization that continued for the next fifty years aiming to relocate freed blacks to Africa. Colonizationists, including Abraham Lincoln at the start of the Civil War, generally thought theirs was a better solution to the slave question than pure abolitionism, which frightened most Northerners by threatening to flood every city and town with emancipated slaves who had no skills and no sense of the American working class they were being, intentionally or not, invited to enter. He was twelve during the local debates in Portland over the benefits of the Missouri Compromise of 1820, which kept the balance between free and slave states by admitting Maine and Missouri to the Union at the same time and prohibiting slavery in the territories above 36° 30' latitude. If Henry as a boy had any strong feelings about blacks and slavery and the South, he kept them to himself. It is more likely that he merely absorbed his family's white, upper-middle-class tolerance tinged with a passive racism that assumed the social order was layered as it should be—at least in Portland.

He did, however, have that one conscience growth-spurt in 1823, when he played the part of the Indian leader King Philip and came to think of the Indians as "a reviled and persecuted race," a people "possessing magnanimity, generosity, benevolence, and pure religion." "See what a noble race have been almost entirely cut off and exterminated from the face of the earth," he had written to his mother, "by the coming of the whites."[101] In 1834, Longfellow toyed with and rejected an idea to write a play on the Haitian hero Toussaint L'Ouverture, the slave who rose to be called the Black Napoleon and led the successful slave rebellion that frightened slave owners everywhere and created Haiti as an independent nation in 1804, the year after L'Ouverture's death. But there had been no embrace of Sumner's brand of antislavery; nothing at least that moved him the way Sumner was moved. Henry's brother Samuel put Longfellow and Emerson into a grouping he called "unclassified 'antislavery men,'" who were neither Colonizationists nor Abolitionists, just people who "trusted to moral influences to lift up the sentiment and conscience of the nation to the destruction of Slavery."[102]

Unclassified or not, in December 1842, with the publication of *Poems on Slavery*, Longfellow put himself firmly and visibly on the side of antislavery, an undisputed member of New England's growing majority that could not and would not tolerate the "peculiar institution" regardless of what the Constitution said or didn't say about it. It was becoming clearer and clearer that slavery (and the South) had to be confronted—and Longfellow, though not the leader Sumner was in the fight, found himself moved to join the battle. Here for the first time in public, he had become an antislavery activist—and in order to drive home the point of his commitment, he donated all profits from the book to the antislavery cause.[103]

There wasn't much in the book to build an antislavery reputation on, but it was enough. Just barely. The powerful first poem was "The Slave's Dream," which showed Freiligrath's exotic African influence in images like "palm-trees on the plain," "tinkling caravans," and "bright flamingoes," all designed to recreate the beautiful natural landscapes of an African king who'd been hunted down as a young man and sold into slavery. He dreamed as he was dying of hearing once again "the lion roar, / And the hyena scream," and then finally he was freed by death from "the driver's whip" and "the burning heat of day." Another of the seven poems was "The Slave in the Dismal Swamp," where an escaped slave "crouched in the rank and tangled grass" to hide from the "bloodhound's distant bay":

> A poor old slave, infirm and lame;
>   Great scars deformed his face;
> On his forehead he bore the brand of shame,
> And the rags, that hid his mangled frame,
>   Were the livery of disgrace.

And in the most dramatic of the group, "The Quadroon Girl," Longfellow wrote a twelve-quatrain narrative about a planter selling his own mixed-race daughter to a traveling slave trader:

> Before them, with her face upraised,
>   In timid attitude,
> Like one half curious, half amazed,
>   A Quadroon maiden stood.
>
> Her eyes were large, and full of light,
>   Her arms and neck were bare;
> No garment she wore save a kirtle bright,
>   And her own long, raven hair.
>
> And on her lips there played a smile
>   As holy, meek, and faint,
> As lights in some cathedral aisle
>   The features of a saint.

The planter "knew whose passions gave her life, / Whose blood ran in her veins," but he sold her anyway:

> The Slaver led her from the door,
>   He led her by the hand,
> To be his slave and paramour
>   In a strange and distant land!

There was nothing subtle about Longfellow's moving *Poems on Slavery*, nothing that rose above the level of propaganda that Harriet Beecher Stowe would employ so well nine years later in *Uncle Tom's Cabin*, but it was sufficient to put Longfellow into the fray on the side of Sumner and antislavery. Maybe even abolitionism. And it was sufficient to earn "a torrent of eulogy," in the words of James Russell Lowell in his February 1843 review of the book in his short-lived *Pioneer* magazine. Most important to Lowell was Longfellow's effort "to make the beauty of the right more apparent."[104]

Praise poured in from nearly every quarter. John Greenleaf Whittier and the new Liberty Party, were so thrilled with Longfellow's entry into the antislavery movement that they pressed him to run for Congress, though that sort of public posturing and self-aggrandizement was the last thing Longfellow wanted. The poems were reprinted widely, with journalist-poet Walt Whitman running "The Quadroon Girl" and "The Slave's Dream" in his *Brooklyn Daily Eagle*.[105] The *Vermont Watchman & State Journal* ran "The Slave's Dream" on its front page on December 30, 1842. The prominent Unitarian minister Henry Ware wrote Longfellow: "Such poems on Slavery are never to be forgotten; and I must not refrain from giving you my heartiest thanks. They are all one could wish them to be—*poetry*, simple, graceful. Strong; without any taint of coarseness, harshness, or passion."[106] The abolitionist Elihu Burritt thought the poems should be "republished & read in heaven"—though they would not be read in the South in 1845, when the Philadelphia publishers Carey & Hart talked Longfellow, who raised no objection, into omitting the slavery poems from their new edition of his collected *Poems* because they feared weak sales.

Lost in the public approval of *Poems on Slavery* was the cooler reading of Margaret Fuller in the *Dial*, who called the poems "the thinnest of all Mr. Longfellow's thin books," and the hotter reading of the Boston-born Southerner, Edgar Allan Poe, who slammed Longfellow's readers as "negrophilic ladies of the North."[107] Nathan Appleton, whose fortune had been built on cheap, slave-produced Southern cotton, probably arched a disapproving eyebrow too. However, taking the good and bad together, Longfellow was content: "Some persons regret that I should have written [*Poems on Slavery*]," he wrote to his father on New Year's Day, 1843, "but for my own part, I am glad of what I have done. My feelings prompted me and my judgment approved, and still approves."[108]

9

The Miracle

Longfellow was in altogether fine fettle as the winter social season in Boston started up in January 1843. His good-humored, often gossipy letters that winter show a man with close friends in the Cambridge and Boston areas (plus a few in New York), a loving family back in Portland, a professorship at Harvard that had its problems but was still better than the one he'd left at Bowdoin, and a balanced composure that put him in good physical and emotional health. He still complained about head colds that he self-diagnosed as "influenza," but he admitted to his sister-in-law Margaret Potter Thacher that his trip to Germany had done him a "vast deal of good" and that his health was "better than it has been for years."[1] He had just published his *Poems on Slavery*, was getting his play *The Spanish Student* ready for the press, and was seeing his *Ballads and other Poems* into its fifth edition. He also published a new poem, "The Belfry of Bruges," in *Graham's Magazine* (January), which would turn out to be the title poem for his next book in 1845.

But though he was constantly busy with his correspondence, his poetry, his Harvard chores, and his negotiations with publishers, Longfellow allowed himself social pleasures that winter too, shaking himself loose from his study at Castle Craigie to attend a regular round of dinners, concerts, and parties. He even stopped in at the Appleton house, mostly to confer with Tom, who was preparing to leave for Europe and needed letters of introduction. But he was careful not to step beyond the proprieties with Fanny. He was still sensitive to the memory of the pain he had suffered for so many years, and he had no reason to suppose her iciness after the *Hyperion* fiasco had thawed. The physical and psychological benefits of the previous summer's water cure were still with him, but he knew better than to risk a setback with the Dark Lady. He'd learned his lesson.

But Longfellow no doubt wondered at the many changes he saw at 39 Beacon Street in the winter of 1843. It wasn't the same place Henry had known in 1837, when he would walk with Fanny and Mary around the Common and then stop in for tea and more talk and maybe a German lesson in the front parlor. Now it was transformed into nursery mode, overrun by 3-year-old Willie and 1-year-old Harriot—and the new Mrs. Appleton, at age 41, was pregnant and due in February. The house's former staid beauty had turned into a livelier, more boisterous home.

Nathan Appleton must surely have felt the changes even more keenly. He was too busy tending to his ever-expanding business interests to be overly attentive to the high-energy of his new family, but it had to occur to him that the last time he'd had a 3-year-old in his house, it was his rogue Fanny in 1820, nearly a quarter century earlier. Not even a full staff of servants and all the ease money can buy, could insulate the 64-year-old tycoon from his new children, completely—which is not to say that he wanted protection from the little ones, only that his quiet refuge on Beacon Street wasn't quite as quiet as it once had been.

Fanny felt the changes too. She'd been transformed from being her father's pet to being the much older sister to two very young half-siblings—with a new baby on the way. She probably felt more like the maiden aunt than the princess of Beacon Street society. The house had a new dynamic, and when Fanny processed the changes, thought about what they meant for her own future, she no doubt took an inventory of available bachelors on the market. But there is no record that winter of any softening toward the professor, who seemed by his travels, literary successes, and good friendships to have found the formula for getting over her. She may have wondered if he'd lost interest.

Frances Elizabeth Appleton was 25 that winter and still a daunting prize—beautiful, smart, cool, rich, and tantalizingly out of reach. One Beacon Hill suitor, Alleyne Otis, wrote in a letter to a friend in 1840: "When I see her come into a room in the ev'g, in full dress, I am on the point of falling in love with her—at any rate with her *distingué* air & fine eyes."[2] At about the same time, James Russell Lowell met Fanny at a party given by William Ellery Channing and remarked to Henry how stricken he was in her presence: "[I] remember keenly the shivering awe with which I plunged into the responsibility of entertaining her. Yet in that conversation (as laborious to her, I doubt not, as to me) she made my heart warm towards her—and it will never grow cold again."[3] Fanny was always on a higher plane—a beautiful and intelligent and uncompromising presence everywhere she went.

It was in February or March 1843 that Fanny began thinking again about Henry Longfellow, perhaps seeing a change in him, a new air of self-assurance, a new strength of mind, body, and heart. She'd been tracking his rising star as a poet, of course, was herself fond of many of his poems, and may even now and then have revisited a pleasant memory or two of him from the summer of 1836. So it is possible that Henry Longfellow had become a little more interesting to her in the winter of 1843, but if so, Fanny didn't tip her hand—and Longfellow wasn't taking any chances during his visits to Tom Appleton. When in February Sam Ward read that Mt. Etna had erupted, he jokingly wondered in a letter to Longfellow if it might not be "emblematic of a revival of the Ashburton" business, and Henry half-joked in reply, "*My* Etna *is* burnt out."[4]

But at the same time that Henry was being cautious with his feelings, there were factors working in his favor with Frances Elizabeth. First, he and Fanny's brother Tom were already brothers in a way that bound Longfellow to the Appletons—in a sense he was already a member of the family. Second, Henry was firmly established at Harvard and in Cambridge—there wouldn't be a wrenching uprooting like the one that had undone her sister Mary when she married Robert Mackintosh, moved to England, had a baby, and then fallen into a deep depression.

Finally, Fanny may well have found herself unintentionally urged to Longfellow by her father, who, occupied by a far-reaching financial empire and a new family, may have softened his opposition to the professor—if he ever had been actively against him. It was past time for his rogue to settle down, and Henry Longfellow, while poor by Appleton standards, was, after all, respectable and solid and gaining more and more international attention as a poet. This would not be a corporate alliance, nor would it be a Beacon Street social coup, but the popular and personable Longfellow was clearly a daunting figure in his own right, still only in his mid-thirties, and seemingly on the cusp of literary greatness. Nathan wouldn't be losing a daughter as much as he'd be gaining access to cultural respectability, always a valuable commodity to captains of industry. Perhaps some of that logic leaked through to Fanny in the winter of 1843, when she began feeling rather unexpectedly that maybe the professor wasn't such a bad choice after all. Something more than a new social season was blowing in the warmer winds of that year's January thaw.

From January to April, Longfellow kept up a steady chatter to friends—to Samuel Gridley Howe and Julia Ward on their engagement and then their marriage on April 26; to Catherine Eliot Norton on a new project, translating the *Divine Comedy*; to Ferdinand Freiligrath on a variety of literary and personal matters; to Hawthorne on an upcoming dinner date; and to his father on his work and health and social life. "On Monday night there is a grand Ball in Boston," he wrote his father on March 26. "I shall go for the purpose of dancing with the *elderly* ladies, who I think are much more grateful for slight attentions than *younger* ones."[5]

And then, on April 13, he was invited to a bon voyage party for Tom Appleton at Shady Hill, the Cambridge home of Catherine and Andrews Norton. Catherine, who had taken a special interest in Henry's thwarted romance with Fanny Appleton back in 1837–38, was still matchmaking, hoping the two might find a quiet place during the evening's festivities to talk. Maybe she sensed a delicate shift in the wind and was trying to help it along. The pair, now 36 and 25, did break away from the other guests that night and sat in a window nook for a while where Henry, still on guard with the Dark Lady, felt an uncustomary warmth and encouragement.[6] It was welcome, of course, but he was no doubt wary of affection from Miss Fanny, the sort of thing he had last experienced in the summer of 1836 in Switzerland—and had yearned for ever since.

With her brother Tom soon heading off to Europe, Fanny said, she would shortly need someone to keep her company, someone to help stave off the loneliness. "You must come and comfort me."[7] For Henry, this was the most stunning moment of his life. After years of suffering with a broken heart, with unsustainable dreams in the face of icy rejections, with a trail of bad decisions published in hard covers, and with seven years of ill-health and psychological collapses—could he be hearing what he thought he heard? Was Fanny Appleton actually smiling at him and inviting him to 39 Beacon Street? If he hadn't heard it all with his own ears and seen her smiling face with his own eyes, he would never have believed it. And why, of all things, would she choose him now, when he had lost more than the first blush of youth? Three years earlier he had despairingly told Greene that "the passion is dead," that he was emotionally "maimed," that he had thrown away "three of the best years" of his life, and had in the meantime grown prematurely old: "my elasticity is nigh gone, and my temples are as white as snow."[8]

Dazed and confused, Henry did call on Fanny and then wrote to tell her there was still time and love enough to put the past to rest and for them to build a future together. His mind was reeling with sensations he had long since buried and now found himself resurrecting—but he worried at the same time about how he had put himself on the line with her once again. Could he survive another rejection? After sending the letter, he waited anxiously for her reply.

On Monday, April 17, Fanny's letter arrived:

> I have just received your note and I cannot forbear telling you that it has comforted me greatly. I trust with all my heart that it is and will be as you say—that a better dawn has exorcised the phantoms for aye [ever], that its cheering, healthy beams will rest as in a perpetual home within those once-haunted walls you speak of. I could not well disguise, I own, how much some of your words troubled me. I should never have ven-

tured to speak so frankly to you had I not believed the dead Past *had* buried its dead and that we might safely walk over their graves, thanking God that at last we could live to give each other only happy thoughts. I rejoiced to see how calmly you met me until Saturday, when I trembled a little, as we are apt to do for a long cherished hope, but I will put aside all anxiety and fear, trusting upon your *promise*.[9]

The letter was cautious, even guarded, as she rehashed earlier "phantoms," "once-haunted walls," "the dead Past," and words that had "troubled" her. But these were balanced by a "better dawn," "cheering, healthy beams," "happy thoughts," and a "long cherished hope." She was committing herself, making herself vulnerable, but she was being careful at the same time, waiting to see if he would make good on his promise to make her happy. It was frightening, but neither one wanted to slow down—only five days had elapsed between reconciliation and rejoicing.

On May 10, less than a month after the Nortons' party, Fanny accepted Henry's proposal and they became officially engaged, a couple at last.

Henry got the good news in a note from Fanny that morning and rushed off on foot to Beacon Street "with the speed of an arrow—too restless to sit in a carriage—too impatient and fearful of encountering anyone!"[10] Fanny's change of heart was seemingly inexplicable, but Longfellow was too happy to dawdle over "why now" speculations. He wrote jubilantly to Five of Clubs member Henry Cleveland:

> Lo! I am engaged to Fanny Appleton! The great vision of my life takes a real shape. I have won not her hand only, but truly and entirely her heart. How this has come to pass, how the magic circle has narrowed and narrowed and narrowed, till at last the cloud of vapor fell, and we found ourselves standing hand in hand—all this I cannot tell you in a letter; but some hints and suggestions, I may perchance breathe into your ear hereafter.
>
> My whole soul is filled with peace and serenity. It returns to her as to its centre. All struggles, all unrest, all indefinite longings—all desires of other things—all that so agitated me, and sent me swinging and ill-poised through the void and empty space, all this is ended; and the heart hath its perfect rest.[11]

A month earlier this outcome had been closer to impossible than improbable, and Henry instinctively understood that he was better off accepting the good news, reveling in it, rather than probing too deeply into it. For whatever reasons, Fanny had finally chosen him—as he had so long ago chosen her. It was more than enough that his heart finally had its perfect rest.

On May 11, Henry wrote to Zilpah in Portland. "I write you one line, and only one—to tell of the good fortune which has just come to me—namely that I am engaged. Yes, engaged to a very lovely woman—Fanny Appleton— for whom I have many years cherished a feeling of affection. I cannot say another word—save that she is very beautiful—very intellectual—and very pious—three most excellent *verys*."¹² Fanny's letter to Zilpah was, by contrast, understandably self-conscious and overly formal: "Would that language could reveal to you how fully I appreciate the priceless blessing God has vouchsafed me in your son's affection, and how fervently I pray to become worthy of it, and to improve my character by his.... We earnestly hope that you will ... bless our future home with a mother's sacred influence."¹³ Fanny couldn't quite manage to make her letter warm, but she did say all the right things as she began to build a bridge between Boston and Portland.

For the next few weeks, the couple broadcast far and wide their plans to marry. To her aunt Martha Gold, Fanny exuded happiness: "Rejoice with me in my great, inexpressibly great joy! I am engaged to Henry Longfellow!"¹⁴ Everyone was aware of her long and stony refusal of him, so Fanny added that the news would "astonish you doubtless, as it is just beginning to many others, but it is nevertheless true." Then she indirectly referred to her own reputation for cool haughtiness by saying, "My heart has always been of tenderer stuff than anybody believed." She thanked God for her good fortune, which she hardly had words enough to speak, but words weren't so important after all, she said to her aunt. "The fact that a nature so noble and gifted and gentle and true has been bestowed upon unworthy me is eloquent enough."¹⁵

Not everyone thought the announced marriage was a good idea. On June 16, a former Boston resident, Mrs. Fanny Calderon de la Barca, wrote to William Hickling Prescott that she didn't think it was a good idea that Fanny Appleton had taken Longfellow after having rejected him: "Fanny Appleton's engagement was communicated to me in her own handwriting, otherwise I should have been tempted to doubt the fact! I confess I am more than surprised. I will tell you the truth. I like the Professor very much, and it may be that he will suit her perfectly; but I do not like her marrying a man whom she has already refused. I say this to you in confidence."¹⁶ There is no telling how many Boston socialites, Harvard colleagues, Cambridge friends, Longfellow and Appleton family members, and others may have secretly agreed with Mrs. De la Barca, but it's fair to think many did. This relationship had died many years earlier, the line of thought went, and maybe it would have been a good idea to let it remain dead.

Henry, however, had other ideas. He wrote to his sister Anne that he could not find the right words to say what he was feeling: "You must see her, and know her, and you will as surely and irresistibly love her.... She is in all things very lovely. I can say no more." But he did: "Life was too lonely—and sad—with little to soothe and calm me. Now the Future opens its long closed gates into pleasant fields and lands of quiet. The strife and struggle are over, for a season, at least; and the troubled spirit findeth its perfect rest."¹⁷ Two days later he wrote to Isaac Appleton Jewett: "I am engaged to your beloved and beautiful cousin—Fanny—*the* Fanny! What powers have brought this to pass—by what hitherto invisible, golden threads of sympathy the Fates have woven this glorious '*Yes!*' into the dark warp of my life—by what magic the mist has fallen, and we find ourselves standing hand in hand in the mystic circle—I cannot venture to tell you."[18] He added that Jewett would undoubtedly "be touched and amused" to see "the interest everybody takes in the matter." It was all his fault, he went on: "Thanks to my heedless imprudence [publishing *Hyperion*], the public has been a kind of confidant in the whole affair. But now, thank God, this imprudence is forgiven and forgotten by the only one of whom I had to ask forgiveness and oblivion of the past."

It was more difficult for Longfellow to break the news of his marriage to the Potter family, but he did so in a measured tone that reassured as it rejoiced. "My life was too lonely and restless," he wrote to Mary's sister Eliza. "I needed the soothing influences of a home; and I have chosen a person for my wife who possesses in a high degree those virtues and excellent traits of character, which so distinguished my dear Mary. Think not, that in this new engagement I do any wrong to her memory. I still retain, and ever shall preserve with sacred care all my cherished recollections of her truth, affection and beautiful nature." He hoped she and her father would understand and approve.[19] As to the judge, he is reported to have laughed out loud when he heard the news. "So he's got the gal at last. He's been after her these six years."[20]

In Fanny's letter to big brother Tom, already in London, she tried her most ambitious explanation. She thought perhaps he'd seen "symptoms" before he left, she said, of her new interest in the "Professor" and that therefore he wouldn't be "altogether astonished," though the speediness of the "consummation" probably had surprised him.[21] "It is only to be marveled at[,] that this blessing did not manifest itself to me long ago, but we have both come to the comforting conclusion that it is best as it is, that our characters have been ripened to appreciate it and receive it with fuller gratitude than if the past experience had been spared us." She then added, "thankful am I to God that I have never been tempted to accept, in the craving for love which often misleads both men and women, an affection which would have caused a great famine somewhere in my heart."[22]

Tom replied that he was indeed "surprised a little" by the news, but was happy because good things should happen to someone with "so warm and noble a heart" as Fanny's.[23] They all knew she'd gone through suitor after suitor, never finding anyone who met her high standards, but now, Tom said, he was pleased that Fanny had discovered that "not all men [are] distasteful": "Pretty specimens you have had, too, in some of them. Your decidedly unpleasant experience in my sad sex will be all the more useful in starting in so sober a race as matrimony.... I feel as if the lover you love ought to be a great deal better than the rest of us and of a very high flight to keep even wing with you. Longfellow I believe to be that man, capable of understanding you and loving you for the very things which would be stumbling blocks to others."

Fanny's sister Mary wrote Longfellow a letter of congratulations from "across the dreary solitude of Sea" that acknowledged what Tom had called "stumbling blocks." She sent along the standard "warm hopefulness for a most happy Future for you both" and said she loved Fanny more than he could know, but then she drifted into a darker place, perhaps coming from her long period of depression, that seemed to touch on Fanny's reputation even within the family for a certain hauteur that had always set her apart: "I have no heart to talk to you of Fanny; if you really know her[,] it is of no use, and if you do not[,] it is too late."[24] Perhaps to compensate for the harshness of that sentence, she followed it with a gentler sentiment: She was afraid Fanny "was too aloof in her goodness and deep directness of Soul from us poor ones to ever find a fitting mate." She rejoiced, she said, that it had turned out to be Henry after all who had been the one "fitted to be her husband."

This was no doubt the most serious stumbling block Tom had referred to, the one that had kept Fanny single for so long: she was so "aloof in her goodness and deep directness of Soul" that it had become hard to imagine anyone soaring high enough "to keep even wing" with her. In all, Tom and Mary were as much relieved as happy that at long last Frances Elizabeth was getting married. And they shared a common joy that Fanny had finally gotten it right by choosing Henry Longfellow.

Longfellow never knew it, but Fanny posed a problem for his mother, who, while apparently the only one in the dark about his seven-year rejection, found in her new daughter-in-law-to-be an intimidating rich girl, the likes of whom Zilpah had never encountered before. Her uncertainty and intimidation by the Appleton fortune was natural. No one, after all, knew exactly how to behave with the entitled children of capitalist tycoons transformed into American royalty—which may account for Zilpah's catty comments on Fanny's looks. She had heard from the mother of Nathan Appleton's new wife that Fanny was "not so *handsome* as many," but that she was, by way of compensation, "a perfect lady" with a "highly cultivated mind" and "a sparkling eye, that lights up when in a conversation."[25] Those words set a tone and a pattern for Zilpah's own correspondence.

When she wrote to her son Sam, Zilpah said, "She is not handsome, I believe, but still she appears so, her eyes are so beautiful and so brilliant when she is engaged in conversation." Handsome or not, however, there was another problem. "She is very tall," Zilpah told Sam, "which made her appear like a maypole among the ladies of the family." The same appraisal of Fanny's beauty was repeated by Henry's sister Mary, who also wrote to Sam: "Her eyes are beautiful, unlike any you ever saw—speaking and full of soul, but the rest of her face is not beautiful." Mary went on, however, to describe Fanny much more lovingly: "Her voice is gentle and clear and sweet, like a summer breeze, and her manners are all refinement, gentleness, grace and heart—her quiet ladylike dignity and the *soul* evinced in every word and motion are her great charms." Sam described his new sister-in-law as "a woman of stately presence, of cultivated intellect, and deep, though reserved, feeling." He paused for a moment, then added that "her calm and quiet face" had a look of "seriousness," but that her beautiful smile "seemed to make the very air bright."[26] The Longfellow family was coming to terms with the rich girl who was marrying Henry: she was perhaps too reserved, not quite beautiful, and a little too tall, all features that were balanced by her sweet voice, her gentle refinement, her "highly cultivated mind," and her "ladylike dignity." Not bad, on balance.

Charles Eliot Norton had perhaps the best take on Fanny Appleton. She had, he said, "great beauty, and a presence of dignity and distinction," adding in a separate context that she had a "fine stateliness and graciousness of manner" and that she was "reserved in expression, but always sweet and kind." He might have excused the Longfellow family reservations, had he known about them, because he realized that "it was only those who knew her well who knew how quick and deep and true her sympathies were, how poetic was her temperament, how pure and elevated her thoughts."[27]

Fanny, unaware of the appraisals being made of her by her new in-laws—and a great many others—pressed on in her letter-writing campaign to win them all over. To Longfellow's sister Anne, she wrote: "I have so recently entered into my new world that I still stammer poorly its alphabet of love.... The holy trust I repose in your brother's long-tried affection, the inexpressible joy which fills my soul in seeing him so happy in mine, after all the pain it was my misfortune to cause him, the stars of hope which illumine the future, the gratitude even for the past, that lifts our spirits ... all this claims your sympathy, and all this, I trust, we may soon talk over together."[28]

Anxious explanations like this were difficult to put down on paper, but it was to Henry that Fanny felt the greatest need to make things right. She'd been genuinely hurt by Henry's use of her in *Hyperion*, but she'd now come around to see his story for what it was—a desperate, last-gasp plea to win her love. And then she had an idea. She took the Swiss sketch book she had used to record the ruined castles she and Longfellow had visited together in August 1836 and gave it to Henry as a wedding gift with the inscription, "Mary Ashburton to Paul Flemming." He was forgiven—and she was asking for forgiveness.

Henry and Fanny were married by candlelight at eight thirty in the evening on Thursday, July 13, in the drawing room of 39 Beacon Street, barely three months after the Nortons' party at Shady Hill had brought them together. Ezra Stiles Gannett, the Unitarian minister who had succeeded William Ellery Channing at Boston's Federal Street Church, presided. The wedding celebration was smaller and more subdued than it might have been owing to the death two weeks earlier of James Amory Appleton, the son of Nathan's brother William, Fanny's first cousin.[29] Though scaled down, the wedding was still a glittering and formal affair ("quietly sumptuous," according to one description) with fifty friends and relatives in attendance, including Henry's closest friends, Sumner, Ward, Felton, and Hillard. The couple had decided "to dispense with so formal an arrangement as a drilled bodyguard," Fanny had written to her friend Mary Dwight to explain why there would be no formal bridesmaids and groomsmen, which also freed Henry from having to pick a best man from among his close friends, although Ward later called himself the "Master of Ceremonies."[30]

Fanny was beautiful in the eyes of Henry's sister Mary in a letter to brother Sam. She wore a "rich and simple and little muslin, trimmed with splendid thread lace," with "natural orange blossoms, a bunch on each side of the skirt—short sleeves, two tiny bracelets on one arm and one on the other." Her veil, adorned with more orange blossoms, was a "plain very delicate lace" that hung gracefully to the floor. "She stood a queen, admired of all."[31] After the ceremony came the wedding supper followed by

Henry Wadsworth Longfellow by Charles Octavius Cole, ca. 1843 (Collections of Maine Historical Society, #4117).

fruits and ices and cake in the back parlor where a couple of large tables were piled high with wedding gifts. Later that evening, the couple retreated to Craigie House for their wedding night. Nathan Appleton had sent his rogue off in high style—the new Mrs. Appleton probably felt it was high time.

After two weeks in Cambridge, the couple went to Portland for a week of introducing Fanny to the family, followed by a short stay at Nahant. Then from August 8–19, they headed off on a formal wedding journey through the Catskills and Berkshires. Longfellow, however, had the self-absorbed and over-dramatic words of Charles Sumner ringing in his ears: "Howe has gone [married] and now you have gone, and nobody is left with whom I can have sweet sympathy.... What shall I do these long summer evenings? And what will become of those Sabbaths, sacred to friendship and repose?"[32] Henry had counted on Sumner's constant presence to get him through years of rejection torment—they had become more than best friends—and he was moved by Don Carlo's own suffering. He wanted to invite Sumner on their wedding trip. So he gently broached the subject with Fanny, who may understandably have been less than fully sympathetic until it came to her that she herself had gone through the same separation suffering Sumner was feeling when her sister had married and left her all alone on Beacon Street. And had she not accompanied the newly married couple to Washington?

If Fanny had lingering reservations about the plan, she kept them to herself, so Sumner went with them on their wedding trip. She may have had second thoughts, however, when on the train to the Catskills the always overserious Sumner regaled the bride and groom with the reading of funeral orations. The new Mrs. Longfellow knew then that, like it or not, her husband's friends were going to be part of her life, part of the daily routine of their marriage—and that their door would always be open to them. Remarkably, she embraced them all.

By the time Fanny moved into Craigie House, she had already refurnished it, adding items like a black walnut chair with "super-fine plush," a "richly carved" rosewood sofa, plus four more chairs, new beds and mattresses, marble-topped commodes, and a Chickering rosewood piano that cost $450 by itself.[33] Soon she would shop in New York for European carpets, risking her father's ire for preferring overseas textiles to those coming from his own New England mills.[34] These purchases were much more expensive than Longfellow could have afforded, even though his income was respectable, averaging nearly $2,000 for the four years before his marriage, and $3,500 for the next nine, all money earned at Harvard and from his poetry.[35]

By Appleton standards, of course, this was woefully inadequate, not even enough to pay for the new furnishings. Nathan therefore took it on himself to insure that his daughter would be more than just comfortable in her marriage to the professor. At first he thought he'd buy or build a place for her, perhaps in the Gothic Revival style she liked (and which his new son-in-law liked as well)—a small reminder maybe of the ruined castles Fanny and Henry toured, together and separately, throughout Europe. But Henry was tied by strands of love to Craigie House and talked Fanny, with the help of his old friend George Greene, into staying there. Fanny wrote to her brother Tom on August 30 that Greene had been staying with them and had "excited" in them an interest in the house's "historical association, or rather reminded us how noble an inheritance this is—where Washington dwelt in every room."[36] She told her father the same thing, and in October 1843, for $10,000, Nathan bought Craigie House and transferred the property over to Fanny—not just the house, but the acres of meadow in front of it spreading lazily down to the Charles River below, for Nathan had made sure that Fanny and her husband would never be threatened by new construction that would spoil their view.[37]

Nathan Appleton also saw to Fanny's portfolio of stocks, which came to over $34,000 by her wedding day, yielding checks of $1,000 twice a year—and then he added enough new money to the investments to bring her total to $50,000. Gradually he added more until Fanny's net worth came to about $66,000 (about $2 million in 2018).[38] "You will perceive that, with your own salary," Nathan explained to his son-in-law, "there will be ample means for sustaining, with a reasonable economy, a comfortable establishment—whilst it will be the dictate of prudence to keep your expenditures somewhat within your income." It's hard to know what a man of his means meant by "reasonable economy."

Despite Nathan's frugal injunction to live within his income, Longfellow knew full well that Appleton money was virtually inexhaustible, though he never spoke or wrote of it. His long and ardent affection for Fanny was all he had ever thought about from the moment they had met in the summer of 1836 until her sudden change of mind and heart in 1843. And yet the enormous wealth she had of her own, the inheritance that would follow on Nathan's death, and Henry's own professorship and very healthy book sales—all combined to make Longfellow unique in American literary history. He was royalty. He wore the mantle of "America's poet" with good grace and generosity for the rest of his life and died before America decided it preferred its poets to be underappreciated, underfed, and under the poverty line, an enduring cliché that is still with us. That had never described Henry Longfellow, not even before his marriage, when he was merely well to do. Afterward, of course, coinciding with his well-endowed marriage, the international poetry-reading community spontaneously elevated him into literary sainthood. The new reality wouldn't take root until the 1850s, but in the meantime, Henry taught his classes, translated endlessly, wrote poems, and basked in Fanny's love.

For her part, Fanny had come full circle on the man she had so unceremoniously broken with in the fall of 1837, and then treated frostily for six long years. In her diary on January 25, 1844, about six months after her marriage, she wrote that she was reading Henry's journal. "How I wish I had the record of every hour of his dear life. I am thankful to glean any part of it that was lost to me—how much through my own strange blindness. It is intensely, painfully interesting to me to see how his great heart rode over the billows of every cruel experience, as over the sunny sea which I trust it will now never lose."[39]

PART THREE: "EVER AND FOREVER, THY FANNY"

10

From Craigie House to Longfellow House

That "sunny sea" Fanny trusted Henry would "never lose" lasted eighteen years—eighteen happy, prolific, socially prominent, and highly profitable years. Not even the over-charged prewar rhetoric could keep Henry and Fanny from growing closer together as a couple, year after year. They were not oblivious to the gathering storm as it picked up strength, but they were nevertheless fully focused on their lives together—family, friends, and Henry's work, both at the college and in his study. Every day after May 10, 1843, the date when Fanny had finally accepted him, Henry counted his blessings, and Fanny wondered why it had taken her so long to say yes.

On the few occasions during the eighteen years when they were apart for business or family matters, their letters to each other have the sound of lovers struggling to get by during unbearably long separations—though they were never apart from each other for more than a few days at a time. In early 1845, when Henry had to be in Portland briefly, Fanny wrote to say she was "forlorn": "I am sitting in the Library, best beloved ... [and] now, naturally, turn to thee to bring thee, if possible, nearer this solitary night."[1] Two years later she wrote to her best friend Emmeline that Henry had gone to Portland for a few days. "I believe I shall never outgrow the thousand fears that beset me when he is absent, nor learn to bear better that wretched sense of a constant want—the hunger of the soul, which I once could endure *tolerably*, but now, through much pampering, get very heartsick under."[2] In the summer of 1860, Fanny was forlorn once again when Henry was in Pittsfield for a few days. Married seventeen years by then, she wrote him with a mock scolding for being "so timid of tender words" in his letters to her and signed herself, "Ever and forever thy Fanny." Taking this gentle rebuke to heart, Henry signed his return letter, "Good night, beloved, A thousand and a thousand times thine."[3]

The worlds Fanny and Henry lived in were on Brattle Street in Cambridge and Beacon Street in Boston, small enough to be parochial and large enough to include theaters, music halls, opera houses, Lyceum lecture rooms, and more. Summers, which usually included a week or two in Portland, were spent occasionally in Pittsfield in the Berkshires but more often at the beach, either Newport or Nahant, the latter becoming such a favorite that they eventually bought a house there, one big enough for themselves and their children, six born between 1844 and 1855, plus a revolving door of friends and relatives.

For eighteen years they remade Craigie House into Longfellow House and raised married life to an art, a thrilling level of happiness that everyone envied. "Of all happy homes theirs was in many respects the happiest," Charles Eliot Norton would later write. "Those who loved them could not wish for them anything better than they had."[4] More ominously, Oliver Wendell Holmes, one undated evening in the late 1850s, rode past Craigie House and said to his companion, travel writer George William Curtis, that he "trembled" when he thought about the Longfellows: "for those who lived there had their happiness so perfect that no change, of all the changes which must come to them, could fail to be for the worse."[5]

Fanny was pregnant two months after the wedding. By May 10, 1844, her secret anniversary (and barely a month before her delivery date), Fanny's transformation into her new twin roles as wife and soon-to-be mother was completed. "What can I say of thee, thou birthday of my new life of love and blessedness? Sacredly and silently must thou be honored in my heart." She also wrote a prayer: "What heart was ever blessed with greater love than mine, given and received!" "How little did I dream what was awaiting me." "O Father! with my whole soul and heart and life let me thank Thee, and for his happiness, my husband's, infinitely more fervently I thank Thee." Later that month, looking out an upstairs window at Henry rowing on the Charles River far below, she thought, "How completely my life is bound up in his love—how broken and incomplete when he is absent a moment; what infinite peace and fullness when he is present. And he loves me to the uttermost desire of my heart. Can any child excite as strong a passion as this we feel for each other?"[6]

On June 9 Charles Appleton Longfellow was born. The next day Henry strutted out a proud single sentence to Sumner, "I have an 'Infant Hercules,' born yesterday."[7]

In all, Fanny was pregnant for six of her first twelve years of marriage. She delivered one more son, Ernest Wadsworth (1845), then four daughters, Fanny (1847), Alice (1850), Edith (1853), and Anne Allegra (1855). Firstborn Charley, however, was the undisputed prince of Craigie House. A month after he was born, Fanny reported to her father that the baby "thrives apace and is growing fatter" by the day and that "all the household are devoted to him and are wretched if he cries."⁸ She herself was doing fine, she added boldly and proudly to her father. Certainly she wasn't an "invalid" any longer, she said, as witness the fact that she was already walking "comfortably, though rather totteringly" through the house and was taking meals with the family again. She also told her father that her quick recovery was owed primarily to homeopathy, which (like hydropathy) was gaining widespread popularity in the 1840s as the latest in alternative medicine and holistic healing. She didn't say what low dosage of what herb had provided the remedy, but she did want her father to know that it was homeopathy, as she put it, that "cured my lameness."

To make a nursery for Charley, Fanny commandeered and redecorated Henry's sunny upstairs study, Washington's old room and the place where *Voices of the Night* and *Hyperion* had been written. Henry reluctantly but resignedly packed his books and moved to the darker downstairs front room where he would for the rest of his days work, nap, entertain visitors, and smoke cigars. He would learn to love his new study, but for a while he sighed and fussed over his loss: "Alas! the old study, now given up as a play-room to noisy Charley, whose feet incessantly patter over my head. Those were lovely days and nights above there! That room is so full of associations. This has none as yet." He complained mildly to Sumner that he "regretted the dismantling of that consecrated chamber. But what can one do against the rising tide of the rising generation?"⁹ But all this grumbling was probably nothing more than a smoke screen of playful chatter because from the beginning, Longfellow was uncommonly devoted to his children, spent endless hours with them, and may even have suggested the upstairs nursery himself.

With Fanny pregnant for the third time in September 1846, a news story about the possible uses of ether caught her and Henry's

Charles and Ernest Longfellow by Eastman Johnson, 1848 (courtesy National Park Service. Longfellow House—Washington's Headquarters National Historic Site, LONG 546).

attention. A Boston dentist, William Morton, had extracted a patient's tooth on September 30, in the first public demonstration of the use of ether as an anesthesia. The widely reported painless extraction prompted Massachusetts General Hospital surgeon John Warren, to have Morton administer ether to a patient of his scheduled for minor neck surgery—a test case in the eyes of skeptical Dr. Warren. The operation was scheduled for October 16 in front of a gallery of interested visitors and reporters. When it was finished, the patient woke and said he felt as though his neck had been merely "scratched," which prompted the respected Warren to pronounce the experiment a resounding success.

The Warren demonstration made medical history, and

Edith, Alice and Annie Allegra by Thomas Buchanan Read, 1859 (courtesy National Park Service. Longfellow House—Washington's Headquarters National Historic Site, LONG 4324).

ether was suddenly promoted from being a recreational party drug used mostly by medical students to a life-saving surgical anesthesia that revolutionized pain control, thus giving doctors for the first time a chance to perform surgeries more slowly and carefully. The Longfellows were thrilled by news of the scientific breakthrough—and they'd heard reports that somewhere in Europe doctors were giving ether to women during childbirth. This was something to think about.

Five months later, after a flu-infested winter that spared no one in the household, Henry made a point to attend an early March discussion sponsored by the American Academy on what he called in his journal, "the great discovery of the age, the Nepenthe—sulphur[ic] ether." A month after that he wrote in his journal that he'd gone over other possible uses of ether with his dentist, Dr. Nathan Keep, an M.D. who had graduated from Harvard Medical School and had chosen dentistry over general medicine.[10] A week later, on April 7, 1847, Fanny went into labor—and consented to taking ether, the first time in America it had been used to ease the pain of childbirth. That night, when Fanny and her baby girl, also to be named Fanny, were resting comfortably, Henry wrote to Sumner: "The great experiment has been tried, and with grand success! Fanny has a daughter born this morning, at ten. Both are well. The *Ether* was heroically inhaled." When he told his mother the next day, he reported that Fanny had been "courageous" and that "the effect was magical": "All pain instantly ceased; though the labor continued." And after writing to his mother, Henry went directly to Dr. Keep's office to have "the stump of a double tooth extracted under the ethereal vapor."[11]

Fanny's heroism, however, was seen by some friends and relatives as foolishly risky. Hillard offered in a letter to Francis Lieber that though Longfellow had shown "courage" in administering the ether, it was also true that no physicians he had consulted had actually recommend it for childbirth. Lieber agreed, saying that Fanny had indeed "immortalized herself," but he asked how they could have been so sure the natural birthing sequence wouldn't shut down under the influence of sleep-inducing ether?[12] There were others who second-guessed Fanny's decision, like sister-in-law Anne, who had written her concerns. Fanny thanked Anne for her "warm sympathy in my new joy and ethereal bravery," and reassured her that she "never was better or got through a confinement so comfortably."[13] She reported the baby had gone through it all perfectly well, too, for she was "very fat," had lots of "very dark hair," and a pair of pretty blue eyes—"I think she will be like Henry." She went on as tactfully as she could:

> I am very sorry you all thought me so rash and naughty in trying the ether. Henry's faith gave me courage and I had heard such a thing had succeeded abroad, where the surgeons extend this great blessing much more boldly and universally than our timid doctors. Two other ladies, I know, have since followed my example successfully, and I feel proud to be the pioneer to less suffering for poor, weak womankind. This is certainly the greatest blessing of this age, and I am glad to have lived at the time of its coming.[14]

When Henry wrote to Anne on May 2, he reported that Fanny was "very well—remarkably well—better than ever before after a confinement; so that *Ether* still reigns triumphant."[15]

But Baby Fan, who had "looked charmingly" at her October christening, according to Henry in his journal, and was described in early January by her mother as a "merry plaything," came down with a cold on January 23: "Poor baby very wretched," Fanny wrote, "wailing in a way that racked all my nerves."[16] She recovered, but at the end of August she was sick again, Henry painfully recording that she was "quite ill" and that she "lies patient and mournful, overcome by the heat." Then for a day or two she rallied, only to take a turn for the worse on September 4: "Little Fanny very weak and miserable," Henry wrote. "Which way will the balance of life and death turn?"[17]

It was a reasonable question for the mid-nineteenth century when twenty-three of every hundred infants died in their first year, the highest rate it had ever been in the United States, or ever would be.[18] Baby Fan was already a little past her first year, but that didn't provide much comfort. Like everyone else, Fanny and Henry knew people who had lost children. Six years earlier Emerson had famously lost his five-year-old son Waldo and had written "Threnody," which Fanny called "a cry of the soul such as has rarely been so well uttered before."[19] Even closer to home, Blanche Lowell, the daughter of Maria and James Russell Lowell, had died at fifteen months, in March 1847, a month before Baby Fan was born. The doctors announced her death had been caused by "dropsy of the brain," which they had treated with leeching and purging, but Fanny believed it was what she called "rapid teething" that had undone the poor child. Overcome with sympathy for Maria Lowell, Fanny wrote that "such a blow must soon sever, I should think, the mother's slender hold upon life."[20]

Fanny wrote to her father on August 31 that her "poor baby" was "very ill with her teeth." She'd been happy and healthy during the family's summer visits to Nahant and Pittsfield, but almost at once upon returning to Cambridge, she'd become desperately ill. "Poor baby drooping today," Fanny wrote in her "Chronicle" on the twenty-ninth, "and at night very feverish with symptoms of dysentery." When the doctor came, he prescribed wet compresses on her belly and head—and later "a little mercury."[21] Fanny reported over the next several days mostly frightened news: "Darling baby very feeble." "Very restless and wakeful." "Poor pale face and hollow eyes."[22] But on the second of September the doctor concluded she was "decidedly better," which prompted Fanny to write that her heart was "lightened a little." But hope gave way to heightened anxiety over the next couple of days, especially when the doctor thought perhaps there had been some "congestion of the brain." Then she improved again on the seventh, though she remained "very very weak." The doctor gave her more mercury on the eighth, but the "poor darling lies perfectly passive," Fanny wrote, "with her large hollow eyes looking up so pathetically." She confessed to the diary that her own courage was "almost broken."

And then on the tenth, "a day of agony unutterable," in Fanny's words, Baby Fan's condition worsened yet again. "The doctor evidently shocked at baby's state, and hope almost dies within me. Another physician watched with us through the long, long night, giving no sign of cheer."[23] Henry wrote somberly in his journal that it had been "a day of agony, of doubts and fears" and that even though "the physicians have no longer any hope, I cannot yet abandon it."[24] Shortly before her little girl died at 4:30 in the afternoon on the eleventh, Fanny broke down as she searched for strength: "Felt a terrible desire to seize her in my arms and warm her to life again at my breast. Oh for one look of love, one word or smile!"[25] Henry wrote: "Her breathing grew fainter, fainter—fainter, and ceased without a sigh, without a flutter—perfectly quiet, perfectly painless. The sweetest expression was on her face. Death seemed lovelier than life."[26] Baby Fan had lived one year and five months.

Fanny and Henry pushed through the difficult days and months that followed, their pain evidenced in letters and journal entries over the next year or more. Fanny's grief morphed into fear for the boys, her imagination appalling her with ever-present images of what they would look like in death. She took the standard Christian consolation that "it is a blessed thing to have a child in heaven," as she put it in a letter to Anne, "a lofty privilege to bring so pure an offering to the Redeemer's feet...."[27] But just as often she was plunged back into inconsolable grief, recording on October 14 that she was "very weary and wretched" and had "lost interest in the future." Three months later, on January 9, 1849, Fanny wrote that she had seen a baby "on an omnibus," which caused another outbreak of fresh grief: "Dreamed my darling Fanny was restored to me; sitting quietly by my side, she said she had been in heaven."[28]

Henry coped in his own way, eventually writing a thirteen-quatrain poem he called "Resignation," which appeared in his 1850 book, *The Seaside and the Fireside*. In the poem, he imagined his baby daughter becoming in heaven "a fair maiden, in her Father's mansion," and he imagined as well the time when he and Fanny would once again "behold her face," but this time "Clothed with celestial grace":

> Not as a child shall we again behold her;
> For when with raptures wild
> In our embraces we again enfold her,
> She will not be a child...

Orthodox Christians weren't sure what to make of this sort of consolation, but the idea of a bereaved father being reunited with his dead daughter had just the right amount of humanity to make the poem heartrending and spiritually hopeful to readers who understood what he was going through:

> There is no Death! What seems so is transition;
> This life of mortal breath
> Is but a suburb of the life elysian,
> Whose portal we call Death.
>
> She is not dead,—the child of our affection,—
> But gone unto that school

Where she no longer needs our poor protection,
And Christ himself doth rule.

In 1853, when a woman wrote to ask him about the poem, Longfellow replied that it had been written shortly after "the event which occasioned it" and expressed the feelings he was having at the time. He said he had never "analyzed" those feelings, "but I remember very well, that the words 'There is no Death!' arose in my mind as a cry, or protest, or if you will[,] a triumphant assertion of immortality."[29]

And then, almost exactly two years after Baby Fan's death, Fanny and Henry had another daughter, Alice Mary, born on September 22, 1850. Henry had been called up to Portland on a family emergency, rushing back as quickly as he could to Fanny, who was due any day. He got back at about midnight on the twenty-first, and at six thirty in the morning, "a daughter made her triumphant entry into Castle Craigie."[30] Six weeks later Fanny wrote her sister Mary that she was "the happy mama of a very nice little girl." She'd taken the ether again and afterward "got up remarkably well." The baby was "fat and vigorous," was "a great laugher," and had "a very expressive little face already, with dark blue eyes." She and Henry were "grateful and happy," as if their "secret prayers had been answered." But she would never be comfortable again with her children's health: "my joy is more tempered than it was formerly, and I dare not trust dwelling upon the future."[31]

What she meant of course was that she couldn't trust a happy outcome as month after month new childhood ailments presented themselves—challenges not only to the children's health, but to their parents' equilibrium as well. She and Henry pressed on, drawing strength from each other, but often on the point of panic. On Erny's fifth birthday, he was down with something unidentified, and Henry noted in his journal that "he looks very ill, and our hearts are very heavy, very heavy. This sudden shutting down of darkness on our joyous sunshine fills us with dismay."[32] Erny recovered and the heaviness receded once again, and then in a stretch between 1852 and 1853, everyone was healthy and Fanny was quick to thank God for the blessing. By then Fanny's life as wife and mother had become so all-absorbing that she confessed to her best friend Emmeline that she couldn't even imagine her old life any more: "My whole life is bound up now in my home and children. I am spoiled by it for society, which seems to me very barren and unsympathetic, giving us only glossy surfaces or sharp corners instead of the genial depth and lofty aspiration we crave."[33]

In January 1853, Fanny was pregnant again. It was a trying pregnancy as her health had been fragile, due she thought in an April letter to sister-in-law Mary, to "an attack of influenza and rheumatism" that had left her "in a state of extreme debility." She'd been forced for a while to sit on a couch without even talking: "I had the consolation of listening, however, but could enjoy nothing from the want of vitality in my veins."[34] By June 24, however, she was feeling a little better physically, though she buckled mentally under the weight of becoming a mother yet again: "I find children such a responsibility as they grow older," she wrote to sister-in-law Anne, "and so difficult to manage rightly, that I shrink from further duties beyond my capacities." The prospect of another confinement coming up on October 1, she told Anne "has depressed me a good deal."[35] Daughter Edith nevertheless arrived on October 22, 1853. Henry rejoiced in an October 25 letter to Fanny's sister Mary over "a wonderful baby, truly ... completely finished, down to the tips of its fingernails!"[36] He reported they were "all in very good spirits here just now." When 36-year-old Fanny reported the birth to her sister on November 22, however, she sounded more relieved than elated: "I am glad to be able to send you a line ... to say that thanks to God, I am nearly well again and am every day gaining new strength"—though she hadn't yet left her bedroom, she said, except for one meal she'd prematurely taken with the family downstairs.[37]

And then, four months later, she was pregnant yet again. Anne Allegra was born on November 8, 1855, but by then Fanny was too busy morning and night with two boys, 11 and 10, and two girls, 5 and 2, to be bothered with letters announcing the new arrival—or even to chronicle entries about her. She'd been pregnant six times between 1843 and 1855 and buried her firstborn daughter and namesake. About her new daughter, she wrote to brother-in-law Sam on January 1, 1856, that the new year had brought her "a new care, but a new darling," adding only that she'd begun feeling like a banyan tree "with all these young shoots springing up round me." Wearily she added "they seem to root me more and more to one spot."[38] She'd become the very heartbeat of a family others admired and envied, but she was also more than occasionally worn down physically and emotionally.

Fanny's love for Henry, however, remained unchanged—had grown deeper in fact as the years moved along. She had known from the moment she accepted him back in 1843 that their relationship was built on firm ground, that she was in love, and that she would spend the rest of her life with him and the children she hoped they'd have together. With two of those children already born, she wrote her sister on December 31, 1845, about her friend Emmeline Austin's wedding the next day to William Wadsworth, which Fanny was not at all sure she approved of: "I cannot crush a crowd of fears which have almost tempted me to forbid the banns. She is not the least in love with Wadsworth, but builds her hopes of happiness on faith in his excellent qualities and the success of others in a like situation; she consoles herself with believing such a marriage as mine is very rare, and though I believe it must be as regards the full sympathy of tastes and tempers, etc., yet I cannot think many venture on such a union without the ardent love which can alone fuse all differences."[39]

Henry on the very same day wrote in his journal about how quietly happy he was in his marriage: "So closes the year 1845.... Not many hopes deceived—not many illusions scattered—not many anticipations disappointed—not many fears realized! But love fulfilled, the heart comforted, the soul enriched with Fanny's affection!"[40] Scattered through Henry's letters and journal entries over the next several years are similar expressions, as on their third anniversary: "Three years of married life, dear Fanny! and you fairer than ever; each year an added grace, and a new charm in you, and in me more love and increase of affection." Or the little observation he made on May 5, 1847, that he walked halfway into town to buy opera tickets, but then returned home "and passed a delightful quiet evening with Fanny, which was more musical than any opera." Or this from his journal of October 22, 1850, when they spent the early evening together in the library: "We were alone and undisturbed, and very happy—very happy, reading and talking."[41] A full fifteen years after Fanny had accepted him, he still celebrated May 10, the "memorable day": "A delicious morning like that of 1843.... The air laden with the perfume of cherry blossoms, and full of sunshine and songs of birds, as it ought to be."[42]

Happy with each other and calm in their love, Henry and Fanny took a walk one day in November 1849 through Mt. Auburn Cemetery, "the sunshine falling warm and bright on all the graves," Henry wrote in his journal. "The place we have selected for ourselves seemed fairer than ever before."[43] The comment was a romantic marriage fantasy—the grave was their symbolic gateway to life everlasting, one they'd spend together arm in arm. But at the same time, a cemetery stroll, coming only fourteen months after Baby Fanny's death, was a sobering symbol of a darker, more unpleasant reality.

Deaths did begin to pile up. Some of them were very public, like Zachary Taylor's on July 9, 1850, just five days after he had presided over a scorching fourth of July celebration at the under-construction Washington Monument—and after drinking what some still surmise was a cholera-laced concoction of iced milk and cherries. Persistent rumors swirled that he was poisoned by proslavery sympathizers furious over his opposition to Henry Clay's proposed Compromise of 1850—that and his threat to lead federal troops against any state in the South foolish enough to try seceding from the Union. His death paved the way for his replacement, Millard Fillmore, who was in favor of the Compromise, to see the measure through Congress and then to sign it into law in September—to the South's great relief as the Compromise allowed for the addition of more slave states into the Union.

That aspect of the Compromise was enough to infuriate Northerners like Henry and Fanny, but it was the section of the Compromise being called the Fugitive Slave Law that pushed them over the top. The new federal law, forcing Northern antislavery activists to return fugitive slaves to their owners, superseded fifty years of Northern state legislation that had been enacted to protect runaways and those who helped them. Now those protected activists were subject to hefty fines and jail time. Making matters worse, the new law denied slaves the right to speak in their own defense or to demand a trial by jury. Longfellow, who was never a political firebrand, became an extremist on this issue, angrily observing in 1858: "If anybody wants to break a law, let him break the Fugitive-Slave Law. That is all it is fit for."[44] But back in the summer of 1850, Taylor's death had spurred passage of the Compromise, including the Fugitive Slave Law, a national tragedy to the Longfellows for political and humanitarian reasons—and for personal ones as well, for they had met the man barely a month earlier in the president's mansion in Washington.

Weighed down by children, an unknown number of servants, and Fanny's stepmother Harriot, the Longfellow entourage spent three days in New York and three more in Philadelphia before arriving in Washington on May 15. During their nine days at the fashionable National Hotel, Longfellow had met with Henry Clay himself, whose rooms adjoined theirs and who was at the time busy putting together support for his proposed compromise. They also met Massachusetts' own Senator Daniel Webster, but they hardly knew what to say to him in light of his defection on March 7 from the antislavery ranks in order to support the Clay compromise. Henry wrote in his journal only that Webster was "ponderous and silent."[45] There were conversations with five other senators, including James Ware Bradbury, Henry's old friend from Bowdoin, who was representing Maine. It was a busy week topped on Friday the seventeenth, when Henry, Fanny, and the children went to meet President Taylor himself.

And now barely a month later, Old Rough and Ready, renowned for his heroics during the Mexican War and a formidable obstacle to the Compromise of 1850, was dead. On July 11, Fanny wrote to her friend Emmeline that Taylor had been "truly loved by all," and that his "firm hand" had been needed to negotiate the terms of a North-South compromise. "Boston," she reported, "was shrouded in gloom."[46]

The gloom deepened two weeks later on July 19, when Margaret Fuller Ossoli and her son and husband were killed, their ship from Italy, the *Eliza-*

beth, having gone down in a storm off Fire Island within eyesight of the shore. "What a calamity!" Longfellow wrote in his journal. "A singular woman was she for New England to produce; original and somewhat self willed; but full of talent and full of work. A tragic end to a rather troubled and romantic life!"[47] The next day Fanny wrote to her stepmother Harriot, "What a tragedy is the wreck of the *Elizabeth* with her precious freight of human beings and works of art! The poor Marchioness' fate is in keeping with her romantic history but very sad for her mother and friends."[48] Fuller had found a lot to be indifferent about in Longfellow's poetry, and had said so, so neither Henry nor Fanny felt bound by ties of friendship or duty to be generous toward her, but after they had read *The Memoirs of Margaret Fuller Ossoli* in 1852, Fanny wrote to Emmeline:

> We have just got through reading the tragic history of Margaret Fuller Ossoli, by Emerson, Channing, etc., various friends taking up her remarkable life with their acquaintance with her. It is deeply interesting and shows forth a woman of nobler heart and brain than I had supposed. There was so much distasteful in her manners we evidently did her no justice, though her friends were of the most devoted kind. Her prophetic longing for foreign life and active benevolence were strangely fulfilled, and the Italian part is very touching, all its struggle and sorrow seeming fitly to close in the grand and solemn beauty of their united death.[49]

The summer of 1850 had claimed yet another important figure and had thus taken another serious turn for the worse.

And then the gloom deepened yet again on August 30, when Fanny and Henry's friend Dr. John W. Webster, the distinguished Harvard professor of Chemistry and Mineralogy and a prominent Bostonian with a socially connected wife and two debutante-age daughters, was publicly hanged for murder.[50] It was the crime of the century, at least according to the Boston *Transcript*, which reported after Webster's arrest, "never in the annals of crime in Massachusetts has such a sensation been produced."[51]

Webster had inherited $50,000 but after putting up an expensive house in Cambridge, he didn't have enough income to pay for the social life he and his family had become accustomed to. He fell into debt and borrowed money from the Boston philanthropist George Parkman, a medical doctor who had inherited money and invested it wisely to create one of Boston's great fortunes. He had even donated the land for the medical school where John Webster worked. Unfortunately for Webster, his debts continued to mount and he borrowed more money using the same collateral for several loans. When Parkman learned that Webster was borrowing more money without having paid back the money owed him, he demanded payment and threatened to go public with the scandal, thus threatening to ruin Webster financially and socially. So Webster invited Parkman to his medical school office—and killed him. He was expert at dismembering bodies and disposed of this one in the building's furnace, but he overlooked the victim's false teeth, which had been fitted out by Dr. Nathan Keep, who could tell that the ones found in the furnace were indeed those of George Parkman. Webster's fate was thus sealed, and he was tried and convicted before his public hanging on August 30, 1850. It was a lurid affair that shook Henry and Fanny, who thought initially Webster must be innocent, only to be persuaded by the mounting evidence that came to light slowly over the course of a year that he had indeed murdered George Parkman. This was a stunning scandal and an unbelievable execution, all played out in the newspapers day after day in the first part of 1850.

All three deaths, Taylor's, Ossoli's, and Webster's, had been public tragedies that the Longfellows nevertheless took personally.

And then there were the deaths that were personal. Henry's brother Stephen died quietly on September 19 of complications from his alcoholism, which he'd never outgrown after his wayward college days at Bowdoin. His wife Marianne had divorced him earlier in the year, and after a half-hearted effort to detox in Brattleboro, Vermont that summer, Stephen was asked to leave and died shortly afterward. He left five children, one of whom, 11-year-old Harry, was taken in by Henry's sister Anne and supported for many years by monthly checks from Henry. It was a messy business all around—a wasted life, repeated failures, unfulfilled promise—all the more difficult for Henry to accept because Stephen was also an amiable, good-hearted companion and a loved brother. At the time of his death, however, his downward spiral had hit rock bottom and the news of his death was neither unexpected nor unwelcome.

Henry lost his father and mother too at about the same time, his father on August 3, 1849, and his mother on March 12, 1851. His father had been a lawyer in Portland and a Bowdoin trustee in Brunswick; he'd gone to the Hartford Convention as a delegate in 1814 and been elected to the House of Representatives in 1823, but he had declined dramatically both physically and mentally after his first attack of epilepsy in 1821, when he was forty-five. Two years later he was already so weakened that he wrote to Zilpah that he felt "uncommonly feeble & exhausted" and that he'd "lost all confidence" in himself. He never fully recovered, never quite achieved the promise of his early years, and by the 1840s he had slipped into a weary routine of leisurely reading, quiet walks, and afternoon naps.[52] As a father, he had always been dutiful if distant, a loving man in his way, and one whom Henry did love, respect, and usually obey. In his journal, Henry recorded his father's death as "a gentle release" from a twenty-seven year "burden of disease and despondency." Six days later, after the burial, he walked quietly one last time through his father's office, which he called a "dusty, deserted, silent place." He could not have missed the irony, for his father's law practice hadn't yielded anything like the prosperity his son was enjoying as a poet. "Here he toiled on day after day. The ledger showed his reward, in page after page of unpaid charges. Alas, for a lawyer in a little town!"[53]

A year and a half later, Zilpah died, the bad news arriving coldly by telegraph: "Your mother died to-day, suddenly." The news came as a surprise, but Zilpah had been delicate for years, sickly to the point where her unmarried older sister Lucia had moved in to help years earlier and then remained to run the household's day-to-day business until her own death in 1864. Zilpah was thus given the opportunity to be a long-term invalid, and when her death came, it was not attended by great drama, just the sense that the inevitable had finally happened. The next day Henry wrote to Fanny from Portland that his mother had died "very tranquilly, as if falling into a swoon.... It was a gradual sinking away of life exhausted, and no disease."[54] He'd be staying for the funeral on Friday the fourteenth, but then he'd be coming home just as quickly as he could. "Kiss my darling boys," he wrote, "and tell them to kiss you a thousand times for me!"

If death seemed a constant companion for several of the eighteen years, there was much more life—like the Longfellow summer vacations, which usually began with a week or two every year in Portland, some time now and then in Newport, irregular visits to the Berkshires, and increasingly as the years sped by at the seaside resort of Nahant. That critical year of 1850 was their first full summer at Nahant, which they had enjoyed on and off during the 1840s, before settling on it as their preferred summer retreat in the 1850s and then buying a place in 1860. Once they settled permanently on Nahant, the family began what became an annual summer routine of packing what they needed from Craigie House, taking a short ride to Boston, and then steamboating to Nahant, not even twenty miles in all. It was very manageable despite the number of people and bags to be moved from one stop to the next. And they all liked the swimming, the boating, and the fishing, along with the beauties of the seascape shimmering before them every day and night. Henry and Fanny both enjoyed the socializing too, for Nahant was popular both with the Beacon Hill crowd as well as the Cambridge intellectuals. Add to that a steady stream of visiting friends and relatives and the result came to good times, a summer refuge and ritual. For Fanny and Henry, however, the best part of their summers on Nahant, was taking their "delicious" late afternoon walks together.

Fanny liked it there immensely. She wrote to Emmeline in the summer of 1851 that there was "a delicious sense of repose" at Nahant that "I can hardly explain, for I am not one of those terribly fussy housekeepers, but still the weight of a big house and of several servants is something so distasteful to my mind that I feel it." When home at Castle Craigie, she said, "I can rarely sit down quietly without being haunted by the thought of something neglected or forgotten, for though I arrange everything as methodically as I can, still my memory is treacherous and I dread its constant faithlessness. This occupation of the mind by petty cares, not dignified enough to elevate or interest it, is very tiresome when one longs for freedom for something better, and here I do enjoy my emancipation and can read and think like a new creature."[55]

Henry liked it there too—most of the time. He complained that it was hard for him to write there, but he always complained about that, even at home. There were the kids who conspired to keep him from his writing desk. And the visitors to Craigie House. And the mountain of correspondence to tend to every day. And of course Harvard. No, there wasn't anywhere he could go for solitude and quiet sufficient to work. He worried that he would never write anything ever again. So Nahant summer houses came in for the same criticism, for as he once put it, he was "shut up in little rooms, without a table to write on, and hardly a place to lay a book"—a calm rant compared to when he complained Napoleonically that Nahant was "a kind of St. Helena on which I am imprisoned."[56] But despite the occasional bursts of self-drama, Henry knew how well he had it and now and then acknowledged the peace and quiet, as he did in his journal on July 12, 1850: "The walks along the shore— the surf—the rocks—the sails that embellish the sea!—books and friendly chat—these make up the agreeable round of the day."[57] And four days later he wrote in perfect satisfaction that "nothing can be pleasanter than our Nahant cottage." His most pleasant moments, however, were the ones he spent with Fanny, especially their late afternoon walks and their occasional days spent together, like the one on July 9: "Sat all the morning on a promontory with wild roses, looking seaward, with my beloved Fanny, who looks fairer and better in this sea air. Oh my beloved! What a delightful morning [this] has been!"

In the summer of 1851, Henry fell under the spell of John Ruskin's *The Stones of Venice* on the city's art and architecture. "There is a certain magnetism about him, which, for the moment at least, makes all he says seem true, however bold his statements." He saw in Ruskin "hints which serve as divining-rods, and grand passages of rhetoric like Iliads in nutshells." But more than anything, reading Ruskin made him itch to write, made him angry with himself for being so unproductive: "This building up life with solid blocks of idleness, as I do here, is a poor kind of architecture. I am getting tired of it."[58]

The idleness of course was a large part of the charm of Nahant, a guilty pleasure which, by itself, could have been borne with patient fortitude, but it was unfortunately accompanied by a steady stream of visitors, what Fanny described to Emmeline as a life of "continued interruptions":

> People call at all hours, and we have many chance visitors from town: one day a lantern-jawed Kentuckian with son and daughters, all greatly desiring autographs, another day some Italian or German refugee hoping for a little advice about their future, another day Mr. Saxe, the huge Vermont humorist, evidently expecting to pass the day, and yesterday a country cousin, or rather the husband of a country cousin of mine, the grimmest kind of Puritan, with a sweet little boy who is called Samuel, and the familiarity of Sam and Sammy he said is never practiced at home! (Consequently I took a malicious pleasure in calling him by the latter the whole time he was here). This is only a specimen of the odd varieties we see (though of course more and odder in Cambridge, for Henry seems to be considered a kind of Helper General to all nations, and his good nature always encourages the idea), but there I can escape a little of it—here my hospitality is more unavoidable and our one salon gives me no place of refuge....[59]

There was no escape, yet none of it detracted very much from the pleasures Henry and Fanny took from the very activities and people that overwhelmed them. And Fanny was mindful too and grateful for the time she got to spend with Henry during the summers. She was sorry every year when it came time to return home because she'd miss, as she wrote to Emmeline on September 3, 1851, "our tête-à-tête walks upon the cliff, our full and perfect enjoyment of each other's society." It was all far better than life in Cambridge, which after eight years, she confessed in a whisper to Emmeline, had become "monotonous" and "dreary" because "so few intimate friends have I there."[60]

Henry took the family to Newport for the summer of 1852, a huge place called the Cliff House, large enough to accommodate twenty-five people (nurses and children counting as halves), for $2,620.[61] The idea was to have friends and family, like Tom Appleton, Julia Ward Howe, George William Curtis, and several others help with expenses and give the house both diversity and divertissement. Fanny told Emmeline in August that the place was "quite filled up and likely to be overflowing" and that she was especially pleased to have Julia Howe with them: "So full of spirits and every variety of talent, her wit rouses us all out of the languor this climate induces, and her singing (greatly improved in Italy), is a perpetual delight."[62] Henry added that his friend and Julia's husband, Samuel Gridley Howe, had come up too, but that he had left soon afterward. It was a good group that encouraged seaside fun and sports, idle hours on the lawn, reading in bedrooms or porches, and conversations everywhere. Afternoons brought regular guests who rang the bell and interrupted naps and other pleasures. In the evening there were games and songs—"and so runs the day away," Fanny wrote to Emmeline. "It is impossible to lead a more sensible life in all this bustle, and in this lazy air all care is softened and all thought becomes a dream...."[63] But all care was not entirely softened, not at least for Longfellow. He wrote to Sumner on August 24, "Newport is very gay and brilliant this year. But such an idle life! Well enough for a week or two; but I have almost too much of it. I wish, with all my heart you were here."[64]

In the group daguerreotype taken that summer, it is Fanny, seated in the center and looking directly at the camera, who brings the portrait into focus. She is slender with a pretty face and a mouth that seems ready to break into a smile. Henry stands behind her looking uncomfortably overdressed in a heavy, dark suit and tall stovepipe hat that hides his hair except for the ample tufts that give him a shaggy look. He is looking gently and lovingly down at Fanny.

The summers of 1853 and 1854 were spent at Nahant, but in 1855 Henry took the family once again to Newport, but this time he needed to work on

A daguerreotype from the summer of 1852 in Newport. Unknown photographer. From left to right: Thomas Gold Appleton, John G. Coster, Julia Ward Howe, Fanny Longfellow, Henry Wadsworth Longfellow and Horatia Augusta Latilla Freeman (courtesy National Park Service. Longfellow House—Washington's Headquarters National Historic Site, LONG 4808).

proofs and couldn't, exploding to his publisher James Fields, that "it is next to impossible to do anything here, with so many people in the house and no school for the children."[65] Then he hit bottom. He wrote Fields with temper: "To-day is very hot. How can I work? If I shut the window blinds—darkness! If I open them—glare! Chamber-maids chattering about—children crying—and everything sticky except Postage stamps, which having stuck all together like a swarm of bees, refuse further duty."[66]

The summer of 1856 was set to be spent in England and the continent. It had all been thought through and worked out in detail, but as Henry boarded the carriage on about June 10 to take him and the family to Boston harbor to set the great trip in motion, according to his own account on July 8, "I struck my knee a violent blow." It was so violent, he reported, that the "surgeon, looking grave, said I must not think of making a voyage until my knee was well." And so the steamer left without the Longfellows, who then gathered themselves up for another summer at Nahant.[67]

Longfellow had already told the story of his knee injury several times by the eighth, had memorized it in fact. Two weeks earlier he had reported it to Sumner: "For the last ten days I have been myself a prisoner, with a lame knee, which I cannot bend to sit at a table, and am forbidden to stand upon. I struck it getting into a carriage." But with Sumner, as always, he could tell the whole truth: "You must not think that our not going to Europe is any great disappointment to me. On the contrary, I am in a very quiet and happy mood of mind. Strange as it may seem to you, when I found myself fairly embarked in this enterprise, the thought of it made me very wretched. I awoke as from a troubled dream, and am glad it was only a dream. The undertaking was too formidable."[68] He wrote to Ferdinand Freiligrath that he wouldn't be going off to Europe any time soon. Just getting the family to Nahant, he said, "with all the go-carts and nurses, warns me of the perils of any longer journey." And to Hawthorne a year later, he was even more forthright. The plan for England "fell through," he wrote, "and has never again been resumed, nor will it be until somebody burns down my comfortable house, or I am in some other way made wretched and restless."

So Henry and Fanny chose the close and familiar and pleasant seaside at Nahant for their vacations, settling, for $450 in 1858, into a house on Willow Road on the shore, facing southwest toward Boston, a place owned by Thomas Wetmore, a 63-year-old Boston attorney.[69] The house was described in a newspaper report much later as a "brown cottage by the willows on the village street," complete with "sea views and sea breezes."[70] Some evenings, from their veranda facing the sea, they watched fireworks flashing across the horizon. It was an idyllic summer retreat.

But even there Longfellow couldn't escape his summer ambivalence. "This is an idle life we are living here," he wrote to James Russell Lowell in July 1858. "It is almost too lazy; but I rather like it, notwithstanding."[71] He still complained about the claims on his attention. "The little leisure I can contrive to secure to myself," he wrote to Sumner, "is filched away from me by unmeaning letters—invitations to lecture; requests to do something or other for somebody I never heard of. Most of them I feel bound to answer."[72] It may have been too "idle" a life or one too crowded with burdensome "invitations," but those were not serious enough as issues for Longfellow to sign up for Emerson's camping expedition in the Adirondacks in the summer of 1858, even though Agassiz and Lowell were going: "Emerson has bought himself a double-barreled shot gun for the occasion," he explained to Sumner, "on hearing which, I respectfully declined joining the party!" He added that the boys had been out ten days already, "and so far we have not heard of anybody's being shot."[73] Regardless of the interruptions and invitations, Henry was actually happy in the brown cottage on Willow Road. And safe from stray shotgun blasts.

Safe, uneventful, pleasant summer retreats—that was what the Longfellows all wanted. Dinner with friends and family was served every afternoon at 2:30; Henry and Fanny walked every late afternoon on the cliffs; and Fanny read to the family every evening. Not even an honorary doctorate from Harvard in July 1859 could pry Henry off the seaside peninsula and into Cambridge for the commencement exercises.[74]

In 1860, a little after landlord Thomas Wetmore died, Henry rented the house on Willow Road once again, but it was being put up for sale, which turned Henry to thoughts of buying the place—or losing it for 1861. He'd thought before about becoming a Nahant homeowner, but Wetmore's death brought the idea into sharper focus. And then, when he went up to Portland in late August 1860, he discovered that it wasn't the same, that it wasn't really home anymore: "This has become to me a land of ghosts and shadows. Within two years people have grown so much older! And so many have departed...."[75] Going there for a part of each summer hardly seemed necessary any more—so buying the Wetmore house where there was youth and liveliness in ample measure seemed more and more like a good idea. It would be an investment in his family's future, not just an island lot with a house. On December 19, he bought it for $5,000—in partnership with his brother-in-law and good friend Tom Appleton. He'd wanted to bargain a little on the price, but there were other buyers interested, so he took the asked-for price and settled gently into the mindset of a man who owned beachside property. He and Fanny were thus settled on the summer house they planned on enjoying with their children far into the distant future.

Almost as a balance to Longfellow's good marriage and happy family life was his hypochondriac's inventory of health issues—some real enough, some exaggerated, some made up. His bad knee in the summer of 1856, for example, was a serious problem that he seems to have exaggerated to avoid a trip to Europe that he didn't want to take. The knee took its place on the life-list of ailments that tormented him, like the regular bouts of what he called "neuralgia in the head" and complained about intermittently in his journal.[76] "It is astonishing how this neuralgia haunts me!" he wrote on March 3, 1851: "Great tides of pain go ebbing and flowing among the piers of teeth, perpetually!" Or this from December 16, 1860: "The demon of Neuralgia raging in my brain. Shiver by the fireside."

But Longfellow's life list of ailments went well beyond headaches and knees. He complained about upper respiratory problems that he lumped together as "influenza"; toothaches that triggered his neuralgia and resulted twice (at least) in extractions; stomach problems that he called "dyspepsia"; occasional lower back pain that he called "lumbago"—plus long stretches of sleeplessness, persistent headaches, and varying degrees of depression. By far his most unrelenting health issue, however, was an eye strain that though never diagnosed with any precision, did pose a threat to his vision for years—and which he therefore took with the utmost seriousness and sought help for.

The problem began, he told Parker Cleaveland in 1844, just when he and Fanny were about to be married a year earlier: "Writing in the twilight, a partial blindness fell upon me suddenly," he wrote. "For some time I walked in a world of shadows, seeing men as trees. By great care (and no coffee) I have now got so far as to write a short letter, and to read at intervals during the day, an hour or two in all."[77] He connected his eyestrain to "writing in the twilight" and overlooked what he took to be the coincidence of the attack coming just when he was to be married, which may in fact have triggered what was once called "hysterical blindness" and is now known as "conversion disorder." Typically this disorder begins with some psychological stress that manifests itself in physical symptoms, temporary blindness among them. The stress in Longfellow's case, according to this line of thought, came from his longed-for and long-delayed marriage to Fanny, which was impossible for him to separate from the guilt he had lived with for so many years over the death of Mary in 1835—and the loss of their child too. His earlier failure as a husband to protect his wife and unborn child, in this interpretation, would have made the stress of his new marriage nearly unbearable. Hysterical blindness was the result.[78]

Whatever the root cause of his eye problems, Henry consulted a New

York specialist, though Fanny was sure the doctor would think the condition minor and "speedily release him," as she wrote to sister-in-law Anne.[79] She was right about the diagnosis, wrong about the speediness of treatment and recovery. The Staten Island doctor was the well known and highly regarded Samuel Elliott, who had treated Louisa Ward, and various Sedgewicks and was, as Fanny continued in her letter to Anne, "the only oculist capable of inspiring much faith."[80] On September 20, barely two months after their wedding, Henry and Fanny arrived at Dr. Elliott's office, spent two long hours stewing in the waiting room, and finally got to see the famous oculist, who examined Longfellow and determined that he had a "strained nerve" from reading in bad light. His condition wasn't very serious—just barely serious enough to warrant a month of three-times-a-week office visits for "dosings and blisterings," in Fanny's words to her brother Tom.[81] She didn't mention the cost.

They got back to Craigie House on October 24 and the next day Fanny wrote to Zilpah that Henry's eyes were only "somewhat better," which is about all one could expect, she thought, after just a month of treatment "under the skill of even such an experienced oculist as Dr. Elliott."[82] She would be in charge of the home treatments, she said, and Henry was to follow a list of "admirable rules" and do prescribed exercises, but in the end the doctor was confident that Henry's eye problems would "disappear entirely." It was so encouraging, Fanny told Zilpah, that Henry could "already read a few pages without pain." Three months later Dr. Elliott visited them at Craigie House and re-examined Henry's eyes "carefully," Fanny reported to Anne, and "pronounced them much better and likely to be fully restored before long!" They were advised, however, to keep up the treatments diligently as this case was especially difficult because "the nature of Henry's pursuits sends much blood to the head and consequently to the eyes," which, according to Dr. Elliott, was why exercise was so essential for "equalising the circulation...."[83]

In August 1845, his circulation apparently not yet equalized and his vision still an issue, Henry sought another avenue of help, this time from hydropathy, the water-cure he believed in, at least in theory and at least some of the time. This time, instead of the 1842 skepticism he received from his friends, he was supported by Fanny, who had herself been converted to homeopathy, a sister branch of alternative medicine in the 1840s. When Dr. Robert Wesselhoeft, a successful homeopathist in Boston, moved in May 1845 to set up his "Aquatic Institute" in Brattleboro, Vermont, Henry determined to go there for treatment of his eyes.[84] Like the rigorous regimen at Marienberg three years earlier, there were excesses of disciplined watering, starting at three every morning when Henry was wrapped in wet sheets and left to sweat for a while before being plunged into cold spring water.[85] Fanny, who had gone to Brattleboro too but could not take the cure because she was pregnant with Erny, wrote to Anne about Henry's routine. After the blankets and ice water, she said, he was given breakfast, then took a long walk "to the douche, which is on the opposite side of the ravine," where he took "divers baths" followed by lots of drinking water and walking until dinner. "At five in the afternoon he has another bath and walk and thus concludes his labors for the day."[86]

The treatment, whether based on good science or bad, did not help Longfellow's eyestrain. Four years later, writing to Evert Duyckinck, the New York editor and anthologist, his eyes hadn't improved: "I still remain half blind," he told Duyckinck, "seeing only at favorable hours and in favorable lights...."[87] And in 1857, he wrote to Freiligrath that his eyes "are neither better nor worse than they have been for some years, since 1843, that is [very bad], for all purposes of work, but otherwise giving me no pain nor trouble. If I let them alone, they let me alone; but when I want them to do me the favor of reading or writing in the evening, they decline."[88]

The failures of the oculist Elliott and watery theorist Wesselhoeft had left Longfellow on his own to deal with his eyestrain. To that end, he routinely restricted his writing and reading to the fewest number of daylight hours that he could—and nighttime reading he avoided almost completely. In November 1843, four months after she and Henry were married, Fanny reported to Anne that because "Henry does not like the trial of lamps," they didn't go out much at night. Instead, they stayed home, enjoyed the silence ("such a blessing"), and received visits from a handful of "dear friends," as she put it.[89]

Strictly speaking, there wasn't much silence because the evening hours were filled with the sound of Fanny's voice as she read book after book, at first just for herself and Henry, then later for the children as well. In effect she became Henry's nighttime eyes. Their books were wide-ranging, like Hawthorne, Homer, Sophocles, Cervantes, Milton, Boswell's *Life of Johnson*, Melville, Coleridge, Cooper, Tennyson, Charlotte Brontë's *Jane Eyre*, Thackeray, Dickens, Emerson, Thoreau, Ruskin, the Brownings, Margaret Fuller, Benjamin Disraeli, Walter Scott, Thomas Carlyle, Victor Hugo, George Sand, and Harriet Beecher Stowe's *Uncle Tom's Cabin*. The list went on, book after book, night after night, and soon the routine grew from eye-saving therapy to treasured family time. As Fanny put it in an August 1847 letter to Emmeline: "I am always sorry to see the summer go like a pretty woman out of my sight, but rejoice to sit down again by my chimney corner for the evening, with book and spouse...."[90] Ten years later, when she was 40 and a confirmed stay-at-home, she described her life to her sister: "As I grow older I think I enjoy more and more my *shell*, like one of Mr. [Louis] Agassiz' venerable turtles.... We very rarely ... go out of an evening, we so dearly delight in our own fireside, and the boys utter such a lament if we do that I have not the heart to cut them off from their nightly readings. Perhaps when my three girls are young ladies we shall be again tempted into society."[91]

Craigie House may gradually have become a refuge from society at large, but not from sociability on a small scale, for though their home life was a constant round of routine family affairs, there were also many visitors to spice up the days, weeks, and years. The close friendships that had stabilized Longfellow's life before his marriage, however, were being reshuffled and rearranged—and there were a few new players to add to the cast of characters. The Five of Clubs had stopped meeting, split on the slavery issue with Sumner, Longfellow, and Howe on one side, Hillard and Felton on the other. But Sumner and Felton continued to visit regularly—Sumner every Sunday for dinner, conversations deep into the night, and his regular sleepover. Henry saw Hawthorne now and then, mostly for dinner at Craigie House, but on occasion in Boston and Salem too. With Emerson, whose Concord home was only fifteen miles away, Longfellow had a long but somewhat distant relationship. On one level they were socially connected with many of the same friends, though Henry was four years younger and light years less complicated than the knotty transcendentalist. But who wasn't? Not many could stand shoulder to shoulder with the Sage of Concord. Longfellow made an effort, however, and did like Emerson the poet and Emerson the lecturer, although he was always measuring the exhilarating moments against the exhausting ones.

On the day after Christmas 1846, Emerson hand-delivered an early copy of his *Poems* to Craigie House: "Fanny read it to me all the evening and until late at night," Henry wrote in his journal. "It gave us the keenest pleasure."[92] He did think some of the poems "Sphinx-like," but he saw in others "bright veins of purest poetry": "Monadnoc," "Threnody," and "The Humble-Bee" were "exquisite" and captured "much of the quintessence of poetry." After they read the book, Longfellow wrote Emerson a complimentary note, Fanny reported to her brother Tom, which had prompted yet another visit from Emerson, who was so set up by Henry's praise that he was actually "very pleasant, and more communicative than usual."[93] Emerson may have been too much for either Longfellow to accept into their inner circle, even if he had wanted to be there, but they liked him and his work well enough to include him in their larger circle of friends, Henry keeping a picture of Emerson in his study.

10. From Craigie House to Longfellow House

A new friend was Swiss-born Louis Agassiz, who had delivered the Lowell Lectures at Boston's Tremont Temple in 1846 on natural history and the next year taken a professorship in zoology at Harvard. He became a new regular at Craigie House, a great favorite of the children. An old friend was Tom Appleton, brother, bon vivant, and charming dinner guest—whenever he was in town that is, and not off in London, Paris, or Rome. Another new friend and popular visitor to Craigie House was Luigi Monti, a Sicilian who had fought in the failed 1848 Italian revolution and been forced to leave his homeland, arriving in Boston in 1850, when he met Longfellow, who recruited the young man to teach Italian at Harvard. At Craigie House the two men enjoyed Italian wines and talked about Italian poets, Dante of course chief among them.[94]

But despite Longfellow's old and new friendships at mid-century, the social life in Cambridge, for Henry and Fanny both, dwindled year after year. In 1860, Fanny wrote to Emmeline that even though there were "so many men of high culture about us," she and Henry didn't have much in the way of "easy, delightful, daily pleasure from them"—not so much at any rate as they might have wished for and would have enjoyed in Europe, she thought. "They are too busy, or too domestic, and hardly one of them but Agassiz is to be relied on for any social purposes. There is no promenade, no Corso where one can meet and exchange a few refreshing words, no gallery to lounge in but the dreary Atheneum, where I rarely meet a soul I know."[95]

These were years too when Henry was out of touch with his old friend George Greene, whose marriage to Maria Carlotta had fallen apart in the 1840s and been dissolved in 1850. Longfellow wrote to Sumner, "What a terrible affair that is. I cannot bring myself to think of it patiently!"[96] Greene went back to Longfellow's salad years of the late 1820s—and Greene's marriage was tied in Henry's heart to his own marriage to Mary. Then Greene had become Henry's desperately needed confidante in the dark years of Fanny's rejection. They did not, however see much of each other anymore, had even given up their correspondence. The divorce had struck deeply into Henry's emotional life, which was further troubled by the 41-one-year-old Greene's second marriage in 1852 to 18-year-old Catherine Van Buren Porter of Catskill, New York.[97] Greene, with his divorce and remarriage, plus his long residence in Italy and then his years living at the family home in Rhode Island, had put himself at too great a distance in miles and affection for Longfellow to keep up with him.

Chief among the cast of characters at Craigie House throughout the 1840s and 1850s was Charles Sumner, a friend so close he had accompanied the newlyweds on their wedding trip in 1843, a man so loved by Henry, and

Fanny too, that he was always welcome whenever he showed up. And he still showed up just about every Sunday he was in town. He sat in his favorite rocker, played with the children, took his regular seat at the dining room table, and even accepted with good grace the family's gentle teasing over his solemn manner. He and Henry would talk deep into the night, and then he would normally stay over until Monday morning. It was a ritual.

Throughout the 1840s, Sumner slowly moved the center of his attention from his Boston law partnership with George Hillard to abolitionism, which led naturally to speech-making and national politics—and an eventual split with Hillard over the slavery question. By 1848, he was speaking for the new Free Soil party, which had come together as a coalition of antislavery Whigs and Democrats, plus abolitionists in the fringe-element Liberty Party; by the mid-1850s, they would all merge into the antislavery Republican Party. All that over-heated, party-forming turmoil was bubbling into creation on October 25, 1848, when Longfellow went to hear Sumner at an antislavery Free Soil rally in Cambridge.

It was a hostile audience, but that didn't trouble the ever-earnest Sumner, who was in full throttle that day—loud and confrontational, probing and provoking—as he had been at the June convention of the new party when he delivered one of the great speeches of his political career, condemning the "conspiracy" between cotton-producing Southerners and New England textile manufacturers, "the lords of the lash and the lords of the loom."[98] (Nathan Appleton, who had kept up a friendly relationship with Sumner because of his friendship with Longfellow, now broke completely with him.) There were catcalls at the October rally Henry attended, and the potential for violence too—a grassroots, bare-fisted expression of American politics. When he got safely home that night, the overwhelmed Longfellow described the event in his journal: "Ah, me! it was like one of Beethoven's symphonies played in a saw-mill! Sumner spoke admirably well. But the shouts and the hisses and the vulgar interruptions were not pleasant. They grated on my ears. I was glad to get away."[99]

Sumner had discovered his element, however, and within days of that speech he agreed to stand as the candidate of the new party for Congress in the Boston district. He lost by a wide margin but was poised to run again, this time for the Senate, in April 1851. On the evening of April 24, Election Day, the Longfellows had a dinner party for the Spanish Secretary of Legation, with Agassiz and Appleton along for entertainment and charm. Before dinner was over, news arrived of Sumner's victory—and shortly after dinner Sumner himself showed up "to escape from the triumph, and be quiet during all the noise in the streets of Boston," Longfellow wrote in his journal. In reality Sumner had come home to celebrate with his family.[100]

Sumner spent the next day at home with the Longfellows, and in the evening Fanny read them all Elizabeth Barrett Browning's 1850 *Sonnets from the Portuguese*, which Henry thought "rather dusky at times—but deep and impassioned."[101] For the rest of the spring and then in the early fall (summer was spent at Nahant), family time was spent as it normally was, with Sumner taking his regular Sunday seats at the Craigie House hearth and table—and his bed at night. On November 23, Sumner spent his last Sunday with the Longfellows, enjoying a final meal and a good night's sleep before heading south to Washington for the winter. "We shall miss him much," Henry confided to his journal, "We sat up late talking."[102]

Three days later, from New York, Sumner wrote to Henry: "I could not speak to you, as we parted; my soul was too full; only tears would flow. Yr. friendship, and dear Fanny's, have been among my few treasures—like gold, unchanging.... From a grateful heart, I now thank you for your true and constant friendship. Whatever may be in store for me, so much at least is secure, and the memory of you and Fanny will be to me a precious fountain. God bless you both, dear ever dear friends, faithful and good. Be happy, and think kindly of me."[103] When he received the letter, Longfellow wrote back at once, "*Alma, soave e cara!*" ["O Soul, sweet and beloved!"][104] "Your farewell note came safe and sad—and on Sunday no well-known footstep in the hall, or sound of cane, laid upon the table! We ate our dinner somewhat silently by ourselves, and talked of you far off, looking at your empty chair—your vacant place!" It would be "many days," he wrote in his journal, before he'd see Sumner's "manly, friendly face by daylight or lamplight!"[105]

Although Henry and Fanny were increasingly anchored at Craigie House by children's health issues, social activities, schoolwork, and special events—plus their own daily rituals and nightly readings, they still managed through most of the 1840s and 1850s to keep up their membership in the Boston social and cultural aristocracy. They took their place together, side-by-side, at a wide range of theatrical, literary, musical, and dance programs. Fanny loved all those cultural outings and loved attending them with Henry, so she was reluctant at first to give anything up just because she was pregnant. A mere two weeks before Charley's birth on June 9, 1844, Fanny drove into town with Henry for the first Boston appearance of the famous Norwegian violinist and composer Ole Bull, whose performance turned out to be near-perfect, Fanny thought. "He is a divine musician," she wrote in her diary, putting "soul into a violin almost angelic.... All other scrapers play from the head only, he from the heart chiefly, with deep pathos and sometimes drollery." She was surprised too that he was so young, only 34, and was thrilled by the "vast crowd and vast applause."[106]

They attended Emerson's lectures religiously, Theodore Parker's too, and Sumner's, among many others. They attended parties and gave them; went to social evenings and received guests at Craigie House; and were nearly always at home for their dearest friends and family. There were piano concerts, dance programs, poetry readings, and a concert in October 1846 by the singing Hutchinson family doing their famous antislavery and temperance songs at the Melodeon.[107] Two months later they went to see John Banvard's popular, three-hour panorama of the Mississippi River at the Armory Theatre: "One seems to be sailing down the great stream," Henry wrote in his journal, watching "the boats and sand-banks crested with cotton-wood, and the bayous by moonlight. Three miles of curves; and a great deal of merit."[108] In January 1847, they went to town for dinner and a program of dancing Viennese children: "A pretty show of some forty or fifty little girls, from six to sixteen years of age," Henry wrote.[109] Nothing escaped their notice and very little escaped their attendance.

It was opera, however, which captured their hearts most completely. For Longfellow, opera in Europe in the 1820s was originally an avenue into foreign cultures and languages, but the sensuous bel canto style that was still popular then converted him completely, whether in Mozart's 1787 *Don Giovanni*, Rossini's 1816 *Barber of Seville*, or in Bellini's 1831 *Norma*. Fanny may have had her opera initiation in December 1835, in Paris, when she heard Giulia Grisi in *Norma*: "I cannot describe the effect of that voice!" she had written at the time. It "floats through my memory as a vision filled with melody not of this earth."[110] Opera became for the Longfellows a passion they indulged by attending performances of traveling companies that were by the 1840s making regular stops in Boston.[111]

On the opening night of Boston's spectacular new Music Hall, November 20, 1852, the Handel and Haydn Society performed. Fanny reported proudly to her brother Tom on December 7 that the hall itself was a "splendid affair" and was "ample enough for the largest audience and perfectly comfortable in all its arrangements, with its forty doors of entrance from the spacious corridors." She added in a letter to her sister on January 2 that there had been crowds every night, "a beautiful sight with the gay dresses of the ladies." The Music Hall was in fact, Fanny wrote to her sister, "finer" than any of the opera houses she remembered in Europe.[112]

For the January 1855 season, Giulia Grisi and her husband Mario (real name, Giovanni Matteo De Candia, one of the most celebrated tenors of the time) appeared together in Bellini's *I Puritani*. Fanny wrote to sister Mary how "exceedingly" they enjoyed Grisi and Mario even if Grisi had "lost the freshness and power of her voice." She still acted and looked "magnificently,"

Fanny wrote: "her Norma was never grander." Henry was taken with her too, despite her diminishment. "Grisi is grand," he wrote in his journal, "with her superb style of acting and her tragic bursts of passion. A splendid woman. Her voice has lost some of its power and freshness—but still she sings right royally, and is Queen of the Lyric Drama." Two days later, he wrote that she was "grander than on Monday." Four days later it was *Norma* once again— and then *Don Giovanni* on the twenty-ninth. He wrote to Sumner the day after to say that they'd been to see Grisi and Mario "almost every night" and that they had liked especially "the trio, '*Protegga il giusto cielo*,'" ["Just Heaven, now defend us"]: "divinely sung—ah, divinely!"[113]

Henry and Fanny were also flush with Jenny Lind fever. A gifted soprano, the Swedish Nightingale had become a prima donna at the Royal Opera in Stockholm in 1838, and then performed for wildly cheering audiences throughout Europe until she retired in 1849—at age 29. A year later the celebrated showman P.T. Barnum lured her out of retirement for an American tour that would begin in New York in September 1850. The terms were simply too good for her to pass up: 150 concerts at $1,000 each plus one-half of the receipts over the first thousand. Barnum also paid all expenses, including the Atlantic crossing, not just for her but her entire party—a woman traveling companion, a secretary, two servants, a composer-pianist Julius Benedict, who earned a salary of $25,000, and a baritone, Giovanni Belletti, who earned $12,500. It came to nearly a half million dollars, all out of Barnum's pocket. And then he agreed to pay all their expenses on tour. It was thus the Swedish Nightingale was lured out of retirement—all that money and a new continent to conquer.[114]

Digging deeper, Barnum blitzed New York with a year-long advertising campaign that produced "Lind Mania" long before her actual arrival, which when it finally occurred on September 1, drew an estimated thirty thousand to the Manhattan pier where she landed. Her first two concerts (a collection of arias) were benefits, which further endeared her to rapturous fans who openly wept at her generosity as well as her performances. But Barnum's big gamble paid off at once with opening night receipts close to $18,000. In the end, the Swedish Nightingale's Barnum-sponsored American tour reaped more than three-quarters of a million dollars for ninety-five dates—which she split with Barnum according to their arrangement.

After three weeks of wildly popular concerts in New York, Lind was off to Boston where she opened at the Tremont Temple on September 27. Longfellow had an opening night gallery ticket that James Fields had managed to get for him, but Fanny was forced to stay home with her five-day-old daughter Alice. Her disappointment was somewhat eased when the twenty-seventh turned out to be a rain-soaked Friday night, but Henry's report of the performance brought the disappointment back: "She is very feminine and lovely," Henry wrote. "Her power is in her presence, which is magnetic; and later takes her audience captive before she opens her lips. She sings like the morning star; clear, liquid, heavenly sounds."[115] The following Tuesday, Jenny Lind's private secretary brought Longfellow an invitation for him to visit the next night at her rooms in the Revere House. He was shown into the drawing room where he and she "had an hour's chat."[116] From the sidelines, Fanny cheered: "What a welcome Jenny Lind is getting. I am glad of it. I like such enthusiasm for an artist and a good creature. No Queen could get it. It is pure love of excellence...."[117]

Eight months later, in June 1851, Jenny Lind returned to Boston, and this time Fanny went to the concerts. She reported to her father, "I did hear Jenny Lind at last in the evening and her voice fully equaled my expectations, though a little husky at times. There is a power and body to it I hardly was prepared for, and the fascination of her whole personality is very remarkable."[118] Fanny was proud that the famous singer (with her replacement pianist and future husband Otto Goldschmidt) came to visit at Craigie House and had "a pleasant half-hour's chat," in Henry's words. He was fascinated by what he called her "soft wildness of manner," the "sudden pauses in her speaking," and the "floating shadows over her face."[119] When she returned five months later, the Longfellows went yet again to hear her sing at the Melodeon: "Jenny's voice rang out wonderfully. We had never truly heard her before," Henry wrote in apparent praise of the Melodeon's acoustics, "though we had heard her often." On the twenty-eighth she sang Mozart's "Deh! vieni, non tardar!" ["Oh come, don't delay"] from the *Nozze di Figaro*, which became Henry's favorite of all the songs she sang. He wrote in his journal, "With what delight Mozart would have listened to her interpretation of his delicious compositions!" At her Farewell Concert on December 6, she once again included "Deh! vieni, non tardar!" "Love, tenderness, longing," Henry wrote to Sumner, "never found a more complete and triumphant expression than in that music, and Jenny's face while singing it!" The next night in his journal, he felt her loss: "Jenny Lind's last concert! Alas," he wrote in rapturous grief, "that we shall never hear that voice divine any more, nor see that radiant face again!"

Another radiant face took her place, however, Fanny Kemble's, she of the triumphant public life in theaters and the tumultuous private life at home. After her stage debut to rave reviews as Shakespeare's Juliet in London in 1829, she toured for two years in America with her father's traveling company, preparing herself mentally in advance for bad manners, a disagreeable climate, frontier conditions, and overall discomfort. But getting to Boston in

1833 had been a revelation. She liked it at once, especially the expensive homes, the gentility of the best people, the beautiful Common, and the Beacon Hill display of wealth and finery. It reminded her of London.[120]

Before she got to Boston, however, Fanny performed in New York, Philadelphia, and Washington, where society figures and venerable politicians lined up to see her—Dolley Madison, John Quincy Adams, Daniel Webster, even the legendary, 78-year-old Chief Justice John Marshall. Fanny brought them all to tears, including Pierce Butler, who was the son of a Georgia plantation family that owned 638 slaves, and who was at that time living in Philadelphia. Starstruck, Butler followed Fanny from theater to theater until she finally took notice—and then allowed herself to fall in love with the persuasive and charming Southern gentleman. A girl could do worse, she thought, than a good-looking rich man who promised to stabilize her life. She'd have to give up her adoring fans, of course, but wouldn't it be worth it to have a couple of permanent homes and a life where she didn't have to scramble around onstage to make a living?

They were married in June 1834, and lived in Philadelphia where Fanny gave birth to two daughters. But in 1838–39 Butler moved his family to the plantations in Georgia where Fanny saw slavery first-hand and close-up. It turned her into an ardent abolitionist—which signaled the end of her marriage. In 1845, he finding real-life with an actress less than he had hoped, and she finding life with a philandering slave owner impossible, Fanny left Butler and returned to England and to acting before discovering she could entertain audiences and support herself handsomely by giving readings from Shakespeare—a simpler and easier business after all than actually acting in the plays. When Butler sued for divorce and sole custody of the children on the grounds of abandonment, Kemble returned to America to keep from being railroaded by the courts. In the end she managed to get the girls every summer, plus $1,500 a year in alimony.[121]

The Appleton sisters met Fanny Kemble in Newport in the summer of 1834, when 16-year-old Fanny Appleton wrote proudly to a friend: "I have got very well acquainted with her and feel myself bound by the spell which attracts everyone to her."[122] They met up again in May 1837 in London, and the following August at the Lenox Hotel in the Berkshires, the Appleton girls wandering off from Pittsfield where they'd been summering with their grandmother Gold, and Kemble escaping Philadelphia's stifling heat—and maybe Butler as well. They got on famously, laughing, partying, and enjoying one another's company, especially at the inevitable poetry readings and recitations from Shakespeare. Fanny Kemble was spellbinding—a mother and a bona fide celebrity too—famous as a stage performer and also as the author of a memoir, *Journal of Frances Anne Butler*, which had appeared to great controversy (and sales) three years earlier, in 1835, when she'd been only 25 years old. This was a modern-day woman to take a girl's breath away, a thrilling, rule-breaking role model who made a lasting impression on the already formidable Fanny Appleton.

It wasn't until after 1845, when Kemble separated from Butler, that she began appearing on Boston stages once again, meeting Henry for the first time and renewing her friendship with Fanny. Over the next fifteen years the Longfellows rarely missed a performance, and often they visited the actress before or after a show, had dinner with her, or visited with her either at her hotel or at Craigie House. In January 1849, Henry wrote in his journal that they'd been to hear her reading of *The Tempest*. "A crowded house—with a reading-desk covered with red, on a platform, like the gory block on the scaffold, upon which the magnificent Fanny bowed her head in tears and great emotion. But in a moment it became her triumphal chariot and her martyrdom became her glory. What glorious reading!" A week later they heard *King Lear*, and Henry reported that "it was her best reading so far. At the close we drove home with her to the Revere House, and had a charming little gay supper." Sumner was there too, "her *chevalier* for the evening."[123] Two nights later, they went again to hear *King John*, "too tragic a play, for those who have any sorrows of their own," Henry thought, only four months after Baby Fan's death. But he thrilled at being the actress's special guest: "We went in at the private entrance before the doors were opened, leaving the expectant crowd outside thundering at the gates."[124]

When Fanny reported to her friend Emmeline on the run of shows they'd attended, she wrote that she felt "delight and wonder" at each one. "I have been to all but two, and have considered the last always the best, though, perhaps, *Lear* is a more astonishing proof of her power and pathos than any.... Last night was *Macbeth*—very grand and ample.... You can have no conception of the sonorous clangor of her voice, nor of its infinite compass and exquisite sweetness." Henry rhapsodized on the sixteenth: "What nights these are!—with Shakespeare and such a reader!"[125] A couple of weeks later, Fanny reported to Emmeline that they'd been to hear *The Merchant of Venice*, Henry escorting Fanny Kemble onstage, and after the program, they all repaired to Craigie House for "a nice little supper," with Sumner, Hillard, and brother Stephen gathered round the table.[126] After supper, Fanny presented Fanny Kemble a bouquet and Henry presented her with a sonnet, "On Mrs. Kemble's "Readings from Shakespeare," which he then read for her. The sonnet was a breathless praise of "precious evenings! all too swiftly sped!" and an ample tribute: "How our hearts glowed and trembled as she read, / Interpreting by tones the wondrous pages / Of the great poet...." Shakespeare's "listening spirit," Henry recited as he handed the paper to Fanny Kemble, must "rejoice / To be interpreted by such a voice!" According to Fanny, the actress was so "much overcome" that she "could hardly recover herself." "Her affectionate nature is easily touched by kindness, and the tears flow at once."[127]

Sponsored by the Mercantile Library Association, Fanny Kemble returned the following season, reading from *As You Like It* on February 12 at the Boston Music Hall to an audience of more than 3,000, Henry reported in his journal.[128] After the reading, however, Kemble surprised the audience by pausing and then saying a few words about a 400-line dramatic poem Boston's own Henry Longfellow had written in the summer of 1849, "The Building of the Ship." What she said, Henry wrote in his journal that night, was "that when she first saw the poem, she desired to read it before a Boston audience; and she hoped she would be able to make every word audible to that great multitude." And she did, "standing out upon the platform, book in hand, trembling, palpitating, and weeping, and giving every word its true weight and emphasis." The audience was overjoyed that the actress had chosen one of their own to honor in this particular way—and Henry and Fanny were both elated and drained. Fanny wrote to sister-in-law Mary that the reading had had a "magnificent effect," but it was nonetheless a "trying occasion for me, sitting in that immense audience of 3,000, but I got through it better than I expected and so did Henry."[129]

For "The Building of the Ship" Longfellow had once again chosen his grand public voice, the one he had used in his 1839 "Psalm of Life," his first popular hit. He was good at these homilies in verse. People loved to read them, memorize them, and perform them. The new lines, rich in rhyme and rolling rhythms, would become a Union anthem in the years to come and would help to cement Longfellow's position as America's unofficial poet laureate—unofficial only because the position wouldn't be created for another 136 years. When contemporary journalist Noah Brooks, who wrote a popular early biography of Abraham Lincoln, recited it to the president in the early 1860s, he reported that Lincoln's "eyes filled up with tears and his cheeks were wet. He did not speak for some minutes, but finally said, with simplicity, 'It is a wonderful gift to be able to stir men like that.'"[130]

The poem had two lines of development, one nationalistic, one romantic, and both openly sentimental. It is the story of a master ship builder and his apprentice at work upon a new ship: "Beautiful they were, in sooth, / The old man and the fiery youth!" The young man stood to inherit the old man's craft and house, and to marry the old man's daughter as well upon the completion of the ship—and thus the completion of his apprenticeship. The "centuries old" ocean ("strong as youth, and as uncontrolled") "waits impatient for his bride," which is the ship "decked with flags and streamers gay":

> On the deck another bride
> Is standing by her lover's side.
> Shadows from the flags and shrouds,
> Like the shadows cast by clouds,
> Broken by many a sunny fleck,
> Fall around them on the deck.
>
> The prayer is said,
> The service read,
> The joyous bridegroom bows his head;
> And in tears the good old Master
> Shakes the brown hand of his son,
> Kisses his daughter's glowing cheek
> In silence, for he cannot speak,
> And ever faster
> Down his own the tears begin to run.

But as sentimentally touching as the father-daughter-bridegroom storyline is, Longfellow from the start had a higher purpose, for this is no ordinary ship: "Sail on," the old man says at the end of the poem, "O Ship of State! / Sail on, O UNION, strong and great!"

> In spite of rock and tempest's roar,
> In spite of false lights on the shore,
> Sail on, nor fear to breast the sea!
> Our hearts, our hopes, are all with thee,
> Our hearts, our hopes, our prayers, our tears
> Our faith triumphant o'er our fears,
> Are all with thee,—are all with thee!

These were the words that would bring Lincoln to tears, but they were a departure for Longfellow, who had always made it a point to avoid politics in his poetry. He'd written that slender, seven-poem book of antislavery poems in 1842, and the peace poem, "The Arsenal at Springfield" in 1845, but he no doubt tempered that not-very-strong impulse out of family considerations—he was after all the son-in-law of Nathan Appleton, a man who depended on Southern cotton for his financial fortune, and the brother-in-law of James Greenleaf, sister Mary's husband, who also made a living from cotton, and split his time between Boston and New Orleans. Henry's own early Whig leanings had given way to the more principled antislavery positions of the Conscience Whigs, but never was he driven to sword points as his best friend Sumner was. But "The Building of the Ship" was a starkly political poem, an emotional and inspirational triumph. It would take a new century too far removed from the Civil War and too poetically sophisticated to be openly sentimental for the poem to lose its impact and some of its appeal, but even now its innocent charm and nimble verse make it a guilty pleasure.

One of Longfellow's harshest critics from the 1920s, Herbert Gorman, wrote that "it would be sheer effrontery not to admit that 'The Building of the Ship' is a dramatic and finely conceived work..., the sort of poem which shows Henry at his best, simple and direct and rising to an extraordinary climax that loses nothing but rather gains by the didactic implications." Though the poem "may be oratory," Gorman grudgingly admitted, it was "better oratory than Sumner's or the lost Webster's."[131] High praise from an unexpected source.

11

Evangeline, Minnehaha and Priscilla

Henry Longfellow was already famous on both sides of the Atlantic when "The Building of the Ship" was published in *The Seaside and the Fireside* (1849), capping off a decade of hit poems and best-selling books that featured perfectly pitched celebrations of village blacksmiths, old clocks, and shipwrecks. He had distinguished himself in the short lyric form, the slightly longer ballad narratives, and then with *Evangeline* (1847), the long narrative poem.

American readers had been following their poet for nearly a decade by the time *Evangeline* was published. *Voices of the Night* (1839), with its centerpiece, "A Psalm of Life," had reached unparalleled heights of popularity. In 1841 he published *Ballads and Other Poems*, which added "The Wreck of the Hesperus," "The Rainy Day," "Excelsior," and "The Village Blacksmith" to his rising reputation. The following December he published *Poems on Slavery*, which besides putting him on the political landscape also had a pair of poems readers connected with, "The Slave's Dream" and "The Quadroon Girl." *The Belfry of Bruges and Other Poems* came out in 1845 and included "The Day Is Done," "The Arsenal at Springfield," and "The Old Clock on the Stairs."

But it took *Evangeline, A Tale of Acadie*, which came out on November 1, 1847, and went through six editions in ten weeks, 35,850 copies in ten years, to make him a household name.[1] Eventually the book would appear in 270 editions, would be translated 130 times into ten languages, and would spread rapidly through popular culture as drama, music, and parody.[2] By the time "The Building of the Ship" came out, Fanny found her herself married to a "literary superstar," as one historian put it, a writer as celebrated as Charles Dickens—or maybe even Jenny Lind, according to another.[3]

Longfellow's was a high-minded poetry, musical poetry, memorable poetry—and it was also carefully crafted poetry rich in literary recollections. And it was being written at a time when poetry mattered to average Americans who memorized poems for public declamations and private recitations. Longfellow was supplying just the right poetry for the age. Maybe as Poe jealously accused, Longfellow plagiarized, and maybe as Margaret Fuller ungenerously claimed, his poems were "thin," and maybe he wasn't so deep as he was polished, but none of that mattered to his devoted public who bought his books, read his poems, and took to their hearts Longfellow's openly didactic and moralistic poems presented in a voice that inspired people "to act, that each to-morrow / Find us farther than to-day" ("A Psalm of Life"). Most important to the rise of Henry Longfellow into America's Poet, however, was the character of Evangeline and the poem named after her.

Evangeline was the first of Longfellow's long narrative poems, and the first of thirteen books that would appear under the imprint of the firm that soon came to be known as Ticknor & Fields. The poem, which ran to five parts in 163 pages in the first edition, had presented Longfellow with two problems, one was physical, the other poetical. The physical problem was his eyesight, so bad that he wrote whole sections of the poem Milton-like, "in the dark," as he put it, scrawling words blindly in pencil on paper that he balanced on his lap.[4] The poetical problem had to do with its musical structure, which he finally decided should be the long lines of Greek and Latin epics, what is called dactylic or "heroic" hexameter lines—fine for the *Iliad* perhaps, but not suited, according to common wisdom, to English poetry. Longfellow thought otherwise. He believed hexameters were the perfect measure for Evangeline's stoic journey through beautiful, barely mapped-out American territories—but he stood alone on this. Even his inner circle, including Fanny and Sumner, were dubious.

By July 1847, however, after she had heard and read so much of the story Henry was then reading in proofs, Fanny changed her mind: "It is a very beautiful, touching poem," she wrote to best friend Emmeline, adding that "the measure gains upon the ear wonderfully. It enables greater richness of expression than any other, and is sonorous like the sea which is ever sounding in Evangeline's ears."[5] After it was published, Francis Lieber wrote questioning the choice of hexameters, and Longfellow defended himself by quoting *The London Examiner*, which had concluded, and Longfellow provided the emphasis, that it was written in a measure "*happily adapted to a narrative in which suspense and expectations are the predominant emotions.*"[6] He had held firm on the hexameters—and he and *The London Examiner* may have been right in the end, for despite the groundswell of well-meaning misgivings and some outright disapproval from critics, the public loved the long sensuous lines, the musical composition matching perfectly the seriousness of the story itself. The poem was as thrilling in its presentation as the magnificent heroine herself, who was adored at once as the tragic, saintly embodiment of pure love and enduring fidelity. Critics be damned.

The events the story hung on were real enough, even though the lead characters were purely fictional, not at all the real people the Reverend Conolly had said they were when he told Longfellow about them in April 1840. The French community in Acadia in the 1750s in the real town of Grand Pré in present-day Nova Scotia was some 15,000 strong, all descended from settlers who had claimed the land and begun farming it a century earlier. But the British were in the ascendency in 1755, and even though the French Acadians were by far the majority population, they were expelled from their homes and homeland and relocated, as mostly unwelcome refugees, to other places in and out of the British Empire, notably to Louisiana, but "scattered," as Charles Calhoun tells us, as far as the Falkland Islands and West Africa.[7] It was a powerful story of a people dispossessed and deported—but it was also personalized, as the Conolly version had come to Longfellow, in the tale of a young couple caught in the middle of events they could not control— and that separated them for a lifetime. In Longfellow's hands, Evangeline spends her life in a devoted search for her lost Gabriel and finds him finally on his deathbed, where they reaffirm their love with a parting kiss. Longfellow knew he had another hit on his hands, a tragic love story with a heroic woman at its center. It couldn't miss, not at least if he could find the words and the form to bring it to the public—which he managed to do.

Four years after *Evangeline* had taken its place in the hearts of readers everywhere, Fanny wrote to her friend Emmeline that Henry had received a fan letter from Louise Stuart Costello, an Irish travel writer, who had gushed out, "How well you understand me!" Fanny wasn't at all surprised by Costello's feelings. "He is truly favored by women," Fanny told Emmeline, "because he does understand and reverence them peculiarly, and has just that tenderness and sympathy in his own nature which sounds the depths of theirs. Most men have a chivalric enthusiasm about women if they have any, but he, though I say it, has that tender sympathy far less common which all feel like magnetism."[8] Magnetism, that was the key to Henry's appeal to women, according to Fanny, and one of the reasons the poem had received such wide approval—and sales.

But that wasn't the only reason. Another was that *Evangeline* tapped into the travel book craze of the time, readers longing to experience vicariously more exotic, faraway, and romantic locations than the ones they lived in. Longfellow had already found success in that line earlier with *Outre-Mer* and *Hyperion*, but this time he would be describing in verse New World locations, from Acadia to Louisiana, from lakes, plantations, and bayous to the Mississippi River and what passed for the far west in the late eighteenth century. Readers embraced Longfellow's story of Evangeline and the places she wandered through and the characters she met along the way—which means they would have been very surprised to learn that, with the exception of Philadelphia, Longfellow had never seen any of the locations he was describing. He had traveled widely earlier—Europe by foot and carriage in the late 1820s, then again in the mid–1830s, and most recently in 1842, but for most of those years he'd been single, exploring European lands and languages for his teaching career. By 1845, however, he was tied to Cambridge by that same career, and by his still-new marriage and his two very young children. And so for *Evangeline* he had to learn about the American frontier from library books— much as James Fenimore Cooper had done in his five Leatherstocking Tales that had been published between 1827 and 1841. When he went to the library on January 7, 1847, to read John Watson's *Annals of Philadelphia* and William Darby's *Geographical Description of the State of Louisiana*, he wrote in his journal: "These books must help me through the last part of 'Evangeline'; so far as facts and local coloring go." Perhaps it was a rueful admission, but he was at least satisfied, he continued, that "for the form and the poetry, they must come from my own brain."[9]

Providing another huge assist in "local coloring" was "Banvard's Grand Moving Panorama of the Mississippi," which John Banvard had first shown to the public in the summer of 1846 in Louisville. He closed the show that October, refined it a bit, and then boldly took it to Boston's Armory Hall in time for Christmas. For his six-month run in Boston, Banvard saw his celebrated painting—complete with piano accompaniment, carefully arranged lighting, and his own colorful narrative of Mississippi River places and people—earn some $125,000. Longfellow was one of the first in Boston to see it, probably with Fanny, on December 19, when he wrote in his journal that he'd seen three miles of the Mississippi plus boats and bayous, sandbags and cotton—and more.[10] He might have added how helpful it all was for him to "see" some of the places he was describing in his new poem—yes, it was a virtual reality, but it was good enough for his purposes

Though he hadn't actually seen much of what he was describing in *Evangeline*, Longfellow was nevertheless feeling secure that he was on the right track when it came to being an American writer. The setting, while American and accurately described from scenes he had read about and seen pictures of, was incidental, he thought, to the epic sweep of Evangeline's quest, after all, the quest that had taken her to a new country and made her into a peculiarly American woman. She was in fact the new American, the one Hector St. John de Crèvecoeur had identified in his famous 1782 *Letters from an*

American Farmer: "What, then, is the American, this new man?" Crèvecoeur had asked. "He is either an European or the descendant of an European; hence that strange mixture of blood, which you will find in no other country." Crèvecoeur had been the first to use the melting pot image, writing that "here individuals of all nations are melted into a new race of men." By 1846, Crèvecoeur's image had long since seeped into the culture, and Longfellow had absorbed it into his own credo, writing in his journal on January 6, "Much is said nowadays of a National Literature. Does it mean anything? Such a literature is the expression of National character. We have or shall have, a composite one, embracing French, Spanish, Irish, English, Scotch, and German peculiarities. Whoever has within himself most of these is our truly national writer. In other words, whoever is most universal is also most national."[11] Of course, he was describing himself.

Walt Whitman, who was percolating ideas and language in the late 1840s that would come together in 1855 as *Leaves of Grass*, would famously write in "Song of Myself": "I am large—I contain multitudes." Longfellow claimed the same largeness. But largeness for him meant absorbing European cultures, their languages, their histories, and their literary forms—the glories of great writers from earlier times and places. *Evangeline* was the much-admired realization of that idea, the harmonizing of a steady baseline of European rhythm over which the melody of American characters, landscapes, and lyrics could play out. And readers everywhere thought Longfellow was on the right track, that this was a giant step in the direction of an emerging American national literature. It didn't matter in the end that he hadn't actually seen much of the New World or that the lines he had poured out were in Old World hexameters.

Samuel Gridley Howe spoke for generations of readers when he wrote a letter to Longfellow barely a week after *Evangeline* was published: "I thank you most heartily for the kind remembrance which you manifested by sending me your little book.... It is not, however, for myself alone that I have to thank you, but as one of many thousands who will read *Evangeline*." This was a book, he said, "that pleases, instructs, improves people—what a gift to the world! ... You feed five times five thousand souls with spiritual food which makes them forever stronger and better." He said he wasn't able to "appreciate the *literary* merits" of the poem, but he understood "the sublime moral, the true poetry," which, he said, included "patience, forbearance, longsuffering love, [and] faith."[12] That was exactly what Henry had been working for—moving, moralistic, uplifting verse that people loved. And bought. In that respect, he was the envy of every poet everywhere—he had found a voice and an audience.

Exactly in the middle of the 1850s Longfellow published *The Song of Hiawatha*. It came out in the decade famously labeled "the feminine fifties" in a book of that title by an early American literary scholar, Fred Lewis Pattee. It was an era dominated by best-selling home-and-hearth novels like Susan Warner's *The Wide, Wide World* (1850), Maria Cummins's *The Lamplighter* (1854), Fanny Fern's *Ruth Hall* (1854), and Mrs. E.D.E.N. Southworth's *The Hidden Hand* (1859)—plus her fifty-nine other novels. Fanny's Aunt Kitty, Catharine Sedgwick, had written *Hope Leslie* in 1827 and was still writing into the 1850s. This was the very same group that had provoked Nathaniel Hawthorne to rail against them as a "damned mob of scribbling women."

When *Hiawatha* appeared, it changed the literary landscape. Suddenly a poet-professor who wrote serious and high-minded verse was competing with domestic sentimental novels for book sales—and holding his own. With advance sales running to 4,000 copies at a dollar apiece, *Hiawatha* had an initial press run of 5,250 copies, when new books of poetry normally ran to about 500. It sold 10,000 in its first month, 50,000 in five months. Seven weeks after its publication on November 10, it was still selling, according to a giddy James Fields, 300 copies a day. That first year alone *Hiawatha* earned Longfellow $3,675 in its American printings.[13]

These were startling, unprecedented numbers, but this was a Longfellow book, a publishing event that was causing industry professionals to rethink their business models. Even six years after its publication, *Hiawatha* was so popular that Ticknor & Fields ordered the nineteenth edition with a press run of a thousand copies. In all, according to Frank Luther Mott in *Golden Multitudes: The Story of Best Sellers in the United States*, *Hiawatha* sold over a million copies, as did the various collected and selected editions of his poems—an unparalleled literary coup. Things were going so well that in June 1857 Longfellow turned down a thousand dollars from the *New York Ledger* for ten poems, saying only that "I do not wish to write for any newspaper."[14]

It would have been difficult for *Hiawatha* the book to be as arresting as its sales figures. It had begun to take shape for Henry on June 5, 1854, when he read, "with great delight," he said, a "charming" Finnish epic poem, *Kalevala* (1849), a painstaking collection of folk songs and legends compiled by the physician-philologist-professor-poet Elias Lönnrot, who had collected the stories that he then refashioned into a poem that identified and defined the Finnish national character. Longfellow was taken with the poem, with its scholar-poet author, and with the inspiration he found there for a similar type of American epic with roots in Native American folklore and history.[15] Two weeks later he wrote that he'd "at length hit upon a plan for a poem on the American Indians," one that would "weave together their beautiful traditions into a whole." When he said "at length," he was most likely talking about recent days and weeks, perhaps even months, but he may also have had in mind a much longer time period. His sympathy for American Indians had been aroused at the 1823 December Exhibition at Bowdoin when he had played the Indian chief and warrior King Philip, whose war-time atrocities Longfellow had come to understand as a last, desperate measure of a "noble race" that had been "most barbarously maltreated by the whites."[16] Now it was 1854, time to set the record straight. And so, with this moral imperative urging him forward, and the *Kalevala*'s music flooding his senses, the stars were finally in alignment for the birth of *Hiawatha*.

When he wrote in his journal that he had "hit upon a plan" for his Indian epic, he added that he'd also "hit upon a measure," the same one used in the *Kalevala*, which he called "the right and only one for such a theme."[17] Here, however, he was on shaky ground—almost everyone disagreed with him. The metrical pattern used in the German translation of *Kalevala* that he had read was called trochaic tetrameter, not far different, after all, from the longer dactylic hexameters of *Evangeline* that had also been condemned by nearly everyone—but loved by the public. It was a trotting measure that sounded singsong except when spoken by experienced readers. It had the singular advantage of moving the narrative along quickly, and—with the inclusion of so many Indian words—slowing it down at the same time. Perfect, he thought, for the rhythm he was after, and as fresh and forthright as its uniquely American subject. And once having committed to the new measure, he held firm; his instincts had not let him down earlier, he reasoned, so why not trust them again? He may have missed the easy and insulting parody possibilities the new measure seemed to invite—or maybe he didn't care and had decided to stand his ground anyway. Not many poets or readers, after all, had as firm a sense of English metrics as he had—or the confidence to use them. It was trochaic tetrameter, for better or worse.[18]

When it came to the actual writing, Longfellow synthesized and compressed the legends he had learned about the Indians, "weaving" was how he phrased it, thus falsifying at the same time he was honoring the peoples he so admired—and inadvertently patronizing them into the bargain. The poem was too much the product of dusty scholarship and creative license to be authentic—too far removed from actual Native Americans to be reliable as either folklore or history. Professor Elias Lönnrot had created an authentic panorama for the *Kalevala* by going into the field eleven times over fifteen years to collect and record the folk tales that until then had existed only in the oral tradition. Longfellow hadn't done anything of the sort, but felt justified in his creative misrepresentations because he saw the process as dignifying Native Americans, not devaluing them. His motives were pure.

If *Hiawatha* misrepresented, it nevertheless pleased the reading public once again on both sides of the Atlantic—and farther. There was a loving fairness to Longfellow's treatment that could not be missed or dismissed. Native Americans had been killed off, enslaved, dispossessed of their lands, herded into strange places, permanently cut off from their hunting and burial grounds. Their civilizations were virtually destroyed. Here was the white man paying tribute to the red, acknowledging the beauty of the Indian people, their cultures, their beliefs, their dignity. *Hiawatha*, despite its flaws, was an apology that the American reading public intuitively understood, accepted as appropriate, and rushed out to buy. It was a balancing of the scales, a national act of contrition as much as an act of national literature. It was a thrilling gesture.

Not everyone thought an apology was necessary. Emerson, for example, when he wrote to thank Longfellow for sending a prepublication copy of *Hiawatha*, which he smugly dismissed as "sweet and wholesome as maize," couldn't resist taking a swipe at Indians, Indian culture—and Longfellow too: "The dangers of the Indians are," Emerson wrote, "that they are really savage, have poor, small, sterile heads—no thoughts.... And I blamed your tenderness now and then, as I read, in accepting a legend or a song, when they had so little to give."[19] Longfellow begged to differ. They had plenty to give, and despite his hodgepodge retelling of folk tales and tribal myths and his wholesale borrowings from European literatures, Longfellow believed his *Hiawatha* true to the spirit of Native American history in all its oversized beauty and nobility.

The poem had taken shape quickly once he had hit upon a theme and measure in June 1854. By mid-July it was pouring out of him. "If I had a hundred hands," he wrote in his journal, "I could keep them all busy with *Hiawatha*."[20] By mid-October he reported that the new poem "occupies and delights me": "Have I no misgivings about it? Yes, sometimes. Then the theme seizes me and hurries me away, and they vanish."[21] When he read pages to a friend in mid-November, the criticism was that the poem "will want human interest," a point which had troubled him too—and Fanny as well. "I must put a live, beating heart into it," he thought as he worked on.[22]

Longfellow may have found that beating heart in mid-January, when the opera season opened and temporarily shut down the writing season. For the next two weeks opera took up large chunks of his time, which he addressed in his journal with the unworried comment that the poem would "get itself sung ... one of these days."[23] On the fifteenth, he and Fanny saw

Bellini's *I Puritani*: "Grisi and Mario!" he blurted out in his journal, "enough for one day," though they went again and found Grisi "grander than on Monday." On the twenty-second he managed to work a little on *Hiawatha* in the morning, but saw Grisi again in *Norma* that night. On the twenty-ninth Grisi and Mario ended their run by combining their talents for *Don Giovanni*, "divinely sung," Henry wrote in his journal. Exhausted and thrilled, and perhaps feeling guilty for losing so much time on *Hiawatha*, he added: "So ends our opera going for the present. Now for quiet evenings at home, and readings by the fireside."[24]

This infusion of opera into his life, just as he was in full stride on what he would purposely call *The Song of Hiawatha*, helps explain how the grand and theatrical and operatic crept into what was already an epic narrative of the American Indian. The music, with its swelling passages, plodding recitatives, and virtuoso arias and duets, added to the elevated sweep of the poem, its mythic underpinning, and its otherworldly libretto. This was the emotional pulse, the "live, beating heart," he'd been looking for. A month later, on February 21, he wrote the last canto, number twenty-two, thereby stretching his song to 316 pages in the first edition, some 5,300 lines. Epic in scope and size. Grand opera.[25]

During the spring and summer of 1855, Longfellow was overwhelmed with page proofs and had trouble maintaining sufficient distance to read the pages, remarking in June that he was "growing idiotic about this Song" and couldn't tell any more "whether it is good or bad."[26] He pushed through and by October 2, when Ticknor gave him a check for a thousand dollars, which was soon followed by a few advance copies, he was anxiously awaiting the first run of five thousand due to come off the presses on November 10.[27] Fanny fretted to brother-in-law Sam a few days before the book went public: "I hope you will like it. It is very fresh and fragrant of the woods and genuine Indian life, but its rhymeless rhythm will puzzle the critics, and I suppose it will be abundantly abused as [Tennyson's] poor *Maud* seems to be."[28] When the tenth finally arrived, the elated publishers told Longfellow "that more than four thousand out of the five of the first edition are sold" and they ordered another three thousand.[29] That much of the gamble had paid off. The poem was an instant hit with the reading and book-buying public, so much so that one twenty-first-century historian called it "the biggest success story in antebellum poetry."[30] The critical response was something else again. He worried on November 18 that while some of the newspaper reviews had "warmly defended" him, others had been "fierce and furious" and had "violently assailed" him.[31]

Longfellow couldn't help worrying when Poe's old charge of plagiarism was raised once again. He was approached by Theophilus Carey Callicot, associate editor of the New York *Commercial Advertiser*, who wanted him to comment on a charge made in the Washington *National Intelligencer* on November 27, accusing him of plagiarizing from the *Kalevala*. It was disheartening and disappointing, but Longfellow patiently replied:

> In *Hiawatha* I have tried to do for our old Indian legends what the unknown Finnish poets had done for theirs, and in doing this I have employed the same meter, but of course have not adopted any of their legends. Whatever resemblance therefore may be found between the poems of 'Kalevala' and mine, in this respect, is not of my creating, but lies in the legends themselves. My authorities will all be found in the notes. All these strange stories are in Schoolcraft and the other writers on Indian matters, and this ought to shield me from any accusation of taking them from Finnish sources.[32]

But the constant tension between exhilaration at the book's success and the "fierce and furious" critical response gave him pounding headaches that were so bad he barely got through Thanksgiving dinner with the Appletons, where, he said, he'd been a "gloomy guest."[33]

On the plus side, George Bancroft had written his warm approval in a letter of November 26, and Henry replied gratefully: "Many thanks for your friendly letter, and your sympathies with *Hiawatha*. You see I am terribly assaulted about the book; but cheering voices like yours are not wanting, and I do not much mind the din of my opponents, who seem to be unusually active this time."[34] Meanwhile, Ticknor & Fields were selling the nine and ten thousandth copies. "Critics may assail as they please," he wrote in his journal on December 6, but *"eppur si muove,"* an echo of Galileo's famously muttered words after his heresy trial in 1633 when he'd been forced to recant his forbidden position that the earth moved around the sun: "And yet it does move."[35]

A week later he wrote to Sumner, "We are thriving here notwithstanding hostile critics. The English papers have come out very strongly in my favor. I have received eleven, warmly on my side; and only one or two of a different way of thinking."[36] Barely making the letter was a line at the end: "Fanny is well and so is the nameless baby," for Anne Allegra had been born on November 8, right in the middle of the *Hiawatha* excitement. Two days after his letter to Sumner, he wrote in his journal that another thousand copies were being printed, bringing the total to eleven thousand.[37] By the end of the month the number was up to thirteen thousand, as he wrote to Lowell: "Some of the newspapers howl like dogs or demons at it; but it only sells the faster; and most of the papers of any name and note are on my side. The English have been particularly generous in their commendations; and on the whole the book has been very successful."[38]

On January 1, Fanny wrote to brother-in-law Sam denying, though she was clearly being less than truthful, that the criticisms had affected them. The book "seems to have roused all the nettles of criticism," she wrote, "but we don't read the disagreeable ones." She added of the ones they didn't read: "The disrespect and impertinence of them strike me most." She didn't expect reviewers "to like all styles of poetry but if the author is known and valued, he should be supposed to be *honest* and to choose even his metre with a good reason."[39] As a family, they were as privately defensive of the criticism as they were publicly heartened by the public's reception.

By the end of January, however, the excitement and agitation were fading, Anne Allegra had a name, and Henry wrote in his journal, "a pleasant kind of lethargy" was settling in. He basked in the sunny words of Hawthorne sent from Liverpool in April: "I have been in all sorts of parties within the last few weeks, and in every single one of them your name was spoken with the highest interest and admiration. Your fame is in its fullest blow; the flower cannot open wider. If there is any bliss at all in literary reputation, you ought to feel it at this moment."[40]

After the first flush of success, a low-grade *Hiawatha*-fever lingered on—for decades. Parodies came in "from all quarters—even from California," Longfellow wrote in his journal on February 18, and in March he commented on the dramatic readings of the poem in Philadelphia and Boston. On the twenty-second, he took the boys to Donald McKay's shipyard for the launching of a ship christened the "Minnehaha," Hiawatha's Indian maiden, followed by a luncheon at which there was another dramatic reading from the poem. In April he wrote to Sumner: "*Hiawatha* rushes onward in readings, recitations and the like.... Thirty thousand have been printed, and five more are going to press immediately."[41] The poem was everywhere, memorized and recited by young and old alike, and it had become indisputably clear by the late 1850s that Henry Longfellow was not merely America's poet, but the world's poet, a bonafide international literary celebrity. In 1857, Sumner, traveling through Scotland, reported back to the Longfellows that he'd been to the estate of art historian William Stirling (Sir William Stirling-Maxwell after 1865), who raised Shorthorn cattle: "Among them," Sumner reported to Henry, "is a famous bull named Hiawatha, and a cow named Minnehaha."[42]

Hiawatha and Minnehaha had in fact become an instantly famous literary couple in 1855, household names—he "the child of wonder," she the "dark-eyed daughter" of the "ancient Arrow-maker."[43] They had met when Hiawatha stopped at Minnehaha Falls, where the arrow-maker lived with his daughter, whom he'd named Laughing Water, after the river and the waterfall. (IV: 147) She was "wayward as the Minnehaha / With her moods of shade and sunshine"—and she also had eyes that "smiled and frowned," a laughter that was "musical," and "tresses" that flowed "like the water." (IV: 147) She won Hiawatha's heart at once:

> Who shall say what thoughts and visions
> Fill the fiery brains of young men?
> Who shall say what dreams of beauty
> Filled the heart of Hiawatha? [IV: 147].

But Hiawatha was a man on a mission at that moment and had to keep Minnehaha a secret passion, at least until he could complete his Herculean tasks, first outfighting Mondamin (who in death gave the gift of maize to the Indians as a guard against starvation), then slaying the sturgeon monster Mishe-Nahma, and finally killing the magician Pearl-Feather, who was guarded by fiery serpents. Once his battles were completed, his fame and honor earned, and the well being of his people secured, Hiawatha turned his attention to the softer matters of love.

When he'd first met Minnehaha, Hiawatha was "perplexed" by his feelings. He found himself "Listless, longing, hoping, fearing, / Dreaming still of Minnehaha, / Of the lovely Laughing Water." (X: 184.) He sorted it out in short order, however.

> As unto the bow the cord is,
> So unto the man is woman,
> Though she bends him, she obeys him,
> Though she draws him, yet she follows,
> Useless each without the other! [X: 183].

His grandmother Nokomis tried to talk him out of marrying Minnehaha ("Bring not here an idle maiden"), but Hiawatha gently insisted, for Minnehaha was not only the "handsomest of all the women" (X: 184), she was also destined to "be your starlight, moonlight, firelight, / Be the sunlight of my people!" (X: 184–85) And with that, Hiawatha returned to the land of the Dacotahs, asked Minnehaha's father for her hand, and waited as she accepted his proposal by taking her seat in the wigwam next to his. Their return journey to Hiawatha's home was slow: "Over wide and rushing rivers / In his arms he bore the maiden; / Light he thought her as a feather." For their wedding night, Hiawatha made "a lodge of branches, / And a bed with boughs of hemlock." From their hidden perches, the squirrel and rabbit "watched with curious eyes the lovers." Longfellow, perhaps suppressing a lusty impulse to say more, satisfied himself by understating the couple's happiness: "Pleasant was the journey homeward!" (X: 190).

From that point onward, Minnehaha makes occasional appearances, as for example when the maize had been planted, at which point

> Hiawatha, wise and thoughtful,
> Spake and said to Minnehaha,
> To his wife, the Laughing Water:
> "You shall bless to-night the cornfields,
> Draw a magic circle round them,
> To protect them from destruction,
> Blast of mildew, blight of insect..." [XIII: 212].

That night in the darkness that protected her from prying eyes, the lovely Minnehaha went naked into the cornfields.

> From her bed rose Laughing Water,
> Laid aside her garments wholly,
> And with darkness clothed and guarded,
> Unashamed and unaffrighted,
> Walked securely round the cornfields,
> Drew the sacred, magic circle
> Of her footprints round the cornfields [XIII: 214].

Repaying Minnehaha for her ritual, the harvest was full that year, and "the merry Laughing Water / Went rejoicing from the wigwam." She gathered up the women and young men, and went about the business of "the husking of the maize-ear" (XIII: 217).

But several years and seven cantos later, "The Famine" tells the story of Minnehaha's death, a canto that was destined to become a performance piece for generations of readers.

> Oh the famine and the fever!
> Oh the wasting of the famine!
> Oh the blasting of the fever!
> Oh the wailing of the children!
> Oh the anguish of the women! [XX: 261].

Minnehaha took ill and took to her bed, "trembling, freezing, burning." (XX: 262) The mighty Hiawatha was powerless to save her. He went into the forest with his bow and prayed for food, but his prayers went unanswered. When he returned to his wigwam, Minnehaha had died:

> And his bursting heart within him
> Uttered such a cry of anguish,
> That the forest moaned and shuddered,
> That the very stars in heaven
> Shook and trembled with his anguish [XX: 265].

After the burial ceremony, Hiawatha took his last farewell. "All my heart is buried with you, / All my thoughts go onward with you!" His consolation was that soon his own life "will be completed" and he'd be following her again, this time "To the land of the Hereafter!" (XX: 266).

The love story between Hiawatha and Minnehaha was as central to the poem as Evangeline and Gabriel's had been eight years earlier. Longfellow had multiple interests in both poems, but he was committed in both to tragic loss as well. Emerson had picked out the brightness of *Hiawatha* and not the darkness when he told Longfellow the poem was "sweet and wholesome as maize." But the poem was more than that as it identified and brought to life not merely Native American customs and tales, but human relationships that readers connected with—and loved. *Hiawatha* was a timeless cross between high culture and pop, between serious poetry and confection. It was Longfellow at his best and worst. But above all, it was a tender and deeply felt love poem. The erudition and scholarship behind the poem was too evident, and Longfellow had made more than one questionable decision, but none of that seemed to discourage readers, who took the story of Hiawatha and Minnehaha into their hearts.

Maybe American readers were saying there is more to being an American poet than simply breaking away from European subjects and literary forms, in the Whitman fashion, which after all didn't really Americanize anyone. Maybe they were simply proud of the way their own Henry Longfellow had elbowed his way to the table of international poetry—and now stood at the top of the list of English speaking poets. For all the world, he seemed the poet America had been waiting for.

One Whitman biographer, trying to be fair in his dismissal of Longfellow, admitted that it is "misleading, of course, to neglect the fact that Longfellow brought alive Native American and New England cultures in popular verse."[44] He also pointed out that while Whitman saw Longfellow as a "smooth imitator of European forms, he could not overlook the immense popularity of his poems," especially as Whitman himself "thirsted for popular acceptance." It was discouraging for Whitman, but his "Song of Myself," the pulsing heartbeat of the first edition of *Leaves of Grass* (also published in 1855), did not capture the imagination or the attention of American readers the way Longfellow's *Song of Hiawatha* had.

It didn't get any better for Whitman in October 1858 when *The Courtship of Miles Standish* was put up for sale by Ticknor & Fields and met with the same success *Evangeline* and *Hiawatha* had enjoyed. By then, however, the numbers were almost expected. It came out on the sixteenth and by noon, Ticknor reported to Longfellow they had already sold five thousand copies in Boston alone—the out-of-town sale couldn't even be estimated yet. That was more than half the original print run of 10,000, with another 10,000 already ordered.[45] On the night the book appeared, according to an announcement in the Boston *Transcript*, English actor George Vandenhoff read from the new poem at the Freeman Place Chapel on Beacon Street.[46] Overall,

Longfellow wrote to Sumner on the seventeenth, *Courtship* "was doing very well" and was "rather a triumph in its way, considering the hard times," a reference to the Panic of 1857 which was taking its toll on discretionary spending. A week later he was able to write in his journal that the new poem "marched steadily on": "Another five thousand are in press; in all, an army of twenty-five thousand—in one week. Fields tells me that in London ten thousand were sold the first day."[47] When Fanny wrote her sister Mary in November, she reported on the book's "great success," which was a relief, she said, because Henry "is so sensitive to any fault-finding."[48]

In fact, not only was the new book well on its way to reaching its projected earnings, it was being spared the angriest critical responses *Evangeline* and *Hiawatha* had sparked. Perhaps the critics were tired of hammering at the citadel that had already become the Longfellow legend. Perhaps they'd grown weary of the fight, or lost interest. Maybe it wasn't fun anymore. The only controversy, Henry wrote to Sumner on December 17, was over Priscilla's spinning wheel: "one party saying that *wool* is never spun on a wheel with a treadle, but only *flax*. The other side says it may be." Then he paused to smile: "Such mighty matters occupy our minds!"[49]

For the new book, Longfellow had returned to the hexameters he'd used in *Evangeline* and made the story into an inverted version of Evangeline's painful saga—a Puritan love story with a happy ending. Moreover, it was much more personal in its focus than the epic sweep of *Hiawatha*, which had taken for its subject the entire course of Native American cultures in the New World. *Courtship* is the much cozier tale of Pilgrims John Alden and Priscilla Mullins, "the Puritan maiden Priscilla," as Longfellow coyly calls her. Perhaps because he was descended from these two *Mayflower* Pilgrims, Longfellow tells their story with warmth and good humor, letting it become at moments an almost comic tale of star-crossed lovers who long for each other but are at least temporarily put at the mercy of John's friendship with the older soldier and statesman Miles Standish, who has set his eye on the Puritan maiden as well. When soldier Standish asks Alden to present his love to Priscilla for him, John was forced by friendship to do so, but as he loved Priscilla too, he was racked with inner turmoil:

> All around him was calm, but within him commotion and conflict,
> Love contending with friendship, and self with each generous impulse.
> To and fro in his breast his thoughts were heaving and dashing,
> As in a foundering ship, with every roll of the vessel,
> Washes the bitter sea, the merciless surge of the ocean! [III: 296-97].

After she has heard Alden present Miles Standish's case, Priscilla, though disappointed, is not deflated or defenseless. Neither was she speechless. In fact,

Longfellow gives her words that have (once again) crept into the national vocabulary: "Archly the maiden smiled, and, with eyes overrunning with laughter, / Said, in a tremulous voice, 'Why don't you speak for yourself, John?'" (III: 306).

Longfellow had imagined into existence a modern woman in Priscilla, one like Fanny perhaps, one who had taken matters into her own hands and chosen John just as Fanny had chosen him—in her own good time and on her own terms. Yes, Priscilla, with her demure beauty and quietly confident independence was the kind of woman Henry liked best. He was pleased with Priscilla and John, with the story he had told, and with the sales figures that kept adding up when, on October 30, 1858, two weeks after *Courtship*'s publication, he attended the next scheduled meeting of the Saturday Club.

By then the Saturday Club had become an exclusive gathering of twenty-odd men meeting on the last Saturday of every month at the Parker House for six hours of good-natured, quick-witted, and often dazzlingly-funny conversation that extended over seven courses paired with perfect reds and whites.[50] One imagines the laughter coming easier and the lips growing looser around the third or fourth course—the sober superheroes of Boston intellectualism shedding inhibitions one bottle of wine after the other. The club had come together in late 1855 or early 1856 with a small core group who set down a few rules, namely that there wouldn't be any rules—except that there had to be unanimous agreement before inviting any new members. And there would be separate checks for dinner. Longfellow, who joined with Felton and Holmes, probably attended his first meeting in April 1857.[51]

Quiet by nature, Henry normally shrank to the background at club meetings where the garrulous Holmes or the magnetic Emerson or any of the other natural talkers entertained for long stretches, but on October 30, 1858, *Courtship* was only two weeks old and already a major addition to the work and reputation of America's Poet, which meant that for one meeting at least, Henry Longfellow was probably not allowed to shrink into the background. He was the man of the hour.

12

July 9, 1861

Even allowing for the unrelenting heartbreak over the death of Baby Fan in 1848, the 1840s and 1850s were good to Henry and Fanny Longfellow, both within the cozy confines of Craigie House and in the outside world of English speaking people who read poetry. But those same decades were marked by the alarmingly violent drift of national politics, a time so explosive that it finally changed both of them. Pacifists in the early 1840s, Henry and Fanny were carried along by the tense rhetoric and dangerous face-offs of the pre–Civil War era to stronger feelings, harsher stances, firmer antislavery sentiments—and a greater inclination to fight for principle as the years wore on. By the end, they both supported the war, specifically the Union's obligation by force of arms to suppress the rebellion—but to arrive at this position, they had to be moved a little at a time by all the North-South flashpoints over eighteen years.

They had both been opposed to President James Polk's Mexican War (1846–1848), believing "manifest destiny" to be a shameful slogan to whip up support for a war that was actually fought just to stack Congress with more slave-state votes. Henry called the war "shabby" and "disgraceful"; Fanny called it "wicked and disgusting."[1] When Alexander Slidell Mackenzie showed up at Craigie House in December 1846, full of "military exultation" that America hadn't lost its "tiger and wolf nature," Fanny was repelled. "It is to me so strangely barbarous to hear a man of years and sense find any glory in that wholesale butchery and murder," she wrote to Emmeline Austin. To her brother Tom, Fanny added that "Polk cannot make an unjust war righteous and fit to be carried on by a Christian people." Henry called it the "unrighteous Mexican War" and was proud of his younger brother Samuel, a Unitarian minister, for denouncing the war from his pulpit and praying for the country "in her hour of shame."[2]

The last of the fighting came in October 1847, followed by the February 1848 Treaty of Guadalupe Hidalgo, whereby Mexico gave up California and New Mexico and agreed to the Rio Grande as the border of Texas. The cost was $18,250,000—plus 1,721 dead from battle, another 12,000 dead from disease, and 4,102 wounded.[3] Its supporters saw the war as an opportunity to extend American boundaries, flex American military muscle, and extend American Protestantism into Catholic territory. Critics saw the war as an imperialist land grab and a transparent political maneuver to gain Congressional seats for the South. There was no middle ground.

Henry and Fanny were also against Henry Clay's Compromise of 1850, with its especially hated Fugitive Slave Bill designed to force Northerners, under the threat of heavy penalties, to return runaway slaves to their Southern owners. Four years later Senator Stephen A. Douglas introduced the Kansas-Nebraska Bill. Designed to navigate the great wilderness into statehood, the Kansas-Nebraska Bill at face value sought to soothe both North and South by leaving the issue of slavery up to the voters—a seemingly impossible-to-criticize, democratically-sanctioned solution. But opponents saw the bill as a way to change the law prohibiting the extension of slavery into the territories, a way in the end to extend slave interests in Congress. Nebraska wouldn't be admitted to the Union until after the Civil War, when the issue of slavery was moot. Kansas, however, was another matter. On January 29, 1861, just as the South was seceding, Kansas was admitted into the Union as a free state, but between passage of Kansas-Nebraska in 1854 and the election of Lincoln in 1860, Kansas was a bloodbath.

Portrait of Fanny in 1859 by Samuel Rowse (courtesy National Park Service. Longfellow House—Washington's Headquarters National Historic Site, LONG 2895).

Longfellow, ca. 1862 (courtesy National Park Service. Longfellow House—Washington's Headquarters National Historic Site, Archives no. 3007-1-2-1-17).

Charles Sumner, whose reputation as an unyielding abolitionist was taking shape in the 1850s, led a small group of congressmen in opposition to slave-owner interests during the vote on Kansas-Nebraska in 1854. His group published "An Appeal of the Independent Democrats" on January 24 in the *National Era*, the same paper that had serialized *Uncle Tom's Cabin* in 1851. The "Appeal" said the bill was "a criminal betrayal of precious rights," the result of "an atrocious plot." Enraged, Douglas rose on January 30 in a packed Senate and called Sumner and his group "the pure, unadulterated representatives of Abolitionism, Free-Soilism, [and] Niggerism."[4] From the sidelines in Cambridge, Henry cheered Sumner on in his campaign against the bill, calling it "the Nebraska Swindle" while Fanny called it "the dreadful Nebraska wickedness"[5] Henry predicted in a letter to Sumner that "the enemy will not prevail" and called the Douglas bill an "abomination."[6] The bill, however, passed easily in the Senate, squeaked by in the House, and was signed into law by President Franklin Pierce on May 30. Kansas was wide open to settlers who would vote at some point on whether they would be a slave state or a free state—but before the voting came the bloodletting.

For two years Missouri "border ruffians" swarmed into the Kansas free-state towns, at first contenting themselves with rigging local elections, but on May 21, 1856, they became so emboldened that they attacked Lawrence for its free-state, abolitionist impudence. A force of some 800 men, facing no resistance, sacked the town, destroying newspaper offices and the Free State Hotel before turning their attention to the homes of elected officials and the stores of local businessmen.[7] Bleeding Kansas, however, had barely begun.

Coinciding with the sack of Lawrence was Sumner's "Crime Against Kansas" speech on the Senate floor. Sumner had told Salmon P. Chase beforehand that Bleeding Kansas had "wrung" his soul and that he intended to "pour it forth," which he did, railing against the "murderous robbers from Missouri" and the "hirelings picked from the drunken spew and vomit" of the South. And then, after two days of sharp attacks and inflamed language, he became a martyr on May 22 when South Carolina Congressman Preston Brooks battered him senseless with a cane in the nearly empty Senate chambers. The assault was so savage and vicious that the war cry of "Bleeding Sumner" soon joined the cry of "Bleeding Kansas." A furious Longfellow wrote to Sumner two days after the attack that his speech had "torn the mask off the faces of traitors"—and he was right when he added that "at last the spirit of the North is aroused."[8] The South had finally managed to unite antislavery people everywhere, most notably a slender 56-year-old abolitionist with Old Testament justice burning in his heart, John Brown.

To many peace-loving abolitionists, violence was, in fact, beginning to seem inescapable. Pacifism wasn't working. The time was right to fight fire with fire. Weren't the border ruffians on record as saying they were willing to substitute the cartridge box for the ballot box? And hadn't they done just that—not only killing abolitionists but scalping them too?[9] The Reverend Henry Ward Beecher of the Plymouth Congregational Church in Brooklyn, had become so incensed over Bleeding Kansas that he raised money in 1855 to distribute rifles to the Free Staters because rifles had more "moral power," he said, than "a hundred Bibles," at least "so far as the slaveholders of Kansas were concerned."[10] "Beecher's Bibles" became symbols of what had previously been thought of as absolutely unacceptable violence, especially for a man of the cloth. But Beecher held his ground, saying that "there are times when self-defense is a religious duty." If Beecher's militant Christianity was unorthodox, his social activism and armed abolitionism seemed long overdue, at least among increasingly angry antislavery Northerners.

Brown, the father of twenty children, was born in Puritan Connecticut in 1800 and by 1846 was living in Springfield, Massachusetts, where he was a member of the African American abolitionist Free Church, which fueled his antislavery sentiments by sponsoring lecturers like Frederick Douglass and Sojourner Truth. An activist from the outset, he helped make Springfield an important abolitionist center and a regular stop on the Underground Railroad. In 1855 he headed west to Kansas with the object of helping defend a few of his sons who had settled there and who were having a hard time coping with the militant proslavery forces.

After the sack of Lawrence, Brown became infuriated that the antislavery residents of the city had not fought the marauding invaders who had attacked them, hadn't even tried to protect their property. His resolve to carry the war against slavery to the Kansas battlefield was taking shape. And then news of Sumner's assault reached Brown and, according to his son Jason, "the men went crazy—*crazy*. It seemed to be the finishing, decisive touch."[11] In the midst of this emotional explosion, someone advised Brown to proceed with caution. "Caution, caution, sir," he replied, "I am eternally tired of hearing that word caution. It is nothing but the word of cowardice."

Brown's plan was simple: to exact a bloody vengeance on slave owners and on the South for its long history of wanton violence against slaves and Indians. The sack of Lawrence and the assault on Sumner, according to Brown biographer David Reynolds, had "converged in his psyche and set off within him an explosion of vindictive rage."[12] In the name of righteousness and answering to a higher power, John Brown was about to strike out against the evil of slavery.

With six men, including four of his own sons, Brown brought his brand of justice to a small proslavery settlement at Pottawatomie Creek some fifty miles south of Lawrence, about ten o'clock on Saturday night the twenty-fourth. They executed five men that night at three different homes. First came James Doyle and his two oldest sons, who were dragged outside and hacked up with recently sharpened broadswords. When the mutilating business was done, John Brown, who had watched as his own sons had inflicted the "justice," fired a single shot into James's head, just to be sure he was dead. Next came Allen Wilkinson half a mile away, who was killed in a similar fashion. Their final victim that night was William Sherman. Like the others, he was taken a short way from his home and slaughtered, his brains lying next to his slashed open head.[13]

Brown managed to escape vigilante justice, and in September, he left Kansas as a well known freedom warrior heading openly to the Northeast on a fund-raising mission for his next foray, a raid on the Harper's Ferry federal arsenal in October 1859, which he envisioned as the start of a slave insurrection in the South. He got to Boston in January 1857, where he conferred with social activist Franklin Sanborn, a 26-year-old schoolteacher in Concord with Transcendentalist connections, about raising $30,000—plus guns and ammunition.

In March he spoke at the Town Hall in Concord, where he was introduced to Emerson and Thoreau, and met with the so-called "Secret Six" who were backing him: Sanborn, Theodore Parker, George Luther Stearns (industrialist and financial supporter of the Kansas free-state settlers), Thomas Wentworth Higginson, Gerrit Smith (who had run for president in 1848 and 1856—and would again in 1860), and Dr. Samuel Gridley Howe. When Brown's October raid at Harper's Ferry ended prematurely with his capture, quick trial, and hanging on December 2, Boston intellectuals took the news badly. Emerson called him a "true hero"; Thoreau said he was a man of "ideals and principles ... unwavering purposes"; Alcott said he was "too noble a man to be sacrificed so."[14] On November 7, Emerson delivered a lecture called "Courage," in which he raised Brown from a flawed romantic hero to a martyred saint—and then he took it up a notch by comparing Brown's impending execution to Christ's crucifixion: Brown was "the new saint awaiting his martyrdom, and who, if he shall suffer, will make the gallows glorious like the cross."[15]

On the day of Brown's execution, there were deathwatches throughout the abolitionist world. They thrilled to the words he had spoken to the judge at his sentencing on November 2: "Now, if it is deemed necessary that I should forfeit my life, for the furtherance of the ends of justice, and mingle my blood further with the blood of millions in this slave country whose rights are disregarded by wicked, cruel, and unjust enactments, I say, let it be done."[16]

A month before the execution, Fanny wrote to Samuel Longfellow, then ministering to a Brooklyn Unitarian congregation, that she'd read a speech of abolitionist Wendell Phillips and found it "electrical." It was "rather too revolutionary for my taste, I must say, though very eloquent. I like Beecher's sermon better, in the Christian spirit it has, although one can't help liking old Brown, so brave and outspoken."[17] Henry may have agreed with his wife that abolitionist rhetoric was "too revolutionary" and perhaps that the still-new Republican party ought to continue with its peaceful antislavery position, but his abolitionist spirit was nonetheless fully roused at Brown's execution: "The Second of December, 1859," Longfellow recorded in his journal, "This will be a great day in history! The date of a New Revolution—quite as much needed as the old one! Even now, as I write, they are leading old John Brown, Ossawattamie [sic] Brown, to execution in Virginia for attempting to rescue Slaves!! This is sowing the Wind to reap the Whirlwind, which will come soon!"[18]

The combustible 1850s, which had already occasioned flash fires over the Compromise of 1850, the pursuit of fugitive slaves in New England and elsewhere, the passage of the Kansas-Nebraska Act, the joint horrors of Bleeding Kansas and Bleeding Sumner, and the elevation of John Brown into sainthood, needed nothing but a single match to go up in flames. Abraham Lincoln provided it.

Events of the summer-long 1860 political season saw rising temperatures as the political parties all maneuvered into place for the November election. In Chicago in May, the still-new antislavery Republican Party gathered at the "Wigwam" where New York governor William Seward was expected to be nominated on the first ballot. But that didn't happen, and the men who were thought to be alternatives all faded, while Illinois Favorite Son, Abraham Lincoln, already known as Honest Abe (born in a log cabin and an actual rail-splitter), had the rabid support of thousands of screaming Wigwammers. He was the living embodiment of the Republican ideal that opportunity and hard work could take a man from rags to riches.

When the balloting began, Seward took a commanding 70½ vote lead over Lincoln, but fell short of the nomination by 59½ votes. Accompanied by ear-piercing support from boisterous Lincoln supporters, the second ballot drew the two men almost even; by the third ballot Seward supporters started jumping ship in earnest until Ohio changed four of its votes and put Lincoln over the top. One contemporary reported that "there was the rush of a great wind in the van of a storm—and in another breath, the storm was there ... thousands cheering with the energy of insanity."[19]

To Southerners, however, this raucous display of American democracy was the final blow that ended their participation in it—or it would be if the

Republican anti-slave, anti–South candidate Lincoln were actually to be elected. But that seemed unlikely early in the election season. As the summer turned into fall, however, political observers began to wonder if the odds might not be shifting in Lincoln's favor. The Democrats split along sectional lines and suicidally put up two separate candidates, one from the North, the Little Giant himself, Stephen A. Douglas, and one from the South, John C. Breckinridge. Then siphoning off more potential pro-slavery Democratic votes was a brand new party, the Constitutional Unionist, made up of leftover Whigs who hadn't joined the Republicans and disaffected nativists who had formerly been Know-Nothings and members of the American party. They nominated John Bell of Tennessee. The impossible was beginning to take shape. When the final votes were tallied, Douglas and Breckinridge polled about two and a quarter million votes between them, which together would have been more than enough to win the popular vote for the Democrats as Lincoln tallied less than two million, though he had a commanding electoral college lead, 180 to 84. Bell's count was not quite 600,000 votes and 39 electoral college votes. When all the votes had been finally tallied, rail-splitter Honest Abe had scored a convincing victory, though he had to run on a practical compromise platform in order to distance the party, officially at least, from John Brown's bloody rampage, which they labeled as "the gravest of crimes."[20] It didn't fool anybody.

Henry Longfellow voted for Lincoln early on November 6. He wrote to his sister Anne, "I am feeling very well and full of faith in the triumph of the good cause, to which you and I belong."[21] And the next day, when the results were in, he wrote in his journal: "This is a great victory. One can hardly overrate its importance. It is the redemption of the country. Freedom is triumphant."[22]

After the election, however, with the Republican Lincoln poised to assume the presidency, Southern leaders redoubled their talk of secession, but there was a new sense of urgency in their voices. The talk sounded less like a threat issued to gain a congressional advantage, more like a grim reality. Six states scheduled conventions between December and February to vote on it. It wouldn't be easy to get the Lower South and Upper South to line up as a single country because each state had its own history and political machinery and self-interest to work out, plus strong Unionist minorities to overcome, but in the end slavery and economics and anger over the insufferable self-righteousness of the abolitionists and their warlike election of Lincoln united the eleven states that became the Confederacy.

One by one between December 1860 and June 1861, each Southern state legislature voted to secede, but though the South thought little of the North's heart for a fight, the new Confederate States of America worried about the belligerent stance Republicans had taken at their nominating convention in May. Secession, the Republicans had said, would be treated as "contemplated treason, which it is the imperative duty of an indignant people sternly to rebuke and forever silence."[23] Battle lines were fixed.

Barely a month passed before Longfellow began worrying. "Congress comes together to-day. The sky looks troubled; and disunion is threatened. I hope the North will stand firm and not bate one jot of its manhood. Secession of the North from Freedom would be tenfold worse than secession of the South from the Union."[24] The next week he sounded even more concerned—and ready for war: "Rebellion stalks through the land. South Carolina talks nothing but fire and fury. She says she will secede this time. Better this than have the North yield; which I am always a little afraid of. I hope we shall stand firm, and so end the matter once for all."[25] When Fanny wrote to her brother the next day, she said they hadn't heard yet if South Carolina's secession was a *"fait accompli."* "The great fear is now of unworthy compromises being extorted from the North—far worse than losing those few troublesome states. I trust, however, the Republicans will stand firm, after such encouragement from the people to do so, and [after] such a struggle and victory...."[26] Once again, Henry and Fanny were standing arm in arm, shoulder to shoulder.

South Carolina voted to secede on December 20, citing Lincoln and the hated abolitionist Republicans as the immediate cause. Four days later, Fanny wrote to her friend Emmeline in France: "I suppose you are anxious to know if we are all falling apart because South Carolina has been crazy enough to vote herself out of our company." They were not, she announced. She predicted South Carolina's "fate will be piteous if she does not speedily come back again." It was just as much President James Buchanan's fault as South Carolina's, Fanny went on, for matters would never have come to this pass if he hadn't been so derelict in his duties: South Carolina seems, "in spite of always having had her own way, and now 'owning the President,' so that he surrenders Fort Moultrie at her wish, thus violating his oath to preserve the Government property (for which it is generally hoped he will be impeached), to have nourished such a hate of us that it will be difficult for her ever to be friends again."[27] Like headstrong children, Fanny went on, the South was behaving like a collection of "refractory states" that had better "come to their senses." "They hope we are in great distress (through this whole trouble showing a most blood-thirsty spirit), but we are not, and are not likely to be with such resources behind us." The North, she predicted, would "stand firm and stand together."[28]

Meantime, life at Craigie House proceeded as close to normal as possible, the most important family issue being whether or not to buy their regular cottage at Nahant, which Henry decided to do before Christmas for $5,000 (in partnership with Tom Appleton), which led to plans for remodeling before their first summer as owners rather than renters. It was to be a long-term family affair. The children, Fanny reported to Emmeline in February, had been well that winter, except for colds. She was especially happy, she said, "teaching my little girls," who were "so good and ready to learn." Six-year-old Annie Allegra "is a droll little thing," playing church with her dolls and preaching to them. She and her 8-year-old sister Edie also "live over every phase of married life with their dolls."[29] Eleven-year-old Alice was not only a "good child," but "so wise she is quite a companion for me." The boys "study at home," she said, "and I read them Shakespeare and Scott to illustrate their history lessons." But balancing the happiness she felt about her children, was news of her father, who was, she told Emmeline, "very feeble this winter, and I cannot but feel that his useful and beloved life will not 'be stretched out on the rack of this rough world' much longer...."[30] Amidst the political turmoil and the daily dose of bad news in the newspapers, Fanny kept her family close.

There was even a new poem that winter. Longfellow had begun it back in April after a long walk with Sumner through Boston's "Little Britain," which included Copp's Hill burial ground and the Old North Church, which especially interested him. He climbed his way up to the top of the bell tower, fighting off "innumerable pigeons" while his ears rang with the chiming of the bells. And from that vantage point, looking out toward the Mystic River, he recalled the old story, that "from this tower was hung the lantern, as a signal that the British troops had left Boston for Concord."[31] The finished poem appeared in the January 1861 *Atlantic*, an early copy arriving at Craigie House on December 20—only by its timing, it sounded as much like a Northern call to arms as the retelling of a Revolutionary War story.[32]

The galloping opening that would be memorized by millions took its place at once in the museum of American literary history:

> Listen, my children, and you shall hear
> Of the midnight ride of Paul Revere,
> On the eighteenth of April, in Seventy-five;
> Hardly a man is now alive
> Who remembers that famous day and year.
>
> He said to his friend, "If the British march
> By land or sea from the town to-night,
> Hang a lantern aloft in the belfry arch

12. July 9, 1861

> Of the North Church tower as a signal light,—
> One, if by land, and two, if by sea;
> And I on the opposite shore will be,
> Ready to ride and spread the alarm
> Through every Middlesex village and farm
> For the country folk to be up and to arm."

Longfellow was rescuing (or creating) Revere's reputation as a Revolutionary War hero, but readers could hardly miss the poem's relevance to the current political crisis and the impending cataclysm. When Revere had ridden "through the gloom and the light" in April 1775, it was clear that "the fate of a nation was riding that night"—and it was again in January 1861:

> You know the rest. In the books you have read,
> How the British Regulars fired and fled,—
> How the farmers gave them ball for ball,
> From behind each fence and farm-yard wall,
> Chasing the red-coats down the lane,
> Then crossing the fields to emerge again
> Under the trees at the turn of the road,
> And only pausing to fire and load.

They were inspirational lines, a reminder of what the descendants of those same farmers might be called upon to do once again, this time against rebelling sister states who had turned against them. Paul Revere's warning resonated in this new context:

> So through the night rode Paul Revere;
> And so through the night went his cry of alarm
> To every Middlesex village and farm,—
> A cry of defiance and not of fear,
> A voice in the darkness, a knock at the door,
> And a word that shall echo forevermore!
> For, borne on the night-wind of the Past,
> Through all our history, to the last,
> In the hour of darkness and peril and need,
> The people will waken and listen to hear
> The hurrying hoof-beats of that steed,
> And the midnight message of Paul Revere.

In the light of worsening national politics, the never-ending talk of secession, and the fearful coming of violent rebellion, Longfellow had latched on to an earlier moment of patriotic nationalism and personal heroism. Paul Revere was suddenly relevant once again. But even with a new patriotic poem and the maintenance of regular family patterns at Craigie House, it was impossible for Henry and Fanny to avoid the political upheavals that were unfolding day by day.

Their letters and journals show how completely involved they were. The secession of South Carolina, Fanny told Tom on January 7, "made very little stir," at least compared to "the spirited act of Major Anderson in leaving Fort Moultrie, which the President [Buchanan] refused to strengthen, and saving his devoted band by removing to Fort Sumter, which is impregnable." Robert Anderson was a Kentuckian put in charge of Fort Moultrie partly as a conciliatory gesture to South Carolina; Northern interests, Buchanan was saying, rested in the hands of a former slave-holding Southerner. But Anderson surprised the South, choosing to defend the North's position in Charleston Harbor by abandoning Moultrie and landing his men at the larger and more strategically placed Sumter. If it came to that, and it certainly seemed that it might, he was going to defend his position against South Carolina's attack. His bravery, Fanny went on, "sent a thrill through all the country, and he is the hero of the hour. Such an act of patriotism was so refreshing amidst the treachery of the Cabinet and the President."[33] The only hope left, Fanny told her friend Emmeline on February 12, was Lincoln's inauguration on March 4. Maybe, she said, Lincoln's "firmer hand will guide us to calmer waters."[34]

On January 28, Longfellow spilled his anger out into his journal. "Six states have left the Union, led by South Carolina. President Buchanan is an antediluvian, an *après-moi-le-déluge* President, who does not care what happens, if he gets safely through his term. We owe the present state of things mainly to him. He has sympathized with the Disunionists. It is now too late to put the fire out. We must let it burn out."[35] The next day in a letter to Sumner, he warned that it was unwise to "have any clause inserted into the Constitution which shall even seem to favor Slavery. Let us make an end of that business once and forever." He ended the letter with, "Yours ever without compromise or concession."[36]

On Sunday, February 3, Fanny and the girls went to church at the Stone Chapel in Boston, while Henry went instead to hear Emerson at the Masonic Hall, which he called Theodore Parker's "parish."[37] Not even the Stone Chapel's beauties and the church's unique connection of Unitarianism, Anglicanism, and Congregationalism could long distract Fanny from the urgency of the political crisis, however. Her tone was becoming daily more and more excitable, anxious, and righteous. "Everything is as unsettled as ever," she wrote to her sister on Monday the 4th. "The southern states go on seceding and helping themselves to all the forts and navy yards they can, and the government, for fear of bloodshed, does little or nothing to stop them." She said Lincoln's election had only been "an excuse for all this treason" and that it seemed the South "had not one sensible man among them" and was instead "over-powered by the threats of the mob, led on by their worst politicians."[38]

On Tuesday Henry observed in his journal that there was nothing but "the usual dreary news in the papers," which he characterized as "the South arrogant and impudent; the North like a giant weak in the knees."[39] On Friday he capsulized the situation for Tom Appleton: "State after State detaches itself and drifts down the Gulfstream of perdition." Meanwhile, he went on, warming to the subject, Buchanan just "sits and twirls his thumbs." He was happier reporting that "the main body of the Republican Party stands firm, and will make no compromise with traitors"—compromise after all being nothing more than "a euphemism for surrender," he said. But then he fell back into frustrated anger: "If for once in their lives the whole North would only go together, it would put an end forever to this nonsense."[40] The chance for peace was in fact dropping faster than the temperature in Boston, which fell sixty degrees in one twelve-hour space on February 8. "It takes one's breath away," Henry wrote.[41]

With Lincoln's inauguration only about a month away, Henry and Fanny allowed themselves a frantic hope that the new president would be able to right the ship. Fanny wrote to Emmeline on February 12: "He has shown such dignified reticence through all this excitement, and is thought very fearless and firm in not compromising with traitors."[42] She told her brother five days later that Lincoln was working his way to the capitol for the inauguration, "making speeches in a hearty Western manner, taking all the enthusiasm as proofs of devotion to the Union, not to him, and carrying the hearts of the people with him. I think he will prove just the man for the hour."[43]

After Lincoln's inauguration on March 4, Fanny was pleased with the Address, which stressed that he had no intention of interfering with slavery where it already existed. Fanny wrote her brother Tom that Lincoln was "strong and sensible, and very conciliatory"; Henry was heartened by what he took to be Lincoln's "firm" manner.[44] Fanny told her brother, with a combination of wishful thinking and worrisome uncertainty that the worst was "apparently" over, that the "back is now broken" of the "well-planned plot." Inauguration Day had spawned hope, even if it was unrealistic.

Five weeks later, at 4:30 a.m. on April 12, South Carolina fired on Fort Sumter, a thirty-three-hour shelling that took its toll on the undermanned and undersupplied forces led by Anderson, who surrendered his partially destroyed and burning fort on the thirteenth. "And so the War begins!" Longfellow wrote in his journal on the twelfth. "Who can foresee the end?"[45]

The attack on Fort Sumter was the final insult that pushed Fanny over completely to the pro-war stance that was sweeping the North. "The spirit of rebellion" had taken over the South, she reported to Emmeline on April 19, "but the people North and West are roused to a state of patriotism which fuses all parties in the one resolve to protect the government, seriously threatened at Washington, and volunteers are pouring south like a spring tide, with all the enthusiasm of '76—men leaving their business and families at an hour's notice—and the poor women (who always have the hardest lot on these occasions), burying their sad thoughts in busy labors—in making shirts for the soldiers, and possibly later will have the sadder duty of preparing for the wounded."[46]

The floodgates were open and Fanny's feelings poured out: It was the South's "atrocious acts" and "vile ambition" that were to blame for this crisis. "I have no sympathy with the thoughts, desires, civilization (if it can be called such) of the South." She knew how jingoistic she sounded and tried to regroup by saying "still I abhor war wherever and whenever produced" and by saying that she hoped this one would be short—but there was a limit to her now worn-thin pacifism. She was already annoyed with Lincoln, who had been in office only six weeks but was already "too long patient and forbearing," she said. The fall of Sumter, "where seventy starved men had to yield to seven thousand and most powerful batteries," she wrote, "has stirred all our hearts with horror and indignation." She was proud that Boston "has been full of the departing soldiers, and the Massachusetts regiments will be the first to arrive to the country's aid."[47]

Ten days later Fanny took up the banner once again in another letter to Emmeline. "Now the North is roused with a glorious heart-beat for liberty." Such a display of Northern loyalty Fanny said, had left the South "amazed and chagrined." They had hoped "we were too divided in opinion to stand against them," but they were wrong. What was more, they couldn't "comprehend the intense love of country ... all classes here display." She said she was "proud to live at such a time" when the people of the North, "risking all for an idea of right," would make "every self-sacrifice to sustain its flag from further outrage." And then she said what she'd been hinting at for months: "It was worth some loss of life and property to behold the heroic virtues so alive after our long dream of self-indulgence."[48] Emmeline may have remembered a letter from Fanny fifteen years earlier about the Mexican War, which Fanny had called "wholesale butchery"; she couldn't bear the thought of American "military exultation." Everything had changed for her. This new war was worth fighting.

As the weather warmed, Fanny and Henry made plans for their annual retreat to what was now their very own summer cottage at Nahant. They hoped they'd be lucky enough to land the charming one-time Brook Farmer George Curtis as one of their summer guests, Henry writing with an invitation on June 8. Curtis was the one they called "Howadji," taken from the Arabic word for "wealthy traveler," because he'd written a popular 1851 book *Nile Notes of a Howadji*. And he'd been their guest before, both at Craigie House (where he had his own room) and at Newport in 1852. Howadji could be counted on to add humor and grace to every party.[49] Henry wrote to Curtis that even though Fanny's father was "very feeble" and "fading away," they still hoped to get out to the cottage—and they hoped he'd be able to join them there for a while.

But when summer arrived they were still in Cambridge waiting for Nathan Appleton to die, every day getting hotter and more uncomfortable. Agassiz came to dinner on July 1. The next day Fanny and Henry took 10-year-old Alice to Boston to see a hippopotamus that *Vanity Fair* was advertising in thirty-two lines of doggerel:

> AY, what's ailing Boston now?
> What a clamor! What a muss!
> Flushed with pride is every brow—
> They have a hippopotamus![50]

On the evening of the third, they stood in the yard and craned their necks to see "a splendid comet in the North, near the Great Bear." There were fireworks, Alice's first, on the fourth, "a very hot, noisy day," Fanny reported to her sister, though "tranquil enough here."[51] On Saturday the sixth, Fanny took Alice into Boston once again, this time for a dental appointment and then to see a whale that was on exhibit. But it was punishingly hot by then. On the seventh, Fanny wrote to Erny, who had already gone up to Nahant with Charley, that "Poor Annie is very droopy with the heat, and Edie has to get her hair in a net to free her neck from its weight."[52] Straining more every day against the oppressive heat, they finally decided to make the move to Nahant. Fanny rationalized that Nahant was only a little farther away from Beacon Hill than Cambridge, after all, and, as she put it in a letter to her sister dated July 5, "I can get up by the boat in an hour to see dear papa."[53] They set the following Thursday, the eleventh, as their day of departure.

On the afternoon of Tuesday the ninth, Fanny and the girls were in the library that served as their family room, while Henry worked and napped in his study a room away, everyone coping with yet another hot and sticky summer scorcher. The household that day was reduced by three, the boys in Nahant with their Uncle Tom, and, according to Henrietta Dana Skinner, a young neighbor whose brother later married Edith, Alice had gone up to Portland.[54] In fact, everyone on Brattle Street who could had already left town by then. The Longfellows were therefore not only hot and sticky, but abandoned too—an uncomfortable summer reality not lost on Fanny or Henry as they waited out Nathan Appleton's death watch with as much grace as they could muster. Fanny may have been saying again to herself what she had written to Erny two days earlier: "We are all sighing for the good sea breeze instead of this stifling land one filled with dust."[55]

The heat bore down on them as the sun rose and peaked at 95 that afternoon, eased just a little by an occasional warm breeze. Fanny decided to cool poor Edith by trimming back a few of her long, blonde, curls.[56] And then, thinking it a good idea to collect a few locks in a sealed envelope—for posterity perhaps or distant relatives or simple sentimentality, Fanny got the paraphernalia ready—the scissors, the envelope, the sealing wax, the candle to melt it, and the matches to light the candle. The two young daughters were the only ones to witness what followed, which means the exact sequence of events in the next seconds will never be exactly known. It may be most likely that one of those warm breezes that afternoon blew in through the open window flickering the candle flame that then licked gently at Fanny's white muslin dress stretched over steel hoops, which then went up immediately into a ball of fire. It was breathtakingly, heartbreakingly, stunningly fast.[57]

When Felton reported the story in a letter to Sumner in Washington, he said that Fanny, "wrapped in a sheet of flame," went "flying from the library to the front room where Longfellow was sitting," perhaps at that moment napping, according to another account.[58] Rising quickly in sudden and confused terror, Henry "threw a rug around her," according to Felton, but it wasn't large enough to put out the fire. Frantically, Fanny broke loose for a few steps then rushed back to Henry's arms. They clutched in an embrace that protected Fanny's face from the flames that had already burned through all the light fabrics of her dress and undergarments—and then burned deeply into her legs and body, an unbearable, unendurable suffering. When the fire finally burned out, Fanny was carried upstairs to her bed and their physician was called. "She bore the agony like a martyr dying at the stake," Felton reported to Sumner. "Poor Longfellow: he was dreadfully but not fatally burned. His hands and face suffered most severely."

Finding a doctor still in Cambridge or Boston that hot summer day was difficult. According to one report, the Longfellow family doctor Morrill Wyman was out of town as was a second unidentified doctor. The doctor who did arrive was the only one available, a Dr. William Otis Johnson. He got to Craigie House as quickly as he could, but it seemed an eternity before pain relieving ether could be administered and before Fanny and Henry could slip off into a restless area between consciousness and unconsciousness for the rest of the night, the temperature at midnight dropping after an evening shower to a still sticky 80 degrees.[59]

In the morning, according to Felton, Fanny asked for coffee, then drifted back into a sleep she never woke from. Only 43, Fanny Longfellow died between ten and eleven, "her face," Felton wrote to Sumner, "pale and calm and sweet, as ever in life."[60] The wife of Dr. Johnson years later reported that according to her husband, Fanny wore an expression "so spiritual, so far removed from this world of suffering, that the physician in ministering to her felt a hushed reverence as if in the presence of a martyred saint."[61]

Henry, under the influence of ether and laudanum, drifted in and out of consciousness, and as Felton put it, "he is growing idiotic, begs not to be sent to an asylum." Felton was barely able to describe the horror: "Was there ever such a woeful scene—such an awful and inexplicable overthrow? God help our dear friend in his unparalleled bereavement. God help us all in this weary world."[62]

On the day Fanny died, the *New York Times* ran a brief notice that Mrs. Longfellow "was melting sealing wax on some envelopes, when a lighted match set fire to her clothing." The burns were so serious "that there is scarcely a hope of her recovery." Prof. Longfellow, the story said, "was seriously but not fatally burned." For a later edition that day, the *Times* reported that "The wife of Prof. LONGFELLOW died from her burns about noon to-day." On the twelfth, the *Times* reprinted a *Boston Daily Advertiser* article on Fanny's death. According to this account, Dr. Wyman had indeed arrived, and with Dr. Johnson and Dr. Henry J. Bigelow of Harvard, famous for his use of ether, they "did all that surgical skill could do." But it was too late. "Mrs. Longfellow rallied a little, but at 11 o'clock she was forever released from suffering."

Felton's is not, however, the only available source for the sequence of events. Another comes from Anne Allegra, who carried guilt over her mother's death for the rest of her life.[63] She was only five at the time, but she remembered the event half a century later with the precision of someone who had gone over and over the horror until the version she recalled, whether accurate or not, became fixed in her memory as the one and only truth. In her version, Fanny was less frantic than in Felton's. Her mother was cutting Edith's hair near the window seat where Annie sat dangling her feet. Annie was holding a box of what she called "parlor" matches, the kind that needed to be scratched on a rough surface to ignite. While she played with the matches, taking them out of and then putting them back into the box, one of the matches fell to the floor, and when she dropped down to retrieve it, either her foot or her mother's landed on the match and ignited it, thus setting Fanny's gauzy white muslin dress on fire. The candle had not yet been lit, according to Anne Allegra. She also remembered that despite her agonies, her mother remained in control of the situation, and that she walked almost calmly into Henry's study, where he was indeed sleeping in an armchair near the fireplace. Henry then sent Annie upstairs to get the servants, thus ending her first-hand observations, although she added that her father took her mother to the front hall where Fanny collapsed into unconsciousness. Henry then ran into the dining room for a pitcher of water. Finally, after Fanny had been carried upstairs by servants and gently put into bed, they sent for a doctor, which proved more difficult than expected. At that point Edith and Anne were taken to the Dana house on nearby Berkeley Street where they spent the next few days. According to Anne, her brothers were indeed at Nahant, but her sister Alice was visiting friends nearby, not in Portland.

Edith too had her memory of the events, and she was convinced that she, not her sister, had been playing with the matches and had dropped one on the floor. But it was Anne who felt the guilt so strongly that she would say flatly for many years after that she had killed her mother, which Henry tried to explain to her was not true. The guilt persisted however, leading Henry at one point to say despairingly that they'd have to change her middle name from Allegra to Penserosa, from happy to sad.[64]

On Saturday the thirteenth, on what would have been her eighteenth wedding anniversary, Fanny was buried at Mt. Auburn Cemetery. (Nathan Appleton died on the fourteenth, and was buried next to her.) At home that day, Fanny's coffin had been placed for viewing in the center of the library on the oak Elizabethan Revival table they had bought just a few years earlier. It was the same room where the fire had started, and which Felton and an endless stream of guests remembered with bitter irony as "the scene of so many pleasures."[65] "Her lovely face [was] untouched by flame or any marks of long suffering," Henrietta Dana Skinner recalled, "unforgettable to all who looked upon it."[66] A wreath of orange blossoms, in memory of what she had worn on her wedding day, had been placed on her head, and a white-rose cross as a symbol of purity and true love rested on her breast. Around the room were large flower arrangements.

Visitors began arriving at noon. "All was still," Felton wrote to Sumner, "hushed—in the presence of death—such a death, and such a victim!"[67] Guests sobbed openly around the room, giving vent to emotions "that even men could not wholly control." There was a service led by Dr. Peabody, according to Felton, which ended without people rising to leave because they seemed "reluctant to take the last look," he said. But eventually the line formed and the mourners began the one-mile procession down Brattle Street to the cemetery—without Henry, who was still wrapped in bandages, under medication, and confined to his bed, unable even to receive the mourners down below much less walk with them to the cemetery.

Felton described the funeral for Sumner, the "short and fervent prayer from Dr. Gannett," the tomb "surrounded by tall trees, now in full leaf," and the bright sunshine that "stole in through the overarching foliage, and fell in bright spots upon the green earth where still lay the open coffin." Fanny had a "placid countenance," he said, "more lovely, at the very last moment, than ever." And then the coffin was closed, Felton walking away with "a weight of sorrow that no words can tell," but at the same time "filled with a sense of the soothing power of nature, the harmony of the scene with the character of Fanny, and the surpassing sweetness of every memory connected with her beautiful and happy life."[68]

No one to that point, Felton told Sumner, had seen Longfellow. "I dread to think of him bereaved of Fanny: she was so perfect a companion of his daily existence, and sharer of his glory."[69] Echoing the thought was a comment of Hawthorne to James Fields in a letter of the fourteenth: "One would think that there ought to have been no deep sorrow in the life of a man like him; and now comes the blackest of shadows, which no sunshine hereafter can ever penetrate! I shall be afraid to meet him again; he cannot be the man that I have known."[70]

Felton reported to Sumner that he had finally been able to see their old friend at Craigie House on Wednesday the seventeenth and found him "in a calm state of mind"; he marveled at how Longfellow's "sweet and lovely nature" could still be in place, even after "this great affliction."[71] Henry spoke "with natural freedom—though with the deepest emotion," Felton went on, and was consoled that Fanny had "been spared a long and lingering decay," which meant he would remember her always "in the perfection of her beauty." Felton was relieved. As to their friend's injuries, he continued, it would be a long time before they would completely heal, and he was for the present unable even to reply to the letters, including those from Sumner, that were pouring in. "His face is still swollen and he cannot yet shave: but the burns on his nose and his left cheek are already healed." But Henry dreaded, according to Felton, his full recovery because then, he said, "I shall have to take up the great burden, and I do not know how I shall bear it."[72]

Longfellow tried for the rest of his life, but never could. Not completely. During the first year after Fanny's death, he managed to function day to day by taking care of the children and deadening his emotional pain under mountains of work. Gradually he resumed friendships and correspondence—and eventually thought about falling in love again. But in the summer of 1861, Henry Longfellow, who had already lost one wife a quarter century earlier, found himself alone once again—this time, if possible, under even more tragic circumstances. He was in the depths of the same despair he had felt after Mary's death and that he had put into "The Rainy Day" in about 1840: "My thoughts still cling to the mouldering Past, / But the hopes of youth fall thick in the blast, / And the days are dark and dreary." The pain was so visibly etched on his face that Annie Fields later wrote that "forever after the death of his wife, he was a different man."[73]

He was different in one very obvious way and one not so obvious. As a visible symbol of how much he had changed after Fanny's death, Longfellow never shaved again. Some said he grew his beard to hide his scars, but it's more likely he was announcing that the man Fanny had fallen in love with was gone forever, just as she was. No longer would he present himself to the world as Fanny had seen him and known him and loved him. From 1861, his fifty-fourth year, Henry Longfellow would grow into the shaggy literary figure W.D. Howells later called "The White Longfellow." The less obvious difference was his private pain, which he marked ritualistically in his journals on May 10 every year, the date of his and Fanny's "secret anniversary," when Fanny had finally accepted his proposal in 1843. On that date for many years after Fanny's death, Longfellow wrote a short line from Dante, from the famous story of Paolo and Francesca, the doomed lovers in Canto V of *The Inferno*. Francesca's lament became Longfellow's: "There is no greater sorrow / Than to be mindful of the happy time / in misery."[74]

By the middle of August, a month after Fanny's death, Longfellow was at the Nahant cottage struggling to provide some semblance of an ordered, normal life for the children. And from there he broke his silence in a long letter to Fanny's sister Mary, a letter he knew he had to write, but was dreading. "How I am alive after what I have seen, I know not," he wrote. He was being "patient, if not resigned," he said, thanking God "hourly" for what he described as "the beautiful life" he and Fanny had shared for eighteen years. All during their marriage, he went on, Fanny had been "an inexpressible delight" to him, and he'd "loved her more and more to the end": "I never looked at her without a thrill of pleasure—she never came into a room where I was without my heart beating quicker, nor went out without my feeling that something of the light went with her." He knew, he said, that he'd "preached resignation to others" and that he didn't want to appear a "cast-away" in the moment of his own deepest suffering, so he told Mary that he was consoled by "infinite, tender memories" and by the "sweetness" that had always come from Fanny. "That noble, loyal, spiritual nature always uplifted and illuminated mine, and always will, to the end."[75]

In 1879, eighteen years after Fanny's death and three years before his own, Longfellow wrote a meditation he called "The Cross of Snow," which wrapped his still-present grief inside the intricate patterns of a Petrarchan love sonnet that wasn't published until after his death:

12. July 9, 1861

In the long, sleepless watches of the night,
    A gentle face—the face of one long dead—
    Looks at me from the wall, where round its head
    The night-lamp casts a halo of pale light.
Here in this room she died; and soul more white
    Never through martyrdom of fire was led
    To its repose; nor can in books be read
    The legend of a life more benedight. [blessed]

There is a mountain in the distant West
    That, sun-defying, in its deep ravines
    Displays a cross of snow upon its side.
Such is the cross I wear upon my breast
    These eighteen years, through all the changing scenes
    And seasons, changeless since the day she died.

Chapter Notes

Preface

1. T.S. Eliot, "Tradition and the Individual Talent," *Selected Essays* (New York: Harcourt, Brace, 1950), 4.
2. Ibid., 8.
3. "addresses itself to our passions": Letter to Caroline Doane. Jan. 22, 1826. *Letters*: I, 144. He was objecting to what he called "sensuality" in a James Gates Percival poem, "The Mind," which had just been published in Boston.

Prologue

1. *Letters*: I, 459.
2. Lawrance Thompson, *Young Longfellow* (New York: Macmillan, 1938), 188–89.

Chapter 1

1. "celebrated": Thompson, 15; "elegantly named": Edward Wagenknecht, *Longfellow: A Full-Length Portrait* (New York: Longman's, 1955), 2.
2. Thompson, 17 and 345, n. 18.
3. Longfellow was certainly not alone gaining early admission: John Adams began at Harvard when he was 16 in 1751; Thomas Jefferson went to William & Mary at age 16 in 1759; Ralph Waldo Emerson was 14 when he entered Harvard in 1817; and James Russell Lowell began there at age 15 in 1834. Starting at Bowdoin the same year as Longfellow, Nathaniel Hawthorne was 17, and Franklin Pierce, the future fourteenth president of the United States, was 16 when he began there in 1820.
4. There are slight variations in the descriptions of the campus in Longfellow's time: Thompson, 24–25; Brenda Wineapple, *Hawthorne: A Life* (New York: Knopf, 2003), 46; Charles Calhoun, *A Small College in Maine* (Brunswick, ME: Bowdoin College, 1993), 40–41; 46; 53. A shortage of dormitory space forced the Longfellow boys to board for their first year with a family off campus on Federal Street. Thompson, 30.
5. Hawthorne: Wineapple, 46; Longfellow: Thompson, 25, 376, n. 11.
6. Thompson, 31–2; 35–36; 41. At recitations students were quizzed on memorized lessons and called on to translate passages they hadn't seen before.
7. Robert Cantwell, *Nathaniel Hawthorne: The American Years* (New York: Rinehart, 1948), 68.
8. *Letters*: I, 33.
9. Thomas Wentworth Higginson, *Henry Wadsworth Longfellow* (Boston, MA: Houghton Mifflin, 1902), 19.
10. "my sweet friend" and "my fair cousin": letters to Caroline Doane. Dec. 31, 1825, and March 13, 1826. *Letters*: I, 141 and 145; "one of the sweetest and most elegant girls, that I ever beheld": To Caroline Doane. Nov. 1, 1825. *Letters*: I, 137; "excellent piece of divinity": To Caroline Doane. March 13, 1826. *Letters*: I, 145.
11. *Letters*: I, 55. December Exhibition: a formal part of the school calendar characterized by Thomas Wentworth Higginson (21) as "a sort of minor Commencement."
12. "The Battle of Lovell's Pond" was Longfellow's first published poem, Nov. 17, 1820. See Thompson, 346–47, n. 23; *Letters*: I, 55.
13. http://beforeitsnews.com/alternative/2010/12/the-grizzly-death-of-king-philip-beheaded-and-quartered-body-tied-in-trees-for-the-birds-to-pluck-316398.html.
14. *Letters*: I, 56, n. 1.
15. Higginson, 21–22.
16. *Letters*: I, 57–58.
17. *Life*: I, 28.
18. Dec. 18, 1824. *Letters*: I, 97
19. June 27, 1830. *Letters*: I, 342. Italics are Longfellow's.

20. Alice Longfellow, "Longfellow with His Children," *Strand* (Sept. 1897): 250. [Clipping]
21. *Ibid.*
22. For descriptions, see Wagenknecht, *Full-Length*, 81; Herbert S. Gorman, *A Victorian American* (New York: George H. Doran, 1926), 61; Higginson, 19; Charles Calhoun, *Longfellow: A Rediscovered Life* (Boston, MA: Beacon Press, 2004), 32.
23. See William Charvat in *The Profession of Authorship in America: 1800–1870* (New York: Columbia University Press, 1968): 100. "It would be difficult to prove that there is any appreciable difference in the public status of poets then and now [mid-twentieth century]. Normal parents and relatives in the nineteenth century were as dismayed as our own to hear a potentially 'useful' future citizen express a predilection for verse-writing; and normal boys, who are always representative of society as a whole, then as now persecuted the sissy who presumed to rhyme and made him think of it as something un- or anti-social. The youthful poet has always been excommunicated."
24. Calhoun, *Longfellow*, 24.
25. March 13, 1824. *Letters*: I, 83.
26. *Portland Advertiser* poems: Thompson, 61 and 354, n. 12; "Lay Monastery": *Ibid.*, 77–78; compromise his calling: "The Literary Spirit of Our Country," part II of "The Lay Monastery" (April 1, 1825).
27. Longfellow's *USLG* publications: Calhoun, *Longfellow*, 37–38; $43.67: Thompson, 62 and 360, n. 13.
28. "since the commencement": *Letters*: I, 83; Benjamin Orr: Thompson, 56.
29. James McHenry: Thompson, 61–62 and 354, n. 13.
30. *Letters*: I, 94–95.
31. *Letters*: I, 98–100.
32. "very pleasant": Thompson, 58–60.
33. Aug. 13, 1825: *Letters*: I, 134–35.
34. Aug. 16, 1825: Thompson, 76 and 358, n. 3.
35. Bryant's praise: Thompson, 359, n. 5.
36. Nothing was in writing: Calhoun, *Longfellow*, 41.
37. The final cost of the trip came to $2,604.24 (Calhoun, *Longfellow*, 42). The inheritance loan was finally paid off in the summer of 1855. See *Letters*: III, 486.
38. Zilpah's letter of May 7 and Stephen's undated letter that follows are both quoted in Thompson, 87–88.
39. *Outre-Mer. Works*: VII, 23–24.
40. *Outre-Mer. Works*: VII, 29–30.
41. $36: June 20, 1826. *Letters*: I, 163.
42. Madame Potet, Thompson, 90–91, Gorman, 122; Madame Potet and her daughters, letter to Stephen, Sr. June 20, 1826. *Letters*: I, 163.
43. *Letters*: I, 173–75.
44. Letter from Stephen is quoted in *Letters*: I, 205, n. 7.
45. Letter of Aug. 11, quoted in Thompson, 97 and 364, n.3.
46. Nov. 19, 1826. *Letters*: I, 204–05.
47. "shelter for invalids": Gorman, 125; "solitude": *Outre-Mer. Works*: VII, 49. The following quotations are found on pages 52–53.
48. *Letters*: I, 191.
49. Oct. 26, 1826. *Letters*: I, 198–99.
50. Oct. 23, 1826. *Letters*: I, 195.
51. Unrecovered, *Letters*: I, 4–5.
52. *Letters*: I, 134, n. 2.
53. Thompson, 385, n. 2.
54. Gorman, 200.
55. "no idea": *Letters*: I, 182. The following quotations are from *Letters*: I, 182–83 and 204.
56. Thompson, 102–03.
57. Oct. 19, 1826, *Letters*: I, 187.
58. "good pronunciation," *Letters*: I, 212.
59. *Letters*: I, 214.
60. Mar. 20, 1827. *Letters*: I, 222.
61. May 15, 1827. *Letters*: I, 234.
62. *Letters*: I, 219. "The Nut-Brown Maid" is an anonymous fifteenth-century poem about woman's love and faithfulness.
63. May 6, 1828. *Letters*: I, 269.
64. El Escorial. May 15, 1827. *Letters*: I, 233.
65. Letters of March 20 and May 15: to his father and sister Elizabeth: *Letters*: I, 222 and 234; "under her attentions": to his father. *Letters*: I, 222.
66. Thompson, 113.
67. "sweetest-tempered," "quite fascinating," and "I confess": *Letters*: I, 239–41.
68. Calhoun, *Longfellow*, 52–3.
69. Florencia as the model of Slidell's Spanish woman: Calhoun, *Longfellow*, 53–54.
70. *Ibid.*
71. Charles Calhoun in 2004 took this line of thought a tantalizing step further by first tracing out what he called Slidell's "fantasy" and then saying it "raises the question of whether Longfellow's infatuation with Spain was linked with a sexual awakening." Calhoun doesn't know exactly when Longfellow lost his virginity, of course, but he does acknowledge Portland as a large enough city to have supported a "demi-monde," although he believes Portland and Brunswick too were both small enough that sexual misadventures would generate rumors and that Longfellow was young enough to care about the ones that were bound to reach his parents.

Paris, three thousand miles away, and an open city where "every pleasure was procurable for a price," as Calhoun puts it, was a more likely place for Henry to lose his virginity, although the young man may have been held back by a small-town moral code he was still afraid to break. Madrid and Florencia were quite another matter, for by then Longfellow was an experienced traveler whose morals may have loosened a little by time and distance. "There is no reason to assume," Calhoun concludes, that by 1828 Henry was still "sexually inexperienced." Calhoun, *Longfellow*, 54.

72. *Letters*: I, 223–24.
73. July 16, *Letters*: I, 237.
74. Calhoun, *Longfellow*, 49.
75. See "Granada": *Papers*: ms. pages 9–19, Nov. 11, 1827.
76. Thompson, 119–20.
77. *Letters*: I, 247–48.
78. Ibid.
79. *Outre-Mer. Works*: VII, 228–29.
80. *Papers*: Dec. 24, 1828.
81. *Outre-Mer. Works*: VII, 231.
82. *Outre-Mer. Works*: VII, 233; LT, 120.
83. See Paul Baker, *The Fortunate Pilgrims: Americans in Italy, 1800–1860* (Cambridge, MA: Harvard University Press, 1964). Details from this paragraph are from Baker, 3, 11, 19–20.
84. *Letters*: I, 249–50; Thompson, 120.
85. March 26, 1828. *Letters*: I, 257.
86. attractiveness of Florence to American travelers: Baker, *Fortunate Pilgrims*, 53.
87. Jan. 18, *Letters*: I, 253; "that glassy river": from "An Italian Scene" by John Pierpont.
88. Romanticizing the Arno: Thompson, 120–21; 370, n. 5. The poem is quoted in Thompson, 121.
89. *Letters*: I, 253; Gorman, 138.
90. Jan. 23, 1828. *Letters*: I, 255.
91. *Papers*: Feb. 9, 1828.
92. *Papers*: Feb. 11, 1828; *Outre-Mer. Works*: VII, 237; Baker, 61.
93. Henry Adams, *The Education of Henry Adams: An Autobiography* (Boston, MA: Houghton Mifflin, 2000), 89. Originally published 1907.
94. *Outre-Mer. Works*: VII, 238–40. The remaining quotations in this paragraph are from pages 239–40.
95. Scholars of the past century vary in the way they report the relationship. Hilen says simply that Longfellow "became romantically interested" in Giulia (*Letters*: I, 259, n. 1);Thompson reports more directly that Longfellow "had lost his heart to Giulia" (125 and 372–73, notes 19 and 20); Wagenknecht would admit only that Longfellow "admired her and was grateful to her" (*Full-Length*, 216); and Calhoun concludes that Longfellow had "a flirtation with his Roman landlord's daughter" (*Longfellow*, 55.) Irmscher does not mention the romance at all.
96. The third daughter was not musically gifted, and the 18-year-old Persiani son, Fabio, went unmentioned. March 26, 1828. *Letters*: I, 256–57.
97. Oct. 1, 1839. *Letters*: II, 177.
98. Jan. 5, 1840. *Letters*: II, 204.
99. Dec. 18, 1828. *Letters*: I, 285.
100. "*antiqua flamma*": old flame. Aug. 2, 1842. *Letters*: II, 452. By then Giulia had remarried and Henry, no longer under her spell, was asking Greene what her new name was merely to indulge in warm nostalgia and idle curiosity.
101. *Letters*: I, 274.
102. Nowhere in his letter to his father does he use the term Roman Fever or malaria, but, assuming he had anything at all wrong with him, that has come to be the accepted diagnosis—at least from this distance. The only published speculation is from Calhoun, *Longfellow*, 56: "Perhaps it was 'Roman fever' (malaria), perhaps it was simply fatigue after so many inns, so many irregular verbs."
103. *Letters*: I, 276–78.
104. *Letters*: I, 274.
105. Thompson calls this lapse "either deliberately twisted or a miscalculation," 373, n. 21. In the same context, Thompson also wrote that "Longfellow was not averse to twisting the facts a bit, whenever it was expedient."
106. *Letters*: I, 277–78.
107. There were likely others that have not been recovered, but that is the count in Hilen's edition of Longfellow's letters. Day-to-day journal entries stopped during the summer and fall 1828 as well.
108. *Letters*: I, 283.
109. Thompson, 127 and 374, n. 26.
110. Calhoun, *Longfellow*, 59.
111. There was another option, of course: he could have used the bad news as an excuse to remain in Rome with Giulia permanently, but if that option occurred to him, it was dismissed straightaway.
112. *Letters*: I, 286–87. Other passages from this letter are quoted in the next two paragraphs.
113. Dec. 20. *Letters*: I, 288.
114. *Letters*: I, 295, 297, n. 5.
115. Calhoun *Longfellow*, 59.
116. *Papers*: Jan. 28, 1829.
117. Feb. 27, 1829. *Letters*: I, 297–98.
118. *Letters*: I, 309–10.
119. *Letters*: I, 312.

Chapter 2

1. Apr. 24, 1829. Calhoun, *Longfellow*, 68.
2. *Letters*: I, 321.
3. Thompson, 148.
4. Thompson, 156; Sloane Kennedy, *Henry W. Longfellow* (Akron, OH: Saalfield Publishing,1903), 39.
5. Chase was the uncle of Salmon P. Chase (1808–1873), the famous governor and senator from Ohio, the Treasury Secretary under Lincoln, and the sixth Chief Justice of the Supreme Court.
6. There is no telling how many girls Henry saw socially when he returned from Europe, although the beautiful and mysterious Susan Codman still thought there might be enough between them for her to break up with him in a letter of March 8, 1830, some seven months after his return from Europe. Three and a half years away from Miss Codman, however, plus at least two intervening romances of his own argue that Henry had little if any romantic interest in her in the winter of 1829–30.
7. Smuggling letters: To Anne Longfellow, *Letters*: I, 346 and n. 1.
8. Early death: See Ancestry.com, D.B. Robinson's Genealogy Database, which identifies the quotation from *Early New England People*, 179.
9. "the learned languages": Higginson, 63.
10. Thompson, 17; Higginson, 60.
11. Kennedy, 40–41; Thompson, 157.
12. "dark hair" and "intensely polite": Gorman, 160, 162; "fragile and appealing": Thompson, 157; "singularly attractive": *Life*: I, 191; "lovely woman": Higginson, 63–64; "chronic ennui": Andrew Hilen, "Introduction" to *The Diary of Clara Crowninshield* (Seattle, Washington: University. of Washington Press, 1956), xxii.
13. Family tradition: Higginson, 60–61; "brown silk dress": Hildegarde Hawthorne, *The Poet of Craigie House* (New York: Appleton-Century, 1936), 75.
14. Thompson, 157; *Letters*: I, 8; Wagenknecht, *Full-Length*, 217.
15. Higginson, 60–61.
16. love letters: In a rash act he later regretted, Longfellow, "being in low spirits," as he put it, burned all but a few of Mary's journals and letters. He explained his decision to Mary's sister Margaret Potter Thacher. Feb. 15, 1843. *Letters*: II, 505–06.
17. *Letters*: I, 346.
18. close friends: Thompson, 158.
19. Thompson, 149.
20. Thompson, 149–50; Gorman, 156.
21. June 27, 1830. *Letters*: I, 341–42.
22. For Longfellow's popularity on campus, including the quotations in this paragraph, see *Life*: I, 182–83; Gorman, 156–57; and Carl Johnson, *Professor Longfellow of Harvard* (Eugene, OR: University of Oregon Press, 1944), 5–7.
23. *Life*: I, 181–82. Quotation from Cyrus Hamlin, later the sixth president of Middlebury College. The following unidentified quotation in this paragraph is from *Life*: I, 182.
24. *Life*: I, 182–83
25. Thompson, 160.
26. Thompson, 169.
27. "Origin and Progress of the French Language" (April 1831), "Anglo-Saxon Language and Literature" (October 1831), a review essay on a new edition of Philip Sidney's *The Defence of Poetry* (January 1832), "Spanish Devotional and Moral Poetry" (April 1832), the "History of the Italian Language and Dialects" (October 1832), and the "Spanish Language and Literature" (April 1833).
28. He had touched on some of the same ideas twice earlier, in "The Lay Monastery" in the *United States Literary Gazette* (April 1825), and in his 1825 graduation speech, "Our Native Writers."
29. Passages quoted in Calhoun, *Longfellow*, 81–83 and Thompson, 172–76.
30. March 13, 1826. *Letters*: I, 145.
31. Thompson, 149–50.
32. *Letters*: I, 322–23.
33. *Letters*: I, 348.
34. Calhoun, *Longfellow*, 91.
35. Wedding announcement: letter to Ann Longfellow. *Letters*: I, 362, n. 3. Martha: daughter of Prof. Cleaveland; Mary: daughter of his Brunswick landlady. *Letters*: I, 362–63, and n. 1.
36. Hawthorne, 77.
37. Thompson, 384, n. 4; Higginson, 61–62.
38. *Letters*: I, 364, n. 1.
39. Jan. 4, 1831. *Letters*: I, 352.
40. *Letters*: I, 361–62.
41. July 11, 1826. *Letters*: I, 170–71, n. 2. Longfellow's emphasis.
42. *Letters*: I, 374–75.
43. Thompson, 190–91.
44. *Ibid.*, 196.
45. Johnson, 4–5.
46. *Letters*: I, 447–48.
47. Thompson, 383, n.4.
48. *Ibid.*, 169.
49. Calhoun, *Longfellow*, 92.
50. Thompson, 184. Charles Calhoun commented that Mary had "suffered at least one miscarriage" by April 1835 (*Longfellow*, 94), but though her delicate health is generally acknowl-

edged, it is not known if it was a miscarriage that confined her to chambers at this point.
51. *Letters*: I, 399.
52. Higginson, 83.
53. Andrew Hilen, "Introduction," *The Diary of Clara Crowninshield* (Seattle, WA: University of Washington Press, 1956), xxiii.
54. *Letters*: IV, 45.
55. For a discussion of Longfellow's translation accomplishment in "To-morrow," see Stephen Burt and David Mikics, *The Art of the Sonnet* (Cambridge, MA: Belknap Press, 2010), 146–49.
56. Thompson, 389, n. 2.
57. Nov. 14, 1832. *Letters*: I, 402.
58. Higginson, 60.
59. *Works*: VII, 20.
60. *Letters*: I, 408.
61. Charvat, 114.

Chapter 3

1. Dec. 2, 1834. *Letters*: I, 459.
2. Letter from Stephen to Henry, Dec. 8, 1834, quoted in Thompson, 206.
3. Hilen, "Introduction," xiv.
4. *Ibid.*, xiv–xv.
5. For Clara's background story, see Hilen, "Introduction," xv–xix.
6. *Ibid.*, xviii and xxi.
7. *Ibid.*, xxi–xxii.
8. Quoted in Clara Crowninshield, *The Diary of Clara Crowninshield*, ed. Andrew Hilen (Seattle, WA: University of Washington Press, 1956), 3. Further references will be identified as Crowninshield, *Diary*.
9. Thompson, 216; 395, n. 13.
10. *Letters*: I, 490.
11. Crowninshield, *Diary*, 6–7. Adelaide was the wife of William IV.
12. May 31, 1835, Higginson, 88–89.
13. Bowring and Bulwer: *Papers*: May 21–22, 1835.
14. Aug. 10, 1835. *Letters*: I, 505.
15. Thompson, 215; 395, n. 11.
16. "sweet": *Papers*: May 21, 1835; "wildflower": Calhoun, *Longfellow*, 102; "talented & accomplished": Higginson, 90–91.
17. Calhoun, *Longfellow*, 101.
18. Crowninshield, *Diary*, 11.
19. Higginson, 92.
20. Crowninshield, *Diary*, 19.
21. *Ibid.*, 27.
22. *Papers*: June 17, 1835.
23. Crowninshield, *Diary*, 34.
24. *Ibid.*, 43.
25. *Papers*: June 29, 1835.
26. *Papers*: July 8, 1835.
27. Letter from Mellin to Nicander, quoted and translated by Andrew Hilen, *Longfellow and Scandinavia* (New Haven, CT: Yale University Press, 1947), 18, n. 3.
28. *Letters*: I, 505.
29. *Papers*: July 12, 1835.
30. Higginson, 93.
31. *Ibid.*, 95.
32. *Letters*: I, 502–03; Higginson, 97–98.
33. *Letters*: I, 505; "beaker full of the warm south": John Keats, "Ode to a Nightingale."
34. Crowninshield, *Diary*, 67.
35. Dec. 1, 1835. *Letters*: I, 526.
36. Sept. 28, 1835. Quoted by Hilen in Crowninshield, *Diary*, 98.
37. "indisposed": July 19, 1835. Crowninshield, *Diary*, 59.
38. Crowninshield, *Diary*, 98.
39. According to the *Online Etymology Dictionary*, "pregnant" did not come into acceptable usage until the 1950s.
40. *Papers*: Sept. 7, 1835.
41. Crowninshield, *Diary*, 104.
42. To Aunt Lucia. Sept. 3, 1835. Higginson, 102.
43. Crowninshield, *Diary*, 110.
44. Higginson, 103.
45. *Papers*: Sept. 10, 1835.
46. Crowninshield, *Diary*, 115. "Apoplexy" was the term then used for "stroke."
47. Higginson, 195.
48. *Papers*: Sept. 1835. See also Crowninshield, *Diary*, Sept. 17–23, 118–23.
49. *Papers*: Sept. 23, 1835.
50. *Letters*: I, 513.
51. Crowninshield, *Diary*, 117.
52. Higginson, 105–06.
53. *Letters*: I, 516.
54. *Ibid.*, I, 526.
55. Crowninshield, *Diary*, 130–32.
56. *Ibid.*, 135.
57. Entry quoted by Hilen in Crowninshield, *Diary*, 137, n. 10.
58. *Ibid.* The narrative from here to Dec. 1, is supplied mostly by Clara's *Diary*, 130–187, with additional details from Longfellow's journal and letters.
59. Crowninshield, *Diary*, 137.
60. Longfellow mistakenly called it forty miles in a letter of Dec. 1. *Letters*: I, 526.
61. "busy street": Crowninshield, *Diary*, 156; "her troubles had returned": Crowninshield *Diary*, 159. The concept of infectious disease had been recognized since ancient times, but in Mary Longfellow's case in 1835, it is not clear that the doctors recognized that she was suffer-

ing from an infection resulting from her miscarriage on October 5, but even if her doctors had seen the connection, there were no effective treatments yet available.

62. Newspapers: *Letters*: I, 522.
63. Crowninshield, *Diary*, 156; 160.
64. *Ibid.*, 161.
65. Crowninshield, *Diary*, 165, 172–73, 176, and 177–78.
66. Bleeding: the conclusion reached by Hilen in Crowninshield, *Diary*, 177, n.13.
67. "agitated" and "How quick": Crowninshield, *Diary*, 178.
68. *Letters*: I, 526.
69. Crowninshield, *Diary*, 180.
70. *Ibid.*
71. To Judge Potter, *Letters*: I, 527.
72. Crowninshield, *Diary*, 181.
73. *Ibid.*, 183.
74. *Ibid.*
75. *Letters*: I, 527.
76. Deathbed dialogue is recorded in Crowninshield, *Diary*, 183–84.

Chapter 4

1. Crowninshield, *Diary*, 184–85.
2. *Papers*: Nov. 29, 1835.
3. *Letters*: I, 528–29.
4. *Letters*: I, 527–28.
5. *Letters*: I, 543.
6. Hilen, "Introduction," xxiii–xxiv.
7. *Works*: I, 25–27.
8. *Papers*: Dec. 4, 1835.
9. *Ibid.*
10. "we had the cabin to ourselves": Dec. 1, 1835. Crowninshield, *Diary*, 187; "Clara is still with me": *Papers*: Dec. 4, 1835.
11. Crowninshield, *Diary*, 190.
12. *Ibid.*, 192–93, 197.
13. To Daniel Raynes Goodwin, April 17, 1836. *Letters*: I, 548.
14. May 8, 1836. *Letters*: I, 550. But see Christoph Irmscher, *Public Poet, Private Man* (Amherst, MA: University of Massachusetts Press, 2009), 45. Irmscher, quoting a line from Longfellow's journal, makes the additional point that he had to get past his original shock at the unsanitary conditions in Heidelberg: "Every front entry smells worse than a stable and I know more than one that smells like a pig sty."
15. For the living arrangements, see Thompson, 227; Crowninshield, *Diary*, 198.
16. Thompson, 230.
17. To Joseph Bosworth. Jan. 10, 1836. *Letters*: I, 535.

18. Jan. 20, 1836. Quoted in Thompson, 232.
19. Longfellow also liked Schiller, Hoffman, Tieck, Heine, and Jean Paul, among others. For a full accounting of his German reading, see James Hatfield. *New Light on Longfellow* (Boston, MA: Houghton Mifflin, 1933), 39–43.
20. Thompson, 229–30.
21. *Ibid.*, 231.
22. Hatfield, 41.
23. Crowninshield, *Diary*, 199.
24. Charles H. Brown, *William Cullen Bryant* (New York: Scribner's, 1977), 24–27.
25. *Works*: I, 43.
26. Thompson, 359, n.5.
27. Crowninshield, *Diary*, 200; 209.
28. Hilen, "Introduction," xxvi–xxvii.
29. "feels solitary": William Cullen Bryant, Jr., and Thomas G. Voss, eds., *The Letters of William Cullen Bryant*, vol. 2, 1836–1849 (New York: Fordham University Press, 1977), 35; "irritated witness": Gilbert Muller, *William Cullen Bryant* (Albany, NY: SUNY Press, 2008), 137.
30. *Letters*: I, 536.
31. Hatfield, 39–40.
32. Ward was the older brother of Julia Ward, who would marry Samuel Gridley Howe in 1843 and write "The Battle Hymn of the Republic" in 1861. Spirited letters: Trying to match Ward, Longfellow wrote letters back that have been described as among "the liveliest and ... the most indiscreet" he ever wrote. Maud Howe Elliot, *Uncle Sam Ward and His Circle* (New York: Macmillan, 1938), 238.
33. Sumner: Elliot, vi; "sixty horse-power": To Greene, *Letters*: I, 542.
34. Elliot, 105.
35. Kennedy, 236.
36. Elliot, 105–06.
37. Crowninshield, *Diary*, 227–35; *Life*: I, 229–30.
38. Crowninshield, *Diary*, 235; William Cullen Bryant, Jr., 14–15, n. 12.
39. Crowninshield, *Diary*, 231.
40. Hatfield, 43.
41. Crowninshield, *Diary*, 260.
42. Crowninshield, *Diary*, 264–86; William Cullen Bryant, Jr., 14–15, n. 12.
43. *Letters*: I, 555.
44. Apr. 27, 1836. William Cullen Bryant, Jr., 17.

Chapter 5

1. *Papers*: 1835.
2. Thompson, 234; *Life*: I, 236–37.
3. July 29, 1836. *Letters*: I, 563.

4. Sept. 12, 1836. *Letters*: I, 566.
5. Frances W. Gregory, *Nathan Appleton* (Charlottesville, VA: University Press of Virginia, 1975), 21; Louise Hall Tharp, *The Appletons of Beacon Hill* (New York: Little, Brown, 1973), 39, 45–46.
6. For Nathan Appleton's connection to the growth of the New England cotton industry, see Gregory, chs. 10–17: Profitable spin-off companies followed the BMC, like the Merrimack Manufacturing Company (MMC) and the Hamilton Manufacturing Company (HMC). Gregory, 174 and 185.
7. "What impressed Dickens were the workers in the mills. Seeing them first just as they were going to their noontime meal, he discovered scores upon scores of healthy, clean, well-dressed young women." Robert F Dalzell, *Enterprising Elite* (Cambridge, MA: Harvard University Press, 1987), 45–46:
8. Gregory, 187. For more on the Lowell factory, see Gregory, Ch. 11, "The Founding of Lowell" and Dalzell, Ch. 3, "Expansion."
9. Gregory, 293; billion dollar industry: Gregory, 194.
10. Feb. 20, 1827. Edward Wagenknecht, *Mrs. Longfellow: Selected Letters and Journals of Fanny Appleton Longfellow* (New York: Longmans, 1956), 4–5.
11. Tharp, 121–22.
12. Tharp, 124.
13. From Fanny's manuscript letters at the Longfellow House.
14. 39 Beacon: Tharp, 104–05. Originally the property had been owned by John Singleton Copley, but Nathan Appleton and a partner hired architect Alexander Parris to raze the existing building and design and build a pair of beautiful three-story brick bow-front townhouses. See the description of 39 and 40 Beacon Street: "How a Short Post becomes a Lengthy Post" (May 2, 2012). https://downeast-dilettante.wordpress.com/category/beacon-hill: "Parris was one of the first New England architects to break out of the box with elegant Greco-Federal designs with oval rooms, curved walls, segmental arched ceilings and other details that gave weight to the aspirations of the early 19th century plutocrats for whom he designed."
15. Tharp, 132–33.
16. *Ibid*.
17. *Ibid*., 134.
18. Wagenknecht, *Fanny*, 7.
19. Tharp, 134.
20. June 11, 1832, and Sept. 2, 1835: Wagenknecht, *Fanny*, 8, 18.

21. Charles to his sisters, Feb. 26, 1833, quoted in Tharp, 142.
22. Tharp, 143–44.
23. *Ibid*., 145–46. Tharp quotes from the joint journal Mary and Fanny kept between them, noting that it wasn't always clear which girl wrote which entry.
24. For the narrative of this trip, see Tharp, 147–52.
25. *Ibid*., 158–59.
26. From Fanny's manuscript letters at the Longfellow House.
27. Sept. 7, 1835. Wagenknecht, *Fanny* 19–20.
28. Tharp, 161–62.
29. *Ibid*.
30. Wagenknecht, *Fanny*, 20–21.
31. The crisis lasted about seven years, during which time Nathan Appleton stepped in to manage company firms in trouble, making them more efficient and ultimately more profitable. Gregory, 200. For the ups and downs in Nathan Appleton's textile empire, and to trace the financial condition of his holdings during this period, see Gregory, 230 and following.
32. See Wagenknecht, *Fanny*, 22–51, and Tharp, Ch. 13, "Europe by Sailing Ship," 164–80.
33. "to explore" and "equaled by Niagara: Tharp, 167–68.
34. *Ibid*.
35. *Ibid*., 169, 172.
36. Wagenknecht, *Fanny*, 25. The remaining diary quotations in this paragraph are from Wagenknecht, *Fanny*, 25–26
37. Wagenknecht, *Fanny*, 26. For further details, see also Tharpe, 171, 172–73, and 189.
38. Tharp, 173.
39. *Ibid*., 173–75.
40. N.d., but early March 1836. Wagenknecht, *Fanny*, 30.
41. *Ibid*.
42. Tharp, 175.
43. *Ibid*.
44. Wagenknecht, *Fanny*, 31–32.
45. June 1 and 2, 1836. *Ibid*.
46. *Ibid*.
47. Tharp, 177.
48. Wagenknecht, *Fanny*, 32.
49. "Learning was the traditionally accepted, and popularly respected, avocation of the gentleman; learning as paid vocation was a dubious cultural status." Charvat, 129–30.
50. *Papers*: July 20, 1836.
51. *Papers*: July 22, 1836.
52. *Papers*: July 24, 1836.
53. July 29, 1836. *Letters*: I, 563.
54. *Papers*: July 31, 1836.

55. Wagenknecht, *Fanny*, 32; Thompson, 235.
56. Tharp, 177.
57. *Papers*: Aug. 1, 1836.
58. Tharp, 177.
59. Wagenknecht, *Fanny*, 33.
60. *Papers*: Aug. 2, 1836.
61. Tharp, 178.
62. *Papers*: Aug. 4, 1836.
63. Tharp, 178.
64. *Ibid.*; Aug. 7, 1836. *Papers*.
65. *Papers*: Aug. 8, 1836.
66. Thompson, 236.
67. *Papers*: Aug. 9, 1836.
68. *Papers*: Aug. 10, 1836.
69. Tharp, 179.
70. *Papers*: Aug. 12, 1836.
71. Tharp, 179–80 and Wagenknecht, *Fanny*, 34–35.
72. Tharp, 180.
73. Wagenknecht, *Fanny*, 35.
74. Crowninshield, *Diary*, 291, n. 10.
75. Wagenknecht, *Fanny*, 35–36; Crowninshield, *Diary*, 291, n. 10.
76. "dungeon narrowing": Wagenknecht, *Fanny*, 35–36.

Chapter 6

1. Both quotations from Crowninshield, *Diary*, 288–89, n. 3.
2. *Ibid.*, 291, n. 10.
3. William Cullen Bryant, Jr., 35, n. 2. This and the following Frances Bryant diary excerpts are found here.
4. Aug. 27, 1836. *Papers*.
5. "Saw the Appletons": Crowninshield, *Diary*, 293; "then they leave": from Fanny's diary quoted in Tharp, 181.
6. Tharp, 181.
7. *Papers*: Sept. 4, 1836.
8. *Papers*: Oct. 8, 1836.
9. *Letters*: I, 568–69.
10. Feb. 1, 1837. *Letters*: II, 13.
11. *Letters*: II, 5.
12. Johnson, 23–27.
13. March 22. *Letters*: II, 15–16.
14. "remarkably youthful": Gorman, 220; "naturally cheerful": Higginson, 146–47; "wine-colored": Thompson, 242.
15. Edward Waldo Emerson, *The Early Years of the Saturday Club* (Boston, MA: Houghton Mifflin, 1918), 138.
16. Dec. 11, 1845. *Papers*. "a dandy Pindar": review of *Poems* (1845) published in the *New-York Daily Tribune*, Dec. 10, 1845. Longfellow unfairly called Fuller's review a "furious onslaught" and a "bilious attack." She did admit to a certain "coolness" to Longfellow's work and saw little to justify the high praise of it that poured in from most other quarters, but she did try to balance her remarks: "Neither have we forgotten that Mr. Longfellow has a genuine respect for his pen, never writes carelessly, nor when he does not wish to, nor for money alone. Nor are we intolerant to those who prize hothouse bouquets beyond all the free beauty of nature; that helps the gardener and has its uses."
17. Anne-Marie Taylor, *Young Charles Sumner* (Amherst, MA: University of Massachusetts Press, 2001), 151.
18. David Herbert Donald, *Charles Sumner and the Coming of the Civil War* (New York: Knopf, 1970), 39–40. This is vol. 1 of the biography; further references identified as *Sumner I*.
19. Paul Baker, 30.
20. David Reynolds, *Waking Giant* (New York: HarperCollins, 2008), 208.
21. David Reynolds, *Walt Whitman's America* (New York: Knopf, 1995), 393.
22. Donald, *Sumner I*, 87.
23. David Herbert Donald, *Charles Sumner and the Rights of Man* (New York: Knopf, 1970), 271. This is vol. 2 of his biography; further references identified as *Sumner II*.
24. Edward L. Pierce, *Memoirs and Letters of Charles Sumner*, 3 vols. (Boston, MA: Roberts Brothers, 1878 and 1893), I, 164.
25. Donald, *Sumner II*, 271.
26. Donald, *Sumner II*, 316. Sumner's marriage: They did not divorce until 1873 and by then Sumner was being regularly attacked in the press by political opponents as "The Great Impotence."
27. Letters of Aug. 29 and Nov. 25, 1840. *Letters*: II, 243, 266.
28. Calhoun, *Longfellow*, 136.
29. Irmscher, *Public Poet*, 80–81.
30. Gorman, 205–06; Calhoun, *Longfellow*, 126.
31. April 1, 1841. *Letters*: II, 293.
32. *Life*: I, 274. Samuel Longfellow wrote that he took this passage from his brother's dictation.
33. For Fanny's time in Paris, see Tharp, Ch. 14, "Appletons at the Courts of Kings," especially 184–186; 211.
34. Wagenknecht, *Fanny*, 36–37.
35. Tharp, 185.
36. *Ibid.*, 186.
37. *Ibid.*, 188. The picture is not identified.
38. *Letters*: II, 6, and note 1. Hilen reports in the note that the poem Longfellow translated

and sent Fanny was Friedrich von Matthisson's "Elegy. Written in the Ruins of an Old Castle," which Longfellow first published in the *Knickerbocker* (September 1839).
39. About March 6, 1837. Tharp, 188.
40. Wagenknecht, *Fanny*, 39; Tharp, 189–90.
41. Wagenknecht, *Fanny*, 45.
42. *Ibid.*, 47.
43. *Ibid.*, 48.
44. *Ibid.*, 51.
45. Dec. 24, 1837. Thompson, 258.
46. Sept. 28, 1837. *Letters*: II, 42.

Chapter 7

1. When Samuel Longfellow edited Henry's note printed with the poem in *Voices of the Night* (*Works*: I, 25), he deleted Fanny's name, an error in judgment corrected by Lawrance Thompson in *Young Longfellow*. The note, as published by Thompson, makes it clear that the poem was intended for Fanny: "The poem will always carry me back to that golden, beautiful Autumn of Fanny's return from Europe. Whenever I read it I live over again that season of love and restlessness, of hope and fear." Thompson, 402. The poem was titled "Flowers" in *Voices*, but "Floral Astrology" in its first publication in the *Knickerbocker* (Dec. 1837).
2. Thompson, 401–02.
3. purple panes: Ernest Longfellow explained that these were from Holland and "were the pride of Bostonians of those days." *Random Memories* (Boston, MA: Houghton Mifflin, 1922), 8. Wrought-iron balcony: Tharp, 197.
4. Thompson, 254–55.
5. Oct. 1837: *Letters*: II, 48.
6. Dec. 10, 1837. *Letters*: II, 51.
7. *Letters*: II, 52, n. 8. Translation by Andrew Hilen.
8. *Letters*: II, 54. The ball is unidentified.
9. Taylor, 158.
10. *Letters*: II, 55.
11. Horatio Greenough, American sculptor, kept a studio in Florence, where he lived and entertained visiting Americans.
12. Jan. 6, 1838. *Letters*: II, 59. Sumner didn't arrive in Rome until May 21, 1839.
13. Thompson, 260, 267; Tharp, 198.
14. Thompson, 267.
15. *Ibid.*, 403–04, n. 20.
16. *Ibid.*, 266.
17. *Ibid.*, 270, 408, n. 16.
18. *Works*: VIII, 275. Also used as the epigraph to the book.
19. Thompson, 414.
20. Sept. 1, 1838. *Papers*.
21. Thompson, 295; 415, n. 25.
22. Tharp, 199.
23. The Poe quotation is from "The Literati of New York City" No. 5 (*Godey's Lady's Book*, September 1846). Taken from http://www.eapoe.org/works/misc/litratb5.htm. The Hawthorne quotation is from a Jan. 19, 1855, letter to his publisher William Ticknor. See Wineapple, 282 and 447.
24. Tharp, 200.
25. Wagenknecht, *Fanny*, 53.
26. Tharp, 200.
27. Wagenknecht, *Fanny*, 52–3.
28. Tharp, 121–22.
29. *Ibid.*, 200–01.
30. Thompson, 406
31. *Ibid.*, 287.
32. "Young men read it": *Life*: I, 282; suicide: Pierce, II, 227; recitation piece: Angela Sorby, *Schoolroom Poets* (Durham, New Hampshire: University of New Hampshire Press, 2005), xiii; schools: In 2017, Longfellow Elementary Schools and Middle Schools remain common everywhere in the country, from Houston, Texas to Riverside, California, to Mitchell, South Dakota, to Columbia, Maryland—and all points in between.
33. Aug. 6, 1838. *Letters*: II, 93.
34. *Letters*: II, 106.
35. Thompson, 275–77.
36. July 23, 1839. *Letters*: II, 158–63.
37. *Letters*: II, 160.
38. The book sold some 14,500 copies through 1864, according to Charvat, 114; see also Calhoun, *Longfellow*, 144 and Wagenknecht, *Full-Length*, 5.
39. July 23, 1839. *Letters*: II, 160.
40. July 23, 1839. *Letters*: II, 161.
41. *Works*: VIII, 160 and following.
42. *Works*: VIII, 190.
43. *Works*: VIII, 205–11; 218.
44. *Works*: VIII, 283–84.
45. Tharp, 203.
46. "old fool" and "new Mamma": *Ibid.*
47. Tharp, 204.
48. *Ibid.*, 204–06.
49. "puzzle" and "worse than Heathenism": n.d., Wagenknecht, *Fanny*, 64.
50. Tharp, 207.
51. *Letters*: II, 192. "Modest" is used here in the sense of "limited."
52. Wagenknecht, *Fanny*, 64–65.
53. *Ibid.*, 64–66.
54. *Ibid.*, 58.
55. *Ibid.*, 63.
56. July 23, 1839. *Letters*: II, 158–63.

Chapter 8

1. Johnson, 34–35.
2. *Ibid.*, 27.
3. *Papers.*
4. Aug. 21 and 31, 1839. Elliot, 253–54.
5. Thompson, 297–98; 415.
6. *Letters*: II, 176. Impossible for Longfellow to see at the time, and certainly something he would have been proud of later on, was his role in the establishment of the academic discipline that took root in the twentieth century, Comparative Literature. His example in the area of European languages and literatures, including his highly regarded translations, textbooks, and essays in the *North American Review*, all provided models of scholarship and literary inquiry that would live long after his death, that would be, in fact, as durable a legacy as the poems he wrote. On Longfellow and Comparative Literature, see Dana Gioia, "Longfellow in the Aftermath of Modernism," in *The Columbia History of American Poetry*, eds. Jay Parini and Brett C. Millier (New York: Columbia University Press, 1993), 76: "Longfellow was the first American poet both to define his literary identity and to build its authority by systematically assimilating European literature.... Longfellow's vision of the American poet's international role was central to both Pound and Eliot, and it remains a dominant force in American poetry."
7. Thompson, 294–95.
8. Testimony to the popularity of *Voices* is widely available; see for example Thompson, *xvii*, 306; 75-cent book: Charvat, 158; also Christoph Irmscher, *Longfellow Redux* (Urbana, IL: University of Illinois Press, 2006), 54 and following; 43,550 copies: *Papers.*
9. "sense of triumph": Higginson, *Longfellow*, 177; "nothing equal": Robert L. Gale, *A Henry Wadsworth Longfellow Companion* (Westport, CT: Greenwood Press, 2003), 104; Ward: Elliott, 251; "These voices of the night": Brown, 256; "elevated place": reviews quoted by Calhoun, *Longfellow*, 138 and Kennedy, 282–83; "Even the Boston papers": Jan. 2, 1840. *Letters*: II, 202. One anonymous reviewer in *Burton's Gentleman's Magazine*, however, accused Longfellow of plagiarism, which set off a flurry of accusations and self-defenses. The reviewer was Edgar Allan Poe.
10. *Life*: I, 350.
11. *Letters*: II, 203–4.
12. Sept. 26, 1841. *Letters*: II, 332.
13. Thompson, 311–12; Reynolds, *Whitman*, 167–68; Brown, 256; and Elliott, 211.
14. Thompson, 312.
15. "oval face": Donald, *Sumner* I, 88. See also Elaine Showalter, *The Civil Wars of Julia Ward Howe* (New York: Simon & Schuster, 2016), passim; "Miss Julia and myself": *Letters*: II, 428; Louisa: Tharp, 231; slight blush: Thompson, 313; Elliott, 375; "my dear Annie" and "not dreaming of me": Thompson, 417, n. 25.
16. July 8, 1840. Elliott, 263; Ivor Guest, *Fanny Elssler* (Middletown, CT: Wesleyan University Press, 1970), 146.
17. Carlos Baker, *Emerson Among the Eccentrics* (New York: Viking Press, 1996), 179–80.
18. *Ibid.*, 181.
19. *Ibid.*, 182.
20. Fanny Appleton attended the same benefit performance, and in a letter she wrote to Isaac Appleton Jewett, she praised the artist instead of defending the woman. Elssler had "excited all the enthusiasm which always leaps up here to welcome first-rate excellence," Fanny wrote. "She has had crammed houses, selling tickets always by auction, and [has had] more discriminating applause, she says, than in any other city." The local Beacon Hill "patriotic dames" weren't sure they liked the idea of taking such a large sum of money "from a foreigner" and most especially "from a pirouetter of doubtful (or rather too well known) character." But the propriety of taking money from a foreigner was less important to Fanny than the evening's performance, which included "the majestic *Cachucha*" that left Fanny as smitten as Ward had been with Elssler's "joyous German smiles and coquettish grace." All of it is on display, Fanny concluded to Jewett, "when she makes the military salute to the audience or when clicking her golden spurs." That was enough, she said, to "drive you crazy." Wagenknecht, *Fanny*, 71.
21. Annie Fields, "Glimpses of Longfellow in Social Life," *The Century*, XXXI (1885–86), 884. Neither one was especially political in college, but their politics would later develop along opposite lines, Longfellow tracing his allegiances along Federalist principles that went back to Washington, Adams, and the Hartford Convention, and would look forward to Whig and Republican principles when they developed, while Hawthorne and his good friend Franklin Pierce were in the line of Jefferson, Jackson, and the developing Democratic party.
22. Hawthorne had published *Fanshawe*, an apprentice novel, in 1828 and been so embarrassed by it that he tried to collect all existing copies in order to destroy them. He was so successful at this that his wife didn't know about the book until after his death. Wineapple, *Hawthorne*, 78.

23. March 7, 1837. *Ibid.*, 94–95.
24. *Works*: VII, 361. The rest of the quotations are also from this edition, 361–67. Longfellow spent five paragraphs of the review explaining that the book, "though in prose, is written nevertheless by a poet."
25. The full review is available online.
26. Rita K. Grolin, "My Dear Longfellow," http://www.hawthorneinsalem.org.
27. Quoted in Calhoun, *Longfellow*, 180. See also, Irmscher, *Public Poet*, 86–87, n. 91.
28. Thompson, 285.
29. *Letters*: II, 244–45.
30. Dana quote in Henrietta Dana Skinner, *An Echo from Parnassus* (New York: J. H. Sears, 1928), 69.
31. Tharp, 215–16.
32. *Ibid.*
33. Wagenknecht, *Fanny*, 66.
34. *Ibid.*, 67.
35. Tharp, 218.
36. July 6. Wagenknecht, *Fanny*, 69.
37. "air burned blue": Tharp, 219.
38. Wagenknecht, *Fanny*, 74.
39. Tharp, 220–21.
40. *Ibid.*, 222–23; Wagenknecht, *Fanny*, 75.
41. Tharp, 225–27.
42. Wagenknecht, *Fanny*, 78.
43. *Ibid.*, 79.
44. Jan. 29, 1841. Thompson, 320.
45. *Ibid.*
46. *Letters*: II, 281.
47. March 21, 1841. *Letters*: II, 291.
48. *Letters*: II, 306.
49. *Letters*: II, 291.
50. Aug. 5. *Letters*: II, 317.
51. Aug. 13. Thompson, 419.
52. Sept. 1. *Letters*: II, 325.
53. *Letters*: II, 331–2.
54. *Letters*: II, 334–35.
55. Thompson, 323–24; Johnson, 43.
56. Reynolds, *Giant*, 231.
57. *Letters*: II, 350.
58. Mar. 9, 1842. Thompson, 327.
59. Johnson, 43.
60. Jan. 24. *Letters*: II, 380.
61. Thompson, 326.
62. Pierce: II, 205–06.
63. Apr. 26, 1842. *Letters*: II, 403–04.
64. June 12, 1842. *Letters*: II, 418–19.
65. Hatfield, 89.
66. June 21, 1842. *Letters*: II, 420–22.
67. June 24, 1842. *Letters*: II, 422–3.
68. As tempting as it may be to attach a sexual meaning to the dream, one does well to remember that Freudian dream interpretation as wish fulfillment has long been disputed.
69. Pierce: II, 208.
70. Aug. 8, 1842. *Letters*: II, 458.
71. To Margaret Boies Bradford Eliot, Sept. 8. *Letters*: II, 467.
72. June 26. *Letters*: II, 425.
73. *Letters*: II, 437.
74. These are all in Hilen's edition of the Longfellow *Letters*, but there were at least two others that were not recovered.
75. *Letters*: II, 415.
76. To Catherine Eliot Norton, July 24, 1842. *Letters*: II, 446.
77. "invariably striking": Hatfield, 91.
78. *Ibid.*, 93–94.
79. Quoted in German in Hatfield, 96 and translated online: http://www.sonett-archiv.com/ef/Freiligrath/gallen-sonette.htm.
80. "not a drop of wine": *Letters*: II, 444; "beautiful Meerschaum" and Maitrank: Jul. 30, 1842. *Letters*: II, 448 and n. 2.
81. Hatfield, 97.
82. "old castles and ruins": July 20. *Letters*: II, 437.
83. "climbed every ruin": *Letters*: II, 457.
84. Hatfield, 97.
85. *Letters*: II, 457.
86. June 28, 1858. *Letters*: IV, 84.
87. Aug. 15. *Letters*: II, 459.
88. *Letters*: II, 441.
89. *Letters*: II, 445.
90. *Letters*: II, 464–65.
91. Johnson, 45–47.
92. Wagenknecht, *Full-Length*, 81.
93. Oct. 16. *Letters*: II, 473.
94. Johnson, 47.
95. Copy included in Longfellow's letter to his father, Feb. 27, 1842. *Letters*: II, 387.
96. Sept. 28, 1842. Copy in *Life*: I, 438–39.
97. http://www.online-literature.com/dickens/americannotes/18/
98. Dec. 29, 1842. Copy in *Life*: I, 452–53.
99. *Letters*: II, 473.
100. Jan. 6, 1843. *Letters*: II, 496.
101. Nov. 9, 1823. *Letters*: I, 57–58.
102. *Life*: I, 444.
103. Charvat, 161; 167, n. 9.
104. https://archive.org/stream/pioneerliteraryc01lowe#page/92/mode/1up.
105. Jerome Loving, *Walt Whitman: Song of Himself* (Berkeley, California: University. of California Press, 1999), 108.
106. *Life*: I, 449.
107. "thin books": Gorman, 238; Gale, 195; "negrophilic": Irmscher, *Public Poet*, 110; Calhoun, *Longfellow*, 157.
108. *Letters*: II, 489.

Chapter 9

1. Feb. 15, 1843. *Letters*: II, 505.
2. Mar. 20. Thompson, 333–34; 421, n.18.
3. Published without a date in *Letters*: III, 83, n. 10.
4. Mar. 2. *Letters*: II, 512.
5. *Letters*: II, 522.
6. Thompson, 335; Calhoun, *Longfellow*, 163.
7. Wagenknecht, *Fanny*, 83.
8. *Letters*: II, 245.
9. Wagenknecht, *Fanny*, 83–84.
10. May 10, 1844. *Papers*. "The tenth of May! Day to be recorded with sunbeams! Day of light and love! The day of our engagement—when in the bright morning—one year ago—I received Fanny's note, and walked to town, amid the blossoms and sunshine and song of birds, with my heart full of gladness and my eyes full of tears."
11. May 22, 1843. *Letters*: II, 537.
12. *Letters*: II, 535–6.
13. May 27. Wagenknecht, *Fanny*, 87.
14. *Ibid.*, 84.
15. *Ibid.*
16. Thompson, 341.
17. May 21. *Letters*: II, 536.
18. *Letters*: II, 537–8
19. May 25. *Letters*: II, 540.
20. Wagenknecht, *Full-Length*, 229, n. 3.
21. May 24. Wagenknecht, *Fanny*, 85.
22. *Ibid.*
23. June 13. Tharp, 233.
24. Undated but June 1843. Thompson, 338–39.
25. This and the following quotations from Zilpah and Mary Longfellow are from Wagenknecht, *Full-Length*, 222.
26. *Life*: II, 1–2.
27. "great beauty": Charles Eliot Norton, *Longfellow: A Sketch of His Life* (Boston, MA: Houghton Mifflin, 1907), 26; "it was only": Charles Eliot Norton, *Letters of Charles Eliot Norton* 2 vols. (Boston, MA: Houghton Mifflin, 1913), I, 240.
28. May 27. Wagenknecht, *Fanny*, 86.
29. Tharp, 235.
30. Wagenknecht, *Full-Length*, 231. There are several descriptions of the wedding: Thompson, 339–40; Wagenknecht, *Full-Length*, 231. Calhoun, *Longfellow*, 165–66; Tharpe, 235.
31. Wagenknecht, *Full-Length*, 231.
32. Donald: *Sumner* I, 95.
33. Purchases itemized from invoices are in Tharp, 236–37.
34. Calhoun, *Longfellow*, 168.
35. Wagenknecht, *Full-Length*, 275.
36. Wagenknecht, *Fanny*, 92–93.
37. *Letters*: II, ix; Calhoun, *Longfellow*, 167.
38. Tharp, 242–43.
39. Wagenknecht, *Fanny*, 104–05.

Chapter 10

1. Wagenknecht, *Fanny*, undated but early 1845, 116–17.
2. Feb. 2, 1847. *Ibid.*, 125.
3. Fanny's letter dated July 24, 1860; Henry's July 26, 1860: Wagenknecht, *Fanny*, 225; *Letters*: IV, 186.
4. Letter to Elizabeth Gaskell, Aug. 12, 1861, Norton: I, 238–41.
5. William Dean Howells, "The White Mr. Longfellow," in *Literary Friends and Acquaintances* (New York: Harper & Brothers, 1901), 195.
6. Wagenknecht, *Fanny*, 111, 102, 112.
7. *Letters*: III, 37.
8. July 11, Wagenknecht, *Fanny*, 114.
9. "'Alas! the old study'": *Life*: II, 47; letter to Sumner: Aug. 14, 1847. *Letters*: III, 139.
10. *Papers*: Mar. 2 and Apr. 1, 1847.
11. "The great experiment": Apr. 7, 1847. *Letters*: III, 134; "double tooth": *Papers*: April 8, 1847. Longfellow on taking the ether: "On inhaling it, burst into fits of laughter. Then my brain whirled round, and I seemed to soar like a lark spirally into the air."
12. Hillard and Lieber: Wagenknecht, *Full-Length*, 243.
13. "warm sympathy": n. d., but mid-April 1847. Wagenknecht, *Fanny*, 129.
14. "I am very sorry": *Ibid.*, 129–30;
15. "*Ether* still reigns triumphant": *Letters*: III, 135.
16. "looked charmingly": Oct. 30, 1847. *Papers*; "merry plaything" and "baby very wretched": from Fanny's "Chronicle of the Children of Craigie Castle": Wagenknecht, *Fanny*, 136–37.
17. "quite ill": Aug. 30, 1848; "Little Fanny very weak": Sept. 4, 1848. *Life*: II, 129.
18. 1850 statistic. See website for the University of California, Davis, "infant mortality."
19. Undated and to an unidentified correspondent, but March 1847. Wagenknecht, *Fanny*, 127.
20. Wagenknecht, *Fanny*, 126; see also, Martin Duberman, *James Russell Lowell* (Boston, MA: Houghton Mifflin, 1966), 90. Dropsy of the brain: Rarely a fatal condition today, it is now called "hydrocephalus," water on the brain.
21. Wagenknecht, *Fanny*, 140; Tharp, 282.
22. Wagenknecht, *Fanny*, 140–41. These and

Notes—Chapter 10

the following quotations about Baby Fan's condition are from these pages.
23. *Ibid.*
24. *Papers*: Sept. 10, 1848.
25. Wagenknecht, *Fanny,* 141.
26. *Papers*: Sept. 11, 1848.
27. Letter undated but Sept. 1848. Wagenknecht, *Fanny,* 142–43.
28. *Ibid.,* 147.
29. To A. E. Warren. May 6, 1853. *Letters*: III, 381–82.
30. To Harriot Sumner Appleton, Sept. 22, 1850. *Letters*: III, 269.
31. Nov. 2, 1850. Wagenknecht, *Fanny,* 174–5.
32. *Papers*: Nov. 23, 1850.
33. April 16, 1852. Wagenknecht, *Fanny,* 186.
34. *Ibid.,* 193.
35. *Ibid.,* 194.
36. *Letters*: III, 398.
37. Nov. 22, 1853. Wagenknecht, *Fanny,* 195–6.
38. *Ibid.,* 202.
39. *Ibid.,* 120.
40. "So closes": *Papers*: Dec. 31, 1845
41. "Three years": *Papers*: July 13, 1846; "passed a delightful": *Papers*: May 5, 1847; "We were alone": *Papers*: Oct. 22, 1850.
42. *Papers*: May 10, 1858.
43. *Papers*: Nov. 22, 1849.
44. *Papers*: May 29, 1858.
45. Clay: *Papers*: May 16, 1850; Webster: *Papers*: May 21, 1850.
46. Wagenknecht, *Fanny,* 172.
47. *Papers*: July 23, 1850.
48. Wagenknecht, *Fanny,* 172. Shortly before their deaths, Fuller is believed to have married Giovanni Angelo Ossoli, an Italian marquis with whom she had a son, Angelino (Little Angelo).
49. Feb. 18, 1852. Wagenknecht, *Fanny,* 183. The book, by Emerson, William Henry Channing, and James Freeman Clarke, was a cleaned-up collection of Fuller's work—texts, letters, and journal entries—plus commentary that misrepresented Fuller by trying to make her appear respectable in light of her relationship with Giovanni Ossoli, who may or may not have been her husband but was the father of her nearly two-year-old son. The book was the number one best-seller in 1852, until it was replaced by Harriet Beecher Stowe's new book, *Uncle Tom's Cabin.*
50. For a discussion of the crime and a record of the trial, see George Dilnot, *The Trial of Professor Webster* (New York: Scribner's, 1928); a more colorful account is in Cleveland Amory's *The Proper Bostonians* (New York: E.P. Dutton, 1947.)

51. Amory, 219–20.
52. "lost all confidence" and reading, napping, and walking: Irmscher, *Public Poet*, 19; 22.
53. "gentle release": *Papers*: Aug. 3, 1849; "dusty, deserted": *Papers*: Aug. 9, 1849.
54. March 13, 1851. *Letters*: III, 290–91.
55. July 14, 1851. Wagenknecht, *Fanny,* 180.
56. Wagenknecht, *Full-Length,* 99.
57. *Papers*: July 12, 1850. The following quotations are from July 16 and July 9.
58. Aug. 27, 1851. *Papers.*
59. Aug. 22, 1851. Wagenknecht, *Fanny,* 181.
60. *Ibid.,* 182.
61. *Letters*: III, 348, n. 1.
62. Aug. 20, 1852. Wagenknecht, *Fanny,* 189–90. See also *Letters*: III, 347 and 348, n. 1; 353–54 and n. 3; Showalter, 106.
63. Aug. 20, 1852. Wagenknecht, *Fanny,* 189–90.
64. *Letters*: III, 353.
65. July 16 and 19, 1855. *Letters*: III, 486–87.
66. July 26, 1855. *Letters*: III, 488–89.
67. Letter to Frances Farrer, *Letters*: III, 545.
68. June 24, 1856. *Letters*: III, 542–43. The following two quotations are from Nov. 3, 1856. *Letters*: IV, 54; Aug. 5, 1857. *Letters*: IV, 44
69. *Letters*: IV, 86–87, n. 1.
70. "brown cottage": When the house burned down in May 1896, the *Boston Transcript* carried a story that was reprinted in the *New York Times* on Sunday, May 31, 1896: "The Burnt Longfellow Cottage."
71. July 23, 1858. *Letters*: IV, 88.
72. To Sumner. Aug. 12, 1858. *Letters*: IV, 92.
73. *Ibid.*
74. Johnson, 92.
75. *Papers*: Aug. 28, 1860.
76. Quotations are identified by date in the Longfellow *Papers*; "neuralgia in the head": April 30, 1848.
77. June 22, 1844. *Letters*: III, 38.
78. Hysterical blindness as a possible cause of Longfellow's eye troubles was suggested to me by a specialist in literature and psychology, Dr. Frank Ancona in 2007.
79. Sept. 19, 1843. Wagenknecht, *Fanny,* 93–94.
80. Louisa Ward and Sedgewicks: Tharp, 240.
81. Oct. 14, 1843. Wagenknecht, *Fanny,* 96.
82. *Ibid.,* 97.
83. *Ibid.,* 103.
84. Calhoun, *Longfellow,* 170.
85. Tharp, 254.
86. Aug. 7, 1845. Wagenknecht, *Fanny,* 119.
87. Wagenknecht, *Full-Length,* 87–88.
88. Nov. 3, 1857. *Letters*: IV, 54.

89. Nov. 10, 1843. Wagenknecht, *Fanny*, 98.
90. *Ibid.*, 133.
91. *Ibid.*, 213.
92. *Papers*: Dec. 26, 1846.
93. Wagenknecht, *Fanny*, 127–8.
94. Longfellow modeled a character after Monti in *Tales of a Wayside Inn* (1863).
95. May 15, 1860. Wagenknecht, *Fanny*, 221–22. See also Irmscher, *Public Poet*, 90.
96. July 28, 1849. *Letters*: III, 208.
97. *Ibid.* See also n. 3.
98. Donald: *Sumner* I, 164–70.
99. *Papers*: Oct. 26, 1848.
100. *Papers*: Apr. 24, 1851.
101. *Papers*: Apr. 25, 1851.
102. *Papers*: Nov. 23, 1851.
103. Nov. 26, 1851. *Letters*: III, 315, n. 2.
104. This was a song of tenor Lorenzo Salvi, whom Henry had heard at a concert in Boston on Dec. 4. Letter dated Dec. 5. *Letters*: III, 315, n. 1.
105. *Papers*: Nov. 30, 1851.
106. Wagenknecht, *Fanny*, 111. Bull became a favorite of the Longfellows, coming often to Craigie House to play for them, and so impressing Henry that he was cast as another major character in *Tales of a Wayside Inn* (1863).
107. To Tom Appleton. Oct. 30, 1846. *Letters*: III, 120–23 and notes 2, 3, 4, 5.
108. *Papers*: Dec. 19, 1846.
109. *Papers*: Viennese children: Jan. 30, 1847.
110. "floats through": Dec. 17, 1835. Wagenknecht, *Fanny*, 24.
111. Opera also encouraged Longfellow to work out his own dramatic, narrative, and musical structures in something like the operatic way of doing business, alternating melodic solos and duets with sections of less lyrical, plot-driven recitative.
112. "splendid affair" Wagenknecht, *Fanny*, 191; "gay dresses" and "finer": *Ibid.*, 201.
113. Fanny: "Grisi has certainly lost": Jan. 2, 1855. Wagenknecht, *Fanny*, 201; Henry: "Grisi is grand": *Papers*: Jan. 15, 1855; *Don Giovanni*: Jan. 30, 1855. *Letters*: III, 466–67.
114. Figures for this paragraph are from Fred Lewis Pattee, *The Feminine Fifties* (New York: Appleton-Century, 1940), 149.
115. *Papers*: Sept. 27, 1850.
116. *Papers*: Oct. 1 and 2, 1850.
117. Wagenknecht, *Fanny*, 173.
118. *Ibid.*, 179–80.
119. *Papers*: June 26, 1851. The remaining quotations in this paragraph are found in *Papers*, Nov. 23, Dec. 1, and Dec. 6, 1851. The letter to Sumner is dated Dec. 7: *Letters*: III, 318.
120. Margaret Armstrong, *Fanny Kemble* (New York: Macmillan, 1938), 170.
121. The divorce was finalized in 1849. Armstrong, 317.
122. To Susan Benjamin. Aug. 20, 1834. Wagenknecht, *Fanny*, 14.
123. "crowded house": *Papers*: Jan. 26, 1849; "her *chevalier*": *Papers*: Feb. 5, 1849.
124. *Papers*: Feb. 7, 1849.
125. Feb. 14, 1849. Wagenknecht, *Fanny*, 148–49; *Papers*: Feb. 16, 1849.
126. March 2, 1849. Wagenknecht, *Fanny*, 149.
127. To Emmeline Austin Wadsworth. March 2, 1849. Wagenknecht, *Fanny*, 149.
128. *Papers*: Feb. 12, 1850.
129. Feb. 14, 1850. Wagenknecht, *Fanny*, 166.
130. Wagenknecht, *Full-Length*, 308.
131. Gorman, 266–67.

Chapter 11

1. 35,850: *Papers*: March 31, 1857.
2. Frank Luther Mott, *Golden Multitudes: The Story of Best Sellers in the United States* (New York: Macmillan, 1947), 108; Gale, 75.
3. "superstar": Irmscher, *Public Poet*, 1; Dickens and Lind: Calhoun, *Longfellow*, 198.
4. *Papers*: Dec. 17, 1846.
5. July 2, 1847. Wagenknecht, *Fanny*, 132.
6. Article dated Oct. 13, 1849. Letter to Lieber: Nov. 18, 1849. *Letters*: III, 226.
7. Calhoun, *Longfellow*, 182. An untold number of French Canadian refugees settled St. Martinville, Louisiana and contributed to Louisiana's Cajun heritage. The local story, elaborately laid out in a fiction that has been passed down as truth, is that Longfellow had a real woman in mind for Evangeline and that she made her way to Louisiana where she lived out the rest of her life, had an unfortunate reunion with Gabriel (both names were changed for the local story), went insane, and was buried at a site still visited every year by thousands of tourists.
8. Mar. 18, 1851. Wagenknecht, *Fanny*, 177.
9. *Papers*.
10. *Papers*.
11. *Papers*: Jan. 6, 1847.
12. Nov. 8, 1847. Quoted in *Life*: II, 97–98.
13. Nearly every nineteenth-century Americanist mentions Longfellow and his sales, but they don't always agree on exact numbers. They do agree, however, on the singularity of Longfellow's success and the phenomenal breadth of his readership. Despite the difficulty pinning down firm and final numbers, two sources are especially useful, Carl Bode's *The Anatomy of Amer-*

ican Popular Culture (Berkeley, California: University of California Press, 1959) and William Charvat's *The Profession of Authorship in America, 1800–1870*. For the numbers in this paragraph, see Bode, 198–99; Pattee, 175; Charvat, 113; Reynolds, *Walt Whitman's America*, 353; Mott, 107. 300 copies: *Papers*: Jan. 1, 1856. Foreign sales figures are even harder to calculate owing to the unknown number of pirated editions in circulation.

14. nineteenth edition: Bode, 198–99; million copies: Mott, 108; "I do not wish": *Papers*: June 20, 1857.

15. "with great delight": *Papers*: June 5, 1854. Longfellow's borrowings from the *Kalevala* and other works created a controversy that is neatly summarized in Irmscher, *Redux*, 106–24.

16. Nov. 9, 1823. *Letters*: I, 57–58.

17. *Papers*: June 22, 1854.

18. "The most frequent criticism [of *Hiawatha*] is of the poem's meter, the trochaic tetrameter line he borrowed from the Finnish *Kalevala*, which has seemed too artificial and formulaic to some readers. The chief advantage of this measure, however, is that it isn't naturalistic. It was an overt distancing device, as was the incorporation of dozens of Ojibway words. These devices continuously remind the listener that *Hiawatha*'s mythic universe is not our world." Gioia, 88.

19. "The dangers of the Indians": Nov. 25, 1855. Quoted in *Life*: II, 294–95.

20. Journal passage quoted and dated July 28 by Hilen in *Letters*: III, 406.

21. *Papers*: Oct. 19, 1854.

22. *Papers*: Nov. 13, 1854.

23. Calhoun, *Longfellow*, 209.

24. Opera quotes are from *Papers*: Jan. 15, 17, 22, and 29, 1855.

25. Christoph Irmscher notes the impact of opera on the composition of *Hiawatha*, particularly in "the careful stage-setting, the stylized interactions of the characters, the repetitiveness of the phrases that are being used, the tragic, yet visually spectacular ending." *Public Poet*, 124–25. First edition information from Jacob Blanck's *Bibliography of American Literature*, vol. 5 (New Haven, Connecticut, Yale University Press, 1969), 494.

26. *Papers*: June 4, 1845.

27. *Papers*: Oct. 2, 1855; Calhoun, *Longfellow*, 211.

28. Nov. 5, 1855. Wagenknecht, *Fanny*, 201. Tennyson's *Maude and Other Poems* had appeared earlier in 1855 and been harshly reviewed.

29. *Papers*: Nov. 10, 1855.

30. Reynolds, *Whitman*, 356.

31. "fierce and furious": *Papers*: Nov. 18, 1855. "warmly defended" and "violently assailed": Calhoun, *Longfellow*, 211.

32. Nov. 29, 1855. *Letters*: III, 503. Schoolcraft: Henry Rowe Schoolcraft had by then published the first four of six volumes of *Information Respecting the History, Condition, and Prospects of the Indian Tribes of the United States* (1851–57).

33. Calhoun, *Longfellow*, 211.

34. Dec. 1, 1855. *Letters*: III, 504.

35. *Papers*: Dec. 6, 1855.

36. Dec. 13, 1855. *Letters*: III, 508.

37. *Papers*: Dec. 15, 1855.

38. Dec. 31, 1855. *Letters*: III, 514.

39. Wagenknecht, *Fanny*, 202.

40. "a pleasant kind of lethargy": Jan. 22, 1856. *Papers*; "I have been": Apr. 12, 1856. Included in *Life*: II, 308.

41. "from all quarters": Mar. 12, 1856. *Papers*; McKay's shipyard: Mar. 22, 1856. *Papers*; "*Hiawatha* rushes onward": Apr. 4, 1856. *Letters*: III, 534.

42. Sir William: letter from Sumner in *Life*: II, 341–43.

43. *Works*: Canto III, 133 and IV, 146. In the following paragraphs, references to *Hiawatha* and *The Courtship of Miles Standish* are taken from Vol. II of *Works* with endnote references identifying Canto and page numbers.

44. "misleading": Reynolds, *Whitman*, 318, 353.

45. *Papers*: Oct. 16, 1858.

46. See letters to Sumner, Oct. 17 and 18, 1858. *Letters*: IV, 98–99; 99, n. 1.

47. *Papers*: Oct. 23, 1858.

48. Nov. 29, 1858. Wagenknecht, *Fanny*, 215.

49. *Letters*: IV, 110.

50. Saturday Club: see Edward Emerson, *The Early Years of the Saturday Club* (Boston, MA: Houghton Mifflin, 1918), 1–20, and Duberman, 184–92.

51. Duberman, 185–86. Longfellow's first meeting with the club has to be deduced from letters and journal entries.

Chapter 12

1. Henry: Wagenknecht, *Full-Length*, 207; Fanny: Wagenknecht, *Fanny*, 123.

2. "strangely barbarous": Dec. 23, 1846. Wagenknecht, *Fanny*, 123; "unjust war": Feb. 28, 1847. Wagenknecht, *Fanny*, 126; "unrighteous Mexican war": *Papers*: June 7, 1846; "hour of shame": To Alexander Wadsworth Longfellow. June 10, 1846. *Letters*: III, 112 and in *Papers*: June 7, 1846.

3. Donald B. Cole, *Handbook of American History* (New York: Harcourt, Brace, 1968), 96.
4. Brenda Wineapple, *Ecstatic Nation* (New York: Harper Perennial, 2013), 66.
5. "Nebraska Swindle": *Papers*: Feb. 12, 1854; "Nebraska wickedness": Wagenknecht, *Fanny*, 198.
6. Feb. 21, 22, 1854. *Letters*: III: 415, 417.
7. James M. McPherson, *Battle Cry of Freedom: The Civil War Era* (New York: Ballantine Books, 1989), 148–49.
8. May 28, 1856. *Letters*: III, 540.
9. Baker, *Emerson Among the Eccentrics*, 378–79.
10. Debby Applegate, *The Most Famous Man in America: The Biography of Henry Ward Beecher* (New York: Doubleday, 2006), 281–83.
11. Reynolds, *John Brown: Abolitionist* (New York: Knopf, 2005), 159.
12. *Ibid.*, 149.
13. *Ibid.*, 171–73.
14. Baker, *Emerson among the Eccentrics*, 382–85.
15. *Ibid.*, 386; Reynolds, *John Brown*, 366.
16. Reynolds, *John Brown*, 354.
17. Nov. 7, 1859. Wagenknecht, *Fanny*, 218–19.
18. *Papers*: Dec. 2, 1859.
19. Balloting information and quotation, McPherson, 220.
20. *Ibid.*
21. *Letters*: IV, 197.
22. Quoted in *Letters*: IV, 198, n. 2.
23. McPherson, 221.
24. *Papers*: Dec. 3, 1860.
25. *Papers*: Dec. 18, 1860.
26. Dec. 19, 1860. Wagenknecht, *Fanny*, 229.
27. Dec. 24, 1860. *Ibid.*, 229–30. Criticism of Buchanan along these lines was widespread. William Cullen Bryant, for example, writing editorials in the *Evening Post* during the first months of 1861 called the president and his cabinet traitors for not protecting federal installations and for not providing reinforcements at Fort Sumter. Brown, 428. Fanny was wrong about Buchanan surrendering Fort Moultrie, although his inaction forced Maj. Robert Anderson on Dec. 26, 1860, to abandon it in order to occupy the larger, more defensible Fort Sumter in Charleston Harbor.
28. Wagenknecht, *Fanny*, 229–30.
29. *Ibid.*, 234–35.
30. *Ibid.*, 233.
31. April 5, 1860. *Papers*.
32. See Jill Lepore's, "Paul Revere's Ride Against Slavery," *New York Times* (Dec. 18, 2010). For a more academic accounting of the poem's popularity in the late nineteenth century, including its promotion by publisher Houghton Mifflin, see Matthew Gartner, "The Cultural Career of Longfellow's 'Paul Revere's Ride,'" in *Reconsidering Longfellow*, ed. by Christoph Irmscher and Robert Arbour (Madison, NJ: Fairleigh Dickinson University Press, 2014), 121–38.
33. Wagenknecht, *Fanny*, 231.
34. *Ibid.*, 233.
35. *Papers*: Jan. 28, 1861. *après-moi-le-déluge*: after me the deluge.
36. Jan. 29, 1861. *Letters*: IV, 212 and n. 2.
37. *Papers*: Feb. 3, 1861. Parker had died some nine months earlier on May 10, 1860 of tuberculosis in Florence, Italy.
38. Wagenknecht, *Fanny*, 232.
39. *Papers*: Feb. 5, 1861.
40. Feb. 8, 1861. *Letters*: IV, 214–15 and n. 4, 216.
41. *Ibid.*
42. Wagenknecht, *Fanny*, 233–34.
43. *Ibid.*, 235.
44. "strong and sensible": *Ibid.* ; "firm": *Papers*: Mar. 4, 1861.
45. *Papers*: April 12, 1861.
46. Wagenknecht, *Fanny*, 236.
47. *Ibid.*
48. *Ibid.*, 237.
49. Letter to Curtis, June 8, 1861. *Letters*: IV, 238.
50. Agassiz: *Papers*: July 1, 1861; Alice: Wagenknecht, *Full-Length*, 253.
51. "Great Bear": *Papers*: July 3, 1861; fireworks: Wagenknecht, *Fanny*, 239–40.
52. Wagenknecht, *Fanny*, 240.
53. *Ibid.*
54. Skinner, 10–11.
55. Wagenknecht, *Fanny*, 240.
56. Temperature from the *Boston Advertiser*.
57. Another possibility is that the hot wax itself ignited the thin muslin. Steel hoops: Calhoun, *Longfellow*, 215. White muslin dress: Fanny is thought to have been wearing what Charles Calhoun describes as a "gauzy summer housedress," very light, he says, "over its steel hoops." The hoop skirt was introduced in the late 1840s and was known as the "cage crinoline" by the late 1850s. See C. Willett and Phillis Cunnington, *The History of Underclothes* (New York: Dover Publications, 1992), 163–68. The outer skirt would have been little more than a layer or two of cool white muslin, just enough material to hide the ridges caused by the steel bands beneath. Because cage crinolines were more comfortable and cooler than the multiple layers of starched petticoats that had been most pop-

ular just a few years earlier, they became almost overnight a fashion craze that was sometimes called "crinolinemania." Deaths by fire and accident, however, became nearly commonplace by 1861. Karen Abbott, a regular columnist for the online magazine *Wonders & Marvels*, has cited several in her "Death by Crinoline" (2015), like the story of a Boston woman who caught fire standing too close to her parlor fireplace in 1858. There were nineteen similar stories in England in one two-month period, she reports, quoting the *New York Times*: "Certainly an average of three deaths per week from crinolines in conflagration ought to startle the most thoughtless of the privileged sex." http://www.wondersandmarvels.com/2015/01/death-by-crinoline-2.html.

See also, http://www.cracked.com/article_16997_6-popular-fashion-trends-that-killed-people.html#ixzz2j46uyAWi.

Diarmid Mogg in another online magazine, *The Penny Newsman* listed numerous examples of death by crinoline in 1861 alone, beginning on January 13, when Miss Maria Eliza Power died. In quick succession there were incidents, mostly fires, but some accidents from carriages and wind, on January 20, February 3, March 4, April 7, April 14, May 26, and June 2, before getting to what he called "The Melancholy Death of Mrs. Longfellow." Mogg's titles include "Injury Through Crinoline," "A Crinoline Catastrophe," "Another Frightful Death of a Female Through Crinoline," and others equally graphic.

58. July 10, 1861. Wagenknecht, *Fanny*, 242. Felton wrote four letters to Sumner, July 10, 14, 19, and 21, that tell the story of Fanny's death and burial. All four are printed in Wagenknecht, *Fanny*, 242–45.

59. Temperature, *Boston Advertiser*, July 10, 1861; Skinner, 12.

60. Wagenknecht, *Fanny*, 242.

61. Skinner, 12–13.

62. Wagenknecht, *Fanny*, 242.

63. For Anne Allegra's story, see Calhoun, *Longfellow*, 217 and n. 275, taken from "Circumstances of Mrs. Longfellow's Death, 1861." Dana Family Papers, Box 44: R. H. Dana III, Massachusetts Historical Society.

64. Calhoun, *Longfellow*, 218.

65. July 14, 1861, Wagenknecht, *Fanny*, 242–3.

66. Skinner, 16.

67. Wagenknecht, *Fanny*, 242–43.

68. *Ibid.*

69. *Ibid.*, 243.

70. Irmscher, *Public Poet*, 87.

71. Wagenknecht, *Fanny*, 244.

72. *Ibid.*, 244–5.

73. Fields, "Glimpses of Longfellow," 887.

74. For many years: Irmscher, *Public Poet*, 158.

75. Aug. 18, 1861. *Letters*: IV, 241–42.

Bibliography

Abbreviations

Works. I have used the Standard Library Edition of *The Works of Henry Wadsworth Longfellow* in 14 volumes (Boston, MA: Houghton Mifflin, 1886), identified in the notes by volume and page number. Longfellow is widely available in paper and online, thus making the "standard" edition perhaps the least available one. The Library of America volume compiled by J.D. McClatchy, *Henry Wadsworth Longfellow: Poems and Other Writings* (New York: LOA, 2000), though not all-inclusive, will serve most needs of most readers.

Letters. Andrew Hilen. *The Letters of Henry Wadsworth Longfellow*. Six volumes. (Cambridge, MA: Belknap Press, 1966–82). Indispensable contribution to Longfellow scholarship. Identified in the notes as *Letters* with volume number and page number.

Life. Samuel Longfellow. *Life of Henry Wadsworth Longfellow, with Extracts from His Journals and Correspondence*. Standard Library Edition. (Boston, MA: Houghton Mifflin, 1891). Three volumes. Identified in notes as *Life* with volume number and page number. This is also indispensable to Longfellow scholarship despite Samuel's protective editing of the original journals and letters. To avoid the bowdlerized journal entries, I worked with digitized and microfilmed originals obtained from Harvard and Rutgers University, which owns a full set of the Longfellow papers on microfilm and makes them available to scholars.

Papers. Longfellow journals (available at Harvard and on microfilm and electronic files): Henry Wadsworth Longfellow Papers (MS Am 1340) at the Houghton Library, Harvard University.

Textual note: I have retained original spellings and punctuation from all sources except for obvious misspellings or typos, which have been silently corrected. In the matter of punctuation, I have avoided Longfellow's habit of doubling up commas and semicolons with dashes, a popular nineteenth-century practice that seems to twenty-first-century readers a distracting redundancy (and which modern computers insist on auto-correcting). I have, however, retained the doubling-up whenever it has seemed necessary, as in the poetry for example.

Abdo, Joseph C. *The Quiet Radical: The Biography of Samuel Longfellow*. Lisbon: Tenth Island Editions, 2007.

Amory, Cleveland. *The Proper Bostonians*. New York: E.P. Dutton, 1947.

Applegate, Debby. *The Most Famous Man in America: The Biography of Henry Ward Beecher*. New York: Doubleday, 2006.

Appleton, Thomas Gold. *Life and Letters of Thomas Gold Appleton*. Ed. Susan Hale. New York: D. Appleton and Company, 1885.

Armstrong, Margaret. *Fanny Kemble: A Passionate Victorian*. New York: The Macmillan Company, 1938.

Arvin, Newton. *Longfellow: His Life and Work*. Boston: Little, Brown and Company, 1962.

Auser, Cortland P. *Nathaniel P. Willis*. New York: Twayne Publishers, 1969.

Baker, Carlos. *Emerson Among the Eccentrics: A Group Portrait*. New York: Viking Press, 1996.

Baker, Paul R. *The Fortunate Pilgrims: Americans in Italy, 1800–1860*. Cambridge, Mass: Harvard University Press, 1964.

Baxter, Maurice G. *One and Inseparable: Daniel Webster and the Union*. Cambridge, MA: Belknap Press, 1984.

Bode, Carl. *The Anatomy of American Popular Culture, 1840–1861*. Oakland: University of California Press, 1959.

Brown, Charles. H. *William Cullen Bryant*. New York: Charles Scribner's Sons, 1971.

Bryant, William Cullen, Jr., and Thomas G.

Voss, eds. *The Letters of William Cullen Bryant.* Vol. II, 1836–1849. New York: Fordham University Press, 1977.

Buell, Lawrence. *New England Literary Culture: From Revolution Through Renaissance.* Cambridge: Cambridge University Press, 1986.

Burt, Stephen, and David Mikics. *The Art of the Sonnet.* Cambridge, MA: Belknap Press, 2010.

Calhoun, Charles C. *Longfellow: A Rediscovered Life.* Boston, MA: Beacon Press, 2004.

———. *A Small College in Maine: Two Hundred Years of Bowdoin.* Brunswick, ME: Bowdoin College, 1993.

Cantwell, Robert. *Nathaniel Hawthorne: The American Years.* New York: Rinehart & Company, 1948.

Charvat, William. *The Profession of Authorship in American, 1800–1870.* New York: Columbia University Press, 1992.

Collison, Gary. *Shadrach Minkins: From Fugitive Slave to Citizen.* Cambridge, MA: Harvard University Press, 1997.

Crowninshield, Clara. *The Diary of Clara Crowninshield: A European Tour with Longfellow, 1835–1836.* Ed. Andrew Hilen. Seattle, Wash.: University of Washington Press, 1956.

Dall, Caroline Healey. *Daughter of Boston: The Extraordinary Diary of a Nineteenth-Century Woman.* Ed. Helen R. Deese. Boston, Mass.: Beacon Press, 2005.

Dalzell, Robert F., Jr. *Enterprising Elite: The Boston Associates and the World They Made.* [On Nathan Appleton.] Cambridge, MA: Harvard University Press, 1987.

Dana, Henry Wadsworth Longfellow. *The Longfellow House, History and Guide.* Pamphlet. Eastern National Park & Monument Association, 1976. Originally published in the April 1948 issue of *Old-Time New England.*

———. "'Sail on, O Ship of State!' How Longfellow Came to Write These Lines 100 Years Ago." *Colby Library Quarterly,* series 2, no. 13 (February 1950): 209–14.

Donald, David Herbert. *Charles Sumner and the Coming of the Civil War.* New York: Alfred A. Knopf, 1960. Vol. I of Sumner biography.

———. *Charles Sumner and the Rights of Man.* New York: Alfred A. Knopf, 1970. Vol. II of Sumner biography.

Duberman, Martin. *James Russell Lowell.* Boston, MA: Houghton Mifflin, 1966.

Elliott, Maud Howe. *Uncle Sam Ward and His Circle.* New York: Macmillan, 1938.

Emerson, Edward Waldo. *The Early Years of the Saturday Club, 1855–1870.* Boston, MA: Houghton Mifflin, 1918.

Fields, Annie. *Authors and Friends.* Boston, MA: Houghton Mifflin, 1897.

———. "Glimpses of Longfellow in Social Life." *The Century,* XXXI (1885–86), 884–93.

Gale, Robert L. *A Henry Wadsworth Longfellow Companion.* Westport, CT: Greenwood Press, 2003.

Gioia, Dana. "Longfellow in the Aftermath of Modernism." In *The Columbia History of American Poetry,* eds. Jay Parini and Brett C. Millier. New York: Columbia University Press, 1993.

Gorman, Herbert S. *A Victorian American: Henry Wadsworth Longfellow.* New York: George H. Doran Co., 1926.

Gregory, Frances W. *Nathan Appleton: Merchant and Entrepreneur, 1779–1861.* Charlottesville: University Press of Virginia, 1975.

Guest, Ivor. *Fanny Elssler.* Middletown, CT: Wesleyan University Press, 1970.

Hatfield, James Taft. *New Light on Longfellow: With Special Reference to His Relations to Germany.* Boston, MA: Houghton Mifflin Co., 1933.

Hawthorne, Hildegarde. *The Poet of Craigie House: The Story of Henry Wadsworth Longfellow.* New York: D. Appleton-Century Co., 1936.

Higginson, Thomas Wentworth. *Henry Wadsworth Longfellow.* American Men of Letters Series. Boston, Mass.: Houghton Mifflin, 1902.

Hilen, Andrew. "Introduction." *The Diary of Clara Crowninshield: A European Tour with Longfellow, 1835–1836.* Seattle: University of Washington Press, 1956. xiii-xxxi.

———. *Longfellow and Scandinavia.* Contains a complete transcription of Longfellow's Scandinavian Journal, June 16–September 24, 1835. New Haven, CT: Yale University Press. 1947.

Howe, M.A. DeWolfe. *Memories of a Hostess, a Chronicle of Eminent Friendships Drawn Chiefly from the Diaries of Mrs. James T. Fields.* Boston: Atlantic Monthly Press, 1922.

Howells, William Dean. "The White Mr. Longfellow." In *Literary Friends and Acquaintances: A Personal Retrospect of American Authorship.* New York: Harper & Brothers, 1901.

Irmscher, Christoph. *Longfellow Redux.* Urbana: University of Illinois Press, 2006.

———. *Public Poet, Private Man: Henry Wadsworth Longfellow at 200.* Amherst: University of Massachusetts Press, 2009.

Irmscher, Christoph, and Robert Arbour, eds. *Reconsidering Longfellow.* Madison, NJ: Fairleigh Dickinson University Press, 2014.

Johnson, Carl L. *Professor Longfellow of Harvard.* Eugene: University of Oregon Press, 1944. No.

5 in the University of Oregon Monograph series.

Kennedy, W. Sloane. *Henry W. Longfellow; Biography, Anecdote, Letters, Criticism.* Akron, Ohio: The Saalfield Publishing Company, 1903.

Longfellow, Alice. "Longfellow with His Children." *Strand* (September 1897): 250–53. Clipping.

Longfellow, Ernest Wadsworth. *Random Memories.* Boston, MA: Houghton Mifflin Co., 1922.

McClatchy, J.D. "Return to Gitchee Gumee." *New York Times Book Review* (October 22, 2000): 39.

McLean, Albert, Jr. *William Cullen Bryant.* New York: Twayne Publishers, 1964.

McPherson, James M. *Battle Cry of Freedom: The Civil War Era.* New York: Ballantine Books, 1989.

Mott, Frank Luther. *Golden Multitudes: The Story of Best Sellers in the United States.* New York: MacMillan, 1947.

Muller, Gilbert H. *William Cullen Bryant: Author of America.* Albany, NY: State University of New York Press, 2008.

Nemerov, Howard. Introduction. *Longfellow.* The Laurel Poetry Series. New York: Dell Publishing Co., 1959.

Norton, Charles Eliot. *Henry Wadsworth Longfellow: A Sketch of His Life.* Boston, MA: Houghton Mifflin Company, 1907.

_____. *Letters of Charles Eliot Norton.* Two volumes. Boston, MA: Houghton Mifflin, 1913.

Pattee, Fred Lewis. *The Feminine Fifties.* New York: D. Appleton-Century Co., 1940.

Payne, Edward F. *Dickens Days in Boston: A Record of Daily Events.* Boston, MA: Houghton Mifflin, 1927.

Pearl, Matthew. *The Dante Club.* Novel. New York: Random House, 2003.

Pierce, Edward L., ed. *Memoirs and Letters of Charles Sumner.* Three volumes. 1811–1845. Boston, MA: Roberts Brothers.

Remini, Robert V. *Daniel Webster: The Man and His Time.* New York: W.W. Norton, 1997.

Reynolds, David S. *John Brown, Abolitionist.* New York: Alfred A. Knopf, 2005.

_____. *Waking Giant: America in the Age of Jackson.* New York: HarperCollins, 2008.

_____. *Walt Whitman's America: A Cultural Biography.* New York: Alfred A. Knopf, 1995.

Roosevelt, Blanche. [Mrs. Blanche Roosevelt Tucker-Macchetta] *The Home Life of Henry W. Longfellow: Reminiscences of Many Visits at Cambridge and Nahant, During the Years 1880, 1881 and 1882.* New York: G.W. Carleton, 1882. Reprint BiblioBazaar Reproduction Series.

Rubin, Joan Shelley. *Songs of Ourselves: The Uses of Poetry in America.* Cambridge, MA: Harvard University Press, 2007.

Rubin, Joseph Jay, and Charles H. Brown. *Walt Whitman of the New York Aurora.* Westport, CT: Greenwood Press, 1972.

Showalter, Elaine. *The Civil Wars of Julia Ward Howe: A Biography.* New York: Simon & Schuster, 2016.

Silverman, Kenneth. *Edgar A. Poe: Mournful and Never-Ending Remembrance.* New York: HarperCollins, 1991.

Skinner, Henrietta Dana. *An Echo from Parnassus, Being Girlhood Memories of Longfellow and His Friends.* New York: J.H. Sears & Co., 1928.

Sorby, Angela. *Schoolroom Poets: Childhood, Performance, and the Place of American Poetry, 1865–1917.* Durham: University of New Hampshire Press, 2005.

Strauss, William, and Neil Howe. *Generations.* New York: William Morrow, 1991.

Taylor, Anne-Marie. *Young Charles Sumner and the Legacy of the American Enlightenment, 1811–1851.* Amherst: University of Massachusetts Press, 2001.

Tharp, Louise Hall. *The Appletons of Beacon Hill.* New York: Little, Brown, 1973.

Thompson, Lawrance. *Young Longfellow.* New York: Macmillan, 1938.

Trachtenberg, Alan. "Longfellow's Radical Americanism." *Los Angeles Times*, December 10, 2000.

_____. "Singing Hiawatha: Longfellow's Hybrid Myth of America." *Yale Review.* 90:1 (Jan. 2002): 1–19.

Wagenknecht, Edward. *Longfellow: A Full-Length Portrait.* New York: Longmans, Green & Co., 1955.

_____. *Mrs. Longfellow: Selected Letters and Journals of Fanny Appleton Longfellow.* New York: Longmans, Green and Co., 1956.

Waggoner, Hyatt H. *American Poets from the Puritans to the Present.* New York: Delta, 1970.

Walthur, Eric W. *The Shattering of the Union: America in the 1850s.* Lanham, MD: SR Books, 2003.

Williams, Cecil B. *Henry Wadsworth Longfellow.* Boston, MA: Twayne Publishers, 1964.

Willett, C., and Phillis Cunnington. *The History of Underclothes.* New York: Dover Publications, 1992.

Wineapple, Brenda. *Hawthorne: A Life.* New York: Alfred A. Knopf, 2003.

Index

Numbers in ***bold italics*** indicate pages with illustrations

Adams, Henry 31
Adams, John Quincy 221
Agassiz, Louis 210, 214, 215, 216
Alcott, Bronson 97, 246
Alden, John 5, 8, 43, 240
Allen, William 6, 41
Anderson, Robert 252, 253
Andrews, James Winthrop 161–62
Appleton, Charles Sedgwick 95, 98, 100, 102–03
Appleton, Frances Appleton *see* Longfellow, Frances Appleton
Appleton, James Amory 188
Appleton, Harriot Coffin (Nathan Appleton's second wife) 103, 143, 144, 160, 162, 179, 186, 189, 202, 203
Appleton, Maria Gold (Nathan Appleton's first wife) 95, 98, 99–100
Appleton, Mary *see* Mackintosh, Mary Appleton
Appleton, Nathan 95–100, 126, 129, 133, 143, 144, 178, 179, 181, 186, 189–190, 194, 197, 216, 224, 255, 258
Appleton, Samuel 95
Appleton, Mrs. Samuel 126, 127
Appleton, Thomas Gold 95, 96, 100, 101, 102, 103, 104, 112, 113, 114, 126, 137, 160, 161, 162, 179, 181, 182, 185–186, 190, 207, ***208***, 210, 212, 214, 215, 216, 218, 242, 249, 252, 253
Appleton, William 104, 108, 112, 113, 114, 124, 126
Appleton, William Sumner 143, 160
"April Day" (Longfellow) 15
Apthorp, Robert 102, 103, 104
"The Arsenal at Springfield" (Longfellow) 224, 226
Astor, John Jacob 151
Athenaean Society 7, 157
The Atlantic Souvenir 153
Austin, Emmeline 100, 136, 144, 147, 162, 163, 192, 200, 202, 203, 205, 207, 208, 213, 215, 222, 227, 228, 242, 249, 250, 252, 253–54

Ballads and Other Poems (Longfellow) 153, 154, 163, 177, 226
Bancroft, George 54, 235
Banvard, John 218, 229

Barnum, P.T. 219
Bartolini, Lorenzo 108
"Battle of Lovell's Pond" (Longfellow) 8–9, 11
Beecher, Henry Ward 245, 247
"The Belfry of Bruges" (Longfellow) 179
The Belfry of Bruges and Other Poems (Longfellow), 226
Bell, John 248
Belletti, Giovanni 219
Bellini, Vincenzo 105, 218, 234
Benedict, Julius 219
Benjamin, Susan 99, 102
Berdan, James 52
Bernini, Gian Lorenzo 32
Berzelius, Jakob 67
Bigelow, Henry J. 257
"Bleeding Sumner" 244, 247
Boccaccio, Giovanni 29
Bonaparte, Charlotte 30
Bonaparte, Joseph 30
Bosworth, Joseph 78, 79
Bowring, John 63
Bradbury, James W. 8–9, 202
Breckinridge, John C. 248
Brooks, Noah 223
Brooks, Preston 244
Brown, Jason 245
Brown, John 121, 244–247, 248
Browning, Elizabeth Barrett 217
Bryant, Fanny 87, 91
Bryant, Frances 87–88, 89, 90, 91–92, 115–116, 127
Bryant, Julia 87
Bryant, William Cullen 15, 85–87, 89, 91, 152
Buchanan, James 249, 252
"The Building of the Ship" (Longfellow) 223–225, 226
Bulwer, Edward 64
Bull, Ole 217
Bunker Hill 123
Bunker Hill Monument 156
"The Burial of the Minisink" (Longfellow) 153
Butler, Fanny Kemble 127–128, 136, 137, 160, 220–23
Butler, Pierce 128, 221

283

Calhoun, Charles C. 123, 228
Callicot, Theophilus Carey 234
Carey & Hart (publishers) 178
Carey & Lea (publishers) 38
Carlyle, Jane 64
Carlyle, Thomas 64
Cass, Lewis 122
Castle Craigie 164, 179, 199, 206; see also Craigie House
"The Castle of Indolence" 6
Channing, William Ellery 7, 97, 146, 180, 188
Chase, Salmon 43, 44
Chase, Salmon P. 244
Clark, Willis Gaylord 64
Clay, Henry 201–202, 243
Cleaveland, Martha Anne 52
Cleaveland, Parker 12, 43, 46, 48, 56, 67, 118, 211
Cleveland, Henry 120, 121, 183
Codman, Susan 7, 21, 27
Cogswell, Joseph 54
Coleridge, Samuel Taylor 45, 112
Connolly, Horace 158–159, 228
Cooper, James Fenimore 229
Coplas de Manrique (Longfellow translation) 153
Cortés, José 24, 62
Costello, Louise Stuart 228
The Courtship of Miles Standish (Longfellow) 239–41
Cowper, William 45
Craigie, Andrew 124
Craigie, Elizabeth Shaw 124
Craigie House 123–124, 130, 164, 174, 189–190, 193, 205, 214, 215, 217, 218, 222, 242, 250, 255, 259; see also Castle Craigie
Crosby, John 101, 125
"The Cross of Snow" (Longfellow) 260
Crowninshield, Clara 60, *61*, 62, 63, 65, 66, 67, 69, 70, 71, 72, 73, 74, 75, 77, 78, 79, 82–92, 93, 94, 106, 110, 111, 114, 115, 116, 127, 141
Crowninshield, George 61
Cummins, Maria 231
Currier and Ives, 161
Curtis, George William 193, 207, 254–55

Dana, Richard Henry 154, 159
Dante Alighieri 30, 34, 154, 215, 260
Darby, William 229
"The Day Is Done" (Longfellow) 226
De Candia, Giovanni Matteo (Mario) 218, 234
De Crèvecoeur, Hector St. John 229
De la Barca, Fanny Calderon 184
De Vega, Lope 57, 58
Dewey, Orville 113
Dickens, Charles 96, 174–175, 226
Dickinson, Emily 46
The Divine Comedy 181
Doane, Caroline 7, 49
Donald, David 122–23
Douglas, Stephen A. 243, 244, 248
Douglass, Frederik 245

Doyle, James 246
Dunlap House 55
Duyckinck, Evert 213
Dwight, Mary 188

Elliott, Dr. Samuel 212
Elmwood 96
Elssler, Fanny 155–56
The Embargo 85
Emerson, Ralph Waldo 97, 131, 154, 156, 176, 197, 210, 214, 218, 233, 239, 241, 246, 252
Emerson, Waldo 197
"L'Envoi" (Longfellow) 153
Erskine, David 68
Evangeline (Longfellow) 159, 226–30
Everett, Alexander H. 24, 54
"Excelsior" (Longfellow) 165, 226

Fales, Mary 52
Felton, Cornelius Conway 53, 118, 120, 121, 134, 155, 158, 163, 165, 188, 214, 256–57
Fern, Fanny 64, 231; see also Willis, Sara
Fields, Annie 157, 260
Fields, James 157, 209, 231, 239, 259
Fillmore, Millard 201
Five of Clubs 120–121, 123, 129, 130, 135, 156, 163, 166, 169, 214
"Flowers" (Longfellow) 130, 153
Folsom, Charles 56, 57
"Footsteps of Angels" (Longfellow) 80–81, 84, 153
Freiligrath, Ferdinand 169–171, 175, 176, 181, 209, 213
Freiligrath, Ida 170
Fuller, Margaret 77, 120, 161, 178, 202–203, 227

Galileo, Galilei 30, 235
Gannett, Ezra Stiles 188, 259
Goddard, Mary 60–61, 71, 79
Goddard, William 79
Goethe, Johann Wolfgang 84, 91, 134, 135, 139
Gold, Martha 101, 184
Goldschmidt, Otto 220
González, Don Valentine 24
González, Florencia 17, 24–25, 29, 34, 93
Gorman, Herbert 224–25
Graces of Bond Street 154
"The Great Metropolis" (Longfellow) 119
Greene, Maria Carlotta 60, 215
Greene, Washington 10, 28, 29, 31, 32, 33, 47, 53, 58, 60, 64, 68, 80, 82, 89, 90, 91, 93, 94, 118, 121, 132, 133, 139, 140, 141, 142, 143, 147, 152, 154, 155, 164, 169, 182, 190, 215
Greenleaf, James 224
Greenleaf, Mary Longfellow (sister) 52, 187, 188, 199, 223, 224
Greenleaf, Patrick 21
Grisi, Giulia 105, 218–219, 234

Hartford Convention 43, 204
Hawthorne, Nathaniel 6, 7, 56, 136, 152, 156, 157–159, 181, 209, 231, 236, 259

Heckewelder, John 9
Hepp, Frau 83, 89, 115
Higginson, Thomas Wentworth 7, 46, 57, 119, 120, 152, 246
Hillard, George 120, 121, 129, 132, 135, 158, 163, 169, 172, 174, 188, 196, 214, 216, 222
Holmes, Oliver Wendell 193, 247
Hosmer, James Kendall 120
Howe, Julia Ward 119, 155, 181, 207, **208**
Howe, Samuel Gridley 121, 122, 181, 189, 207, 214, 230, 246
Howells, William Dean 260
Hutchinson Family 218
"Hymn of the Moravian Nuns" (Longfellow) 15
Hyperion (Longfellow) 135, 139–143, 146, 152, 153, 159, 163, 164, 174, 179, 185, 187, 185, 187, 194, 228

The Inferno 260
Irmscher, Christoph 123
Irving, Pierre 22
Irving, Washington 4, 22, 23, 24, 29, 38, 58
Isabey, Jean-Baptiste 104
"Italian Scenery" (Longfellow) 30

Jackson, Andrew 54, 62, 98–99, 160
Jacquard, Joseph-Marie 106
Jewett, Isaac Appleton 104, 127, 146, 160, 161, 185
Johnson, Dr. William Otis 256–57

Kalevala 231, 232, 235
Keep, Dr. Nathan 195–196, 204
Kemble, Fanny *see* Butler, Fanny Kemble
King Philip (Metacom) 8–9, 176, 232
King Philip's War 8

"The Lay Monastery" (Longfellow) 12
Ledyard, Henry 125, 126, 127
A Legacy for Young Ladies 45
Lieber, Franz 143, 145, 146, 196, 227
Lignell, Karl 67
Lincoln, Abraham 122, 223, 243, 247–249, 252, 253, 254
Lind, Jenny 219–220, 226
Longfellow, Alice Mary (daughter) 10, 193, 199, 250, 255
Longfellow, Anne (sister) 8, 45, 46, 53, 55, 56, 69, 169, 184, 187, 196, 200, 204, 212, 248
Longfellow, Anne Allegra (daughter) 193, 206, 235, 250, 255, 257–58
Longfellow, Charles Appleton (son) 193, 194, 217, 250
Longfellow, Edith (daughter) 193, 200, 250, 255, 258
Longfellow, Elizabeth (sister) 24, 37, 40
Longfellow, Ellen (sister) 60
Longfellow, Ernest Wadsworth (son) 193, 199, 213, 250, 255
Longfellow, Frances (daughter "Fanny") 193, 196–199, 201, 222, 242

Longfellow, Frances Appleton (wife) 93–116, **95**, **106**, 125–148, 151, 159, 164, 166, 169, 173, 179–225, **208**, 241–261, **243**
Longfellow, Henry Wadsworth: "April Day" 15; "The Arsenal at Springfield" 224, 226; *Ballads and Other Poems* 153, 154, 163, 177, 226; "Battle of Lovell's Pond" 8–9, 11; "The Belfry of Bruges" 179; *The Belfry of Bruges and Other Poems* 226; Bowdoin College 6–16, 47–50; "The Building of the Ship" 223–225, 226; "The Burial of the Minisink" 153; and Charles Sumner 120–123; *Coplas de Manrique* (translation) 153; *The Courtship of Miles Standish* 239–241; "The Cross of Snow" 260; "The Day Is Done" 226; "L'Envoi" 153; *Evangeline* 159, 226–230; "Excelsior" 165, 226; and Fanny Appleton 109–114, 130–148, 182–191, 193–201, 254–260; Five of Clubs 120–123; "Flowers" 130, 153; "Footsteps of Angels" 80–81, 84, 153; "The Great Metropolis" 119; at Harvard 3–4, 118; "Hymn of the Moravian Nuns" 15; *Hyperion* 135, 139–143, 146, 152, 153, 159, 163, 164, 174, 179, 185, 187, 185, 187, 194, 228; "Italian Scenery" 30; "The Lay Monastery" 12; in Madrid 23–27; and Mary Storer Potter 42–47, 50–52, 59–78; "Mezzo Cammin" 173, 175; "Moral and Devotional Poetry of Spain" 4, 59; "The Old Clock on the Stairs" 226; "On Mrs. Kemble's Readings from Shakespeare" 222; "Our Native Writers" 15; *Outre-Mer* 28, 31, 39, 57–58, 62, 109, 124, 143, 159, 228; in Paris 17–23; "Paul Revere's Ride" 250–51; *Poems on Slavery* 175–178, 224, 226; "Poetry of the Dark Ages" 13; Portland Academy 5, 10; as professor at Bowdoin College 15–16, 42; "A Psalm of Life" 134–135, 138, 139, 151, 152, 153, 154, 156, 223, 226, 227; "The Quadroon Girl" 177, 178, 226; "The Rainy Day" 226, 259; "Resignation" 198; in Rome 28–39; *The Seaside and the Fireside* 198, 226; Sidney, Sir Philip, *The Defence of Poetry* (review essay by Longfellow) 49–50; "The Slave in the Dismal Swamp" 177; "The Slave's Dream" 176, 178, 226; *The Song of Hiawatha* 231–239; *The Spanish Student* 155–156, 179; "The Spirit of Poetry" 153; "Sunrise on the Hills" 15; "The Village Blacksmith" 161, 163, 226; *Voices of the Night* 81, 152–154, 156, 164, 194, 226; "Winter" 11; "The Wreck of the Hesperus" 153, 154, 226
Longfellow, Marianne Preble (brother Stephen's wife) 52, 204
Longfellow, Mary (sister) *see* Greenleaf, Mary Longfellow
Longfellow, Mary Potter (first wife) 42–47, **44**, 50–52, 55–56, 60, 63, 64, **65**, 66–78, 79, 80, 82, 83, 84, 87, 93, 94, 103, 106, 111, 114, 115, 118, 141, 153, 185, 211, 215
Longfellow, Samuel (brother) 138, 176, 186, 187, 188, 235, 242, 247
Longfellow, Stephen (brother) 5, 7, 19, 52, 176, 204, 222

Longfellow, Stephen (father) 5, 14–15, 17, 20
   22, 23, 25, 27, 29, 34, 35, 36, 37, 38, 39–40,
   43, 44, 50, 53, 59, 62, 73, 119, 163, 164, 165,
   168, 178, 181, 204–05
Longfellow, Stephen (grandfather) 5, 43
Longfellow, Zilpah Wadsworth (mother) 5, 7,
   9, 10, 17, 20, 24, 26, 30, 32, 34, 36, 37, 38, 40,
   44, 55, 60, 62, 63, 65, 68, 176, 183, 184, 186,
   196, 204–205, 212
Longfellow House 193
Lönnrot, Elias 231, 232
Lovewell's Fight (Battle of Pequawket) 8
Lowell, Blanche 197
Lowell, James Lowell 124, 177–178, 179, 197, 210,
   235
Lowell, Maria 197

Mackintosh, Sir James 144
Mackintosh, Mary Appleton 95, 99, 100, 101–
   102, **106**, 107, 125, 131, 132, 134, 135, 137, 143,
   145, 160, 162, 165, 179, 181, 186, 199, 200, 218,
   221, 240, 250, 260
Mackintosh, Robert 144–146, 160, 162, 181
Madison, Dolley 221
Mann, Horace 154
Manrique, Don Jorge 56, 58, 59
Marshall, John 221
McHenry, James 13
McKay, Donald 236
Mellen, Frederic 11
Mellen, Judge Prentiss 11
Mellin, Henrik 67, 69
Metacom (King Philip) 8–9, 176, 232
Mexican War 242–243, 254
Meyerbeer, Giacomo 117
"Mezzo Cammin" (Longfellow) 173, 175
Michelangelo 30
Miscellaneous Poems Selected from The United
   States Literary Gazette 12
Miss Cushing's seminary (also called her "fe-
   male school") 45, 61
Monti, Luigi 215
"Moral and Devotional Poetry of Spain"
   (Longfellow) 4, 59
Morris, George 55
Morton, William 195
Motley, Anna 110
Motley, Thomas 110
Mott, Frank Luther 231
Mozart, Wolfgang Amadeus 91, 218, 220
Muller, Gilbert 89
Mullins, Priscilla 6, 43, 240
Mussey, Reuben 56

Nathan, Isaac 105
New York Review 15
Newcomb, Charles 156
Nicander, Karl 67, 69
Nichols, the Rev. Ichabod 52, 53
North American Review 4, 44, 58, 59, 119, 157,
   266n27

Norton, Andrews 77, 169, 182
Norton, Caroline Sheridan 21
Norton, Catherine Eliot 169, 181, 182
Norton, Charles Eliot 187, 193
Novalis 84

"The Old Clock on the Stairs" (Longfellow)
   226
"On Mrs. Kemble's Readings from Shakespeare"
   (Longfellow) 222
Orr, Benjamin 13
Otis, Alleyne 180
Otis, Harrison Gray 143
"Our Native Writers" (Longfellow) 15
Outre-Mer (Longfellow) 28, 31, 39, 57–58, 62,
   109, 124, 143, 159, 228
Owen, John, 153, 175

Packard, Alpheus 52
Parker, Theodore 218, 246, 252
Parkman, George 203–04
Parsons, Theophilus 12, 14–15
Pattee, Fred Lewis 231
Paul, Jean 131
"Paul Revere's Ride" (Longfellow) 250–51
Payne, William 107
Peabody, Elizabeth 97, 161
Perkins Institute for the Blind 121
Persiani, Giulia 17, 32–37, 40, 93, 172
Persiani, Innocenzo and Marianna 31–37 pas-
   sim
Peucinian Society 7, 9, 13, 157
Philippe, Louis 125
Phillips, Wendell 247
Pierce, Edward 122
Pierce, Franklin 7, 244
Pierce, George Washington 72, 84
Poe, Edgar Allan 81, 136, 178, 227, 234
Poems on Slavery (Longfellow) 175–178, 224,
   226
"Poetry of the Dark Ages" (Longfellow) 13
Polk, James 242
Porter, Catherine Van Buren 215
Portland Academy 5, 10
Portland Advertiser 12
Portland Gazette 10
Potet, Madame 18–20, 117
Potter, Barrett 44, 45, 46, 47, 51, 60, 69, 73, 77,
   78, 80, 185
Potter, Eliza 62, 185
Potter, Mary Storer *see* Longfellow, Mary
   Potter
Potter, Margaret *see* Thacher, Margaret Potter
Preble, Edward 36, 37, 39
Preble, Marianne (brother Stephen's wife) *see*
   Longfellow, Marianne Preble
Prescott, William Hickling 184
Priessnitz, Vincenz 165, 167
"A Psalm of Life" (Longfellow) 134–135, 138,
   139, 151, 152, 153, 154, 156, 223, 226, 227

"The Quadroon Girl" (Longfellow) 177, 178, 226
Quincy, Josiah 3, 59, 119, 149, 166, 172, 173, 174

"The Rainy Day" (Longfellow) 226, 259
"Resignation" (Longfellow) 198
Revere, Paul 250
Reynolds, David, 121, 122, 245
Richter, Jean Paul 139 154
Rossini, Gioacchino 105 218
Rousseau, Jean-Jacques 18
Rowell, Elizabeth 61
Ruskin, John 206

Sanborn, Franklin 246
Saturday Club 241
Schmitz, Dr. 167, 168, 171, 174
Scott, Sir Walter 6, 128, 250
The Seaside and the Fireside (Longfellow) 198, 226
Sedgwick, Catharine Maria 136, 137, 231
Sedgwick, Charles S. 147, 231
Seward, William 247
Shakespeare, William 128, 220, 221, 222, 223, 250
Shelley, Percy Bysshe 45
Sherman, William 246
Sidney, Sir Philip, *The Defence of Poetry* (review essay by Longfellow) 49-50
The Sketch Book 22, 58
Skinner, Henrietta Dana 255, 258
Skinner, Mary 63
"The Slave in the Dismal Swamp" (Longfellow) 177
"The Slave's Dream" (Longfellow) 176, 178, 226
Slidell, Alexander 24-25, 29, 50, 242
Smith, Gerrit 246
The Song of Hiawatha (Longfellow) 9, 231-39
The Sorrows of Young Werther 84-85
Southey, Robert 128
The Spanish Student (Longfellow) 155-156, 179
Speed, Joshua 122
"The Spirit of Poetry" (Longfellow) 153
Standish, Miles 9
Stearns, George Luther 246
Stirling, William 236
Storer, Anne 44
Storer, Eben 18
Stowe, Harriet Beecher 177
Stuart, Lispenard 100-01
Sumner, Charles 90, 120, 121-123, **122**, 132, 133, 138, 140, 143, 163, 164, 166-167, 168,170, 171, 172, 174, 176, 180, 188, 189, 193, 196, 208, 209, 214, 215-217, 222, 235, 236, 240, 244, 252, 256, 258, 259
Sumner, Harriot Coffin *see* Appleton, Harriot Coffin
"Sunrise on the Hills" (Longfellow) 15

Taglioni, Marie 125
Taylor, Zachary 201-02

Tennyson, Alfred Lord 131, 234
Thanatopsis 86-87
Thatcher, Margaret Potter 77, 179
Thompson, James 6
Thompson, Lawrance 84
Thoreau, Henry David 246
Ticknor, George 3-4, 26, 27, 54, 59, 118, 129
Ticknor & Fields 227, 231, 235, 239
Toussaint L'Ouverture 176
Truth, Sojourner 245

Uhland, Ludwig 112, 113
"Ulalume" 81
The United States Literary Gazette 12, 13-15, 30, 87

Van Buren, Martin 119, 160
Vandenhoff, George 239
"The Village Blacksmith" (Longfellow) 161, 163, 226
Voices of the Night (Longfellow) 81, 152, 153, 154,156, 164, 194, 226
Von Gall, Louisa 170, 172

Wadsworth, Lucia (aunt) 27, 71, 72, 205
Wadsworth, Peleg (grandfather) 11, 43-44
Ward, Anna 154, 156
Ward, Julia *see* Howe, Julia Ward
Ward, Louisa 155, 212
Ward, Sam 90, 91, 145, 151, 152, 154, 155, 164, 165, 166, 169, 181, 188
Ward's Tavern 7
Ware, Henry 178
Warner, Susan 231
Warren, John 195
Washington, George 123, 190, 194
Watson, John 229
Webster, Daniel 202, 221
Webster, Dr. John W. 203-04
Wesselhoeft, Dr. Robert 212
Wetmore, Thomas 209-10
"The White Longfellow" 260
Whitman, Walt 122, 230, 239
Whittier, John Greenleaf 178
Wilkinson, Allen 246
Willis, Nathaniel Parker 63, 64, 111
Willis, Sara 64, 231; *see also* Fern, Fanny
"Winter" (Longfellow) 11
Wollstonecraft, Mary 137
Worcester, Joseph E. 124
Wordsworth, William 113, 200
"The Wreck of the Hesperus" (Longfellow) 153, 154, 226
Wright, Fanny 160
Wyman, Dr. Morrill 256

Yale, Mr. and Mrs. 144
Young, Edward 45

www.ingramcontent.com/pod-product-compliance
Lightning Source LLC
Chambersburg PA
CBHW051211300426
44116CB00006B/520